The Pleasure of Modernist Music

Eastman Studies in Music

Ralph P. Locke, Senior Editor
Eastman School of Music

(ISSN 1071–9989)

Additional titles in Music of the Nineteenth and Twentieth Centuries

The Pleasure of Modernist Music

Listening, Meaning, Intention, Ideology

Edited by

Arved Ashby

UNIVERSITY OF ROCHESTER PRESS

First published 2004
Reprinted in paperback and transferred to digital printing 2010

University of Rochester Press
668 Mt. Hope Avenue, Rochester, NY 14620, USA
www.urpress.com
and Boydell & Brewer Limited
PO Box 9, Woodbridge, Suffolk IP12 3DF, UK
www.boydellandbrewer.com

ISSN: 1071-9989
Paperback ISBN: 978-1-58046-375-1
Cloth ISBN: 978-1-58046-143-6

Library of Congress Cataloging-in-Publication Data

The pleasure of modernist music : listening, meaning, intention, ideology /
edited by Arved Ashby.
    p. cm. — (Eastman studies in music ; v. 29)
  Includes bibliographical references and index.
    ISBN 1-58046-143-3 (hardcover : alk. paper)
    1. Music—20th century—History and critcism. I. Ashby, Arved Mark. II.
Series.
ML197.P57 2004
780'.9'04—dc22

                                        2004011370

A catalogue record for this title is available from the British Library.

This publication is printed on acid-free paper.

For my parents

and in memory of Jong, music lover and dear friend
(August 23, 1968–February 20, 1997)

Contents

Introduction

Arved Ashby

The nice thing about an -ism, someone once observed, is how quickly it becomes a wasm. Some musical wasms—academic-wasm, for example, and its dependent varieties of modern-wasm and Serial-wasm—continue to linger on artificial life support, though, and continue to threaten the increasingly fragile classical ecosystem.
—Richard Taruskin, *New York Times*, March 10, 1996

Fortunately, we are witnessing the growth of a grass-roots movement comprised of composers and performers who, having peeked over the fence surrounding this dungheap [of the New Simplicity and the New Romanticism] have determined that shovelling shit is not to be their fate, and who are lovingly dedicating their lives to the seemingly endless, often agonizing labor which the production of challenging new works entails.
—James Boros, *Perspectives of New Music*, Winter 1993

Who knows what the new century holds for music? I predict that we will bury most of the musical modernism of the 20th, with its need to shock and cause distress.
—Donald Vroon, *American Record Guide*, March/April 2000

This is a book about twentieth-century art music with popularity problems. We haven't set out to draw all-encompassing, general conclusions on music of the previous century, or its listeners and contexts, but focus instead on specific repertoires long felt to be elitist and unapproachable. The music discussed is varied, stemming from different aesthetics, places, and decades. But what ties these pieces together is that they have all been recognized, from first hearing—or even from first rumor of their existence!—as challenging the ear and mind. Over the years they have therefore been praised (as liberating and healthily demanding of close attention) or vilified (as elitist or worse fraudulent, because their complexities resist perception). This debate over modernist music has continued for almost a century: such pro-modernist writers as Webern, Adorno, Varèse, René Leibowitz, Babbitt, and Boulez (as well as books and critical articles of Paul Griffiths, among others) have been answered, sometimes belatedly, in such frankly anti-modernist essays as Henry Pleasants's *The Agony of Modern Music*, George Rochberg's *Aesthetics of Survival*, and spirited publications by Susan McClary, Richard Taruskin, Fred Lerdahl, and Roger Scruton.

Our aim in this volume is to negotiate a varied and open middle ground between these polemical extremes, to map out new areas of discussion by opening up new questions of meaning. Our project is to trace the kinds of import, usually not the meanings the composers themselves would recognize, that these works have held for a significant number of listeners of different kinds. This music has never achieved much success and acceptance, beyond the *succès d'estime* that rules the Pulitzer Prizes and university appointments—or long did. But this doesn't mean that modernist music hasn't found an audience and couldn't find *more* listeners if we took a fresh look at its fabled difficulty—if we stopped approaching modernist works as pseudopositivist experiments to be praised or censured for rejecting conventional ideas of musical "coherence." Possessed of a certain useful naïveté, the contributors to this book go beyond questions of difficulty to ask what these compositions might mean, what their importance might be in daily life, and what role their creators played in constructing those meanings.[1]

In short, we have developed postmodern approaches to modernist music, sketching out the possible significance of a repertory that in past discussions has been deemed either evasive or iconic, meaningless or beyond describable structural meaning. And as with any pioneering attempt to offer new explanations, this book is by necessity preliminary and exploratory: we devise no taxonomies of interpretation, but instead put forth some possible directions for future thought. This study looks forward to a reconsidered future, but we also found it necessary to look back and revisit some familiar questions that still demand answers. And we felt compelled to take on this dual project in the most straightforward language possible, keeping in mind a non-specialist readership. Those readers not blinded by partisanship or turned away by the often dense expository styles of its advocates likely came to this music fairly recently, and that clientele calls for a less assuming mode of address.

Like anyone attempting to negotiate between warring factions—whether in law, business, or international diplomacy—this volume by its very nature risks incurring the wrath of all factions, but does so in pursuit of a higher good. It may endear itself neither to modernist composers nor to those who have an axe to grind with modernism, both of whom may castigate these writers simply for succeeding with what they set out to do. Modernists will likely decry the approaches to the music, and anti-modernists the music thus approached. The former will doubtless consider various of the essays simplistic, and the latter will likely dismiss the whole effort as both outdated and defensive. As much as this book will displease those with the biggest franchises in arguing for or against modernism, the volume will—or so it is hoped—speak to a quiet majority who are more interested in the music than in the composers or the politics surrounding, and often engulfing, them.

Our project, far from being idly revisionist, addresses a cultural and political emergency. The future of human culture—our bodily survival, even—may well depend on cultivating empathy across ideological battle lines, since our age sees ever more divisive factions, each increasingly sure of its own monopoly on virtue. There has developed in the public sphere a syndrome marked by such self-empowerment, such a sense of vindication and inability to entertain other points of view, that psychiatry has seen fit to give it a name: Cornell psychiatrist Robert B. Millman is preparing a book on the affliction he calls "acquired situational narcissism."[2] Thirty years ago, Brandeis historian David Hackett Fischer diagnosed a slightly more scrupulous condition among scholars, something he called the "genetic fallacy" of ethical historicism. "Another contemporary variant of the fallacy of ethical historicism," Fischer writes, "might be diagnosed as Carr's disease, after an English socialist scholar who seems to think that morality marches triumphant through history, always on the side of the big battalions. Carr marches through history with them, too."[3]

Hubris of the kind under consideration here is found in the pro-modernist (or, more loosely, high humanist) convictions that systematic reason can solve all or most problems; that artworks can have permanent, inherent, and absolute value; and that the "new" atonality of the early- to mid-twentieth-century supplanted the "old" tonality of the common practice period. On the anti-modernist side, a similar sense of chronological privilege imbues millennial conclusions that, for example, capitalism has trounced socialism, that the unwitting sexism of earlier writers should be pointed out by attaching a [sic] to their indefinite male-gendered pronouns, and that the "new" tonality of the later twentieth century supersedes the preceding "old" atonality.[4] This editor feels that the world needs no more doctrinaire polemics on modernism and complexity in music after Susan McClary's "Terminal Prestige: The Case of Avant-Garde Music Composition" and James Boros's contradictory "Why Complexity?"[5] The contributors to the present book believe that no one stands to benefit from restricted access to the modernist compositional projects of, say, Stravinsky, Martino, Ferneyhough, or Ruth Crawford Seeger. Unlike ethical historicists, we find it more fruitful and honest to see a Webern or Stockhausen composition not as an icon of indescribable importance or a hopeless relic, but as something inbetween: perhaps an important relic or describable icon. There is no reason to exclude modernist works from the current mandate of finding cultural meaning.

1. Listening

The title of our book invokes pleasure—not a sensation many would link with modernist music, but therein lies an important point regarding our volume. American critic Henry Pleasants excoriated modernism under the title *The Agony of Modern Music*, a study he published in 1955.[6] Referring to pleasure up-front in our own title highlights the fact that we have, in effect, come up with a broad-minded response to Pleasants's old book. The word also emphasizes the non-academic nature of our approaches: we complement Pleasants in that we, while sharing some of his aesthetic-historicist misgivings, arrive at different conclusions because we generally choose to approach modernist issues through listening—"listening" in the broadest possible sense—and find pleasure rather than agony therefrom. But it is perhaps a particular kind of pleasure that we discover: pleasure in the sense of *jouissance*, as the term was used by post-Freudian psychologist Jacques Lacan.

The word translates literally as "enjoyment" or "pleasure." But as invoked by Lacan, *jouissance* is more specifically the silent, unspoken possibility that drives desire.[7] All-fulfilling but also all-destroying, it is to be both aspired to and defended against: all desire *believes* it is striving for *jouissance*, yet actual arrival at *jouissance* would entail pain and anxiety, even psychosis. Indeed, the subject will subconsciously work to avoid fulfilling the *jouissance*—getting intimate with the most attractive girl in class, say—in order to continue his own desire. And what the subject really desires is the beautiful girl's desire for him as he imagines it. In this way, pleasure and *jouissance* are at the same time overlapping, intertwined, and at odds with one another.[8] The whole Lacanian circuit of desire manifests itself in processes of language and signification, so the formulations become all the more difficult to place in any parallel musical examples. Psychoanalyst and philosophy scholar Levi R. Bryant has described music as neither a language nor any kind of intuitive or hermeneutic system, but as a mark-based, problem-solving method like mathematics. In such a context, the Lacanian terms of pleasure and desire would become all the more difficult to formulate.

Yet it seems inescapable that music, modernist music especially, enshrines a peculiar dialectic of pleasure and *jouissance*. Because it is not a language, and also because it inspires unique feelings of empathy or even ownership ("*how* could you possibly interpret/analyze/play Schubert/Bartók/Ellington/ Prince *like that* . . . !"), music is able to conquer the Real of *jouissance*, it offers a way of touching on and dislocating the *jouissance* that might otherwise invade us.[9] What might that *jouissance* be? Modernist and antimodernist partisans tend, in equally forced ways, to present modernist music as either a familiar text or as the Other: modernist music either makes no special demands (or at least none that should not be made), or it presents an alien and unnatural way of thinking. To pursue the polarity further: the music either represents an utterly organic system, a viable re-designing of nature itself, or it draws a frame around chaos and pathology. Many of us will admit Modernist music as Other, but also say that by definition it is a necessary, constructive, or even erotic impetus—like *jouissance*, in short. The faults that many critics find in it—its lack of hierarchy, goal-oriented motion, and closure—are the very Other-characteristics that keep desire-potential open and active. Courtesy of obscurity and novelty, modern music becomes a bottomless well of possibility: a good compositional example offers new discoveries with each visit, always promising and never entirely satisfying any listener.

By definition, modernist music is the most conflicted that we have. More than any other kind of music, except maybe for rock 'n' roll, it offers each listener a unique, volatile, high-stakes dialectic of inseparable pleasure and pain, reward and risk—with the final formulation doubtless unique to each individual who writes and hears it. As such, modernist music is closest to the Lacanian idea of the Real, and is indispensable in the way that it mirrors and plays out basic psychological processes. It is a music of extremes, and its closeness to reality—as opposed to Lacan's realm of the more manageable and easily conceivable Symbolic—means that it has cut too close to the heart of the matter for many listeners.

As we have already mentioned, the reference to listening in our title separates us from the aesthetic-based polemics of a Henry Pleasants. But then listening does not come up often in polarized discussions of modernism, since it might seem as inappropriate to a high humanist project within a history of ideas as it would to an exclusionary denial of music's "universality" of language. We advocate the term "listening" as opposed to "hearing," the first defined by the *Oxford English Dictionary* as "giving ear to" and the second as "perceiving, having cognizance of by means of the ear." A listener participates in the construction of meaning while a hearer apprehends or (re)cognizes pre-existing meaning. As such, the listener follows connotation rather than denotation. Modernist composers, on the other hand, are generally keen on the idea of denotative communication—on hearing. As Judy Lochhead tells us in her chapter on the modernist program of hearing, the composer presumes a "program of objective structure or sound" that listeners are supposed to apprehend. "I intend it in such a way," goes the modernist idea, "and you should hear it in that same way." In its most extreme form, modernist hearing entails worshipful discussion of the music for its abstract, formal, and stylistic properties, including its degree of coherence, unity, and originality (seen as a kind of inherent good, along the models of technological-scientific progress). Our book works to avoid such aesthetic hagiography; listening to the music is our attempted means of escaping it. Such discussions lead some contributors to alternative listening strategies for modernism, alternative in that they bear no connection to the composer's thinking, documented or inferred. Those contributors affirm Leonard Meyer's statement that there is no necessary reason that principles of listening should relate to the specific principles followed in composition of a piece.[10]

Accordingly, none of us takes up the usual mandate of "educated listening" to modernist works: the notion that a person can appreciate "difficult" music if given enough time, college courses, readings on composition and aesthetics, and ear-training. Certainly none of us believes that it behooves the listener to make such efforts, that they are necessarily "good for" him or her, or that such labors will reveal some key element without which the work will not be "understood." This is not an aural skills book, nor do we develop a program for understanding large-scale musical forms in the twentieth century. In short, we don't formulate a musical equivalent to what modernist art scholar Philip Yenawine calls "directed looking": focusing on the artwork with "a spirit of open inquiry" and "us[ing] our eyes in a more demanding way than is normal." Under the heading "I Know You Can Do It," he makes the promise that "the more visually and intellectually rich the work, the more there is to grasp and ponder."[11] His first chapter ("Looking for Meaning") then goes on to give art history students the conceptual and analytic tools of perspective, line, color, shape, and form that they will need in their journey. By contrast, our own book is a corrective that concerns itself more with personalization than poiesis and methodology.

Here we arrive at the issue of "intention" also alluded to in the title of the book: do the composer's thinking and agenda have any bearing on the listener's search for meaning? Does an author mean what he or she *intends* to mean? Listeners with no idea of a composer's methods or intentions have proved able to reach some kind of consensus on aesthetic value, and this points to avenues of significance beyond those deemed appropriate by the composer or the academy. Most of the chapters that follow deal with the issue of compositional intention, if often implicitly and by another name. Greg Sandow brings up intention neither as a term nor an idea. But he dissipates the illusion of unity that Schoenberg created for his mature music, and this allows him to discuss disorder—which the composer recognized neither as an aesthetic nor a musical possibility—as a characteristic element of this composer's language. Martin Scherzinger adopts the particular anti-intentionalism of Marxist theory—more specifically, the ideas of Walter Benjamin and Bertolt Brecht as well as the critical thinking of T. W. Adorno and the Frankfurt School, who heard musical works not as abstract compositional achievements but as records of social and aesthetic struggle. Amy Bauer sets aside the idea of a compositional grammar, a fundamental intentionalist construct, and in doing so opens the door to metaphorical approaches. Pierre Boulez focuses on processes of writing, denying perhaps the most basic intentionalist assumption: that transcription of a thought, the ostensibly simple act of writing it down on the page, can serve as a transparent and neutral transmission of that thought. In a similar way, William Bolcom denies the idea that a compositional discipline (invertible counterpoint or a twelve-tone row, say) enables the composer to exert greater command over his or her musical results, but finds instead that it serves productivity and inspiration by pulling the artwork away from the composer's control. Intention foils intention, with beneficial results.

I have made a case for empathy and compromise between pro-modernist and anti-modernist causes. One specific rapprochement made by many of the authors in this book is to deny the composer his or her authority as cardinal source of meaning (a more-or-less universal postulate in twentieth-century music) but at the same time admit that specific works can be of signal importance by reason of their modern-ness. In this way, the authors (with the exception of Toop and possibly Mead) defy creative authority in a domain that has been long constrained by intentionalism. The thought has long been that the modernist composer, systematic and rationalist by definition, knows best when it comes to his or her modus operandi—whether it be the generalized combinatorial methods of Babbitt or the Biblical narratives of Messiaen—and has worked to maintain the relevance of those systems for the music.

The ideological freedom of "naive" listening is to be contrasted with the supposed freedom from ideology embodied in absolute music, which demands that the work be contemplated "for its own sake," as abstracted from the listener's thoughts, aims and desires. This vision of absolute music is rooted in Kant's concept of aesthetic disinterestedness, as described in his *Critique of Aesthetic Judgment*. But I hope the reader will note early on that the contributors to this book don't subscribe to a Kantian conception of listening. Indeed, we believe that decisions regarding musical and aesthetic value should be individual and personal ones, and that the same goes for listening. Ours tends to be an inclusive and subjective conception of listening—involving the mind as well as the emotions and the listener's sense of identity.

Is it possible to arrive at an apolitical hearing of a musical work, since such an idea would seem basically at odds with searches for cultural meaning? I would prefer to call it a descriptor-free hearing. Music-historical authorities usually believe they use -isms as mere descriptors. Even if they acknowledge the political import of their terms, they often fail to see the direct effect that ostensibly "descriptive" term has on musicians' and listeners' senses of aesthetic identity: the descriptor becomes a heuristic, in a word, especially as it has by this time become all but useless *as* aesthetic-historic descriptor. In referring to psychotherapy, Levi Bryant has pointed to the counterproductive nature of the term and idea of "addiction," which simply propitiates the addiction by defining the patient's identity around it, and, by force of terminological duality, makes it all the more difficult for the person to go from addict to "non-addict." For our own purposes, it would be as simple as it would be instructive to substitute the word "modernist" for "addict" in Bryant's statement: "The signifier 'addict' doesn't simply describe what I am, but initiates a way of relating to myself that informs how I relate to others."

Along these lines, it would be as helpful for the music listener to ignore the terms "modernist," "postmodernist," "academic," "serialist," "atonalist," or "tonalist" as it would be for the psychologist to refuse the title "addict" when the couch is taken by someone who washes his or her hands obsessively or abuses drugs. In both cases, the focus would shift from the person's need for cleanliness or intricate compositional systems to what their needs tell us about them as social beings. "We should treat substance abuse," Bryant writes, "as being on par with any other sort of symptom (in the psychoanalytic sense) and as being something to be *interpreted* (not treated) like anything else." In the same way, it is surely less useful to try to "treat" modernism and romanticism than it would be to work toward an understanding of them.

2. Whose Modernism?

By necessity, we walk a fine line in this volume between defining a modernist aesthetic and common focus of discussion around a modernist repertory, and working to resist the usual aesthetic terminology and the boundaries and political impasses that attend it. Our conceptions of "modernism" range far and wide—the composers discussed range from Schoenberg and Berg to Hindemith, Babbitt, Ligeti, Brian Wilson, Lou Reed, and Bernard Herrmann. And so prefatory remarks are needed on modernism and just how we have found it necessary to deviate from the traditional aesthetic terminology. In other words, we need to give some specifics up-front before we can try to re-appropriate terms or set them aside.

Authors of standard volumes on the subject have emphasized several defining aspects of modernism over the years. In *Children of the Mire* Octavio Paz described modernism as "a tradition against itself," and Matei Calinescu picked up on this paradoxical movement-basis when he defined modernism as "a conscious commitment to modernity, whose normative character is thus openly recognized."[12] Jochen Schulte-Sasse differentiated between modernism and avant-gardism in his foreword to Peter Bürger's *Theory of the Avant-Garde*, where he ascribed different social-aesthetic roles to modernist and avant-garde artists, declaring the former someone who chooses to attack traditional ways of writing and the latter a figure who opposes the very institutions and business of art.[13] More recently, Fredric Jameson has listed those aspects of modernism that were no longer thought desirable in full postmodernity: "The asceticism of the modern, for example, or its phallocentrism (whether it was ever altogether logocentric I am a little less sure); the authoritarianism and even the occasional repressiveness of the modern; the teleology of the modernist aesthetic as it proceeded on triumphalistically from the newer to the newest; the minimalism of much that was modernist as well; the cult of the genius or seer; [and] the non-pleasurable demands made on the audience or public."[14]

The musicians discussed in these pages are perhaps modernists in that they have carved out and followed conscious paths toward modernity, and thus practiced a certain asceticism and technical introspection. (Cage and Steve Reich qualify as modernists in that they are unusually concerned with method; and Lochhead discusses them from that perspective. It is interesting in this context that Jameson should cite minimalism as an aspect of modernism.) The modernists generally operate within bourgeois channels and institutions. This operating-from-within-the-industry quality, as described by Schulte-Sasse, is one modernist characteristic that allows us to stretch that term to include popular culture figures like Herrmann, Pete Townshend, and John Cale. But our musicians are defined by their individualism, whether it be covert or overt, and share a basic urge toward disruption of musical discourse: they attack traditional standards of writing and discourse and make anomalies a necessary part of their would-be language. As Scherzinger cites Lydia Goehr in these pages, the modernist premise lies in a "critical gap" between artist and society.[15] In this respect, the modernist re-enacts the project of Schoenberg, who in Robert Morgan's account "attempted to transform musical language from a public vehicle, susceptible to comprehension by ordinary people (but thereby also limited to more or less ordinary statement), to a private one capable of speaking the unspeakable. Music became an incantation, a language of ritual that, just because of its inscrutability, revealed secrets hidden from normal understanding."[16]

All that said, the contributors to the present book tend to play loose with tried-and-true dualities of modernism and avant-gardism. Readers may also fault some of these essays for pursuing no systematic distinction between modern and "postmodern." A few contributors resist these distinctions, or even use the words within these dualities interchangeably— and thus fly in the face of respected thinking on modernism by Renato Poggioli and (as we have seen) Calinescu.[17] In this respect, our terminology is less like Calinescu's and Poggioli's than George Perle's in *The Listening Composer*, where he uses several designations to circumscribe the same (as he sees it) peculiarly novel body of twentieth-century music: Perle refers in the same sense to "the art music of our century," "the new music," and "twentieth-century" and "modernist" works. The revolutionary music he describes makes use of "a scale that comprehends the total pitch-class content of that universal set [of twelve pitch classes]." As we do in our own book, Perle sees the operative conflict not between nineteenth- and twentieth-century aesthetics, but between those of the twentieth and twenty-first: he refers to a "classical" body of music by twentieth-century composers, musicians who remain at the start of the twenty-first century "problematical and controversial as to the substance and meaning of the foundational elements of their musical language, as Mozart and Beethoven certainly were not to Brahms and his generation."[18]

In loosening our terminology in such a way, we are acknowledging the decreasing relevance and usefulness of these old dichotomies (as Perle, hardly a careless judge, would seem to concede). After all, Calinescu, Poggioli, and Schulte-Sasse produced their influential accounts of modernism some thirty years ago. One could even ask if avant-gardism exists at all after the Cold War, as a movement or even as a historiographical term. The word originated in military history, and in this day of "smart bombs," terrorism, and waging war with microchips, old ideas of a front line—along with spatial differentiation in deploying the forces of war, or even the idea of war itself in any conventional sense—are increasingly irrelevant, at least for a rich superpower like the United States. One can't escape a similar conclusion in culture and the arts. And with no current, practicing sense of avant-gardism, do we know it well enough even to use it in good conscience as a term for past projects? And then there is the wholesale repackaging of the modernist impulse in recent decades, and its impact on historical-aesthetic terminology. There was a time after World War II when modernism went mainstream in the academy and the art museums. But then came (neo-)conservative and spiritedly commercial times, and modernist and avant-gardist impulses alike were forced underground, to the point where they became synonymous—like besieged political parties forced to become one in order to survive. In the sense that Greil Marcus has talked about "alternative histories," smaller histories that have transpired alongside and in spite of the grander historiographical narratives, avant-gardism has been subsumed into modernism, and all such subversion has become what could be called "alternative modernisms." In the aesthetic fabric of today, such telltale rumples can be found in, for instance, the non-syntactic qualities of Philip Glass's film music, the Noise phenomenon in Japanese dance clubs, and the crudity of draftsmanship in the popular cartoon *South Park*. (The essays toward the end of the book by Lochhead, Bernard, and myself pursue the idea of alternative modernisms further.)

There is also a necessary and symbiotic relationship between our inclusive conceptions of modernism and our continuing belief in the modernist impetus. To that extent, several chapters put forth arguments about terminology: are Steve Reich, early Paul Hindemith, or John Cale to be described as modernists, postmodernists, or perhaps neither? The radicalness of our aesthetic-historical terminology comes to a head in my own conclusion in chapter 15, that Glass's soundtracks for *Koyaanisqatsi* and *Naqoyqatsi* are modernist: they are basically tonal, yes, but the structure and semantics of the music are just as radical as those of Ligeti and Wolfgang Rihm. Glass has shown the new "alternativity" of modernism: in his film scores, subversion (a latterday version of what Hanns Eisler called "the new musical resources") has found a way to survive, find a public, even make some money, when paired with appropriate visual images. An even more imposing example might be John Cage, who is single-handedly responsible for much of today's alternative modernism, and himself the subject of heated debate: was he a postmodernist or a modernist? In her chapter Judy Lochhead claims him as a modernist. But the arguments are sure to continue, which in itself is a sign of the durability and immediacy of Cage's aesthetic.

3. About the Writers

Taking the described platform as a given, I set out to compile a diverse list of contributors including scholars of comparative literature, composers, musicologists, cultural historians, and—yes—some music theorists. In this or any other book, there is no benefit in lining up writers along the same aesthetic, perspective, or form of address. To the contrary: I cannot help but be suspicious of compendia where the outlook is uniform, the writers sharing sympathies beyond what is necessary for a book simply to cohere under a title, and their essays converging toward similar (or even the same) conclusions. Consensual books, like political rallies in a one-party state, protest too much: they beg the questions of what dissenting voices are excluded from the discussion, and what hidden circumstances of discontent necessitate such line-toeing.

The present book sprawls constructively, and its diverse roster is a strength. I can only feel that the variety of our writers and approaches—even the conflicts and contradictions that arise between chapters—is testimony to the continuing influence of modernist repertories and their relevance to different contexts. The only belief all authors share is the conviction that works of the twentieth-century modernists represent a vital if not definitive aspect of our cultural past, present, and future. That shared belief does not necessarily make us disciples of music theory. Not everyone who takes an interest in modernist music is a "music theorist": at most, four of the thirteen contributors could be described as music theorists, whatever that might mean in this day and age. Accordingly, this is not a book about music theory. The volume as a whole is neither "pro-theory" nor "anti-theory," and I did not see how politicizing our project across-the-board in such a way would attract readers to it.

Neither does our common conviction necessarily make us partisans of modernism, or even defenders of that cause. Several authors single out aspects of modernist thought they feel continue to serve as examples, but most of us would not claim that modernist goals and artistic-aesthetic criteria are themselves still viable at the turn of the twenty-first century. Many are too young to have known modernist ideals in any incumbent form. Most of the authors weren't around to witness the epochal Darmstadt *Ferienkurse für neuen Musik* in their heyday or even the American network TV airing of Stravinsky's late mystery play *The Flood*. To work on the book half of the authors interrupted projects on topics as diverse as Joni Mitchell, the Pet Shop Boys, Zimbabwean mbira songs, Frank Zappa, film and video, and Miles Davis. Half of us, and not necessarily the same half working on popular culture topics, are more likely to remember *Dark Side of the Moon* and the Sex Pistols as decisive musical influences. Greg Sandow, Jeremy Tambling, William Bolcom, and Lloyd Whitesell are particularly ambivalent about modernism as a musical-aesthetic project, and it proves mutually illuminating to juxtapose their perspectives with the views of Andrew Mead, Jonathan Bernard, and Richard Toop.

Some of us—perhaps most—have contributed to this book because we love the music and find the telling of that love, the process of fathoming its beauties and its depths, to be both personally fulfilling and a powerful advocacy for the music. In chapter 12 Andrew Mead, long an articulate expositor of the compositional aspects of serialism and twelve-tone music, shows the empathy he feels for Babbitt's music (and that of Sessions, Carter, and Schoenberg). Mead hears this composer's work as something larger, broader, and yet more personal than Babbitt's own edicts would allow. A composition like *Philomel* induces the most urgent searches for meaning: "I find myself seeking sense from the dazzle and glitter of the sounds I am hearing." But Mead primarily laments a fault of the technical terminology which Babbitt's devotees use to discuss his music: that this kind of "shorthand," like most forms of shoptalk, tends to hide the fact that it is describing human experience, that the very specificity of that terminological evolution has politicized the musical experience and alienated people from it.

Babbitt has stood at the center of arguments over academicism and modernism for many years, and any new study of those subjects must perforce continue those Babbittian debates. Greg Sandow has long been interested in Babbitt, for musical and affective reasons rather than aesthetic-historical ones: he clearly loves this music as much as Mead, if for different reasons. His work on Babbitt dates back to the early 1980s, and I have elected to reprint his 1982 essay "A Fine Madness" in this volume for the simple reason that it has become an underground classic of new music criticism. Marked by real enjoyment of Babbitt's music, but perplexed and even angered by the composer's daunting pronouncements on just *how* it is significant, this essay represents one of the very first inquisitions—perhaps *the* first—into the extrastructural meaning of this composer's work. Indeed, Sandow was doubtless the first to talk about Babbitt's music as something *listened to* rather than heard or heard about. In his second, entirely new essay, Sandow goes in a different direction and chooses to argue specifically against institutionalized forms of music theory and analysis as dominant vehicles of meaning in modernism. He ends here with a specific example of how much we stand to lose by assuming such approaches to be exhaustive and definitive. According to him, academic discussions have blinded us to a basic—also poignant, and highly modernistic—characteristic of Schoenberg's music, and perhaps that composer's legacy: his fracturedness, the very *dis*unity of his art.

Like Sandow, Fred Maus attends to qualities of the sounding music and stresses the almost universal tendency to limit the qualities of Babbitt's compositions to those denoted and connoted by the composer's own polemics. As Maus would have it, much of the conflict between music and discourse stems from the hidebound dualities and institutions of our time— particularly the "musical museum" mechanism which has conflated diachronic differences into synchronic dichotomies and conflicts, and which has propitiated the music-aesthetic dualities that have become so intertwined with twentieth-century socio-sexual dualities. Maus has written about music from the perspectives of theory, aesthetics, and gender and sexuality. It is therefore appropriate that his discussion of power structures and power relations should recall Foucault, who writes in the introductory volume to his *History of Sexuality* that power places human activity in an irrevocably binary system: licit and illicit, mainstream and stigmatized.[19] Music and sex become analogous playing fields for this kind of opposition, since they are both experiences hinging on intimacy, vulnerability, transcience, and inexplicable pleasure.

Maus discusses the actual duality mechanism behind the tonal-vs.-atonal and heterosexual-vs.-homosexual oppositions, and their ideologies. In a related inquiry, Lloyd Whitesell investigates some of the metaphors that have cloaked the traditional-vs.-modern dichotomy through the twentieth century and shows us what they reveal (and what they hide). Like Maus, Whitesell explores the idea that people have generally encountered twentieth-century modernist music only through the prism of ideology. In short, ideological positions—one's situation within the essential Foucauldian duality—have conditioned how modernist music has been heard. And yet Whitesell ends by wondering if an escape from ideology is even possible: in his view, compositional ideologies can be propounded ad infinitum, and ideology is inseparable from style.

At least one chapter in our volume, Amy Bauer's, goes beyond local ideologies of reception and intention to take on the very assumption that "listening" is necessarily an obverse, recursively plotted process to "composing." Bauer argues that comprehensibility of compositional processes is a non-issue with modernist music, or any other. In doing so, she argues against music cognitionist Fred Lerdahl, who conceives music as a grammatical construct founded on the dual notions of compositional and listening grammars. Lerdahl faults modernist composition for the discrepancy it produces between the construction of a modernist work and the mental representation that "comprises the 'heard structure' of the piece." Though the dichotomy itself can be traced to modernism, Bauer offers a powerful counterargument to this persistent idea that listening to a modernist work must involve tuning into its one specific compositional grammar: working from Gilles Fauconnier and Mark Turner's models of conceptual blending, she argues that music is intrinsically a polyvalent experience that requires the listener to mix metaphors from different aesthetic- and thought-domains.

A rather different inquisition into the relevance of signifying and signification is offered by Jeremy Tambling, a scholar of comparative literature with particular interest in opera. Tambling considers any misconnection between modernist composition and hearing not from a compositional or cognitive perspective, but as a *necessary* and grammatical disjunction between signifier and signified, as the modernist breakdown of "unitary meaning." He considers it similar to schizophrenia in that respect, and focuses his discussion on Berg's *Wozzeck*, a repertory staple that illuminates these breakdowns in meaning—partly because of the fact that it is an opera, a theatrical genre that is schizoid in itself, but also because it happens to be a modernist opera *about* schizophrenia. But the second side of Tambling's investigation concerns itself with Berg's (compensatory?) structural obsessionalism, his need to effect balance and unity in his work. In Tambling's analysis, Berg's *Wozzeck* offers a unique perspective on the paradoxes and ambiguities of musical modernism.

Toop, a composer and musicologist who worked as assistant to Karlheinz Stockhausen in Cologne in the early 1970s, is also concerned with the breakdown in communication between composer and listener. But he differs from other authors in the book, most obviously Bauer, in saying that comprehension of compositional processes and "audible form" is an issue. In addition to discussing compositional structure, though, Toop addresses the problem of a common wisdom about modern music that has nothing to do with compositional thinking. Turning to Stockhausen's *Kreuzspiel*, for instance, he finds a structure that proves distinctly audible without virtuoso listening, but which is not usually noticed "since the work is, by repute, 'pointillist,' 'totally serialized,' etc. Here, listening may be not so much a matter of tuning in as switching off." Much of the misunderstanding of modernism can, in Toop's estimation, be attributed to misconceived notions that "since innate capacities to recognize form and coherence in certain kinds of music are apparent from a very early age, these form the essential, nature-based template for all future musical perception."

Boulez follows Roland Barthes (more specifically, his influential monograph "Writing Degree Zero") by choosing to discuss the "writtenness" of composition as something distinct from its "hearedness."[20] By invoking "writtenness" Boulez defines writing as act and condition, as a separate agency that participates in the creation of meaning. He contradicts the idea that the written form of a musical work—its score, in most cases—functions only as a means of transmission of the musical thought, which passes unimpeded from the author to the listener. (He writes: ". . . since writing is so overloaded with intentions, the question is no longer even, 'should we

listen naively,' but rather, 'can we still do so?'") Boulez believes that the
"writing" of a piece of music is more than mere transcription of ideas
already present in the mind of the composer. In fact, writing is an object or
activity in its own right, and composition involves a two-way process in
which the writing participates in the creation of the piece.

William Bolcom—compositional polystylist par excellence, pupil of
Milhaud, and editor of George Rochberg's postmodern polemic *The Aesthetics of Survival*—presents conceptions of authorship and writing that
are surprisingly similar to Boulez's. In an April 1996 letter to the arts editor
of the *New York Times*, Bolcom defended serialist Donald Martino against
an indictment penned by Richard Taruskin; and his essay in the present
book grew from that short rejoinder. In both his original letter and the later
essay, he speaks of modernism as an arbitrary period that was generally
hostile to art and to the very idea of listenable music. (And non-listenable
music is beside the point, he would seem to argue, while leaving listenability
undefined.) But Bolcom saves his sharpest arrows for Taruskin's diatribe
against compositional disciplines per se. Contrary to Taruskin, he portrays
a compositional discipline as a catalyst for mystical and possibly wonderful happenings that lie beyond the immediate understanding of composer
as well as listener. "I must defend one of the best examples of academic
modernism in music," Bolcom wrote in his original *New York Times* letter.
"I have always felt that the music of Donald Martino is proof that a strict
twelve-tone composer can still make sensuous and passionate music. A
musical ear can transcend any stricture."[21]

Martin Scherzinger supplied the necessary overview of what modernism
represents in larger terms. A student of Edward Said and Andreas Huyssen,
he is one of few authorities who can defend modernist aesthetics while
working from an intimate knowledge of postmodern as well as modernist
precepts. As previously averred, his essay differs from the others: Scherzinger
is not concerned with meaning per se, except insofar as the modernist musical work takes on socioeconomic rather than purely aesthetic significance
by resisting conscription into commonplace "meaning." He is concerned
with the modernist ideal of autonomy for the artwork, and how misunderstood this idea has become in postmodernity. Against a background of
Adorno and Benjamin, Scherzinger argues that to reject modernism's elevation of aesthetic autonomy today is shortsighted, counterproductive,
willful, and arbitrary. At the very least it is a misrepresentation to argue
against autonomy while ignoring the fact that the modernist work owes its
particular power to this very distance between music and society. "By resisting absorption into the terrain of everyday meaning," Scherzinger writes,
"the inherently non-discursive, absolutely musical work defied the ideological hold of such meaning." Postmodern incentives, on the other hand,
"fetishize differentiality over totality," caught up as they are in imperatives
of late capitalism. The natural outcome of a business conglomerate, an

increasingly verticalized market is, perhaps paradoxically, a market oriented toward a multitude of equalized products (fragmented narratives) rather than a selective hierarchy of products (the meta-narrative).

Our book concludes with three essays that explore the boundaries of modernism as it confronts—and, in some cases, coalesces with—postmodernist aesthetics, popular culture, and commercialism. These contributors bring to their topics expertise in pop and rock, popular culture, and questions of listener agency in modern and postmodern music. Although Steve Reich's thinking of the 1960s was rooted in the idea of compositional process, Judy Lochhead describes how he—like Lerdahl—questioned whether compositional structures are *hearable* in themselves. While Reich's conceptions of compositional process and structure have roots in modernist thinking, then, he and George Rochberg did help mark a basic turn in the mid to late 1960s toward a "postmodern" conception of listener agency. Reich talks about *hearability* as an objective quality but doesn't ask if the listener can or should *make* it a *priority* to hear structure. Which is to say the listener that Reich describes has agency but that agency is to some extent indeterminate: the compositional object lies with the listener's perception rather than the grammar instituted by the composer.

The essays by Jonathan Bernard and myself are concerned with the possibility of modernism within popular, "postmodern" creative cultures—and more generally with the difficult and complex relationship between avant-gardism and the marketplace. I discuss the latterday modernism heard in many movie scores and, conversely, what I call the "phantasmagoric" concert styles resulting from the influence that modernist soundtracks have had on such composers as Penderecki and John Corigliano. Bernard finds remnants of early-century modernism in certain rock currents of the 1960s and 70s, and traces a particularly telling lifespan as those impulses fought briefly but tellingly for survival in a commodity-driven field. His essay and mine are complementary. We both follow up on Adorno's declaration that the modernist impulse is irrevocably transformed and commodified when it enters its second generation. In short, we both wish (Bernard with his "psychedelic" or "progressive" rock and me with my "phantasmagoric" acoustic music) to decide just what kind of legacy these modernism-remnants represent. Would Adorno's malediction of "pseudo-individualization" apply to them? Bernard concludes that yes, some of the music does effect false novelty. But he also maintains that the avant-garde element was redirected rather than nullified in the case of Deep Purple, Pink Floyd, and the British "progressive rock" bands—groups characterized by "stylistic consolidation and retrenchment, if not outright retreat from the avant-garde."

A Hegelian, almost deterministic sense of history leads me to the more extreme belief that recent film-inspired modernism has both supplanted and validated earlier art-music modernism.[22] American formalism and academia proved bankrupt when it came to invoking or supplying meanings for modernist music, perhaps because they have until fairly recently made it their business to take a positivist, fact-based approach rather than a hermeneutical one. At the same time, popular culture has stepped into the breach and instituted its own codes through the sociogenetically powerful mechanism of film. (Jeremy Tambling has similar things to say in his own chapter about opera's relationship with modernism.) Against early modernist expectations, it is popular culture that promises to carry modernist styles—albeit in altered form—well into the future.

4. Acknowledgments

The greatest debt is of course owed to the contributors, who so eagerly took up the premise and showed immense patience as the book was assembled, edited, and seen through publication: half of these essays were finished by 1999. We all owe much to Joseph Auner and Leo Balk, who took an interest in the book early on. Ralph Locke helped the volume along with his wisdom and unflagging support just when they were most needed, and we are all most grateful for his advocacy and encouragement. I am also very thankful for Tim Madigan's time and advice, and editor Louise Goldberg's guidance and wisdom. I thank the Society for Music Theory and especially the College of the Arts at the Ohio State University for their generosity in providing copyright and publication subventions just when they were urgently needed; as Associate Deans at the latter office, Judith Koroscik, David Butler, Esther Beth Sullivan, and the late Jim Hutchens were particularly gracious with their help and time. I also owe many thanks to Christian Bourgois for permission to translate and republish Boulez's "L'Écriture du musicien: Le regard du sourd," as published and copyrighted by him in the volume *Jalons* (Paris: Christian Bourgois, 1989; the essay originally appeared in 1981 in the journal *Critique*). In addition I am thankful for Jean-Jacques Nattiez's advice and help in procuring the necessary permissions to bring the Boulez essay into English, and for Robert Samuels's painstaking translation and discussions over its critical contexts. Jane Warburton worked tirelessly and extremely dependably as editorial assistant, checking citations and not letting up in the seemingly endless process of finalizing copyright permissions. Keith Dippre's skill in putting together the musical examples graces a good many of these pages. Finally, the book would not likely have been conceived or brought to fruition if it weren't for the encouragement and input of Yoshiaki Yoshinari, Philip Rupprecht, Amy Bauer, Dina Lentsner, Josh Heaphey, Rena Iwai, and a number of other friends and colleagues. Not only am I grateful for their moral support, their hypothesized readership was a constant point of guidance—and I hope very much they will enjoy the final product and decide that it was worth the wait.

Notes

1. By way of analogy, I offer my own first period of intoxication with Mahler. When I was searching for meaning in his music at that time, I found my search thwarted by his banality, which seemed an evasion of meanings as I then understood them. The Mahler literature that I found failed to discuss this aspect of his music, and therefore left me dissatisfied. The commentary on Mahler by T. W. Adorno and Carl Dahlhaus helped me through that impasse, but there are few if any such expositions on Schoenberg's restlessness, Xenakis's primitiveness, Ferneyhough's hermeticism, and other "extramusical" connotations in modernism that dare not speak their names.

2. "The Year in Ideas," *New York Times Magazine*, December 9, 2001, 50.

3. Fischer, "Fallacies of Narration," in *Historians' Fallacies: Toward a Logic of Historical Thought* (New York, Evanston, and London: Harper & Row, 1970), 155–57.

4. For a relatively brief account of general modern/postmodern oppositions, see N. J. Rengger, *Retreat from the Modern: Humanism, Postmodernism and the Flight from Modernist Culture* (London: Bowerdean, 1996).

5. McClary, "Terminal Prestige: The Case of Avant-Garde Music Composition," *Cultural Critique* 12 (1989): 57–81; Boros, "Why Complexity?" *Perspectives of New Music* 31, no. 1 (1993): 6–9; Boros, "Why Complexity? II," *Perspectives of New Music* 32, no. 1 (1994): 90–113.

6. *The Agony of Modern Music* (New York: Simon and Schuster, 1955).

7. In Levi R. Bryant's description, the *jouissance* is "the inverse side (mobius strip) of [the subject's] desire and that which causes his desire to function as it does." Bryant, personal communication, March 21, 2004.

8. In *The Lacanian Subject*, Bruce Fink defines the Lacanian understanding of *jouissance* as the situation devised in fantasy, "this pleasure—this excitation due to sex, seeing, and/or violence, whether positively or negatively viewed by conscience, whether considered innocently pleasurable or disgustingly repulsive." *The Lacanian Subject: Between Language and Jouissance* (Princeton, N.J.: Princeton University Press, 1996), p.60.

9. In this way modernist music differs from sado-masochism, in that pain is not directly or consciously aspired to, and therefore not experienced. I thank Prof. Bryant for suggesting these Lacanian descriptions of music. Levi R. Bryant, personal communication, March 21, 2004. I am also grateful to Amy Bauer for much information on Lacan, and for engaging in a number of most helpful and provocative Lacanian discussions.

10. Leonard B. Meyer, "Perception and Cognition in Complex Music," in his *Music, the Arts, and Ideas: Patterns and Predictions in Twentieth-Century Culture*, republished with a new postlude (Chicago: University of Chicago Press, 1994), 311.

11. Yenawine, *How to Look at Modern Art* (New York: Harry N. Abrams, 1991), 7.

12. Calinescu, *Faces of Modernity: Avant-Garde, Decadence, Kitsch* (Bloomington and London: Indiana University Press, 1977), 86.

13. Schulte-Sasse, Foreword to Peter Bürger, *Theory of the Avant-Garde*, trans. Michael Shaw (Minneapolis: University of Minnesota Press, 1984), xv.

14. Fredric Jameson, *A Singular Modernity: Essay on the Ontology of the Present* (London and New York: Verso, 2002), 1.

15. Lydia Goehr, *The Quest for Voice: Music, Politics, and the Limits of Philosophy* (Berkeley, Los Angeles, and London: University of California Press, 1998), 37–47.

16. Morgan, "Secret Languages: The Roots of Musical Modernism," in *Modernism: Challenges and Perspectives*, ed. Monique Chefdor, Ricardo Quinones, and Albert Wachtel (Urbana and Chicago: University of Illinois Press, 1986), 49.

17. Poggioli, *Theory of the Avant-Garde*, trans. Gerald Fitzgerald (Cambridge, Mass. and London: Harvard University Press, 1968).

18. Perle, *The Listening Composer* (Berkeley, Los Angeles, and Oxford: University of California Press, 1990), 42–43, 53.

19. Michel Foucault, *The History of Sexuality*, Volume 1: *An Introduction*, trans. Robert Hurley (New York: Random House, 1978), 83.

20. Barthes, *Writing Degree Zero*, trans. Annette Lavers and Colin Smith (New York: Hill and Wang, 1968). Barthes defines writing as that which goes beyond grammar (which is universal) or style (which is dictated by historical period) and remains the distinctive *choice* of the writer. The fact that Boulez insists on writing as an ideal or virtual construct, whose capabilities go well beyond the containment of the work's meaning, also recalls Derrida's discussion of writing. In particular, the writing of a piece demonstrates that it does not have one "present" meaning, but is always radically in need of interpretation; it also participates in the creation of meaning, instead of awaiting use by an author who already holds that meaning fully in mind prior to the creation of the (musical) utterance. I thank Robert Samuels for his helpful observations on the Boulez essay and its necessary situation in the contemporary French intellectual debates.

21. Bolcom, Letter to the Editor: "In Defense of Dodecaphonism," *New York Times*, 7 April 1996, section 2, p. 7.

22. Or perhaps I am influenced by Merleau-Ponty's phenomenological perspective on history: "My existence does not stem from my antecedents, from my physical and social environment; instead it moves out toward them and sustains them, for I alone bring into being for myself (and therefore into being in the only sense that the word can have for me) the tradition which I elect to carry on. . . ." Maurice Merleau-Ponty, "What is Phenomenology?" in *Phenomenology of Religion: Eight Modern Descriptions of the Essence of Religion*, ed. Joseph Dabney Bettis (New York: Harper & Row, 1969), 15.

Part One

Reception & Politics

1

Intention and Meaning in Modernist Music

Arved Ashby

I am not very sympathetic to certain theses associated with postmodernism, such as that of the death of the author, or that according to which all works of art/cultural phenomena rightly impact the understanding or appreciation of all others, so that, for example, the music of Beethoven is properly heard differently after Kubrick's Clockwork Orange.
    —A distinguished aesthetics scholar, when shown an early precis of this book

Little is left to the imagination [with Boulez's third recording of Pli selon pli*], except the unanswered question of how and why our ears and minds perceive this music—as powerful yet elusive in syntax and semantics as the poetry of Mallarmé to which it pays tribute—as clearly as they do.*
    —Nicholas Williams, BBC Music Magazine, August 2002

[The music of Boulez and Stockhausen] makes no statement. It's music for after-the-bomb-drops. Boulez would fit perfectly for an atomic waste-dump. But could they write about the love of a child for his mother? I think not.
    —James Galway, Symphony Magazine, June-July 2003

1. Music, Intention, Interpretation

Should the listener laugh at the apparent march parody in Xenakis's *Jonchaies,* when the work was put together on statistical premises? Would it be worthwhile to hear the untraditional syntax of Boulez's *Marteau sans maître* or Babbitt's *Dual* as an evocation of schizophrenia, when these composers are among the eminent rationalists of their time? What cultural mechanisms would a listener confront in making such readings? What would be the rewards of such interpretations, and what new limitations would be introduced?

One feels compelled to ask such hesitant questions only when it comes to twentieth-century music, particularly modernist works of the past one hundred years. And these questions of meaning and intention point out one of the more volatile confrontations between modern and "postmodern" sensibilities. Such inquisitions into individual reaction and meaning can embarrass American academics, because they cut so strongly against the way these authorities have been trained to discuss this music. But why? Autonomy from the everyday world was a founding rationale for post-Enlightenment modernism. But most would now say such high-humanist autonomy never was, and never could be, a possibility—especially in this least obviously semantic of the arts, the one therefore most imbued with social meaning. As for the importance that compositional ideologies have for listeners in postmodernity, it should be noted that the opera-going public has for some time now (at least in Europe and some parts of America) largely kept Wagner's own hateful ideologies from impeding the aesthetic pleasure it finds in his music. In earlier periods, and with twentieth-century music in more accessible styles, these widespread searches for meaning became an important part of reception history. Scott Burnham's book *Beethoven Hero* details the history and continuing usefulness of such approaches with regard to Beethoven's Third Symphony.[1] Nicholas Cook in *Analysing Musical Multimedia* has described Franz Fröhlich's detailed nineteenth-century explanations of Beethoven's Ninth Symphony as a man's struggle against deafness; about which Cook writes, "To trace the reception of the Ninth Symphony through responses like Fröhlich's is to see musical meaning in the making."[2]

Before getting into my main discussion, I should offer a more detailed idea of what "meaning" might be in music. The questions of what instrumental music (music without the denotative specificity of words) can mean, and where such meaning might lie, have of course been topics of heated argument since the late eighteenth century. As one analogy for discussion of musical meaning, I offer philosopher Gary Iseminger's three categories of observations about a literary text. As Iseminger introduces them, these represent three avenues toward finding meaning in a poem by Gerard Manley Hopkins:

> *interpretation*:
> (1) Hopkins's poem "Henry Purcell" refers to a famous English composer.
> (2) The poem "Henry Purcell" expresses the wish that Purcell shall have good fortune.
> *description*:
> (3) The first line of "Henry Purcell" contains two occurrences of the word "have," two occurrences of the word "fallen," and three occurrences of the word "fair."
> *evaluation*:
> (4) "Henry Purcell" is a great poem.[3]

Translating these categories into musical terms would present obvious and not-so-obvious problems, depending on just how one thinks music is or is not expressive. (For one, would I be interpreting or describing if I took the last two movements of Beethoven's "Pastorale" Symphony to represent a storm followed by peasants' merry-making at its passing? The question is not easy to answer since this is a famously programmatic work: I could simply be relaying the fact of the composer's own interpretation, which would make my role that of a describer.) Still, Iseminger's analogies help clear up my semantics. The idea of meaning in music would seem to coincide primarily with Iseminger's "interpretation" category. And this is also the kind of statement among the three types that is most difficult to make about a piece of music. Rather, such "interpretations" are *easier* to make about a piece of music than "descriptions" and "evaluations," but they are (for what it's worth) harder to substantiate. Iseminger's "interpretation" would seem the effort that the listener brings to the table, a kind of obverse to the music's capacity for expression; in other words, music *expresses* something which we then read through the act of *interpretation*. (The process is more complex than all that, of course, as I get into when I discuss the idea of authorial intention below.)

The literary critic Monroe C. Beardsley came up with a rather more polemical category that I could add to Iseminger's three: namely, the category of "superimposition." (Beardsley's description appeared in print thirty years ago, and today's post-structuralist critics would surely come up with a more charitable designation.) As an example of "superimposition," Beardsley's example is reading the children's tale "Jack and the Beanstalk" as Freudian symbolism or a Christian allegory.[4] To add a "superimpositional" claim to Iseminger's statements about Hopkins's poem, one could come up with an assertion like:

superimposition:
(5) "Henry Purcell" is a poem about homoerotic desire.

Such a "superimposition" is to be differentiated from Iseminger's other interpretations (or at least from interpretation and description) by the fact that it is less grounded in the semantics and specific denotations of the text. In statement (5), such is indicated by the phrase ". . . is about . . . ," which becomes a liberating interpretive tool but also invites vagueness: it moves us from denotative meaning to connotative meaning, and its new possibilities and dangers. Fröhlich practiced superimposition when he heard Beethoven's Ninth.

Post-Kantians have worked to define meaning in music. But the kinds of meaning sought out have changed. Iseminger's five categories help us generalize about the changes in how people have thought and written about instrumental music since the late eighteenth century. In brief, since the time of Fröhlich's writings about Beethoven's Ninth and, say, Adolph Bernhard Marx's writings about Beethoven's Third, "professional" discussions of

music have seen a marked shift from such superimpositional, interpretational, and even evaluative statements toward the purely descriptive. Clearly,
such changes have mirrored the rise of logical positivism, and the rise of
modernism itself. Eduard Hanslick, the Viennese formalist and aesthetic
opponent to Wagner, played a role in this. His treatise *Vom musikalische
Schönen* (first edition 1854) is a polemic for description over interpretation: Hanslick believed it impossible to make interpretive statements about
music, with the exception of what he called dynamic states. His philosophy
proved influential, well into the second half of the twentieth century. And
particularly with regard to newly written music, probably for the reason
that its composers had become largely synonymous with its intellectuals
and aestheticians. It is possible to hear the preponderance of *descriptions*
of twentieth-century modernist music, and the allergy toward *interpretations* and especially toward *superimpositions,* as an after-effect of Hegelian
accusations that music is especially handicapped by its inability to express,
"mean," or embody anything specific, that it has no semantics. The compositional avant-garde had to negotiate such formalist polemics through
the nineteenth century, continuing on (by way of Hanslick) through to the
Weberns and Babbitts in our own century.[5]

The argument boils down to the concept, one that inspired strenuous
debate in literary circles but has been virtually ignored in music, of authorial *intention*: does an author mean what he or she *intends* to mean? The
subject is an old one among literary critics: the middle of the century saw
the rise of the New Criticism in literary thinking, as presaged by Wimsatt
and Beardsley's famous "Intentional Fallacy" article (1946), whereby what
a reader found in a text was declared to have no necessary connection to
what the author of that text actually conceived or believed, and in any
event intention itself was deemed irrelevant and unknowable. This essay
apparently marked the first appearance of the critical term "intentionalism,"
which Wimsatt and Beardsley were of course arguing against.[6] Finally, in
the 1970s the intentionalist–anti-intentionalist debate was remade with the
arrival of Jacques Derrida, Paul de Man, and deconstructive approaches to
a text—a juncture in textual analysis where intention was at once subsumed and left behind as a concept because the critic took its limits as a
point of departure.[7] Indeed, post-structuralists would recognize none of
Iseminger's categories—believing, rather, that meaning lies behind the written
text, or in its interstices.

The rise (and subsequent fall, some would say) of anti-intentionalism
has somehow bypassed those who discuss music of the twentieth-century
modernists, though it is difficult to ask whether a basic emphasis on description over interpretation propitiated this oversight or is merely symptomatic of it. Because they are so often covertly anti-intentionalist but
phrased in intentionalist terms, theoretical discussions of twentieth-century music tend to have a particularly strange, even bigamous, relationship

with intentionalism and anti-intentionalism. (Ethan Haimo surely confused the issue further in a recent *Music Theory Spectrum* article where he proposed a basic intentionalist–anti-intentionalist difference between certain descriptions of music, when more often than not the differences in his examples are purely semantic.[8]) Institutionalized discussions of twentieth-century music were founded on the dual platform of twelve-tone theory and Fortean pitch-class set analysis—two scientistic methods of investigation that for the most part advance supra-intentionalist arguments, many very useful ones among them, in a vocabulary of compositional-theoretical intentionalism.[9]

1. "The Death of the Author"

One particular essay encapsulates anti-intentionalist thinking, and provided a phrase that became a commonplace in philosophy and literary aesthetics. Post-structuralist linguist and critic Roland Barthes—and particularly one Barthes essay with a title that quickly became a commonplace phrase in philosophy, history, and literary aesthetics. Barthes wrote "The Death of the Author" ("La Mort de l'auteur") in 1967.[10] Whether by reason of its intellectual virtuosity or *bon mots,* the article defined the beginning of an epoch, and some have even called it an augury of postmodernism, despite the fact that much of what Barthes said had already been laid out by, among others, Wimsatt and Beardsley and by Georg Steiner (*Language and Silence*).[11] The fiercely intentionalist E. D. Hirsch even saw the decades before Barthes as "a heavy and largely victorious assault on the sensible belief that a text means what its author meant."[12] But it was Barthes who had the éclat (the sensationalism, some would say) to use the decisive metaphor of death for the fate of the author as source and nexus of a text's meaning. He invoked death because he wanted to echo Nietzsche and his pronouncement of the death of God, and thereby show the author's demise to be profound and irreversible. In short, Barthes—like Nietzsche—was writing more than a prouncement on literary study, he was writing an obituary for something deep within ourselves and our culture.

What exactly did Barthes say and want? Like Nietzsche, he called for a revolution: to free the text "from any authoritarian control" by reducing the figure of the "Author-God" to the level of mere "scriptor," and thereby ceding the text and its meanings to the reader. ("The reader is the space on which all the quotations that make up a writing are inscribed without any of them being lost; a text's unity lies not in its origin but in its destination."[13]) But he was also describing a situation that, chez Barthes, was already well in existence with Mallarmé and Paul Valéry: a situation where "it is language itself that speaks, not the author; [and] to write is . . . to reach that point where only language acts, 'performs,' and not 'me.'"[14]

More specifically, Barthes was eager to differentiate between God-like Author and proletarian scriptor, and to ensure polyvalent meanings for a text. "We know now that a text is not a line of words releasing a single 'theological' meaning (the 'message' of the Author-God) but a multi-dimensional space in which a variety of writings, none of them original, blend and clash. The text is a tissue of quotations drawn from the innumerable centres of culture."[15] Just as important, he declared the critical task of deciphering "a 'secret,' an ultimate meaning" to be just as moribund as the figure of the author:

> Once the Author is removed, the claim to decipher a text becomes quite futile. To give a text an Author is to impose a limit on that text, to furnish it with a final signified, to close the writing. Such a conception suits criticism very well, the latter then allotting itself the important task of discovering the Author (or its hypostases: society, history, psyché, liberty) beneath the work: when the Author has been found, the text is "explained"—victory to the critic.[16]

To describe the new process of reader-based explanation, Barthes suggested we replace the idea of deciphering with the less directional notion of "disentangling." Or, to return to Beardsley and Iseminger's categories as I spelled them out earlier, we could call Barthes an advocate of "superimposition": at least this is the closest thing in my fairly conservative terminology thus far to Barthes's idea of the text as a reader-based "multi-dimensional space," his conclusion that "a text's unity lies not in its origin but in its destination."

The predictions of Barthes have been realized most conspicuously by the joint critical projects of marxism and feminism. Along with their offspring of gender and ethnic studies, these two lines of inquiry have tried to institute a hermeneutics with no transcendant, text-based meaning; or, in the case of Derrida- or Paul de Man-ian styles of deconstruction, a hermeneutics based on denial of such meaning. These paradoxical critical projects have by no means been universally accepted. Indeed, a good number have found them philosophically and rationally unsound, and many have seen them as an invitation to a kind of interpretive meltdown: the path toward concluding that *The Tempest* is really about incest or *Moby Dick* an allegory about castration. Still, whatever the residual structuralist resistance, the Barthesian multiplicities of textual meaning—and the marxist and feminist projects more generally—have become a permanent and undeniable fact of critical life.

Barthesian techniques of "disentangling" have become a necessary part of understanding music, at least to post-structuralists. However, and here I return to the main thrust of my essay, they have played a very limited role in approaching modernist music of the twentieth century. Adorno, apologist for Schoenberg and the Viennese avant-garde, is perhaps an exception.

But even Adorno, as a composition student (once-removed) of Schoenberg, retained some of what Barthes deprecatingly called authoritarian control—a telling pun that equates authorship with fascism. When discussing Schoenberg in *Philosophy of Modern Music* and elsewhere, Adorno was still concerned to some extent with questions of authorial intent, compositional technique, and even the reification and distraction of authorship that he called "the compositional subject." And there is certainly a contrast to be drawn between, say, T. S. Eliot's *The Wasteland* and Ezra Pound's *Canticles* and pieces of music written at about the same time such as Schoenberg's Violin Fantasy and Xenakis's *Metastasis*. The difference concerns something literary theorists call *critical monism,* or the notion that a text can fulfill or embody only one meaning or interpretation. If the T. S. Eliot and Pound are "about" any one thing, it would seem to be refutation of critical monism; these works are designed to elude any one interpretation, and their very modernism resides in this aspect. The Schoenberg and Xenakis, however, are in the eyes of the musicologist and theorist a kind of composing-out of a single meaning imputed explicitly or implicitly to the composer: the Schoenberg manifests twelve-tone combinatorial relations, and the Xenakis a specific manifestation of stochastics, or probability theory. Anything beyond that is a derelict or adjunct meaning. (This is undoubtedly an oversimplification, in that these are manifold issues that can never be "solved" or answered absolutely. But they are rarely broached with any such caveats, and the complaint could be made that a kind of infinite but monodirectional inquiry has crowded out manifold questions—be their potential answers more or less "deep" than those of the structuralists.)

2. The Non-Death of the Composer

I averred a moment ago that Barthesian multiplicities of textual meaning have become permanent aspects of reading a text. Recent intentionalist philosophers and aestheticians would argue with this. Indeed, the importance of authorial intention has "come back to life" in recent years in the eyes of many aestheticians. In a word, the author has been restored to health—never feeling better. Several recent studies carry clever and epigrammatic titles on the "Death and Rebirth of the Author" theme, and intentionalist thinkers have run out of ways to work the phrase "premature autopsy" into their titles. Yet the modernist composer barely caught him- or herself a sniffle over this ideologically volatile span of time. The modern author returned from the dead under the aegis of literati like E. D. Hirsch and Stein Haugom Olsen,[17] while the modernist composer more or less retained impeccable control over the search for meaning in his or her work. How has the modern musical creator stayed so unequivocally "non-dead," so robust and healthy, in the Barthesian sense? I believe there are three main reasons.

The Musical Work

Much of the lack of freedom felt in interpreting music of the twentieth-century modernists is owed to some peculiarities of the musical—as opposed to literary—work. The compositional "Author-God" is so much more an insistent presence than the literary author, and this mostly has to do with the more difficult logistics of "reading" a piece of Western concert music. Textless "classical" music, compared to the other arts, offers a strange combination of immediacy and intangibility. The person wanting to encounter Joyce's *Ulysses* need only go to any reasonably sized bookstore and buy a mass-produced paperback in any one of several editions, at least one of them no doubt printed in a typeface or layout that the author would have disapproved of. But performances and recordings of Boulez's *Pli selon pli* or *Répons* remain the domain of Boulez himself. (His first two recordings of the former differ substantially in tempo, and in some ways the piece itself thereby seems to have changed between 1969 and 1981.) As a result, when we hear *Pli selon pli* we insistently see and hear the composer himself bringing the music to sounding form, seeming to create it before our very ears and eyes—seeming to compose it anew, thereby retaining his authorial authority over the work. (I have vivid memories of Boulez conducting *Répons* in Chicago in 1985, and since that evening have even found the way he turned the huge pages of the score to be an indelible part of hearing that composition.) Even when the composer is not a performer, he or she remains a kind of unspoken collaborator in the performance in a way unique to the twentieth century: it is a sign of the continued sway of the twentieth-century composer that a performance of Elliott Carter by the Chicago Symphony could make headlines in the mid-1980s when the conductor gave a few pre-concert words on the music that caused the composer to storm out of the hall. Or that Messiaen's music should be accompanied so persistently by the composer's incredibly monistic, and also singularly unrevealing, program notes. Or that Babbitt's writings and analyses could continue to be so fascinating and intimidating decades after they were written.

One can only wonder if the passage of time and the eventual passing of these "author-gods" from the scene will make a difference in interpretation and reception. Their presence actually resides in two places: in their physical or media appearance, and in the authorial consistency of their work as a whole (itself a modernist characteristic, and only the first of these will really disappear along with the author-god's bodily presence). Literary theorist Alexander Nehamas, unhappy with the Barthes-Foucault doomsday prognosis of authorial death, proposed a duality of writer (the physical figure) and author (the figure-through-the-text) and claimed that "what a text means is what it *could mean* to its writer."[18] More specifically, Nehamas sees an interrelated chain of writer, text, work, author, and interpretation. "Writers produce texts," he says. "Some texts are subject to interpretation:

Understanding them involves seeing them as the products of idiosyncratic agents. Interpretation construes texts as works. Works generate the figure of the author."[19] In this sense, then, any possible meanings deduced from the work will have to pass the test of consistency with what we know of author and oeuvre as "idiosyncratic agents."

The limited availability of modernist musical "texts" has also sustained this filial relationship between work and composer. Or, better said, there has developed a symbiotic relationship between that limited accessibility and that close affinity. At this point in history, the supposedly inherent, musical inaccessibility of a modernist work—the "difficulties" it presents *in hearing*—pales into insignificance compared to the logistical difficulty of getting access to the text—finding *a way to get around to* hearing it. That aforementioned second recording of *Pli selon pli* is a good deal harder to find on the shelves than Joyce's *Ulysses*. Whereas a 32-bar pop standard is malleable in meaning and owes this multivalence to its transmissability, its ease of physical-aural access, its omnipresence, a string quartet by Ferneyhough is far less likely to be found in a music store, record store, on the radio, or whistled on the subway. Even if the modernist composer were very much alive and kicking, and polemical, wide public success and dissemination of a work by him or her would cause its textual meaning to quickly spin out of his or her control—or away from any one person's authority, for that matter.

Music Analysis and Composition

The particularities of music analysis have also helped the modernist composer retain his or her authorial health. If the twentieth-century composer is more present in word and body than the twentieth-century literary author, this has something to do with institutionalized methods of analysis—his or her presence in analytic schools. A modernist composition is generally felt to require "professional" explanation, and a restricted one at that. Music analysis, to return to Iseminger's categories, is a language of *description*. If someone were to sponsor the unusual idea that the Schoenberg Fantasy, Op. 47, was "about" relating the two whole-tone scales or parodying a particular style of violin playing, he or she would invite confrontation with an authority who claimed connection, direct or indirect, with Schoenberg's own thinking. Or by someone who claimed, through their familiarity with the Schoenbergian twelve-tone system, to know just what the composer was trying to "do" in this piece. And both these kinds of testimony would differ in essence from a scholar substantiating claims about Beethoven's music, say, by citing that composer's letters or metronome markings.

It is easy to see such monistic projects as the very basis for modernism in music. For example, Schoenberg and Webern took exception to the innate variability and plurality of *Ästhetik*—to its "softness" and variability—and insisted instead on unalterable, natural laws as a model for discussing art. In his *Der Weg zur neuen Musik* (1932–33), Webern all but declared the twelve-tone row a monism, an escape from the arbitrary interpretative wills and wiles of aesthetics.[20] Even as late as 1964, Susan Sontag could say of the avant-garde art of her own time, that it "may be understood as motivated by a flight from interpretation."[21] Given such a basis and the ostensible difficulties posed by a hearing of modernist music, it is easy to understand why the authorial declarations of the composer might appear the most attractive option—or model, at least—for anyone now wishing to "read" the music. (Certainly, it is interesting to compare Schoenberg, Webern, Babbitt, or Nono with the likes of T. S. Eliot, Pound, Joyce, or Braque, who did not leave behind such a clear monistic legacy for future interpretation of *their* work. In Hirsch's eyes, Eliot and Pound were responsible for the very inception of the idea that a poem was autonomous from its author.[22])

Babbitt has developed a particularly influential and monistic view of music theory and analysis, describing the ideal apparatus as the one that uncovers a basic and constant aspect of the work and produces replicable results. The right approach is an objective one; he writes that music theory must provide "an adequately reconstructed terminology to make possible and to provide a model for determinate and testable statements about musical compositions." His ideal analysis betrays a monistic mindset, in that its specificity and precision work to circumvent the fact that "infinitely many true statements can be made about a musical composition."[23] Babbitt's approach is monistic; but it is more work-driven than composer-driven, and this distinguishes it from the Schoenberg school's philosophy.

As if in response to such monistic approaches, a particular listener-oriented brand of music theory has developed: semiotics, or the study of signs, has come of age as a post-Barthesian strategy. One could say similar things about narratology, the study of the functional units that create something similar to a literary sense of narrative. Here I refer to the work of, among others, Jean-Jacques Nattiez, Anthony Newcomb, and Eero Tarasti. The multivalence and immediacy of semiotic readings might still rescue modernist music and its analysts from author-heavy irrelevancy. But such listener-based inquiries into this music have yet to appear, despite the fact that semioticians assume the mechanisms of language to be well outside the purview of authorial intent. It is easier to attribute this semiotic and narratological hesitancy to the politics discussed above than to any incompatability or semiotic insufficiency in the music itself, and semioticians and modernist compositions alike would benefit from such explorations.

Modernism and semantics

Third and last among the reasons for the modernist composer's consistent Barthesian health are the peculiarities specifically underlying the mortality of the literary rather than musical author. The "death of the author" project in literature was motivated at least in part by people who wished to demonstrate the semantic autonomy of written language, the notion that language need not convey any closed and definite meaning. Any such project would be harder to define and locate in music. Unless it would be an attempt to demonstrate how music can "work" when free of tonal constraints, but then advocates of atonality generally upheld the idea of authorship, and recent decades have seen greater incentive to show the cognitive and cultural rootedness of musical languages. The impetus now aims in the other direction, and scholars are at pains—especially in the realm of pitch—to find a musical semantics, or at least a particular set of meanings, and the phrase "tonal language" has become an acceptable one. Nowadays, there are more obvious contradictions to the idea that music might be free of semantics: specifically, the popular notion that "meaning" in music resides primarily in its tonality (or, more generally, pitch), and that the prime (the only?) true language-character of music lies in its tonal language.

Discussions of tonality have surfaced in various attempts to challenge modernist—and, more specifically, serial—projects in music. The most stringently argued of these is Lerdahl's and Jackendoff's *Generative Theory of Tonal Music*.[24] These authors approach music and meaning from a grammatical perspective. In brief, Lerdahl and Jackendoff assert that pitch (and harmony) is the only aspect of music that can be grammatical because it is the only aspect that can be *hierarchically* ordered. According to their thinking, one can properly speak of a "pitch language" or "harmonic language" but strictly speaking not a "rhythmic language" or "timbral language," because it is not possible to create hierarchies of rhythm or timbre. (For instance, one can speak of secondary dominant relationships in harmony, or even gradated relations through chains of fifths, but a certain rhythm cannot relate to another through a secondary-dominant-type of relationship.) In a later essay titled "Cognitive Constraints on Compositional Systems," Lerdahl follows up on this argument with the idea of reciprocal compositional and listening grammars, describing the incongruity between the two that proves frustrating and finally ruinous for a person trying to listen to modernist music.[25] According to him, the modernist composer generally contravenes the cognitive or perceptual constraints necessary if the listener is to understand and follow the piece (though Lerdahl does not claim outright that one, two, or all of these are necessary for the listener).

I don't believe music, even serial music, need be limited to a grammatical-linguistic conception of meaning. I would go further and say that modern art—or art in any period, for that matter—need not function grammatically. The work of Mallarmé and the Symbolist poets tends toward the oblique: they take lexical items (words) and ask that we process them not lexically, denotatively, but at a musical (or at least metaphorical) level. If we were to take a Lerdahlian approach to these writers, we could reach some absurd parallel conclusions: by analogy to Lerdahl's tacitly intentionalist thinking, one could go so far as to try and discredit the Symbolists for being ungrammatical, or say that they produced works that are "unsuccessful" because of an anomaly between the language at their surface and the means by which they are to be taken in. Lerdahl might say that I'm comparing apples and oranges, and respond by saying that Boulez's work is avowedly and necessarily grammatical at a compositional level, that the compositional language *is* perforce the listening language, while Mallarmé's is not. He takes Boulez's *Le Marteau sans maître* as his prime example of a serially conceived grammar that does not observe the cognitive constraints necessary if it is to be hearable. *Marteau* must, or so Lerdahl might say, make sense on a musical-grammatical level, because (unlike the Mallarmé) there is no other level it can make sense on. Its musical level *is* its grammatical level. But I would again respond by denying the *necessity* of a grammatical "understanding" of a piece of music; and if I felt the need to concede Lerdahl the necessity of musical "communication," say that we would also need to consider codes and signs that have nothing to do with compositional systems. Any claim that *Le Marteau sans maître* is more a grammar-based entity than, say, Mallarmé's *Coup de dés jamais n'abolira le hasard* would require a more detailed exploration of precisely how important the composer thought the compositional system was in the larger reality of his work—in short, just how "serial" *Le Marteau* actually is.

3. Listening

To determine how important the compositional system is for experiencing a piece, one would have to determine what other communicative systems, sponsored by composer or listener, the work might contain. Boulez himself disavows the relevance of his own compositional thinking to the listener, and says, in a riposte that sounds almost as if it were aimed at Lerdahl and Jackendorff, that there are other, more important levels to the experience:

> When I first got the score of Schoenberg's Piano Concerto I did a kind of routine analysis—identifying all the permutations of the note-row—but really that's not very interesting. The form is conveyed *above* that level. If the analysis is creative it will go beyond matters of vocabulary. People have gone through my works identifying rows and the like, and they think that they have somehow found the "secrets" of my music, but however much the things they discover may have helped me, they don't help the listener. This approach doesn't "explain" my music—not even the beginning of it![26]

Along these lines, one could fault Lerdahl for failing to differentiate between things one *could* follow and things an auditor *should* or likely *does* follow, and for implying that it is the former that tells us which listener will "understand" which composition. I don't believe most listeners hear many tonal details that are essential to the compositional structure of works from the common practice period, but that doesn't invalidate those structures and relations. The finale of Beethoven's Op. 110 Piano Sonata is based on a fugue in two parts, the first based on the uninverted version of the theme, and the second on its inversion. Beethoven starts each of these two parts slowly and clearly and with the melody alone, obviously encouraging the listener to hear the inversion relationship. One might even say that the finale is *based on* this uninverted-then-inverted idea, and that it is a kind of compositional-structural stratagem. But I don't imagine most people who enjoy listening to this sonata are aware of this relationship, and least of all the simplicity of the connection.

Given his reasoning, Lerdahl would seem to question the validity of such a work—one whose compositional premises are more often than not overlooked by listeners. Lerdahl would at least say, to introduce some of his own terminology, that there is a discrepancy in the Beethoven between compositional and listening grammars as concerns "parallelism of event sequences." He might respond by saying that Beethoven compensates for any such anomaly or ambiguity of pitch-understanding with obviously audible returns to the register, phrasing, and texture of the original, uninverted statement of the theme. In truth, Beethoven's structural-compositional premise is no less or more important to the Op. 110 finale than Berg's row-relations are in his Violin Concerto, or Boulez's manipulation of set-complexes in *Marteau sans maître*. Although the music in all three examples is in some ways dependent on these compositional premises, in even more important ways it is not.

In the introduction to this book, I invoked listening as a means of "escaping" compositional ideology, or at least music-aesthetic descriptions: in doing so I am not claiming that the listener can avoid ideology altogether when he or she presumes to forget compositional dictates. But listening philosophies are less nefarious than compositional mindsets for the simple reason that they are based in connotation rather than ideas of denotation. There are half a dozen perspectives for hearing a composition, but only one compositional ideology (or, better said, one compositional perspective). Listening may play host to ideologies, but they are more fragmented, more arguable, more amenable ideologies. And this fragmentation occurs when the composer lets his or her listening influence the composition, or (to follow a thought of Barthes) if the actual process of writing happens to circumvent or subvert compositional doctrines. Perhaps the best summary is to describe listening as a fundamentally naïve activity, and say that composers are naïve insofar as they let their listening selves influence their composing selves.

George Perle writes, "I think the listening experience is extraordinarily complex, spontaneous, intuitive, naïve, and sophisticated, all at the same

time, and that the composer already participates in the listening experience
in the process of composing. And I believe that the component of naivete is
at least as essential a part of it as any of the others."[27] The composer's work
as listener is manifest either naively or consciously, in service of what David
Schwarz calls the "listening gaze." He adopts Jacques Lacan's binarism of
eye and gaze in devising a duality of "listening look" and "listening gaze."
The listening look maintains a clear division between observing subject
and musical object. With the listening gaze, however, the "object" seems to
have thought ahead and commandeered an aspect of the experience, such
that the musical object momentarily "becomes" the subject.[28] The surprise
in the second movement of Haydn's Symphony No.94, clearly designed
from a listener's rather than a composer's point of view, could serve as an
example of the latter.

As mentioned earlier, the naive listener (and composer!) would wish to
elude the journalistic handles used to discuss and dismiss modernist music—or any other kind of music, though such quick-and-easy terms are less
commonly applied to other repertories. "Atonal" or "tonal"? "Serial" or
"chromatic"? "Combinatorial" or "tropic"? Twentieth-century listeners
did not complain about Bach being too "contrapuntal" to be understood
(with the notable exception of Thomas Beecham, who, so the story goes,
once derided Bach for "too much counterpoint—and what's more, *Protes-
tant* counterpoint"). Just as we frequently do not hear basic twelve-tone
transformations or invariances in Schoenberg's music, we don't necessarily
hear the details of Bach's polyphony. Yet we allow ourselves to hear the
music in it, in contrast to "atonal" and "serial" repertories.

4. Modernism and the Critical Monism

Admonishing music scholars for inattention toward literary fashion or the
listener's requirements is in itself not too convincing an argument for getting away from intentionalism in talking about modernist music. Additional persuasion might be found in the fact that the very future of this
music is threatened by hidebound intentionality: Babbitt, Boulez, Varèse,
and Stockhausen are close to becoming irrelevant at the turn of the twenty-
first century, a time that values art for immediate and individual relevance
but at the same time denies itself what Harold Bloom idealistically calls
"the reader's solitude, a subjectivity that has been rejected because it supposedly possesses 'no social being.'"[29]

It is hard to escape the conclusion that the critical monism set up around
modernist music by both its friends and its enemies—i.e., its rigidity or
monodirectionality of interpretation—has to a large degree contributed to
its fall from currency, its impending extinction. I choose Babbitt as an example yet again, for the simple reason that much ink has been spilled over

his music and thought, and this allows us to see in some detail the passions stirred up when one tries to define musical meaning. Babbitt describes the kind of meaning he would like the listener to establish for his own music, as follows: "not that kind of understanding which reduces the rich manifestations, the rich ramifications, of musical relationships to some mundane banalities, not some sort of many-one mapping of all those wonderfully rich ramifications of musical relations to some sort of representation of the world out there. . . ."[30] The composer's own highly developed terminology is a kind of calculus devised to prevent "mundane banalities" from encroaching on discussions of the music. Susan McClary is right to declare Babbitt's prose exclusionary, repressive, even a bit delusional. It is so highly developed to such a specific end, like a particular kind of forceps used for vascular microsurgery, that it is useful only for that one precise purpose. Like those microsurgical forceps, it is also developed to work perfectly anytime and every time, with minimal possibility of malfunction or contradiction.[31] Its arrogance is the functional and rationalist arrogance of the hardworking medical specialist, or more generally the single-minded presumption of Cold War science.

But in facing off with Babbitt, McClary effects an exclusionary arrogance equal to her subject's. She makes the incontestable assertion that "no musical repertory can truly be autonomous from social values and networks," but takes this to mean that social values are the *only* possible source for musical meaning. In her words, Babbitt would rather "go down with the ship than to admit to meaning,"[32] when it would have been more accurate to charge the composer with excluding *non-structural* or *extracompositional* meaning. With this accusation, McClary seems to miss her own important point: that "social values" necessarily constitute an inclusive category, and it follows from this proposition that artistic or intellectual values have their own social aspect. It would have been more honest for a person invoking social values to castigate Babbitt for failing to acknowledge the social consequences of his intellectualizations. As further support for her accusations of narrowness, McClary induces a second meaning from the *Philomel* text that pertains to the horrors of rape, but then faults the composer for not explicitly espousing such an interpretation.[33] Her interpretative imagery is polemical, a beneficial way of goading music academics away from theoretic-analytic discourse, if only to defend it. But the interpretive approach she suggests, whether better or worse than what music theory has to offer, begs important questions: why hold the composer responsible if you should choose to limit your reading of the piece? Why fault the composer's critical monism and at the same time thrash about in it? If you find the composer's written polemics not useful, and you are an advocate of extracompositional meaning, why not throw away the polemic and find your own meanings? Andrew Mead states the case eloquently in his own account of *Philomel* in the present volume: "I certainly don't want Babbitt's writings to limit how I hear his music, and I simply refuse to be discouraged by them!"

Stravinsky is usually the exception to every rule, and he was less of a monist—fascinatingly enough, he seemed more conciliatory when it came to musical meanings than when it came to performance practices. Just as he had a strangely ambiguous relationship with modernism (defying his critics as well as his partisans, even if it meant making dramatic and sudden changes in stylistic and aesthetic direction), he came to make concessions to populist avenues of meaning. Insofar as it is possible to generalize at all from Stravinsky's prose, for which he usually called upon a ghostwriter or dual author, his relationship with his public and his own oeuvre changed over the years. First, let us take the early Stravinsky—the modernist and *poseur*. In the famously selfless remark on *Sacre du printemps*, that he was "the vessel through which the *Rite* passed," Stravinsky dramatically sacrificed himself—and authorship itself—at the altar of his most famously avant-garde composition. After Koussevitsky's disastrous premiere of the *Symphonies of Wind Instruments* (1921), he assumed his well-known performer-as-mere-conduit philosophy. In *Chroniques de ma vie* (1935–36), the attitude is more Schoenbergian in that the work is said to result from the composer's train of thought, which the listener might come to reject or at least misunderstand:

> Liking the music of *L'Oiseau de Feu*, *Petroushka*, *Le Sacre*, and *Les Noces*, and being accustomed to the language of those works, [the great mass of my listeners] are astonished to hear me speaking in another idiom. They cannot and will not follow me in the progress of my musical thought. What moves and delights me leaves them indifferent, and what still continues to interest them holds no further attraction for me. For that matter, I believe that there was seldom any real communion of spirit between us. If it happened—and it still happens—that we liked the same things, I very much doubt whether it was for the same reasons. . . . Unfortunately, perfect communion is rare, and the more the personality of the author is revealed the rarer that communion becomes. The more he eliminates all that is extraneous, all that is not his own, or 'in him,' the greater is his risk of conflicting with the expectations of the bulk of the public, who always received a shock when confronted by something to which they are not accustomed.[34]

Stravinsky penned those lines, with the help of Walter Nouvel, at about the time he wrote the Concerto for Two Pianos and the extremely approachable *Jeu de cartes*. Strangely enough, he guarded compositional intentions less jealously in his program note for the more "difficult" orchestral Variations of 1963–64:

> So far as my own music is concerned, the twelve-part variations are the main novelty of the opus; and the one for *ponticello* violins, which sounds a little like

the sprinkling of very fine broken glass, is probably the most difficult music to analyse aurally in its entirety that I have ever composed. The listener might think of these three variations as musical mobiles, whose patterns change perspective according to the different dynamic characteristics of each performance.[35]

The *Chroniques* are transparent enough when it comes to their aesthetics, or studied, *echt*-modernist lack thereof. But just what is going on in Stravinsky's later description of the Variations? On one level, he makes few concessions on meaning: the composer summons analysis as his final witness, and is proud of the newness and impenetrability of some of the music. At the same time he offers similes to aid in hearing it, but—it should be emphasized—the "sprinkling of very fine broken glass" and "musical mobiles" are offered only as analogies. It is doubtful that he was trying to start a glass-based hermeneutic tradition for the Variations, let alone for any other work. There is precious little interpretation (as opposed to "description") going on here, as is underlined by Stravinsky's statement a bit further in: "I do not know how to guide the listener, except to urge him to listen not once but repeatedly."

And yet, Stravinsky's descriptions are telling. I believe he offered glass and mobiles in 1964 as a listener's heuristic, choosing analogies that were helpful in their specificity and universality. They are a palm frond, a peace offering made by an elder statesman in a modernist age of sclerotic meaning. The glass and mobile images are admittedly dispassionate, emotionally neutral, and quasi-controlled: glass shatters and mobiles move according to specific physical laws rather than the will of human beings. These images and objects also evoke all-purpose properties of things modern: objectivity, brilliance, and changeability of form. It was the new possibility of manufacturing affordable large glass sheets that had enabled Philip Johnson to open his Farnsworth House to the surrounding landscape, thereby removing the fig leaf that shielded private life from public scrutiny. And so the glass and mobile analogies are modern but also universal, accessible, and visually concrete; when Stravinsky sprinkles broken glass in his *ponticello* variation, his metaphor titillates the aural as well as the visual imagination. The proportion of his concession becomes even more evident when one considers how foreign these metaphors are to the creative act: it is difficult to believe that these descriptions were faithful to the Variations as they might have been "his own, or 'in him.'"

What's more, these analogies are provocatively erotic in the sense that Sontag advocated: in the same year Stravinsky finished the Variations, she made the declaration that "In place of a hermeneutics we need an erotics of arts."[36] Her erotics are sexual only insofar as they advocate undirected sensual pleasure rather than the linguistic exercise, the intellectual and monodirectional search for truth that is hermeneutics. Sontag's erotics are also concerned with the here-and-now rather than the "shadow world of 'meanings'" that the intellect has spitefully devised "to impoverish, to deplete the [real] world."[37] It is almost as if Stravinsky devised his broken glass and mobile metaphors to expressly satisfy Sontag's search for "the sensuous surface of art without mucking about in it," and "really accurate, sharp, loving description of the *appearance* of a work of art."[38]

By now, in disposing of the idea of intention so intently, I have probably exasperated all but the most sympathetic readers by thoroughly exploring so many ways that modernist music should *not* be heard. I have tried to debunk a number of systems of interpretation, if only to say they should not serve as the only means of listening. So how *should* modernist music be listened to? I find an ideal perspective in Sontag's "erotics of art." Certainly no pocket-description better describes the way I usually listen to the music of (say) Nono, Birtwistle, Rihm, Per Nørgård, Colin Matthews, and Elisabeth Lutyens—not to mention the Stravinsky Variations. Her erotics appeal largely because it is not a system. Moreover, Sontag's description allows a fairly wide avenue of meaning: she uses the indefinite article, and her alternative to hermeneutics is not writer-based, text-based, or (necessarily) reader-based. It does not involve deciphering, disentangling, author-gods, or analytic legacies.

It thereby offers some promise of that elusive and golden ideal: a pristine listening, a hearing unencumbered by ideology, even the ideological non-ideology of Barthes. Sontag is not an academic, and only a non-academic would have the courage and sense of perspective to say that we must give up both system and the search for the kinds of universal, sacred, singular meanings that are modeled on reading scripture. She made a critical statement forty years ago that musicology apparently failed to hear: that such sacred, as opposed to secular, "interpretations" are a thing of the past, incompatible with or least dishonest to modern life. Our manic and often contentious practices of interpretation have all but killed off our own abilities to feel and experience. Sontag writes:

> Interpretation takes the sensory experience of the work of art for granted, and proceeds from there. This cannot be taken for granted, now. Think of the sheer multiplication of works of art available to every one of us, superadded to the conflicting tastes and odors and sights of the urban environment that bombard our senses. Our is a culture based on excess, on overproduction; the result is a steady loss of sharpness in our sensory experience. . . . What is important now is to recover our senses. We must learn to *see* more, to *hear* more, to *feel* more.[39]

An interpretive "erotics" would be non-systematic, depending more on qualitative than quantitative thinking, and would center around textural, visual, and tactile metaphors. Art historians have a term that we could well borrow in suggesting a musical erotics: *facture,* used by the observer of graphic art to describe the quality, weight, and grain of paint as applied to the canvas. (The term is larger and more general than discussions of brushstroke, though it does subsume them.) Facture is non-hierarchical and presumably operates "beneath" the artist's conscious thought and intention, because creator and observer commonly consider it more a means than an end. Yet it is a prime aspect of individual style: one art history text contrasts the "aesthetic" of Dali's "neat, tight Vermeerish facture" with that implicated in Picasso's "bold, plangent, viscous brushwork."[40] I can think of many examples in the graphic arts that call for such an erotics of interpretation, a subjective approach that would not involve intentionalist concepts like composition, shape, and line. The person who views one of Paul Klee's more intricate "taking a line for a walk" drawings is free to enjoy such a work as a graphic surface, as a textured two-dimensional space rather than vectors—and such a viewer would likely get more from that kind of reading than the other, in part because it would be easier to pursue. In a rather different example, the art-lover who sees Seurat's pointilism purely as a novel method of representation, without seeing it as an abstract series of blots that need bear no necessary or functional relation to one another when seen close-up, misses something important. An interpretive erotics, a delectation of the colors or even flavors of sounds and words, would also be important in reading the Symbolist poets.

Focusing on facture, the music erotician wouldn't search for the most elegant analytic system, but the most appropriate and revealing metaphors: instead of imitating the mathematician or chemist, he or she would devise a kind of working taxonomy of poetry. (Structuralist music analysis is itself based in metaphor, but the metaphors used—involving ideas of line, shape, pattern—are usually simple enough to be amenable to moderately broad conceptions of intentionalism.) We owe any resistance to such "soft" eroticist analogies to the Hegelian and Schopenhauerian legacies of music as the art form least bound to concrete and worldly meaning. Thus Fred Maus, in describing Babbitt's piano works of the 1980s and 90s as "extreme, even reckless, in their delicacy and transparency,"[41] reveals more through his powers of empathy than his choice of metaphors. It comes as no surprise that music analysts have come closest to an erotics of music when working with John Cage and the New York School of composers, all of them closely allied in aesthetic and method with painters of the time. Catherine Hirata, for instance, has proposed a non-hierarchical, concertedly asystematic analysis of Morton Feldman's early music.[42] In an aesthetic comparison of the New York composers and painters, Dieter Gutknecht speaks of an "aural eyeness."[43]

Such approaches are still amorphous enough to leave some musicians dissatisfied. The unsympathetic reader could even bounce any perceived interpretational deficiencies back to questions of meaning and hearability in modernist music. "The modernist work has a stunted reception history and limitations of approach not because of politics or textual problems," he or she might say, "but because the modernist's language and meanings are so remote that no one cares about them." The only way I can answer such a charge is to refer to my own experience and say that I have had intense and fulfilling reactions to modernist music since I was a teenager, and contrast that with the propaganda, pro and con, that I have seen many people repeat without listening to the music. I say "difficulty" and "unlistenability" are non-issues, but the charges at least beg the question: which came first, the listening or the politics, Schoenberg the composer or Schoenberg the aesthetic lightning-rod?[44] I believe the relative lack of recordings and broadcasts meant many early modernist compositions became trapped in their composers' ideologies: newspapers and journals often spread the polemics faster than musicians disseminated the scores. (How different things might have been if cheap LPs were available at the time of Schoenberg's *Erwartung,* or if Franz Kline had access to cheap full-color poster reproductions!) I can only hold onto the hope that modernist sounds will gain a wider audience as music gains the possibility of even wider and easier dissemination and modernist politics recede. As the noise of interpretation dies down, we may yet realize how easy many modernist composers made it for us to understand music according to Sontag's ideal description: "The aim of all commentary on art now should be to make works of art—and, by analogy, our own experience—more, rather than less, real to us."[45]

Notes

1. Scott Burnham, *Beethoven Hero* (Princeton, N.J.: Princeton University Press, 1995).

2. Cook, *Analysing Musical Multimedia* (Oxford: Clarendon Press, and New York: Oxford University Press, 1998), 93–94.

3. Iseminger, Introduction, in *Intention and Interpretation* (Philadelphia: Temple University Press, 1992), 1–9.

4. Monroe C. Beardsley, "The Authority of the Text," in *Intention and Interpretation,* 37–38.

5. In contradistinction to Hanslick's formalism, Wagner justified his avant-garde tendencies with the Schopenhauerian idea that humanity was learning to express its deepest feelings through music while "in modern prose we speak a language we do not understand with the feeling . . . we cannot discourse in this language according to our innermost emotions, for it is impossible to *invent* in it according to that emotion." Wagner, "Das Schauspiel und das Wesen der dramatischen Dichtkunst," trans. William Ashton Ellis as "The Play and the Nature of Dramatic Poetry," in *Opera and Drama,* 2nd ed. (London: K. Paul, Trench, Trübner, 1900; reprint, University of Nebraska Press, 1995), 231; as cited by Robert P. Morgan, "Secret Languages: The Roots of Musical Modernism," in *Modernism: Challenges and Perspectives,* ed. Monique Chefdor, Ricardo Quinones, and Albert Wachtel (Urbana and Chicago: University of Illinois Press, 1986), 33–34.

6. The essay is anthologized in *On Literary Intention*, ed. David Newton-de Molina (Edinburgh: Edinburgh University Press, 1976), 1–13. The arguments for and against intentionalism have since devolved to the point where those debating the issues apparently cannot agree on what intentionalism *is*. The ironies and cross-purposes reached comic proportions when Morse Peckham re-read the Wimsatt and Beardsley in 1976 and declared the text so poorly phrased that it did indeed "seem to advocate" what E. D. Hirsch had described earlier as the "popular misreading" of the essay: "that what an author intended is irrelevant to the meaning of his text." See E. D. Hirsch, Jr., *Validity in Interpretation* (New Haven, Conn., and London: Yale University Press, 1967), 11–12; and Morse Peckham, "The Intentional? Fallacy?" in *On Literary Intention*, ed. David Newton-de Molina (Edinburgh: Edinburgh University Press, 1976), 140–41; as cited in Ethan Haimo, "Atonality, Analysis, and the Intentional Fallacy," *Music Theory Spectrum* 18, no. 2 (Fall 1996): 177. For a clear and well-argued discussion of intention from a perspective somewhere between the extremes of Hirsch and Wimsatt and Beardsley, see Joseph Margolis, "The Intention of the Artist," in his *Art and Philosophy* (Atlantic Highlands, N.J.: Humanities Press, 1980), 165–89.

7. See Seán Burke, *The Death and Return of the Author: Criticism and Subjectivity in Barthes, Foucault and Derrida*, 2nd ed. (Edinburgh: Edinburgh University Press, 1998), 138–49.

8. Haimo, "Atonality, Analysis, and the Intentional Fallacy," 167–99. As Haimo avers, the only instance where intentionalism has been debated with regard to modern music was the interchange between Allen Forte and Richard Taruskin over the validity of pitch-class set analysis (more specifically, whether it bears any connection with composers' intentions, and whether or not that question might be important); in this instance, the debate was founded on the assumption that post-tonal music is post-syntactical music. For the opening salvoes in this argument, see Taruskin's review of Forte's *The Harmonic Organization of the Rite of Spring* in *Current Musicology* 28 (1979): 114–29; and Forte's answer in "Pitch-Class Set Analysis Today," *Music Analysis* 4 (1985): 36–37. See also Haimo, "Atonality, Analysis, and the Intentional Fallacy," 167; and Robert P. Morgan, "Secret Languages: The Roots of Musical Modernism."

9. Regarding this aspect of twelve-tone music, see Arved Ashby, "Schoenberg, Boulez, and Max Weber's Ideal-Type: Toward a Conceptual History of Twelve-Tone Composition," *Journal of the American Musicological Society* 54, no. 2 (Summer 2001): 243–90.

10. Barthes, "The Death of the Author," in his *Image, Music, Text*, trans. Stephen Heath (New York: Hill and Wang, 1977), 142–48.

11. "In that great discourse with the living dead which we call reading, our role is not a passive one . . . to read well is to take great risks." Steiner, *Language and Silence: Essays on Language, Literature, and the Inhuman* (New York: Atheneum, 1967).

12. Hirsch, "In Defense of the Author," in *Validity in Interpretation* (New Haven, Conn., and London: Yale University Press, 1967), 1

13. Barthes, "The Death of the Author," 148.

14. Ibid., 143.

15. Ibid., 146.

16. Ibid., 147.

17. Hirsch, *Validity in Interpretation,* and *The Aims of Interpretation* (Chicago: University of Chicago Press, 1987); Olsen, *The Structure of Literary Understanding* (Cambridge and New York: Cambridge University Press, 1978).

18. Nehamas, "The Postulated Author: Critical Monism as a Regulative Ideal," *Critical Inquiry* 8 (1981): 149; quoted in H. L. Hix, *Morte d'Author: An Autopsy* (Philadelphia: Temple University Press, 1990), 26. Emphases added.

19. Nehamas, "Writer, Text, Work, Author," in *Literature and the Question of Philosophy,* ed. Anthony J. Cascardi (Baltimore, Md.: Johns Hopkins University Press, 1987), 281. As H. L. Hix notes, this is the reverse of Foucault's view in "What Is an Author?": according to Foucault, the author's name confers unity on his or her body of work, while Nehamas believes the body of work to define the name.

20. I have little interest in the possible objection that Schoenberg himself denied the "twelve-toneness" of his twelve-tone music: if he really stood in such opposition to the idea of twelve-tone technique, why did he in fact use the description? Schoenberg's rejection of "twelve-toneness" in his prose is a clear example of a defensive action. His polemical objections to the phrase and the description exemplify a fact that Carl Dahlhaus noted in his twelve-tone period: namely, Schoenberg's tendency to turn to aesthetics in order to make it clear that "his works are music in the same sense as those of Beethoven or Brahms, against the tendency of the critics, both well-meaning and hostile, to cling to the manner in which they were made." Dahlhaus, "Schoenberg's Poetics of Music," in his *Schoenberg and the New Music* (Cambridge and New York: Cambridge University Press, 1987), 74–75. See also Ashby, "Schoenberg, Boulez, and Max Weber's Ideal-Type."

21. Sontag, "Against Interpetation," in her *Against Interpretation* (New York: Delta, 1966), 10.

22. Hirsch, "In Defense of the Author," 1.

23. Babbitt, "The Structure and Function of Musical Theory," *College Music Symposium* 5 (1965); reprinted in *Perspectives on Contemporary Music Theory,* ed. Benjamin Boretz and Edward T. Cone (New York: W. W. Norton, 1972), 10–21.

24. Lerdahl and Jackendoff, *A Generative Theory of Tonal Music* (Cambridge, Mass.: MIT Press, 1983).

25. Lerdahl, "Cognitive Constraints on Compositional Systems," in *Gnerative Processes i Music: The Psychology of Performance, Improvisation, and Composition,* ed. John A. Sloboda (Oxford: Clarendon Press, 1988), 231–59.

26. "Pierre Boulez Talks to Stephen Johnson," *Gramophone* 63, no. 756 (May 1986): 1376.

27. Perle, *The Listening Composer* (Berkeley, Los Angeles, and Oxford: University of California Press, 1990), 22. Like Perle, I mean nothing negative by the word "naive."

28. Schwarz, "Peter Gabriel's 'Intruder,' a Cover, and the Gaze," in *Listening Subjects: Music, Psychoanalysis, Culture* (Durham, N.C. and London: Duke University Press, 1997), 87–99.

29. Bloom, *The Anxiety of Influence: A Theory of Poetry,* 2nd ed. (New York and Oxford: Oxford University Press, 1997), xxv.

30. Babbitt, "The Unlikely Survival of Serious Music," in *Milton Babbitt: Words about Music,* ed. Stephen Dembski and Joseph N. Straus (Madison: University of Wisconsin Press, 1987), 182; as cited in Susan McClary, "Terminal Prestige: The Case of Avant-Garde Music Composition," *Cultural Critique* 12 (Spring 1989): 65.

31. See Babbitt, "The Structure and Function of Musical Theory," *College Music Symposium* 5 (1965); reprinted in *Perspectives on Contemporary Music Theory*, ed. Benjamin Boretz and Edward T. Cone (New York: W. W. Norton, 1972), 10. For Babbitt's views on the more general pitfalls and possibilities for failure in talking about music, see Babbitt, "Contemporary Music Composition and Music Theory as Contemporary Intellectual History," in *Perspectives in Musicology: The Inaugural Lectures of the Ph.D. Program in Music at the City University of New York*, ed. Barry S. Brook, Edward O. D. Downes, and Sherman Van Solkema (New York: W. W. Norton, 1972), 151–73.

32. "What if underneath all that thorny puzzle-playing and those displays of total control," asks McClary, "there lurked the fear and confusion (clearly recognizable in all the defensive quotations already cited) that mark most other forms of contemporary culture? In other words, one could, as Sandow does, explain on many levels how this music is meaningful in other than quasi-mathematical terms. But the point is that such an agenda would violate the criteria of prestige the avant-garde has defined for itself. Better to go down with the ship than to admit to meaning." McClary, "Terminal Prestige," 65–66. One might say that in reducing compositional thought and meaning to "thorny puzzle-playing and displays of total control," McClary did some necessary polemicizing in response to Babbitt's (and others') own entrenched and violently-defended views. But then one could say the same of Babbitt: that he "went over the top" in an attempt to refute the aestheticians of the early century.

33. McClary, "Terminal Prestige," 74–75. McClary's polemic succeeded in that sense: whether or not it says anything useful about how modernist music is to be understood and discussed, "Terminal Prestige" has caused ripples that, when all is said and done, can only prove beneficial for the neverending project of trying to understand music.

34. *Chroniques de ma vie*, translated as *An Autobiography* (New York: Simon & Schuster, 1936), 175.

35. Stravinsky and Robert Craft, *Themes and Conclusions* (Berkeley and Los Angeles: University of California Press, 1972), 63.

36. Sontag, "Against Interpretation," 14.

37. Ibid., 7.

38. Ibid., 13. My italics.

39. Ibid., 13–14.

40. Herbert Edward Read, ed., *Surrealism* (London: Faber and Faber, 1936), 63.

41. Fred Everett Maus, liner notes to *Milton Babbitt: Piano Music since 1983* (New York: CRI, 1997), 7.

42. Catherine Hirata, "The Sounds of the Sounds Themselves: Analyzing the Early Music of Morton Feldman," *Perspectives of New Music* 34, no.1 (Winter 1996): 6–27.

43. Dieter Gutknecht, "Aural Eyeness: Gemeinsamkeiten von Musik und bildender Kunst in Abstract Expressionism und New York School," in *Glasba in Likovna Umetnost/Musik und bildende Kunst Ljubljana* (Festival Ljubljana, 1996), 187–98.

44. In one Ivy League music appreciation course with a large enrollment, the instructor prefaces a hearing of *Pierrot Lunaire* by asking for a show of hands: those of you who hate this music, raise your left hands; those of you who like it, raise your right. This serves as an introduction to modernism for 300 undergraduates each year.

45. Sontag, "Against Interpretation," 14.

2

The End of the Mannerist Century

William Bolcom

In March of 1996 the composer Donald Martino came under attack from the musicologist-critic Richard Taruskin, who in a *New York Times* article on twelve-tone composition excoriated Martino as one of its more perniciously academic practitioners.[1] All this only occasioned by the reissue, mind you, of a Nonesuch record of around twenty years before; it's as if someone, now, decided to ambush a prizefighter walking by for winning a controversial match in 1965. The attack seemed certainly out of proportion for the occasion, and I rose to Martino's defense in print.[2] This eventually brought about a reacquaintance between Martino and me; I'd known him in seminar at Tanglewood in 1966, and we'd seen each other at odd times, but this public crisis occasioned a pleasant correspondence between us. Don very kindly sent some of his own music, and listening to it confirmed what I had remembered—that here is not only one of the most tonal of "atonalists" but also a composer extremely musical and natural of utterance. The intellectual rigor involved with serial technique never exposes itself for its own sake in his work. But it always is there.

To summarize Taruskin's argument would take up more space than this essay can spare, but one can note his two main (though unrelated) points: that 1) Modernism's stranglehold on music has lessened, as it has in the visual arts, and good riddance too; and 2) there is a lack of connection between Martino's super-controlled language and what Taruskin calls its "primitive and simplistic" expressive gestures. (One could attack especially the late Schoenberg for the same thing; Boulez's early-1950s essay "Schoenberg est mort" jumps on him for using Viennese periodicity and gestures—the very things that make a performance of his music coherent if recognized and nonsense if ignored.[3])

Taruskin's screed against what is now anything but a current musical style—so many years after its hegemony—must come from a long-pent-up anger at what was, in its time, an almost fascistic doctrine of historical inevitability adopted by some serialists. One would think that a composer like me, a Stanford graduate student in the early 1960s who quickly became interested in ragtime, popular music, and simple tonal gestures, would also rejoice at the death of the dodecaphonic witch. It *is* wonderful now not to have to worry about two hundred composers looking over your shoulder disapprovingly if you dare to write a triad. (I remember a dinner in 1965 in West Berlin with Louis Andriessen at the apartment of Luciano Berio, who was directing Boulez's *Domaine Musical* that summer—I was one of the group's pianists. Afterward, Luciano summoned up the courage—helped with quite a bit of shared cognac—to sit down and play what would later become *Wasserklavier,* a rather sweet piano piece clearly in F minor. No wonder we needed so much cognac in that musical climate! This was heresy.)

We are now distant from those times, however, and the issues are too complex and far-reaching to imagine that we can simply reject twelve-tone, or any type of musical rigor. Whatever need Donald Martino has had as a composer to interact with a discipline—whatever discipline—is essentially the same as any one of us needs in some form. Forty years ago the serialists held the greatest intimidating force in the small world of modern composition; then there was a terrific rebellion against many of its assumptions—I was certainly part of that rebellion—and now it is OK to attack all serialists, indeed all the new music of the period roughly between 1950 and 1975. And it is true that much ugly music of that time, written with the help of complex pseudo-mathematical processes, really doesn't need rehearing. Why then is Martino, for an example, worth separating from the crowd of so much shrill musical logical positivism? Because it *sounds* good, and not necessarily because of the tonal implications, but because there is a truly sensitive ear at work here, strongly imprinted with Renaissance chordal spacing and counterpoint and married to a Classical proportional sense; there is an epic power in some of his music, *Paradiso* for example, that draws me immediately to the world of my most beloved Italian so-called primitive painters. (The art-history "primitive" classification has always puzzled me, particularly when one remembers that painters under its rubric like Castagno and Della Francesca were fascinated with newly explored science in their art, something one easily forgets while reeling openmouthed from the emotional power of, say, Piero's Arezzo frescoes.) What made Bach's fugues "truly poetic creations" to Schumann was only incidentally their intellectual brilliance; yet the structure of fugue cannot be discounted in the whole impact of the piece, and this is also true in the very best serial music of our time.

The twentieth century has been obsessed with language—the invention, the destruction, the arbitrary building, of language—and this may be the easiest way to grasp whatever modernism means. We have become enormously dependent on the word, the explicated concept, the published manifesto. For example, it took Frank Stella years of writing a large amount of obfuscatory prose to herald his stylistic change from minimalism to an exuberant maximalist style; I love the result as much as I did his earlier art, and I regret that he needed to confuse *Artforum* so totally in order to avoid being hooted down for his new work, but that's the world today.

It seems, however, that schools of painters, composers, or writers in the more distant past were much more defined by geography than by precept. The landlocked J. S. Bach's excursions into French and Italian style, seen from the perspective of a pig-knuckle-eating Leipziger, can be understood as his— perhaps slightly desperate—attempts to break out of locale. And although many twentieth-century schools have defined themselves nationally (Jeune France of the thirties, De Stijl in current Dutch music), one senses an effort of will as each movement labels itself in the pursuit of a discrete identity, which reinforces their spiritual oppositeness to Bach's attempts at internationalism.

What we have called modernism in this century has usually been an art divorced from locale—although we recognize different aspects of modernism as being rooted in particular cities and countries—and whatever can be called pure modernism has hit several crests and valleys throughout these hundred years. Periods after our major wars often have been the times when artists wanted to start over from scratch. Perhaps the major reason for Arnold Schoenberg's relative silence between *Pierrot lunaire* and the dodecaphonic works of the twenties was the First World War, and the twelve-tone system, like the post-Webern efflorescence of imposed musical procedure after the Second, may have been a source of needed comfort after those ordeals. (Bach's fascination with order has been thought to stem from the Pietistic hunger for control after the horrors of the Thirty Years' War, even though that had been a considerable time before—changes were slower in that era, one supposes.)

I think the major difference in art movements today from those of the past is in our overwhelming need to publicize; it is ever so much greater because there are so many artists, schools, factions around us now that it is impossible to keep track, and whoever shouts loudest is the only one heard—until some- one else shouts even louder. This has escalated our need for polemic, for self- advertisement, for marketing, to unprecedented levels, and our horn-tooting abilities grow every day as Web pages sprout all over cyberspace. The danger in spouting rhetoric about art is that one day one might come to believe one's own words, and that is the beginning of the end of that artist's vitality. Any artist has a modus operandi. We understand our own way of working well enough to be able to continue, but we can't understand the whole picture; thus our attempts to explain ourselves to ourselves and others are hobbled by our final inability to know what's really going on in us, and that's probably what saves whatever is valuable in our work from drying out totally.

1. Manner vs. Substance

I am often saying nowadays that ours has been a Mannerist century. Man- nerist periods are known and recognized throughout art history more often than in music; they are moments when the *how* of art overwhelms the *what*, and they are often rich times, full of promise, new ideas, and invention sometimes seemingly for its own sake. Although the usual notion is that Mannerist periods in art come as transitions between the great stylistic epochs, I don't find that Mannerism in music necessarily coincides with our music-history notions of period. We consider Nenna and Gesualdo Renaissance composers, and Monteverdi an early Baroque one; yet these three and their common or contingent decades share the instability of musical upheaval in certain ways not shared with those preceding or following. (I've always wondered how one can lump Monteverdi and Bach together in the same bin, as music history texts insist.) One could rightly term the turn of the seventeenth century Mannerist (bridging our usual Renaissance and Baroque classifications), one reason being that their music still shares the power to shock—a quality shared with the best Mannerist art (from Piero di Cosimo to Fuseli) and architecture.

What is the distinction between modernism and Mannerism? Modernism is really a subset of Mannerism, involving principally the shedding of past references. But usually we are talking of the renunciation of terribly recent references when we look at the great expanse of history. (Remember that the isms of our time are mostly the children of concepts less than two centuries old.) The Mannerist impulse in architecture is stronger in Antonio Gaudí than, say, Philip Johnson (no matter how many stylistic hats the latter has worn in his long career), partly because their assumptions are different, but much more because by the time Johnson appeared, so much ground had been broken by Gaudí, the Secessionists, and the Bauhaus that the newness of it all had diminished somewhat. What fun it must have been in 1900, for example, to be the first to try out things with film, to know that no one could possibly have done it before! Film today can do anything—the technological breakthroughs of *Who Framed Roger Rabbit?*, so stunning a few years ago, elicit yawns today—and this is symptomatic of the end of Mannerist periods.

What was once new and frightening is old suddenly. Having spent so much energy on *how* we're doing something, we become aware of the fact that *what* we're doing feels meaningless. This mood is intensified by our recalling the sound of our own shrill voices hawking our wares, hawking ourselves, trying to be noticed—what was it all for? Why did we have to ally ourselves with Serialism, Minimalism, Neo-this and Neo-that, now that our self-labeling in the pursuit of identity seems so hollow in retrospect? Our disgust with our recent past has led to a wholesale rejection of music of that past. Add to this the sense of glut—book publishers and record companies are finally cutting down on numbers of releases because there is so much stuff around that consumers are tuning out—and it is no wonder that, with our boredom with what is now shouted as new, we are not necessarily wild either about what was once new a few decades ago. We are getting tired of Manner; what we crave is Substance.

But Substance needs Manner to express itself. We depend on the pathfinders of the past who found disciplines that would become our vocabulary. And this is the whole history of music, from technique to technique, from organum and Ars Antiqua to the New Complexity. The point is that time and usage have eventually always transformed the found disciplines, by a natural process of wearing away of inessentials and the gradual disappearance of underlying dogmas, into language that we could use to say something. To throw out what is useful in our century's exploration is to cripple our future. We are not, I expect, going to be as obsessed with process as eastern U.S. and Californian university composers of forty years ago were, and thank God. But what I hope for fervently is that, in future, musicians will absorb a portion of our twentieth-century disciplines in the same way as we study sixteenth-century counterpoint and eighteenth-century harmony today. We do not, for instance, configure isometric harmony from the tenor in the same way Zarlino did, but we use the chord-forms he describes in much the same manner, and we have felt meaning in sequences of these chords. Is this meaning imposed, evolved, or what? Our musical structure could all have been otherwise—there have been so many historical accidents down the long road to our time—but for some reason we have agreed on musical meanings in our culture to a surprising extent. What is also amazing is that the music we have produced—at least that of the past—often carries significance to cultures other than our own, and we are finding that music from elsewhere means something to us in ways we (and musicians from elsewhere) hadn't anticipated.

All this seems to indicate that, having conquered vast new territories in musical language, we must now reconquer them using intuitive means. What this involves is paying attention to how a musical effect affects us as composers, and then deciding whether it will become part of our musical vocabulary. This is wildly different from the cult of originality that has been a tenet of much twentieth-century Mannerism. The best artist has often been perceived as the most separate stylistically from all others, and this notion usually is an indication of our blindness to how much that artist really did owe to what was around. (The so-named post-Webern era was largely predicated on our misapprehension of Anton Webern; far from being as divorced from history as many postwar composers had wished, his music turns out to be deeply rooted in both late Romanticism and the Renaissance. There is a famous description by pianist Peter Stadlen of hearing Webern play his new Piano Variations for the first time; Webern pedaled through the huge silences and employed wildly romantic rubato throughout, a far cry from the white-coat-and-stethoscope Webern performances by Robert Craft we grew up with in the sixties.[4])

In the end we may be alone as artists, but we can't avoid our time, either by eschewing the ephemeral in the interest of eternality *or* by trying to elevate the ephemeral to something it's not. What we can revel in is the enormous breadth of musical vocabulary open to us, now that we are in touch with so much of the surrounding world. I do feel however that our mistake in how we perceive multiculturalism has been to accept distinctions between styles as they are presented to us, by either the artist or the hype surrounding the art or both. (Distinctions are surely there, however, and not recognizing or invoking them flattens out the rhetoric of any art.) In every one of the musics around us are elements that can find commonality with other musics, and their collision and merging are the stuff of musical meaning, because they expand communication (just as Bach's espousal of French and Italian elements reduces his own musical parochialism). This marriage of musics eventually leads to a broader understanding of ourselves and love of others—I truly believe this—but I also note that enforced juxtaposition of styles and elements, in order just to make a big bang, doesn't seem to have much power any more: a deeper link needs to be found.

There are thoughtful critics who bemoan the recent lack of innovation in music. Where are the Stravinskys, the Messiaens, the Xenakises, the Nancarrows? It must be admitted that at the moment many younger composers are churning out a lot of neo-Romantic treacle, much of which seems very tired to me, even though it is succeeding a little better with audiences than the stuff from twenty years ago. But there must be a deep emotional reason for such apparent regressiveness, as more and more composers have turned to past styles in an effort to communicate emotionally and spiritually—a pursuit that is common to John Tavener's embrace of Eastern Orthodox church music and George Rochberg's evocation of Beethoven or Mozart. In my own case as a composer, I've explored past styles of American popular music. Why are we doing this? should be the question, more than Should we do this or not? It's very easy to take the position some critics have, that composers are doing this purely to win audiences in some sort of sellout. The fact is, however, that for many composers today the music we of my generation once felt impelled to write out of peer pressure doesn't mean much to us now. (Some of us are ashamed of our earlier formalist effusions; now *that* was academic music, Professor Taruskin, not the juicy sensualism found in Martino.) As far as winning audiences to new music is concerned, I haven't noticed an enormous groundswell of public interest in it now that so-called accessible music is more common. And as far as the sellout argument goes, as the painter George Grosz once answered to someone accusing him of it (in his later, lyrical, less angry period, after he had given up images of scarfaced World War I veterans decapitating whores), "I've been trying to sell my soul to the devil for 30 years, and he hasn't even come around to make me a price!"

2. What Will Survive?

Will the future eschew whole sections of the past, in a sort of artistic holocaust? It isn't impossible—who could blame the young for feeling crowded out in our time?—and the impulse to destroy the past is one of the oldest in human society. (To see this, visit the Edfu temple on the Nile and see with what violence someone has brutally hammered out any bas-relief representations of the bird-god Horus.) We've been such packrats in our Mannerist century, with one hand pushing for newness at any cost, and the other hand just as avidly preserving and unearthing our history to be saved for ever and ever, that I wouldn't blame some twenty-first-century artistic terrorists for setting fire to all those dead rivals to their own hegemony. I would have to put the recent 100-best-movies list issued by the American Film Institute and Taruskin's violent attacks on Prokofiev and Martino in the same bracket, that of an arrogant, millenaristic need to weed out what is considered extraneous material for our supposed future benefit. Perhaps we can circumvent such arbitrary apocalypses by doing some weeding ourselves as artists. Of course we do this every day: as a composer I use various elements of music around me and ignore others, and even if this selectivity is a purely personal (and, alas, generational) process, it turns out probably to be my principal means of communicating to others and is perhaps what makes my music mine. But I can't say I hold out much hope for avoiding something more violent in our future artistic history on a worldwide level, as conglomerate mass-market venues trample out human individuality increasingly each day, state and private support for non-commercial art dries up in country after country, and artists of all stripes and persuasions censor themselves into a universal grayness.

We forget that the serious music of the recent past, zealous as it often was in declaring the death of tonality, of continuity, of whatever else it decided was dead, still depended for the most part on traditional instruments, conservatory-trained executants, and the concert-hall ethic that is perceived today as down-at-heel. This may be the principal reason, much more than any stylistic rebarbativeness, that the Martinos, Wuorinens, Stockhausens, and Boulezes may mean little to succeeding generations: all of these composers took for granted some semblance of the traditional performer-listener axis, their attempts to violate it actually confirming an unconscious belief in it, so that now—when the whole equation seems to be changing because of electronic advances in world communication—their music may well be swept away with the global electronic tide. (That goes for my music too, yours, and most music in any time, despite our greater ability to preserve things.)

What will survive is what nourishes us emotionally and spiritually, probably to the detriment of what is merely interesting. What distinguishes Bach fugues from, say, the vast majority of ricercars and canzonas of the previous century is the emotional and spiritual meaning Bach carries to us through a form clearly derived from, and respectful of, its musical ancestors. We may regard the workings of his music as secondary to its spiritual impact on us. But Bach didn't; he clearly loved and needed the disciplines of the past to make his designs. I hope that some of the designs that our Mannerist century has happened upon will be of use to our own musical future, and this will be only if we find some music in our vast catalogue that we truly can love, that we really need in order to go on living. "Art is what is irresistible," the writer William Saroyan once said to me, and I have yet to find a better definition of it. Only time will tell whether we have made irresistible music during our Mannerist century. I think some of it is, of many genres and provenances, and what we select will have a commonality and signification that will be the basis for the music of the world's future.

Notes

1. Richard Taruskin, "How Talented Composers Become Useless," *New York Times*, 10 March 1996, section H, p. 31.
2. Bolcom, Letter to the Editor: "In Defense of Dodecaphonism," *New York Times*, 7 April 1996, section 2, p. 7.
3. Reprinted in translation as "Schoenberg is Dead" in Boulez, *Notes of an Apprenticeship*, trans. Herbert Weinstock (New York: Knopf, 1968), 268–76.
4. Peter Stadlen, "Serialism Reconsidered," *The Score* 22 (February 1958): 12; cited in Hans Moldenhauer, in collaboration with Rosaleen Moldenhauer, *Anton von Webern: A Chronicle of His Life and Works* (New York: Knopf, 1979), 484.

3

A Fine Analysis

GREG SANDOW

1. Music as a History of Compositional Technique?

I wrote my 1982 Milton Babbitt essay "A Fine Madness," reprinted else-where in this volume, in a single night. And even, or so I'd like to think, in a single breath, though that can't be true, because writing is never that easy. But why did I write in such a fever? Because, back then, I was a critic covering the "downtown" music scene in New York—Philip Glass and beyond. And I was, along with a few other people (Susan McClary was an important ally), locked in a battle with what I came to call "the compli-cated music gang." These, of course, were the "uptown" guys, the atonal composers—Babbitt, Charles Wuorinen, and the rest—who dominated contemporary classical music in New York, and influenced a good share of the funding, commissions, and faculty appointments that composers might get, anywhere in America. Early in the 1970s, when I was a composition student at the Yale School of Music, I followed the gang's lead myself for awhile, and assumed that new music ought to be atonal. Later I heard Britten's *Death in Venice* at the Metropolitan Opera, and discovered that, on the contrary, a contemporary work could in fact be both tonal and thoroughly modern.

Back then, uptown composers generally hated "downtown" music, and in both concrete and symbolic ways stood in its way, even though (and of course partly because) some of it had a thousand times the audience they had. Babbitt was generally fingered as the leader of the gang, and, after I'd read the dusty analytic stuff about him in the first edition of Paul Griffiths's *Modern Music,*[1] I was delighted—blazing with delight, in fact—to take an alternate approach to the man who pioneered, embodied, and (politically, in those days, within the contemporary music world) even helped enforce the view that analysis and music might as well be the same.

That view, it seemed to me, informed Griffiths's book, or rather drained information out of it. More precisely, Griffiths (in recent years a critic for the *New York Times,* and often a sensitive and poetic one, no matter how strong our disagreements) seemed to treat the history of music as if it were the history of composition, and then treated the history of composition as if that, in turn, were largely the history of compositional technique. He could have asked who listens to the music he dissects, or who funds it, or why so much of it is so hard to play, or (arching over all these smaller questions), what the music means, and where it fits in our larger contemporary culture. But instead he shut nearly every window to the world outside, and wrote almost nothing about the juice of music, about music as a living activity, pursued by people with emotions, people who get hungry, thirsty, wry, ironic, desperate, joyful, lost, and (inevitably, in our time) convulsed with many contradictory feelings all at once. He might just as well have written a book about sex, and filled it with the structural formulas of organic chemistry. If Griffiths had responded, he might have said that "modern music" isn't meant to be expressive in romantic ways, and thus should be discussed objectively. But that would still leave its aesthetic dimension untouched, no matter what aesthetic the music embodies, as if—to suggest a more modernist metaphor—Griffiths had written a book about Marcel Duchamp, and gotten lost in Duchamp's brushstrokes, or in the materials he used in his artworks that aren't paintings.

But of course Griffiths wasn't the only serious writer on music at that time who didn't ask what new styles of music tell us about ourselves and the world. These inquiries, as it happens, are staples of rock criticism, and when they don't show up in discussions of classical music today—even about the standard repertory, at a time when the very existence of classical music seems to be threatened—I get suspicious. Are people in this field afraid that classical music (and especially modernist classical music) has no meaning? Or are they comfortable taking the meaning for granted, knowing, perhaps unconsciously, that if the meaning of the music isn't stated, then it can't be challenged?

At this point in my argument, I was reminded by a friendly colleague that Schoenberg and Webern set the stage for the kind of discussion Griffiths typifies, by talking about analytic details in their own music. But it's clear that both composers, however detailed their analytic writing, thought music had a deeper, and in fact mystical side. "My personal feeling," wrote Schoenberg in his 1946 essay "Criteria for the Evaluation of Music," "is that music conveys a prophetic message revealing a higher form of life towards which mankind evolves."[2] Nor did he want analysts to pull his twelve-tone structures apart: "I find this diligence applied in the wrong place," he wrote, this time in 1936, about the work of someone who'd published an analytical essay about his use of rows:

> I foresaw the confusion that would arise in case I were to make publicly known this method. . . . What I feared, happened. Although I had warned my friends and pupils to consider this [only] a change in compositional regards [by which he means, as he'd previous explained, a change in method, but not a new

compositional theory], and although I gave them the advice to consider it only as a means to fortify the logic, they started counting the tones and finding out the methods with which I used the rows. . . . [T]heorists always fall into the error of believing their theories to be rules for composers instead of symptoms of the works, rules which a composer has to obey, instead of peculiarities which are extracted from the works.[3]

And didn't Schoenberg write *Moses und Aron,* in which he strained to convey a "prophetic message," reaching toward truths—wrenching, deep, unutterable—that can never be explained empirically? That last point, of course, lay at the center of the opera, in the conflict between Moses, owner of the truth that can't be uttered, and Aron, the glib explainer. If we reduce Schoenberg's music to analysis, don't we follow Aron's lead, worshipping his golden calf, in flat disregard of Schoenberg's most heartfelt spiritual concern?

As for Webern, he trembles with emotion, as anyone can understand even without hearing his music, simply by looking at the texts he set, like this one, given in translation, from the last of his *Three Songs on Texts by Hildegard Jone,* op. 25:

Stars, you silver bees
of the night, circling the flower of love!
Truly, the honey from it
shimmers on you.
Let them drop in the heart,
in the golden honeycomb.

He'd also sketch outlines of prospective works, not only of their twelve-tone structure, but also of their emotional content. These are sections of the third movement of what became his Quartet for Violin, Clarinet, Tenor Saxophone, and Piano, op. 22:

I   Coolness of early spring.
II   Dachstein, snow and ice, crystal clear air.
III   The children of ice and snow.
IV   Outlook into the highest region.[4]

And nobody could have been more emotional about how he wanted his music to be played. Peter Stadlen, a pianist who worked with Webern on the op. 27 Variations, reports that Webern refused to talk about twelve-tone structure, saying this was nothing performers had to know.[5] What he wanted, instead, was emotion:

For weeks on end, he had spent countless hours trying to convey to me every nuance of performance down to the finest detail. As he sang and shouted, waved his arms and stamped his feet in an attempt to bring out what he called the meaning of the music, I was amazed to see him treat those few scrappy notes as if they were cascades of sound. He kept referring to the melody which, he said, must be as telling as a spoken sentence. . . . It was shaped by an enormous amount of constant rubato and by a most unpredictable distribution of accents. But there were also definite changes of tempo every few bars. . . .[6]

But why, then, would Webern care so much about analysis? Stadlen acutely observes that the composer had a "dual attitude to his music":

[O]n the one hand his urge to express extra-musical contents went to such extremes that the notes had become almost incidental and were only regarded as carriers of expression; at the same time he strove to free music from this very bondage and to restore to it that autonomous structural sense it had tended to lose during the romantic period.[7]

Music, from Webern's point of view, had gotten uncontrollable. And it had from Schoenberg's point of view, too; writing free atonal music, he famously said, was like swimming in boiling water. So the point of twelve-tone writing—and, I think, of analytic talk about music—was to bring order, to (re)establish standards, and of course to bring the traditions of the past forward into the present, by creating a structural atonal equivalent to the structural coherence of tonal harmony.

But as we'll see, this last agenda might be impossible, which makes me even sadder about the approach Paul Griffiths took. Schoenberg said (in a 1946 lecture, "Heart and Brain in Music") that "everything of supreme value in art must show heart as well as brain."[8] But by the time Griffiths's book came out, the contemporary music world had traveled so far from Schoenberg's balanced view that *Modern Music* seemed not just normal, but even more accomplished than most books about music, precisely because most of it was about compositional procedures. That made it elevated, even (as many people thought) artistic.

So that's another reason I stayed up all night—I felt I was reclaiming dead land, bringing blighted soil back to life. If I'd been a rock critic (which in fact I later became for awhile), I might have asked what Little Richard's screams mean in "Tutti Frutti," his most famous song and one of the great happy assaults of the rock & roll revolution in the mid-1950s. One answer might be that the screams are one of many cues—along with Richard's piled-high pompadour, his rough lyrics, the sandpaper in his gospel vocal style, and his way of almost eating a piano alive while he played—that told us rock & roll really *was* a revolution. White Americans, it's true, were already used to music with a beat, served up by endless swing bands of the 1940s; the Andrews Sisters' "Boogie Woogie Bugle Boy," a familiar hit from 1941, is even built on the same blues chord progression as "Tutti Frutti." But "Boogie Woogie Bugle Boy" was accomplished music, cleverly arranged, with sophisticated lyrics. "Tutti Frutti," by contrast, was an explosion—an eruption of something black and primal, aimed at the heart of white America (with only one concession, a quick rewrite of its lyrics in the recording studio, so they wouldn't be out-and-out obscene.) Times were changing; that's one message of Little Richard's screams. White (and by extension western) hegemony was under attack, culturally and even politically; it's no coincidence that the civil rights movement rose up at the same time as rock & roll, a generation after Schoenberg had tried to restore the foundations of western classical music.

So it was in this spirit (though I might not have fully understood it at the time) that I asked what the sound of Milton Babbitt's music might mean:

> At a lecture-recital sponsored by the New York University Composers Forum ... Babbitt spoke calmly, with his usual affable grace, about the structure of the music to come. But he didn't prepare us for what we actually heard, at least not for the torrents of notes, jumping from one end of the piano to each other, shifting speed every few seconds (though the notated tempos are generally constant: changes in apparent speed are produced by difficult to perform and always varying subdivisions of the constant beat); he didn't mention that his music lacks both regularity and any connection to everyday emotional and musical life.

I went on to discuss structural reasons for all this irregularity—it helps highlight pitch relationships, since pitches now can stand by themselves, without getting caught up in irrelevant rhythmic patterns. But, as the end of my quotation suggests, there's a cultural dimension as well; it's hard to pretend music has a purely objective existence when the sheer sound of it seems so outrageous:

> [Babbitt's] music [I wrote] and the whole school he represents, are products of the 1950s, as much symptoms of the eruption of tumultuous subterranean forces into aboveground life as monster movies, rock and roll, the beat generation, and abstract expressionism. But in Babbitt's case the eruption is controlled, disguised, and unmentioned, the secret nobody will acknowledge or even name.

Babbitt's music, in other words, embodies both an attempt to bring unprecedented order to western music, and, at the same time, an echo of wild disorder. Not, by the way, that we should pretend that Paul Griffiths, in his book—and even Babbitt himself, who (as a proudly self-described "logical empiricist") only wants to make "verifiable" statements about music—don't in their own way engage in this cultural discussion. They do it by omission. By not dealing with the simplest emotional reactions to how his music sounds, Babbitt is making his own cultural statement, one that Griffiths seemed to accept. To his credit, he's taken a broader view in recent years, but back then they both might have been saying, "Let's pretend that the western musical tradition is still intact, and contemplate it as we retreat from the wider world." It's no coincidence that serial music arose at more or less the same time as rock & roll.

2. Analysis and Meaning

I should note once more that everything I've said applies far more to Griffiths's book than to his criticism. In his *Times* reviews, and in conversation, his emotional reactions to modernist works have been very touching. But then in some ways this makes *Modern Music* seem more strange. Did Griffiths, a man full of feeling, think (at least in 1981) that he had to put emotion aside, to be academically respectable?

But then maybe his emotional reticence was also a sign of the musical times. Things have changed since then, and Griffiths in fact has updated *Modern Music,* producing a more fluid, less conclusive sequel called *Modern Music and After,* which in his own words takes a "broader" (or, as I might put it, a more forgiving) view of what music should be.[9] Minimalism, for instance, gets far more respect (due in part, perhaps, to its success in the years that separate the two volumes).

And one passage about Babbitt now sports a qualification that might sound familiar to anyone who reads my own Babbitt essay. Quoting John M. Peel, evidently a rapt Babbitt scholar, Griffiths leads us into a familiar verbal thicket, full of thorny phrases about "ordered subsets or segments [that] form a larger, more complex ordered set which itself may then be regarded as a new or derived line subject to the same transformations and the same interpretation in a musical dimension as a fundamental line." In the first *Modern Music,* Griffiths typed these same words with a straight face, going on from them to quote something analogous from Babbitt himself. But in *Modern Music and After,* he steps forward from the thorns to remark: "This sort of writing, maintaining accuracy at the risk of appearing defensive, has taken command of most discussions of Babbitt's music, but it fails to reflect the clarity and humor of his own prose (in the same way that many of his composing imitators have missed those same qualities in his music)."[10] Who, I wonder (my smile blooming into a grin), said this first?

But analysis of a strikingly reductive kind can still pop up in the classical music world, as it does in Michael Steinberg's program note on Beethoven's Fifth Symphony, which I encountered at a New York Philharmonic concert. Steinberg, of course, has been America's most respected program annotator, and gave a keynote address at the 1999 convention of the American Symphony Orchestra League, where he urged orchestras to play the analysis-friendly works of Elliott Carter and Pierre Boulez.

That event seems distant now; American orchestras these days are preoccupied more with accessibility than with modernism. But their program notes can still bristle with analysis, as can program notes for other classical events (William Kinderman's notes for Daniel Barenboim's cycle of Beethoven sonatas at Carnegie Hall in 2003 were strikingly inscrutable). Some orchestras might still reprint Steinberg's exegesis, in which he just about turns Beethoven into Carter. Speaking of the first movement, he notes that Beethoven added the fermata in the fourth bar—at the end of the second da-da-da DUM—as an afterthought. Originally, there were just two half notes, tied together; then Beethoven put a fermata on the second one. Steinberg finds an analogue to that extended note, in the horn call at the start of the second subject:

> An interesting detail about the horn call is that the fourth note, B-flat, is held for 13 measures so that it serves as a bass to the *dolce* violin melody that follows. This corresponds to the extra length of the D at the beginning of the symphony, and no doubt when Beethoven had the afterthought of lengthening that D it was to clarify this relationship. As for the violin melody, the first two measures outline the B-flat/E-flat dyad (though in reverse order), and the third and fourth outline F and B-flat. In other words, it uses the same pitch vocabulary as the opening and the horn call, and again the link in the middle is E-flat/F.[11]

In my view, there are numerous problems here, starting with the slippery word "corresponds." In what way, exactly, do two tied half notes with a fermata on the second one "correspond" to thirteen half notes tied together? In what way are they similar? Only, I'd think, because each lasts longer than a single measure, which really isn't much foundation for a structural relationship. (Especially since most conductors don't hold the fermata very long. Are they supposed to stretch it out until the note gets as long as the later D?) And then there's Beethoven's "afterthought" of lengthening the D. He lengthened it, Steinberg says, to "clarify" the relationship between the two long notes—which barely existed before Beethoven added the fermata! Up to then, in fact, only one of the two notes had been long. Steinberg's thinking seems to me a little muddled.

But something else strikes me even more strongly. Even if we grant Steinberg his none too clear analysis, when he tells us why he thinks Beethoven added the fermata he has yet another problem: He falls into the intentional fallacy, something I was warned against by my rock-critic editors at the *Village Voice*. If we take Steinberg's words at face value, he more or less clearly says that Beethoven *purposely* created those analytic goodies: "[N]o doubt when Beethoven had the afterthought of lengthening that D it was to clarify this relationship."

But how does Steinberg know what Beethoven was thinking? How can there be "no doubt" of his intentions? Did Beethoven ever talk or write about these passages? Composers create all sorts of microrelationships in their music, even complex ones, but usually by instinct, demonstrating not any formal or informal plan, but only the coherence of their unconscious thought.

To avoid an intentional fallacy of my own, I'll readily concede that I have no idea what Steinberg was thinking. Maybe he didn't *mean* to speak for Beethoven. But his words, taken in their simplest, most literal sense, seem to pry open Beethoven's inner mental space. They also threaten to transform it, by remaking Beethoven as a composer working with a post-Schoenberg consciousness of structure. Only in the wake of Schoenberg did a small if influential minority (notably including Babbitt) consciously create the kinds of microstructures theorists like to talk about. (It's clear, I trust, that I don't mean macrostructural entertainments, like canons, fugues, and Haydn's games with sonata form, which composers obviously did plan.) If Steinberg thinks Beethoven was an exception, he needs to prove it. But all he offers, to back up his assumptions, is verbal sleight of hand—his offhand, almost sly "no doubt."

And beyond that is something I find even more unfortunate. Who's likely to understand the Steinberg passage I've just quoted? Surely it's incomprehensible to most of its intended audience, the loyal but musically untrained people who go to symphony concerts. "The first two measures outline the B-flat/E-flat dyad," Steinberg writes. How many New York Philharmonic subscribers know what a "dyad" is?

These two errors—the intentional fallacy, and writing things the audience can't understand—are related. Both have the same effect; they make readers think analysis (of the most limited kind) is crucially important. After all, Steinberg doesn't simply say that *he* thinks those two extended notes are linked. Beethoven, he seems to say, thought so, too; now we're forced to pay attention. And why, respectful readers might well ask, would Steinberg detail analyses that we can't understand, unless they were surpassingly important? Evidently (or so an innocent music lover is likely to conclude) this "B-flat/E-flat dyad" must be something every trained musician talks about, which mere civilians shouldn't think they'll comprehend. Of course, this also means that ordinary music lovers can't expect to comprehend the concerts that they hear, but then many of them (cowed by the glory of classical music and by all the complex talk about it) have always suspected that. Now Michael Steinberg has confirmed their expectation, and they can listen to Beethoven with even more blind reverence than before.

Which (in an echo of my thoughts about Babbitt and Paul Griffiths) suggests one reason why the classical music world has privileged analysis too much. Or at least it's one way analysis pays off. In an age when popular culture has not just a bigger audience, but also more prestige, analysis seems to prove that classical music has deep and timeless meaning, At Juilliard, where I teach a graduate course called "Breaking Barriers: Classical Music in an Age of Pop," my students all say they listen to pop. But when I've asked some of them which kind of music is better, many of them say classical. And when I ask why classical is better, some of them invoke analysis. Classical music, they say, is analytically complex; that's why it's better than rock, or dance music, or hip-hop.

So that's one way classical music can defend itself against the pop onslaught—pop sells more records, but we've got dyads. The truth, though, is that much classical music isn't compositionally complex, that rock has its own compositional niceties, and above all that rock is likely to be complex in other ways—in its texture, for instance, in its "groove" (the precise inflection of standard rhythmic patterns), and in its range of stylistic and cultural reference, all of these still largely untouched in the analysis of classical music. We still, to cite just one example, find people saying that classical music has thoughtful rhythms because they change, while rock rhythms, repeated over and over again (or so the notion goes), have to be crushingly inane. Rock listeners, though, hear subtle changes in the groove, which will vary from player to player and create an intangible discourse, something very much like body language, which even the best classical musicians (in concrete cases that I know about) can't quite grasp.

Even Beethoven is hurt by this analytical emphasis. We lose sight of him as a human being, we misunderstand him as a composer, and we diminish him as an artist. With astonishment I read a paper by Geoffrey Block, "Organic Relations in Beethoven's Early Piano Concerti and the 'Spirit of Mozart.'" Mozart, says Block—citing analyses by Charles Rosen—built relationships between the first and last movements of some of his piano concertos. And so did Beethoven, even though, astonishingly, he "did not have the advantage of being able to study with Mozart or read [*sic*] Rosen's illuminating chapter on Mozart's piano concerti. . . ."[12] As if Beethoven needed Charles Rosen to teach him to compose! (A contention that Rosen would surely find as ludicrous as I do.)

Block's absurdity may be extreme, but there's a whiff of it in Steinberg, too. Does Steinberg congratulate himself for divining Beethoven's intentions, or—subtly—does he congratulate Beethoven for being as smart as Michael Steinberg?

3. What Does Schoenberg's Music Mean?

And now a little more about Schoenberg. If he's not quite the one who got us into this analytic pickle—it would hardly be fair to say that, especially since (as we've seen) he resisted attempts to tear open the twelve-tone structure of his works—he did invent the compositional system that has most tempted people to confuse analysis with music.

His supporters, and even some of his opponents, suffer from that confusion. See, for instance, Joseph P. Swain's discussion of twelve-tone music in chapter 6 of his book *Musical Languages*. Apparently Swain thinks serial structures fail because they're supposed to be audible, and aren't. "A strict sequential arrangement of the twelve available pitch classes," he writes (stating what he believes to be a basic principle of serial music), should be "an integral musical organization sufficient to supplant the perceptual anchor of a tonal center."[13] He might be giving tonal centers too much credit—obviously, a cadence is a "perceptual anchor," and we're used to hearing final cadences in the same key the piece began in. But tonal pieces can conclude in keys they didn't start in. And in large-scale works that do return to their opening key, composers tend to reinforce that return by also returning to their home-key musical material, typically (in sonata-form recapitulations) the opening theme. What's the perceptual anchor—the theme or the key?

Moreover, Swain skips a step in the evolution of serial music. Free atonal writing—which of course evolved before serial systems—has no tonal center, but can be full of perceptual anchors. Why wouldn't serial works have similar audible landmarks—motifs, rhythms, gestures, the whole grab-bag of contextual cross-references we find in free atonal music—with the serial skeleton functioning as a substructure, not necessarily audible and not important to performers or listeners? (That seems to be what Schoenberg and Webern thought it was.)

Or does Swain think free atonal music is a failure, too? The differences—analytically and perceptually—between serial and free atonal music are fascinating to think about. (Consider harmonic rhythm, apparently locked, in twelve-tone works, to recurring twelve-tone aggregates, and thus typically moving much more swiftly in allegro movements than in adagios). But Swain, by leapfrogging these questions, seems to do exactly what some serial advocates have done—he talks as if serial analytic structures need to be the most important musical facts in a serial piece. What would he do with the first movement of Webern's Symphony, op. 21, where the row unfolds very slowly, in four simultaneous horizontal statements? These four statements, in turn, are deployed as two canons, and it's the unfolding of these overlapping canons that—rather than the row—creates the succession of pitches that we hear. To put this differently, the piece of course remains twelve-tone on paper. But in performance, we hear pitches in an order governed essentially by Webern's ear; we could never deduce the row if all we did was listen to the horizontal progress of the piece. What, then, is the function of the twelve-tone system in this music? This question implies a deeper one, which Swain dismisses far too quickly: Why do composers use serial techniques at all? Swain doesn't ask, for instance, whether a consistent play of intervals, which serial structure guarantees, will provide coherence by itself, whether or not it's consciously perceived.

But these issues won't be my focus here. If analysis can hide the meaning of Babbitt and even Beethoven, it can do the same thing with Schoenberg—

it can blind us to what his music might say to us if we'd just listen to it. Twice in recent years I've gone to Schoenberg retrospectives, one at Merkin Hall in New York, and the other at Bard College. At both, written and spoken commentary took an analytic view—so much so at Bard that one listener asked if he was "crazy" to think that Schoenberg's Serenade might be amusing. The festival's program book might have encouraged his confusion, with passages like this, from the program note about the Serenade:

> In the essay "My Evolution," Schoenberg draws two examples from the Serenade to illustrate significant advances in twelve-tone composition. . . . [He] calls our attention to the middle section [of the *Tanzscene* movement] in which the six tones used in the accompaniment, drawn unordered from the movement's opening mandolin theme, are complemented by the six tones supplied by the main theme in the clarinet.

Nowhere in this program note (apart from one rushed suggestion that "the mandolin and guitar create the flavor of serenading musicians") are we told what the music might feel like.

At the New York retrospective, Milton Babbitt spoke on a panel, along with his twelve-tone colleague Charles Wuorinen. Both—even after so many years of changes, one of which is that Babbitt and I are now friendly colleagues at Juilliard—were deferred to as spokesmen for Schoenberg, which guaranteed that structure would get more votes than feeling. Babbitt was charming—delightful, in fact, as he always is. Certainly he doesn't seem to be forcing ideological agendas these days. But Wuorinen made me especially sad when he asserted, as he often has, that a new generation of composers isn't making music "everything it can be." What does he mean? Does he want music as simple as it can be, as moving, as shocking, as ironic, or as vivid as reflection of our culture as it can be? Of course not. He wants music to have complex pitch relationships (twelve-tone style), with complex structures growing from them, and while there's nothing wrong with that, it's only one aspect of music, elevated (in familiar, analysis-privileging style) to become the main event. Maybe Wuorinen or Babbitt might say that pitch relationships can be studied objectively, and hence can support verifiable statements about what's going on in music. Which to me would mean that their music was about a world in which only objective statements are allowed, in which emotions are so painful that they're banned.

What does Schoenberg's music mean? At both retrospectives, some people said that that we should move past analysis, and simply enjoy how Schoenberg's music sounds; one speaker at Bard even said we should listen to Schoenberg as if he were Schubert. But that, in its own way, redoubles the damage analysis did. Analysis, as it's usually practiced, suggests that there isn't any problem with Schoenberg, that his music is structured and orderly. Now we're told that listening to him isn't a problem, either. But, as one member of the audience said during the question period at a panel discussion at Bard, Schoenberg *isn't* Schubert. His music really does pose problems, and these, I think, run much deeper than mere complexity.

The Serenade, for instance, may be a witty piece—and I love its wit—but when I heard it at Bard, it bothered me. At the start (as I wrote in a review I later published in the *Wall Street Journal*[14]), no music could have been more delightful, dancing with a Viennese lilt while it teased my attention with wonderfully poised complexity. (All those quirky instrumental blends, overlays of tasty counterpoint, and phrases that never go where you think they will!) But later, as movement followed movement, I realized with a shock that Schoenberg wouldn't stop. He wouldn't let me go, much like someone you meet at a party who first seems like a sparkling conversationalist, but after half an hour starts to fluster you because he's so obsessive.

There might be, in other words, a disproportion between Schoenberg's method and his content. Maybe that's because Schoenberg moves in the kind of painful depths Adorno explored in *The Philosophy of Modern Music*:

> The seismographic registration of traumatic shock becomes . . . the technical structural law of music. . . . Musical language is polarized according to its extremes: towards gestures of shock resembling bodily convulsions on the one hand, and on the other towards a crystalline standstill of a human being whom anxiety causes to freeze in her tracks. It is this polarization upon which the total world of form of the mature Schoenberg—and of Webern as well—depends.[15]

Schoenberg, according to Adorno, does in his own way what I said Babbitt does—he tries to create order, but can't stop the disorder of the world at large from creeping in. He keeps propounding wit and order at such great length that both wit and order disappear, swamped by an inner need to express something that might be far more troubling.

Or, to put this more mildly (though in a way I think Adorno would readily understand), there's something very private about Schoenberg's work. Webern's music, of course, is even more private. But—with his concision, his ecstasy, his love of pure silence, and his compression of musical materials until every gesture becomes a variation on one basic cry—Webern embraces his privacy. Schoenberg doesn't do that. His move to twelve-tone writing came with a move toward established, public genres (orchestral variations, suites, string quartets, a piano concerto, a violin concerto, a wind quintet). Immediately there's a conflict implicit in his work. I noticed this conflict at the New York retrospective, when Robert Craft conducted the Chamber Symphony, op. 9, in a performance that was vivid (rhythmically, at least) and precise, but didn't have much dynamic variation. There wasn't much difference between *forte* and *piano* passages; there also wasn't much human feeling.

What was missing, in other words, was poetry. Much of the Chamber Symphony sounds like a frighteningly intimate transformation of Wagner, Strauss, or Mahler. So why wasn't it played with more of Wagner's and Mahler's emotion, turned ferocious by Schoenberg's deeper exposure of himself? Craft didn't indicate nuances in his conducting, so maybe that was part of the problem. But a larger part, as a panel discussion afterward made clear, was the sheer difficulty of the work. Craft, Gunther Schuller, Charles Wuorinen, even James Levine, one of the world's great conductors (who demonstrated his honest love of Schoenberg by serving on the panel with no publicity, and no self-importance)—all of them said that this and other Schoenberg scores are forbiddingly difficult. Schuller thinks they can't be properly played without weeks of rehearsal; Levine said musicians need to play music like this repeatedly, for many years, before they really learn it.

But then what's the meaning of music that, even after nearly a century, still can't be played? In 1859, when Wagner wrote *Tristan und Isolde,* it too was unperformable. Yet in no more than forty years it was mastered, at least to some extent, and even got popular. By contrast, Schoenberg's Chamber Symphony—ninety-eight years old, and not even as challenging as his later works—still eludes both fully realized performance and fully realized comprehension.

And here I'll draw my last moral, one that listening can teach us, but analysis can't. As I've noted earlier, Schoenberg said he felt like he was swimming in boiling water when he wrote free atonal music. To get back to dry land, he invented the twelve-tone system, in an attempt to bring order to his work, and to restore what he believed was the traditional structured discipline of classical music.

But that task was impossible. One study of modern culture, a 1982 book by Marshall Berman, is entitled *All That Is Solid Melts into Air,*[16] and that's a plausible headline for the twentieth century. Music historians routinely agree that the language of classic Western music was dissolving even before Schoenberg's time. More crucially, Schoenberg himself, a Viennese Jew, lived through World War I and the resulting collapse of central Europe; he fled from the Nazis, and spent the last decades of his life in the alien climate of the United States.

Could Schoenberg—simply by devising the twelve-tone method—put our broken century together, when nobody else could? Of course not. And because he so desperately tried, his music can sound awkward, at war with itself, and, like the Chamber Symphony, so fiercely private that he might not (unconsciously, at least) have cared whether anyone could play it. Schoenberg's fiercest current partisans seem never to think of this, even though Theodor Adorno put ideas like this on the table many years ago. Instead, Schoenberg's defenders often flee from reality, by focusing mostly on structural abstractions.

By doing that, they might unconsciously confess their own artistic alienation. And they do nothing to teach the classical music world where it stands, now that its own traditions have fallen apart.

Notes

1. Paul Griffiths, *Modern Music: The Avant-Garde since 1945* (New York: George Braziller, Inc., 1981).

2. Arnold Schoenberg, "Criteria for the Evaluation of Music," in *Style and Idea: Selected Writings of Arnold Schoenberg*, ed. Leonard Stein (Berkeley: University of California Press, 1984), 136.

3. Arnold Schoenberg, "'Schoenberg's Tone-Rows,'" in ibid., 213–14.

4. Hans Moldenhauer, in collaboration with Rosaleen Moldenhauer, *Anton von Webern: A Chronicle of His Life and Works* (New York: Knopf, 1979), 423.

5. Ibid., 485. Webern, as Stadlen is also quoted saying, "acted as if he himself were not aware of the serial aspect of his work, or at least never thought of it when playing or discussing it."

6. Moldenhauer, *Anton von Webern*, 484.

7. Ibid.

8. Arnold Schoenberg, "Heart and Brain in Music," in *Style and Idea*, 75.

9. Paul Griffiths, *Modern Music and After* (Oxford: Oxford University Press, 1995), xiv. This book should not be confused with Griffths's *Modern Music: A Concise History* (New York: Thames and Hudson, 1985; revised ed., 1994), which is a much less technical history of musical developments from Debussy onward.

10. Griffiths, *Modern Music*, 157; *Modern Music and After*, 67.

11. A slightly different version of this passage appears in Steinberg's collection of his symphonic program notes, *The Symphony: A Listener's Guide* (Oxford: Oxford University Press, 1995), 27. Curiously, the version in the book doesn't use the expression "B-flat/E-flat dyad," and thus is easier to understand than the one in the New York Philharmonic's program book (which you'd think should be simpler, since it's going to be read by casual concertgoers).

12. Geoffrey Block, "Organic Relations in Beethoven's Early Piano Concerti and the 'Spirit of Mozart,'" in William Kinderman, ed., *Beethoven's Compositional Process* (Lincoln and London: University of Nebraska Press, 1991), 72.

13. Joseph P. Swain, *Musical Languages* (New York: W. W. Norton, 1997), 132.

14. Greg Sandow, "When the Solid Dissolves," *Wall Street Journal, September 17, 1998, section A, p. 20.*

15. Theodor W. Adorno, *Philosophy of Modern Music*, trans. Anne G. Mitchell and Wesley V. Blomster (New York: Continuum, 1973), 42. Adorno is writing about *Erwartung*, but leaps, at the end of the passage I've quoted, to generalize his remarks, so that now they're about "the total world of form of the mature Schoenberg."

16. Berman, *All That Is Solid Melts into Air: The Experience of Modernity* (New York: Simon and Schuster, 1982).

4

In Memory of a Receding Dialectic: The Political Relevance of Autonomy and Formalism in Modernist Musical Aesthetics

Martin Scherzinger

One must not expect too much from people who use the word "form" too fluently as signifying something other than content, or as connected with content, whatever, or who are suspicious of "technique" as something "mechanical."

—Bertolt Brecht, "Against Georg Lukács"

The uncompromising radicalism of the works [of the most important artists of the age], the very features defamed as formalism, give them a terrifying power, absent from helpless poems to the victims of our times.

—Theodor Adorno, "Commitment"

Introduction: The Ethics of Memory

This paper is concerned with the postmodern reception of modernist musical aesthetics and proposes a reassesment informed, on the one hand, by the historical conditions of modernism, and, on the other, by current political themes. The postmodern stance hotly contests certain tenets of modernist music. Modernism, the argument goes, subscribes to the ahistorical principle of aesthetic autonomy for high art (in the sense of a tradition of music that was no longer tied to practical or moral purposes, and existed instead in an abstract realm of self-sufficient signification), and thus buttresses an insular and rationalist elitism that disavows certain social responsibilities and thus maintains the social status quo.[1] Instead of engaging the role of art in the context of a living social praxis, modernist music, and its critical elaboration, is charged with an overly narrow engagement with the immanent development of purely artistic forces of production. There is scarcely a critical musicological account in the last ten years that fails to lambaste at least one aspect of what are perceived to be modernism's surviving intellectual practices—the structural analysis of formal musical notes alone (i.e., treating musical works as if they were self-sufficient totalities), for example, or the teleological approach to music history (i.e., writing as if some utopia in waiting lay ahead).[2] Occasionally, musicologists even take this ideological condition to be embodied in actual modernist musical works, thereby venturing, paradoxically, to galvanize their apparently hermetic claims.[3]

In this paper I will argue, first, that to reject modernism's elevation of aesthetic autonomy today is no longer self-evidently a progressive position. Rather, it may be yielding to yet another unspoken ideology: various pressures produced by the processes of capitalist modernization. In an age where the canon of autonomous high art no longer holds the privileged position it once did, critique of the above sort may be advancing in obsolete terms. Second, I will argue that such critique codifies modernism's aesthetic autonomy into a narrow dogma that does not line up with its meanings in its original historical context. The separation of art from social functions during the first half of the twentieth century was less an absolute denial of a relationship between the two and more a forging of a peculiar linkage between the two that was complex and dialectical. Broadly, what has been disregarded in recent critical accounts is the socially critical and provocative side of the formulation of aesthetic autonomy as it was elaborated within a dialectical tradition. In other words, the *antagonistic* side of aesthetic autonomy, which was tied to notions of critique and negativism, has largely been forgotten. What should be remembered is that, by resisting absorption into the terrain of everyday meaning, the inherently non-discursive, absolutely musical work also defied the ideological hold of such meaning. This distance between music and society, which Lydia Goehr calls a "critical gap," *was* its social praxis.[4]

I will argue that modernism sought to heighten the tension between various extreme dialectical tendencies in an effort to arrest critical space in an increasingly administered world. While it insisted on its self-sufficiency and its ability to disclose truths about the world (principally in negative terms), modernism's adversarial impulse also claimed art as an agent for social change (or resistance to unwanted change). This kind of critical thinking was perhaps exemplified by high modernists such as the Schoenberg circle. While my argument will focus on the nexus between Adorno and Schoenberg, I want to suggest that a dialectical attitude was, in fact, widespread during the wars in Germany. It is true that musical production during the wars was extremely diverse, often giving rise to incompatible and contradictory styles. For example, the critical stance adopted by Adorno's interpretation of the music of Arnold Schoenberg advanced a musical understanding that involved immersion in the wholly immanent structural features of the musical work, whereas the critical stance adopted by Paul Hindemith's Heideggerian conception of musical use, involved immersion in the worldly side of musical production (the vernacular of popular culture, for example). But this immediately apparent aesthetic difference should not obscure the underlying critical affinity between the two.

So, while it is fairly obvious that the surreal mockery of Hindemith's *Kammermusik* No. 1 differs politically and aesthetically from, say, the proto-twelve-tone experimentation of Schoenberg's Serenade, I contend that, to the extent that both endorsed the critical potential of a dialectical situation, these diverse tendencies can be legitimately subsumed under a single notion of critical modernism. Despite the striking differences between these composers then, I argue that there is what Daniel Albright calls a "kinship relation" established by their respective philosophical elaborations.[5] Philosophically speaking, both Adorno and Heidegger took a stand of calculated disloyalty to the Enlightenment project that grounded their philosophical positions. Musically speaking, both Schoenberg and Hindemith dialectically engaged traditional musical tropes in their works to forge a space for social critique. In Schoenberg's music, this was achieved through a dialectical jostling between the general structures of musical material handed down by historical tradition and the subjective intervention forged by the music's recalcitrant and unique aspects. Hindemith's music shared this general philosophical strategy, but differed in the details. By dislocating various traditional musical devices from their historical domain of practical use (i.e., by rendering them fleetingly autonomous), Hindemith's music effectively illuminated their mystified second nature and thus opened a space for something new.[6]

Already within the opening measures of the first *Kammermusik,* certain pertinent philosophical categories are brought thematically to the ear (see figure 4.1). First, by sounding out a limited pitch collection lacking certain notes, the opening draws attention to a musical grammar that has fallen into disuse. If the music is in B major, it is a malfunctioning B major. Second, the overly active rhythmic dimension, almost vertiginous in movement (in which binary rhythms run agilely alongside three-beated ones, for example) brings a kind of traditional Baroque motoric figuration into strife with itself. Neither rhythmic grouping assumes ascendancy and yet both are in full *fortissimo* flight. Thus, rhythmic layers are both preserved and annulled, resulting in a negation of propulsive rhythmic movement. A complex stasis remains. Third, the quasi-Cubist rendition of the trill in the piano unmasks the claimed "naturalness" of its ornamental eighteenth- and early-nineteenth-century form. The trill has morphed into its exchangeable commodity form, mechanized and stiff, at once denaturalized and denatured. It is removed from its felicitous world (where it was associated with cadences that marked music's formal divisions) in order to reveal the assumptions of formal balance and symmetry on which that world rested.

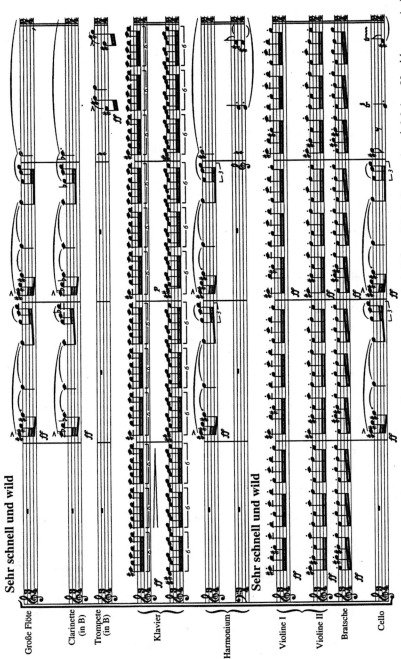

Figure 4.1. Hindemith, *Kammermusik* Op. 24, No. 1. First movement, mm. 1–4. Schott Music International, Mainz. Used by permission.

Hindemith may be polemically gaming with traditional music's rhetorical devices of beginning and ending. By sounding a gesture of closure at the beginning of the piece, as Stravinsky was to do a year later in his first truly neo-classical work, the Octet, Hindemith lays bare the arbitrary face of these naturalized devices.

This is not to say that such critique is still operative or adequate to the task of transformative political praxis today, but that postmodernism's selective memory of modernism has severed a vital dialectic between politics and art. Far from indicating modernism's lack of political ambition, then, this limited memory reflects the postmodern sensibility that art cannot be an agent for social change or resistance after all. By fancifully depoliticizing modernism (perhaps because of its historical association with the political failures of the 1930s and 1940s), postmodernism risks instituting its own aestheticist trend and recapitulating the very failures it seeks to transcend. For example, the blanket refusal of the concept-metaphors of autonomy, organicism, and formalism (indeed, "the tyranny of all wholes" in the words of Ihab Hassan) in order to decenter the unity of reason, the subject, and art, is also an attribution of a limiting self-identical significance (free from contextual determination) for these concept-metaphors.[7] Such a critical orientation identifies an ideological capacity with the concept-metaphors *as such* instead of with the social *use* to which they are put. When ideology is located by virtue of employing a kind of language itself (rather than by virtue of its workings in particular times and spaces), the dialectical tendencies of that language recede and the possibility of harnessing such language for strategic political concerns dissolves. This essay attempts to retrieve the dialectical component of modernism not for its own sake but in order to shed light on various political predicaments in postmodernity. Phrased as a question: How do we forge a new link between culture and politics that is adequate to our times?

Modernism in Context: Aesthetics under Siege

After a decade of prosperous capitalism in North America at the end of the twentieth century, it has become easy to forget the traumatic economic and political crises that befell Europe in the wake of the June 1848 massacres of the proletariat by the monarchy, crises that culminated in what Eric Hobsbawm calls "the age of catastrophe"—Europe's 31-year war from 1914 to 1945.[8] The kaleidoscopic proliferation of new styles, manifestos, and artistic "isms" at this time—symbolism, impressionism, expressionism, suprematism, futurism, cubism, surrealism, to name a few—was itself a testimony to a new and peculiar condition of modern art in the context of massive social upheaval. The sustained and radical questioning of the very artistic medium was often understood as an attack on the tyranny of sedimented habit and belief. Modernism sought out radically new modes of expression and representation along every conceivable trajectory (except perhaps the middle one, as Adorno might say). Indeed, cutting-edge experimentation became a privileged category. Consequently, the concept of "style," increasingly contested and in doubt, became inherently provisional. Modernism became an art of extremes reaching out to various stylistic limit-points. In the words of Albright, it became a "testing of the limits of aesthetic construction: volatility of emotion (expressionism); stability and inexpressiveness (the new objectivity); accuracy of representation (hyperrealism); absence of representation (abstractionism); purity of form (neoclassicism); formless energy (neobarbarism); cultivation of the technological present (futurism); cultivation of the prehistoric past (the mythic method)."[9] These extreme pairs registered the crisis of style in almost opposite ways. Once again, take the expressionism/new objectivity opposition: On the one hand, Schoenberg proclaimed that the true musical idea (*musikalische Gedanke*) transcended the exigencies of style, and he wrote compositions for the high canon of serious music. On the other hand, Hindemith endorsed a self-conscious provisionality of style and (in his work of the early post–World War I period) wrote music that adopted a motley assortment of styles (including current dance crazes such as the foxtrot, boston, shimmy, and ragtime) whose lifespan was calculated to be short.

The shortlived Weimar Republic was a particularly volatile zone for the polarization of the arts. Social discontent and resentment analagously polarized the political field. Not only were extreme left and right parties considered serious political options, but the left itself fractured into communists and democrats. By the time the unified politics of the leftist popular front appeared, the crack in the left had already opened the way for the Nationalist Socialists. As if to reflect the enforced democracy that could not last, many forms of Weimar art were predicated on a rejection of all principles of permanence and thus tended towards the extremes of radical expression. Artists often felt that even the most radical forms of aesthetic production were insufficiently responsive to the social crisis. For instance, Hugo Ball, the Dada poet of the Cabaret Voltaire, found that, much to his disappointment, one could not *not* make sense in the domain of language. While his poems, like the infamous "gadji beri bimba" (1916), were shocking in their defiant destruction of all semiotic norms, Ball despaired over the impossibility of absolute linguistic freedom. Like Walter Benjamin's interpretation of Paul Klee's *Angelus Novus* as an ineffectual opponent to progress, Ball's sputtering sound fragments could not resist the force of the ordering "storm of progress." The anxious and dynamic search for new forms of artistic expression reflected the often paradoxical mood of the 1920s, relief and a taste for the new (in the face of war weariness) combining oddly with cynicism and disenchantment (in the face of continued social and economic hardship). This is not to say that artists forged overt

political allegiances. In fact, aside from the Italian futurists' right-wing celebration of war heroism, or the tenuous links between various artistic
movements and the communist party (such as the surrealists or the Brecht
circle), the political dimension of artistic activity was largely defined precisely by a separation from the politics to which it was averse. This is also
not to say that culture passively reflected the social world from a hermetic
distance, but to acknowledge that it was concretely (albeit often antagonis-
tically) bound up with it. The new emphasis on aesthetic simplicity and
fragmentation, the prevalence of chamber music, the short comic sketches
in one act, the mixing of high and low art, the modest new performance
venues (such as the Cabaret Voltaire and the music festivals at
Donaueschingen and Baden Baden) were the result of the new, straitened
economic circumstances of the 1930s.

The rise of fascism in Germany ignited an intense interest in the role of
aesthetic production in political critique. Marxist rationalism, with its over-
emphasis on the socio-economic base, was inadequate to the task of analyzing the success of the Nationalist Socialists, who exploited irrational
and obsolete traditions to outline a utopian society based on religious allegiances, family values, and emphatic notions of homeland (*Heimat*). Traditional Marxism failed to capture the material roots of these myths and
their powerful artistic elaboration (in the form of mass spectacles—monumental rectangles of marching soldiers at the Nuremberg Party Conventions, and so on). In a related, but not identical way, Stalin incorporated
elements of the constructivist avant-garde of the 1920s to assert the dogma
of socialist realism (in the form of monuments to heroic labor in the fields
and factories, and so on). The signing of the two-year-long Hitler/Stalin
pact in 1939 forged a paradoxical allegiance between these politically opposed forms of dictatorship. For theorists like Benjamin, Stalin's act was a
betrayal of the socialist cause. Stalin's use of art for political purposes
amounted to an aestheticization of politics in the manner of the fascists,
whereby the need for social change was falsely satisfied.[10] Against orthodox Marxism, Benjamin felt that the role of art was continuous with, indeed organic to, political state formation. Society could not be reduced to
economic relations in the last instance. Similarly, for Adorno, totalitarianism was not an irrational eruption in an otherwise progressive continuum
of Enlightenment logic, but a refinement of some of its central tenets. The
Nazi industrialization of death, for example, was both a perversion and an
embodiment of the instrumental principle of efficiency and self-interest.[11]
For Adorno, Enlightenment reason needed to remain allied to other ("non-
identical") concepts of truth and ethics if it was, politically, to resist the
power of the totalitarian state, and, economically, to resist the movements
of brazen monopoly capital. This is where the principle of aesthetic autonomy played a pivotal role.

Aesthetic Autonomy in the Thought of Modernist Dialectics

Adorno considerably invested autonomous modernist artworks with the ability to resist undesired political and economic developments. Art's very aesthetic autonomy freed it from the instrumental reason that operated only to secure the ends of certain (market-driven) means. In the words of Adorno, "The uncalculating autonomy of works which avoid popularization and adaption to the market, involuntarily become an attack on them."[12] The formal structures of composers like Schoenberg and writers like Samuel Beckett challenged the illusions of Enlightenment reason and revealed the workings of unacknowledged contradictions of the modern human condition. The hermeticism of Beckett's works, for example, had nothing to do with "conceptual or logical abstraction" per se, but were calculated to make people shudder. And yet, wrote Adorno, "no-one can persuade himself that these eccentric plays and novels are not about what everyone knows but no one will admit."[13] Likewise, the atonal works of Schoenberg put into question their very own compositional procedures. That is, Schoenberg's works questioned what Adorno called "structures perfected within themselves which might be exhibited for all time in museums of opera or concert."[14] Hence, the formalist autonomy of these works rendered them recalcitrant to permanent (and therefore exploitative) values. They were a dialectical "challenge [to] the lying positivism of meaning."[15] In other words, the formal aesthetic dimension, however hermetic and receding in itself, was relevant to aspects of political struggle.

To the chagrin of some postmodernist critics, Adorno thought that the emancipatory potential of art lay almost exclusively in the high modernist art of Europe. In contrast, critics like Benjamin and Siegfried Kracauer recognized this kind of potential in mass culture as well. This has led to the simplistic notions that Adorno was an elitist mandarin and that Benjamin, the champion of modern media, provides the better analytic model of cultural critique today. But such a media-triumphalist reading ignores the shared interests of Adorno and Benjamin, which are arguably more relevant than their differences. Like Adorno, Benjamin favored the dialectical method in his analysis of art: "[P]enetrating into depth," he wrote in one of his conversations with Brecht, "is my way of travelling to the antipodes."[16] Essentially, both critics forged a materialist theory of art and both valued an autonomous moment in its production. It is true that Benjamin did not vividly distinguish between what he called "autonomous" art and "tendentious" art, especially in his early essays that owed a debt to Brecht. But, by arguing that the political relevance of autonomous art also rendered it tendentious, Benjamin's position was never far from Adorno's effort to articulate the political aspirations of modernist art.[17] And in his later writing, Benjamin increasingly recognized the necessity of autonomy for concentrating genuine critical attention. For example, in his essay on Baudelaire, Benjamin restored the progressive role of art's "aura,"[18] whose withering he had celebrated in his earlier essay on the work of art in the age of mechanical reproducibility.[19] Here, the aura, which "invest[s] [an object] with the ability to look at us in return," was an essential part of a genuine experience of art. Indeed, the auratic experience impugned the objectified and exploitative "rhythm of production on a conveyor belt."[20] Analogously, in his essay on the problem of music analysis, Adorno wrote that "one must let [the music] assert itself, in order to be able to enter into its structure analytically."[21] For both critics, then, an authentic critical encounter with an artwork entailed furnishing it with the capacity to impose itself auratically on the beholding subject, which, in turn, entailed granting it a certain irreducible distance and autonomy from that subject.

Even in his discussion of the philosophy of history, Benjamin stressed the necessary autonomous "configuration" required for revolutionary intervention.

> Where thinking suddenly stops in a configuration pregnant with tensions, it gives that configuration a shock, by which it crystallizes into a monad. A historical materialist approaches a historical subject only where he encounters it as a monad. In this structure he recognizes the sign of a Messianic cessation of happening, or, put differently, a revolutionary chance in the fight for an oppressed past. He takes cognizance of it in order to blast a specific era out of the homogeneous course of history—blasting a specific life out of the era or a specific work out of the lifework.[22]

Rejecting the legitimacy of all historical "facts" that emerge in the logical context of a "causal connection," Benjamin furnished thinking (figured as a radically specific and self-sufficient "monad") with revolutionary energy.[23] The concept of the monad, which Benjamin borrowed from Gottfried Wilhelm Leibniz's seventeenth-century philosophical writings, involved an internally self-regulating and unified body that could not be acted upon by any external agent. In his chapter on monadology, Leibniz wrote: "Monads have no windows, by which anything could come in or go out. . . . [T]he natural changes of monads come from an *internal principle,* since an external cause would be unable to influence their inner being."[24] Although it appeared *as if* monads acted upon one another, in fact they were wholly free from the temporal dynamics of cause and effect. For Benjamin, the monad was the autonomous, indeed anti-historical, aspect without which a dialectical materialist history could not result. Its recalcitrant and static separation from the homogeneity of standard historical accounting could wrest the latter from its own processes and illuminate a future. In short, like Adorno's progressive evaluation of the autonomous artwork (hibernating, perhaps, in the winter of capitalism), the category of autonomy played a constitutive role in Benjamin's account of social change.

Similarly, for Bertolt Brecht the effort to secure a political role for the arts involved a deep respect for their autonomous formal dimension. In response to Georg Lukács, the high conscience of Soviet realism who was hostile to purely formal experimentation in art, Brecht craftily rearticulated the charge of "formalism" in terms that would chafe at the anti-formal organicist stance of Lukács's realism more than it would the formal productivist stance of his own artistic assemblages. Brecht asked, "What is formalism [in 'everyday life']? Let us take the expression: *Formally he is right*. That means that actually he is not right, but he is right according to the form of things and only according to this form."[25] Thus, Brecht recoded "formalism" in terms of the socially false and not in terms of aesthetic technique. And the question of a form's truth or falsity could not be settled on an *a priori* basis but needed to be answered via experimentation with a variety of forms. Brecht came up with a simile: "The actors may not use makeup—or hardly any—and claim to be "absolutely natural" and yet the whole thing can be a swindle; and they can wear masks of a grotesque kind and present the truth"[26] In short, progressive aesthetics, as he defined them, involved a political end whose means varied according to the contingencies of changing historical contexts.

While Brecht favored the formal techniques associated with defamiliarization (collage, montage, etc.) over the organic vitalism of Lukács's realism, his aesthetic position was inherently flexible and open to the tactical reworking of many different aesthetic forms. In a simple rhetorical reversal, Brecht demonstrated how his formal adaption of cubist and constructivist strains could produce precisely the effects Lukács was looking for in realism. They too were capable of "discovering the causal complexes of society, unmasking the prevailing view of things as the view of those who are in power . . . making possible the concrete, and making possible abstraction from it."[27] Indeed, for Brecht, all organic natural law and behavior was already surreptitiously artificial and arbitrary. The artist's obligation lay in creating new objective forms and new realities. His realism should be the result of a "purposely distorting imagination" (to borrow a phrase from Benjamin). In other words, for Brecht, the artist was less an imitator of the (artificial) natural world, than he was a producer of new worlds. Brecht rejected the traditional Marxist "reflection" model of base/superstructure relations (whereby art, as superstructural, could provide a mediated mirror of social relations but could not concretely effect their change), and instead adopted a "productive" model (whereby the mediations between base and superstructure were mutual). For Brecht, the productive potential of art lay in its ability to effect functional changes in systems of signification (*Umfunktionierung*) in the social world. Thus, a longing for a future world informed the philosophical ground of that branch of aesthetic modernism that came to be called the "New Objectivity" (*Neue Sachlichkeit*).

It should come as no surprise that the writing itself of the Frankfurt School and other contemporaneous cultural critics who sanctioned theories of political modernism often took on the very formal characteristics of modernist art. That is, this body of writing also took on a self-reflexive attention to its own medium. For instance, levels of content and form were uncoupled in the syntax; pithy aphorisms that posed a challenge to decipherment became a key mode of expression; the writing asserted itself as autonomous; multiple angles of vision were simultaneously cast on phenomena; linguistic devices producing rhetorical hyperbole, gray zones, transitions, ruptures, transgressions, disunities, and fissures were valued; and cryptic concepts like shock, dream, catastrophe, and distraction ran the philosophical arguments. As Max Paddison observes regarding Adorno's book *Minima Moralia* (1951): "Although not a "text on music," it is certainly a most musical "text," with its wordplays, grammatical inversions and ellipses, its exaggerations and analogies taken to extremes."[28] The prevalence of tersely constructed antitheses and hyperbolic assertions in Adorno's output was a symptom of the extreme pressures of the time. In his essay on Brecht, for example, Adorno made no attempt to soften his earlier pronouncement (made in 1949) that writing poetry after Auschwitz was barbaric.[29] Instead, he exaggerated the exaggeration by calling into question the very possibility of "living" with dignity after Auschwitz.

The point I wish to make here is that modernist critics of culture also incorporated what Albright calls the "strong thrust toward the verges of the aesthetic experience" in their effort to think social transformation.[30] Startling juxtapositions of contradictory elements (like outmoded debris and utopian progress) became a key rhetorical device in many of these writings. By way of analogy, Ernst Bloch felt that the pastiche of everyday junk and decay found in modernist montage could produce a perceptual rupture, which, in turn, created space for social change. This was art that strove "to exploit the real fissures in surface inter-relations and to discover the new in their crevices."[31] And this was criticism that radically questioned eternal values and principles of permanence. Relatedly, Kracauer insisted that the promise of the new lay in a peculiar perceptual faculty—a kind of "distracted vigilance"—that operated in the field of "inconspicuous surface-level expressions."[32] Distracted (instead of contemplative) attention to objects of mass culture, such as the then well-known Tiller Girls, was the surest way to resist their domestication into falsely organic unities. Benjamin's dialectical images also wrenched elements of the everyday from their function and placed them in strange and defamiliarized constellations. Like the surrealist coupling of images that did not normally belong together—the most famous of which may be the Comte de Lautréamont's chance encounter between an umbrella and a sewing machine on an operating table—Benjamin's enigmatic prose was a jolt to ordinary syntax, and could thereby send thinking in motion. In short, philosophy had transformed itself into politically strategic artistic practice.

To sum up, it seems to me that, for all their individual differences, these cultural critics shared the conviction that aesthetic modernism had a significant adversarial role to play in society. They viewed the artistic avant-garde as a contestatory moment, one that produced various shocks and jolts that would push through the catastrophe of the past toward a new social formation. In all cases, the political challenge was grounded in dialectical thought. I will now demonstrate these dialectical tendencies in the context of a specific example, namely the music of Schoenberg. Although my argument will develop in tandem with Adorno's categories, I will revise Adorno's disparaging reading of Schoenberg's twelve-tone music by callling attention to the dialectical oppositions at work in this music. Thus I will briefly outline the way Adorno figured dialectics in Schoenberg's atonal works before making a parallel argument on the terrain of Schoenberg's twelve-tone works.

Dialectical Tendencies in the Music of Modernism: The Adorno/Schoenberg Case

Schoenberg's status as a "dialectical composer"—elevating his musical ideas by, at once, radically negating the musical past and conservatively preserving it—is fairly widespread and well known to writers on modernism.[33] Already in Schoenberg's atonal works, Adorno identified the unfolding of a progressive dialectical argument. Adorno located the truth content of the musical work in the dialectical tension between, on the one hand, the general layers of historically mediated "material" (i.e., aesthetic norms and conventions) on which the composer drew, and, on the other hand, its "subjective" articulation, contextualization and organization in a particular composition. The composer's response to the current state of the pre-formed material resulted in a simultaneous embrace of its inherent tendencies and a critical negation of its handed-down character. For Adorno, the authentic musical work retained this twofold character of development and disintegration. Like Hegel's dialectical progress of spirit, Adorno's exemplary work embraced the dialectical progress of the musical material, but unlike Hegel's spirit, Adorno's exemplary work was not readily elevated to higher levels of musical unity. Schoenberg's *Erwartung*, for example, retained the "scars . . . which have become fixed in his music . . . as the heralds of the id against the compositional will." They can be heard as disruptive moments in the otherwise seemingly organic whole. Indeed, "The heteronomy of the scars—and the blotches—challenges music's facade of self-sufficiency."[34] For Adorno, *Erwartung*'s images of past and future flashing in the "now" of recognition functioned as a kind of dialectical image. Thus, the authentically critical musical work strove for formal unity and its negation, thereby revealing the historically contingent nature of that unity.

Listening to Schoenberg with Adornian dialectics in mind involves a kind of double consciousness. In Schoenberg's atonal music, for example, musical structure was defined by a unique network of referential associations that straddled tonal expectations and non-tonal organizational principles. Often a unique unordered cell, which Schoenberg called a *Grundgestalt* ("basic shape"), provided the motivic/intervallic unity of the piece. From Adorno's perspective, the *Grundgestalt* represents the logic of the unconscious subjectivity that threatens the surface veneer of conventional tonality. Schoenberg's atonal music reflects this kind of dialectical jostling between two levels. In the last of his Six Little Pieces for Piano, op. 19, for example, the music is precariously poised between a gradually unfolding symmetrical sonority built on stacked fourths and residual traces of functional harmony (see figure 4.2). This tension is present already in the sound of the opening two chords, the first of which suggests a dominant seventh on B and the second a symmetrical trichord built on fourths. Oscillating back and forth, these chords interpenetrate throughout the piece, and (alternately trading places on strong and weak beats of their respective measures) draw constantly changing meanings out of each other. For example, the first linear movement in the left hand seems to momentarily

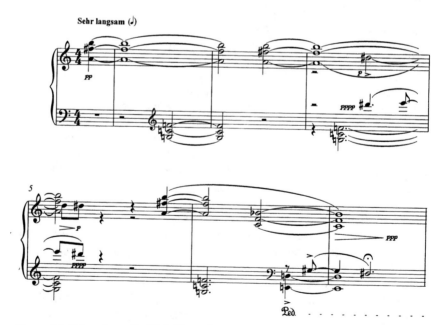

Figure 4.2. Schoenberg, Six Little Pieces for Piano, Op. 19, No. 6, mm. 1–6. Copyright © 1913, 1940 by Universal Edition A.G., Wien / UE 30775. Used by permission.

"resolve" the leading tone (D sharp) of the implied dominant in mm. 3–4. But, against this interpretation, the sounded "tonic" E also extends the logic of unfolding symmetrical fourths in a giant symmetrical chord pivoting around A. In other words, E sounds both like a resolution to the dominant on B *and* like the next fourth above the B of the first chord. The latter hearing is encouraged by the first new chord in the left hand (m. 5), which sounds D below G of the second chord, thus extending the symmetrical unfolding downwards. Like a Wittgensteinian duck-rabbit (derived from Jastrow), the music yields to a two-fold interpretation that disconcerts the unity of the whole. In Adorno's terms, the historically beholden functional "material" and the "subjectively" unique symmetries mark the poles of the music's doubleness.

In Adorno's view, this kind of gap between the music's double logic was essentially a critical gesture for it undermined the ascendency of any totalizing structural order. In fact, the work's truth content lay in subverting what had become falsely naturalized (a process whereby social conventions are experienced as second nature). Thus, authentic music reversed the scheme of things to which mass music conformed socially and thus functioned as social critique. But, for Adorno such subversion could never be total because the unfettered deviation from music's historical material paradoxically empowered that material as its negative imprint. In the spirit of Hegel's master/slave dialectic, Adorno argued that when the subjective destruction of music's "illusion" (of naturalized material) became a single-minded goal, the music paradoxically elevated that illusion and became a slave to it: "In the final analysis the radicalism with which the technical work of art destroys aesthetic illusion makes the illusion responsible for the technical work of art."[35] According to Adorno, this is what happened in Schoenberg's twelve-tone music. In its effort to check the unhindered ascendance of any particular musical style, tonal organizing principle, or internal musical parameter, twelve-tone technique collapsed the distinctions between "polyphonic fugal structure and homophonic sonata form," between "the essential and the coincidental," and between "harmony and melody."[36] By rationally undoing these instinctive historical oppositions, Schoenberg's twelve-tone technique effectively "actualizes the sensitivity of musical dynamics in the face of the unconscious recurrence of the same."[37] Adorno's analogy between the recurrence of tones in tonality and Nietzsche's principle of the eternal return of the same suggested that a progressive music should resist the force of such unconscious recurrence. But the radical de-differentiation of musical dichotomies (which Adorno also called the "musical domination of nature"), "suddenly turns against the subjective autonomy and freedom itself, in the name of which this domination found its fulfillment."[38] Instead of maintaining the extreme tendencies within the work itself, Schoenberg's absolute elevation of the subjective dimension paradoxically objectified that subjective dimension. In Adorno's view, the structure of twelve-tone music thus became "correct" instead of "meaningful;" its "absolute variation" became "infinitely static," and its "rationality" became "superstition."[39] Through its outright break with the blind domination of tonal material, twelve-tone music allowed this material enigmatically to command the compositional scene, and thus gave in to a "second blind nature."[40] Twelve-tone music had reproduced the fate it attempted to elude and thus degenerated into its opposite. It was as if Schoenberg's battle against "style" in the name of "idea" was suddenly transformed into style *par excellence*. His music became a historical disaster.

In his essay "The Concept of Twelve-Tone Technique" Adorno wrote, "[the 'row'] refers to an arbitrarily designated ordering of the twelve tones available to the composer in the tempered half-tone system, as, for example, c♯–a–b–g–a♭–f♯–b♭–d–e–e♭–c–f in the first of Schoenberg's published twelve-tone compositions."[41] Here Adorno overstated the "arbitrariness" of the row. First, in the cited example (which refers to Schoenberg's op. 23, no. 5) the row is made up of two hexachords that are pitch-class inversions of one another (around c/b or f/f♯). This made possible the subjective play of various (dis)connections within the row and between successive presentations of row forms that were neither wholly "arbitrary" nor wholly presupposed by the "ordering" of all twelve tones. Indeed, for Schoenberg the musical "idea" lay in the manner in which balance and unity were restored to the music's inherent condition of "imbalance" and "unrest." This was the subjective component of twelve-tone composition. And it could take various expressive forms. In *Klavierstück*, op. 23, no. 5, for example, motivic connections (such as the upward dotted-note melodic figure in m. 1 as it is recalled in m. 6) are not aligned with the unfolding of the twelve tones. Motivic ideas, that is, take on a life that is independent of the demands of the row. Similarly, in mm. 22–27, for example, the parallel two-bar gestures are articulated by fourteen notes. The aggregate is thus exceeded by two notes within the phrase. By circulating pitches in a way that keeps the phrase structure out of sync with the row structure, Schoenberg's row was less like Adorno's "arbitrary designation" to be deafly followed and more like a vehicle for projecting motivic linkages through developing variation.

While Adorno took a firm stand on the matter, the question whether Schoenberg's twelve-tone music failed to sustain a genuinely dialectical musical situation has not been definitively settled. Indeed, Schoenberg viewed himself as a dialectical composer. Like Heidegger and Adorno, Schoenberg spoke about music in terms of cultural critique and truth telling.[42] He also subscribed to the Hegelian idea of the historical progress of art and situated his music at the cutting edge of modernity. For Schoenberg, this progress involved a dialectical encounter between conflicting tendencies, such as "tradition" and "innovation," "heart" and "brain," or "style" and "idea." Like Adorno's dialectic between musical "material" and subjective "composition," Schoenberg's elusive concept of "idea" (*Gedanke*), for example, involved a dialectic between preservation and negation, old and new. A musical idea was the establishment of "sheerly musical" relations "between things or parts between which no relation had existed before that establishment."[43] An idea was therefore always new. Following a lightning-like moment of inspiration (*der blitzartige Einfall*), the composer set out to realize the conception materially. Schoenberg described the compositional process in terms of reckoning with an inherently unstable scenario: "The method by which balance is restored seems to me the real idea of the composition."[44] Schoenberg's emphasis on the unique manner in which organic unity is achieved was an endorsement of the notion of originality as a sign of artistic autonomy, which, in turn, was analogous to the emancipation of the bourgeois subject. But, for Schoenberg, to be genuinely original involved a persistent consciousness of tradition. According to Hermann Danuser, Schoenberg's paradoxical paradigm is best understood if we "take as our point of departure the idea of a dialectical form of art production, one that favors the unorthodox and in which the rationally deducible is found alongside the unexpected, and recourse to compositional and genre tradition alongside bold inroads into new musical and music-historical territory."[45] In short, Schoenberg and Adorno may have differed in the way they progressed but not in their general direction.

The fact that Adorno failed to hear a dialectical struggle between contradictory criteria in Schoenberg's twelve-tone works does not mean Schoenberg was not thinking dialectically. It is therefore necessary to scrutinize Adorno's negative assessment of Schoenberg's twelve-tone practice in light of actual musical examples. By focusing exclusively on the relationship between twelve-tone music and functional tonality, Adorno may have overlooked the fact that the twelve-tone idea arose more out of a desire for new ways of ordering tones than the avoidance of a tonic. In the earlier movements of the *Klavierstücke*, op. 23, for example, Schoenberg used ordered groups of notes comprising five, six and nine notes. The music, in turn, tends to seek out embedded relationships between different ordered sets and their transformations rather than venerate the sets' linear ordering as such. In op. 23, no. 1, the startling appearances of the "Bach" motive in different voices, transformations, and referential contexts, for example, exceeds the objective of mere hexachord formation. Likewise, in the Piano Suite, op. 25, the music draws attention to the unique connections forged between three unfolding tetrachords. In the Prelude, for example, the canonically imitating tetrachords (separated by a tritone) produce unexpected linkages. There are countless examples: The second half of m. 1 yields a harmonic "sonority" that is then linearly unfolded by the second tetrachord over mm. 1–2; the C–A motive initiating the second tetrachord (in the middle voice of m. 2) is prominently echoed in the second and third notes of the third tetrachord (in m. 3) as if to draw attention away from the polyphonic unfolding as such and towards un-implied motivic connections between non-imitating tetrachords; and so on.

Even in his fully developed twelve-tone works Schoenberg's music seems preoccupied with relations within and between presentations of the row that are not automatic.[46] For example, in his Variations for Orchestra, op. 31, Schoenberg explored various connections between two (transpositionally related) hexachords that were going on simultaneously in the music. Let me illustrate one of these connections (see figure 4.3). The piece begins by elaborating increasingly complex oscillating sonorities that gradually complete the row (mm. 1–9). These sonorities are exact pitch inversions of one another, except for the final pitches of the two hexachords (A and A flat) in mm. 9 and 10 respectively, which break the inversion pattern. This break is effected by the *Hauptstimme*, which elaborates the first five tones of one of

Figure 4.3. Schoenberg, Variations for Orchestra, Op. 31. Introduction, mm. 8–18. Copyright © 1929 by Universal Edition A.G., Wien / UE 12196. Used by permission.

the (hitherto oscillating) hexachords an octave below in the low instruments. Thus the pitches A and A flat (dynamically emphasized in the music) are related only by pitch-class inversion (see figure 4.4). But the music immediately restores the broken inversional relation in the succeeding passage (mm. 10–11), which is a pitch inversion of mm. 9–10. Thus a relation that once held between simultaneous passages holds between consecutive ones. The point is that there is nothing inherent to the "ordering" of the row form that determines this compositional choice. Nor is it therefore an entirely "arbitrary" choice because it restores a kind of unity (between successive row forms) that was subtly disrupted (within a particular row form) in m. 9. At the same time, this momentary disruption prepares the way for increasing levels of abstraction as the music progresses. The *Hauptstimme* in the low instruments in mm. 12–13, for example, presents a differently ordered version of the hexachord sounded by the bass throughout mm. 1–11 (see figure 4.5); or the inversion relation that holds between the *Hauptstimmen* in mm. 16–17 and mm. 17–18 is no longer one that produces complementary sets, but rather one that recalls the opening pitch-class interval and reinterprets it as an oppositely directed pitch interval (see figure 4.6). It is as if the introduction to the Variations gradually pries

Figure 4.4. Schoenberg, Variations for Orchestra, Op. 31. The broken inversion pattern in mm. 9–10.

Figure 4.5. Schoenberg, Variations for Orchestra, Op. 31. The re-ordered pitch-class set in mm. 12–13.

Figure 4.6. Schoenberg, Variations for Orchestra, Op. 31. The non-complementary inversion relation between *Hauptstimmen* in mm. 16–18.

apart both pitch relations to yield pitch-class relations and order relations
to yield unordered relations and then reunites them again in various ways
at various points. None of these relations are "determined by this row" as
much as they are expressive options made possible by a dialectical play
with it, or better, by hearing the presentation of the row in various subjective ways. As Joseph Dubiel might say, this is a twelve-tone piece that does
not acknowledge its twelve-tone-ness.[47] The crucial point is that the dialectical interplay functions critically. That is, the intense interest in precise
pitch symmetries at the opening of the Variations deconstructs the historically traditional perception of music via the framework of pitch-*class*, which
had/has become second nature. By elaborating a dialectical struggle between contradictory tendencies in its materials, modernist music attempted
to critically engage the world, thereby raising the listener's social consciousness and conscience. In this way, art had a key role to play as an agent of
social transformation.[48]

The Afterlife of the Modernist Debates

In the early twenty-first-century North Atlantic context (with its drastically new political formations and technological media), the connection
between aesthetic avant-gardism and social change is largely lost. For
postmodernism, the category of the "new" has lost its privileged role of
envisaging new modes of social organization. John Barth describes
postmodern literature as the "literature of exhaustion"; Arthur Danto announces the "end of art" in a post-historical era; Jean François Lyotard
attacks the utopian aspirations of all "meta-narratives" (or representations
of the world as a totality); and Frederic Jameson describes aesthetic practices in terms of the "cultural logic of late capitalism."[49] It is as if Benjamin's
enchantment with the ability of auratic objects to "look back" at us has
become disenchanted once more. For French poststructuralists (like Jacques
Lacan, Michel Foucault, and Julia Kristeva), the reciprocity of the gaze is
largely transformed into something oppressive, imprisoning, and aggressive. In short, the postmodern rearticulation of modernism has been stripped
of its political, epistemological, and idealist ambitions.

One result of this postmodern rearticulation has been the deconstruction
of the distinction between the high and the low arts purportedly upheld by
modernism. The difference that was felt to exist between autonomous and
mass culture in the 1920s and 1930s (and especially in the 1950s) does not
matter in quite the same way today. It is true that the opposition still operates in some factions of today's culture, but its significance in terms of lived
lives has dwindled. The social function of high art is no longer tied to
systems of political legitimation, such as the identity of nation states, to the
extent that it was in the nineteenth century and the first half of the twenti-

eth century. The problem with lambasting the institutions of high culture today is that it shields from view the increasing verticalization of the institutions of "popular" culture. Music and movies of the "top twenty" are not identical to "mass culture" as Benjamin, say, understood it. Rather, they are part of various hierarchized and domineering structures, like Time Warner (who bought out America Online in January 2000) and Clear Channel Communications (who accumulated over 1,200 radio stations in the last seven years), which function in turn as ideological transmission belts for cultural values, beliefs, and modes of identification and pleasure. While Horkheimer and Adorno's critique of the culture industry may seem overdrawn, many of its motifs actually ring truer in the 2000s than they did in the 1930s.[50] The problem is that certain forms of cultural production are being wiped out by new forms of distribution. Witness, for instance, the decline of independent bookstores and cinemas in recent decades in the United States, Europe, and various African countries. Studies of culture today need to be alert to the possibility that the erosion of the high culture/low culture distinction might amount to the erosion of all culture. Alas, just when these discussions are needed most, it has become taboo to raise the question of autonomy and aesthetic value in current literary and cultural studies, no less than in progressive musical studies. Terry Eagleton's apocalyptic call for "the death of literature" in service of "Political Criticism" is the apogee of such thought.[51]

Not only is it mistaken to sacrifice aesthetic value on account of its supposed reactionary elitism (still less on grounds of its alleged connection to fascism à la Eagleton on Paul de Manian deconstruction), but the very idea that this is an advance over modernism's belief that high art was supposed to uphold a certain criterion of truth is based on a threefold factual error. First, the conservative lament about the closing of the American mind on account of the withering status of the high canon is lodged in hypocritical terms. The debate concerning the study of high culture pertains only to a few elite universities and not to the educational apparatus at large. Allan Bloom is not advocating the scholarly study of Socrates, Boethius, Gesualdo, Shakespeare, or Beethoven in the public schools of Harlem. More importantly, Bloom is not advocating the opening of these American minds to the *radical dimensions of social critique* elaborated by Socrates, Boethius, Gesualdo, Shakespeare, or Beethoven. To figure high art in narrowly Bloomian terms therefore necessarily misses the value such art may have today.

Second, many modernists, in fact, took a sustained interest in "low" forms of art (which is not to say they uncritically embraced them). In addition to the work of composers like Hindemith, Weill, and Hanns Eisler (who was deported from the U.S. in 1947 in the McCarthy drive against communists), Kracauer wrote politically oriented popular film criticism, Bloch wrote about the progressive potential of pulp fiction, and Benjamin's argument was run by a dialectical interplay involving various kinds of "low" culture (auratic art vs. mass-produced art, cult vs. exhibition value, individual genius vs. collective creativity, aesthetic autonomy vs. aesthetic tendency, etc). Benjamin's reason for focusing on mass culture was his belief that new technological modes of production altered the way we touched, heard, saw, and smelled things in the world. In other words, he argued that human sense perception was organized historically and needed to be assessed in light of technological and political developments. This last point may serve cultural music studies better than a triumphal celebration of the victory of the low arts over the high arts in postmodern times. The victory may be an imagined solution to a real problem.

Third, the work of those modernists that did in fact ostensibly renounce the "low" arts maintained a paradoxical link with them. For example, the rejection of mass culture by modernists like Schoenberg, Berg, and Webern was already a reaction-formation against its encroachment. Like Gustave Flaubert's Madame Bovary, who dies from reading commercial pulp fiction, the Schoenberg circle felt that the competition of the free market destroyed the space for true music. In a contribution to a symposium published by Adolf Loos in 1919, Schoenberg wrote: "Concert life must gradually cease to be a commercial business. . . . The basic fault in public concert-life is competition."[52] With the foundation of the Society for Private Musical Performances in 1919, the circle staged a temporary retreat from commercial venues. In short, the phenomenon of high art was not so much prior to that of low art. Rather, the two were historically interlinked.[53]

What then is the relevance of aesthetic modernism today? Of course, there is no fixed or stable understanding of modernism. The truth resides in the layers of perception that inform different readings over time. Twentieth-century dealings with the modernist debates of the 1920s and 1930s have passed through at least three key stages. The first of these, the Cold War period of the 1940s and 1950s, witnessed a move to depoliticize modernism in England, France, Germany, and the United States. The Central Intelligence Agency (CIA) was active in promulgating modern art on both sides of the Atlantic. Various exhibitions and concerts, as well as academic and critical journals (including *Der Monat,* in which Adorno's essay lambasting the socialist realism of Lukács appeared), were actively funded by the CIA during this period. The use of formally "radical" or "polemical" culture as a propaganda tool became widespread. Serge Guilbaut writes, "The Cold War was being waged furiously [in the 1950s], its weapons had been chosen and honed. Cultural magazines published in Europe with CIA funds mushroomed. The American liberal spotlight [also] . . . focused on art and intellectuals."[54] Radical aesthetic modes of operation, such as Pierre Boulez's total serialism and Jackson Pollock's action painting, became an emblem of art in a free, rather than totalitarian, society. The emancipated affront of abstract expressionism of the West contrasted vividly with the gagged realism of art in China or the Soviet Union. It was as if the productive tension between avant-gardism and realism during the 31-year war (1914–45) became less complex—more dichotomous, separated by an Iron Curtain—during the Cold War. The intense interest in the autonomous medium, which was able to lay bare its own musical and painterly processes, was now paradoxically harnessed as an instrument of national power.[55] In other words, the material support for "controversial" freedom of expression in these increasingly abstract artworks played out an illusory tolerance for an illusory dissent. Indeed, what functioned in the 1920s and 1930s as a politically progressive abstraction—a radical questioning of the ability of art to describe the world in naively positive terms—threatened to be co-opted in a kind of "swindle" (which even Brecht could not have foreseen) in the Cold War period. It is against this background that the purely formal approach to the study of literature, art and music at this time should be analyzed.[56] Better still, this background should be studied in dialectical juxtaposition with the immanent processes and historical developments of these arts.

A second major period in the reinscription of the modernist debates came in the 1960s and 1970s, which witnessed a renewed interest in the (repressed) political dimension of the arts. The informing context included the protests against the war in Vietnam, the success of the civil rights movements, the student uprisings in the U.S. and France, the rise of rock 'n' roll, and the generation of Beat poetry and counterculture. It is also the time when Derrida, Barthes, and Foucault launched a sustained critique of structuralism, when writers of the Frankfurt School were translated into English and French, and when new directions were taken in the arts. In music, for example, anti-modern styles came to the fore (such as minimalism, New Romanticism, and various kinds of accessible experimentalism), which menaced the binaries between high and low art, performer and listener, abstraction and pastiche. Like Barthes, whose poststructuralist work of the 1960s juxtaposed the "writerly" (mass cultural, consumerly) with the "readerly" (reflexive, eternal), composers like Philip Glass fused sophisticated, developmental compositional techniques with banal, static ones. The pedestal of high art was withering. Drawn up as a critique of modernism at large, postmodernism was, in fact, the *enfant terrible* of the high modern period—a modernism of its own kind. For instance, Lyotard's attack on meta-narratives in the late 1970s—recapitulating an early modernist motif—was a rejection of what had become a progressivist figuration of history under the high modernism of the 1940s and 1950s and drew its strength from opposition to that earlier phenomenon.

A third moment in the history of the reception of modernism, one that heralds the end of the Cold War, has emanated from a critique of postmodernist thinking as it might be seen in the context of global modernity. The argument goes something like this: Wholly shorn of utopian aspirations, postmodernism fetishizes differentiality over totality, cultural specificity (under the title "diversity") over economic and structural generality, and local over global historical tropes. The intense specialization of autonomous fields of inquiry in academic institutions permitted the kind of hermetic critique that is no longer obliged to engage in dialectical comparison. Development of new subdisciplines of music study in the U.S. in the 1960s—music theory and ethnomusicology—or, more recently, of new disciplines in the Humanities, such as Cultural Studies, has increasingly fractured the ranks of critique. It is an era that has witnessed the withering of some important distinctions (not only of the theoretical deconstructive sort). In Cultural Studies today, for example, there is a risk of replacing an analysis of economic and political relations with that of cultural phenomena in isolation. The wholesale rejection of "totalities," whereby such concepts as "aesthetic autonomy," "mass," "society," and "globalism" are read as false abstractions, has led to an overvaluation of the contrast cases, "aesthetic heteronomy," "identity," "minority," and "localism." The reductive emphasis on The Fragment has produced a new totalization that marches in step with the demands of late-capitalist niche marketing. What was once a "dialectical image," a Benjaminian "tiger's leap" into the past to secure a present that saw itself in novel and productive ways, risks becoming memory and novelty for its own sake. Jonathan Kramer and Glenn Watkins observe that postmodern quotation and pastiche in music differs from its modernist counterparts in their lack of Harold Bloomian influence-anxiety about the past.[57] Works such as John Zorn's *Forbidden Fruit*, Weird Al Yankovitch's *Hooked on Polkas*, Carl Stalling's *To Itch His Own*, and Jonathan Kramer's *Notta Sonata* announce their references plainly, without irony, without any trope of distorted misreading. What, in the third ritornello theme of Gustav Mahler's Seventh Symphony finale, was a complicated allusion to Richard Wagner's *Die Meistersinger* Overture becomes, in Zorn's *Forbidden Fruit*, a seemingly unmotivated series of literal quotations (Mozart's B-flat Major Piano Sonata, Beethoven's *Grosse Fuge*, and so on) in a musical circuit of eclectic exchangeability.[58]

In his essay, "On the Fetish-Character of Music and the Regression of Listening" (1938), Adorno said that the then new music increasingly and regressively "recall[ed] incomprehensible rites and surviving masks from an earlier time . . . [through the use of] prepared material ready to be switched on," and thereby actually anticipated the postmodern condition of music that takes ready-made quotation as one of its representative moments.[59] While he held out the hope that composing with "vulgarized fragments" might produce "something new" (notably in the case of Mahler), for Adorno untransformed quotations paradoxically served to naturalize the canons of the past. One reason Adorno insisted on the dialectic between music's historically given (pre-formed) "material" and the subjectively formed "composition" was precisely to bring to the ear the once subjective (and hence historically contingent) nature of that material. Though some postmodernists might argue that the fragment from the past, however untransformed in itself, is radically changed by its new musical surroundings, Adorno's challenge remains suggestive if only because his ideal artistic quotation renders history itself hermeneutically debatable, whereas the frozen postmodern fragment hermeneutically secures it. In other words, the untransformed quotation posits a certain determined past and then reckons with it instead of unhinging the very determination of the past. Thus, the former paradoxically naturalizes the past. Still, whether or not we agree with Adorno about the specifics, the general point is that just as aesthetic autonomy could be co-opted by political forces in an earlier age, so too can memory and novelty be instrumentalized in our present age. The current interest in the music of the past—"authentic performances" in art music, or "classic rock" re-releases in popular music—has been shored, in significant measure, by the logic of the profit margin. That is, there is a significant (global and unified) corporate interest in the localized and fragmentary social terrain that postmodernism so often lauds and cloaks in the pluralist metaphorics of "diversity."

This is not to say that all commodified cultural activity bears the mark of instrumental reason in an equivalent way. Rather, it is to say that there are always complex relations between part and whole, however refractory and broken those relations appear within any particular historical conjuncture. The operative analytic distinction should not be between totalization and fragmentation, so much as between various examinations of their dialectical interplay. This interplay changes over space and time. For example, the kind of dialectical montage found in the work of Sergei Eisenstein or John Heartfield can be found in every television advertisement, Hollywood movie, fashion magazine, and store window today.[60] In other words, the liberatory potential of this technique has been partly overwhelmed by the grammar of marketing and styling, its "shocking" aspect absorbed into what Kracauer called a delusional "artwork of effects."[61] Similarly, Horkheimer and Adorno argue that metaphors of radical rupture, transgression, and subversion (which have become a mantra for postmodernism) are easily transformed into a mere performance of taboo-breaking.[62] Already in Sade's writing, they argue, the sacrilegious element had become the mere inversion of the sacramental one—indeed, the same reasoning controlled Sade's staging of subjection, mutilation, and murder. Brecht's concerns have also become relevant today: "oppressors do not work in the same way in every epoch, . . . there are so many means for them to avoid being spotted."[63] Systems of oppression have changed. Louis Althusser, Foucault, and more recently Judith Butler, observe that the oppressive moment in late-capitalist society largely depends on a complex mechanism of internalized psychic subjection. For Butler, the promise of political agency is mired in the internalized "subordination" of the subject, which is "understood as the deprivation of agency." In tandem once again with the modernist principle of non-identity, Butler argues that the force of subordination can be overcome in the interstices of psychic behavior—when the psyche "*resists* the normative demand by which subjects are instituted."[64] The problem with Butler's model today is that sectors of society have different access to such deviations from the norm.[65] In other words, not all resistance is equivalent in the tilted social playing-field of global modernity.

This is why the modernist critique of unchecked reason remains relevant today, even if new historical conditions have dated many of its specific themes. Yet Lukács's statement is still valid: that the underlying unity of the socio-economic system is revealed in moments of crisis.[66] For example, ruptures like the Asian financial crisis of the late 1990s (resulting from vast speculative flows of finance capital), or the economic downturn in the U.S. in the early 2000s (betraying disconcerting alliances between corporate capital and government), or the gangster capitalism in Russia today (where the intense economic flux is counteracted only by invented categories like "ethnicity") give the lie to the postmodern world's motley *laissez-faire* pluralism. While the countervailing forces may be stronger in the West than in some of these regions, late modern critical practice should be put in global terms as well, particularly with respect to the widespread failures of decolonization in neo-colonialism. When the TRIPS Agreement (Trade-Related Aspects of Intellectual Property Rights) sets out to patent rules that hinder access to AIDS medication for approximately 90 percent of the world's infected population (residing in countries ranked in the lowest 10 percent in terms of Gross National Product), the question again arises as to whether the instrumental principles of profit and efficiency have dangerously absolved themselves of concern for ethics and truth.[67] In the words of Sidney Hook (who was writing well before the AIDS epidemic): "It would be absurd to try to settle, by the pressures of the market place, what medical theories should guide medical practice or what educational theories should guide educational practice."[68] It is absurd, too, to settle, by these pressures, which ideologies should guide artistic practice. The modernist debates are useful wherever cultures of barbarism loom.

Again, as far as the arts and the media are concerned, Max Horkheimer and Adorno's critique of the culture industry (in the *Dialectic of Enlightenment*) has gained, instead of lost, in significance. In an age of mega-media industries like Disney and Time Warner, and of media moguls like Rupert Murdoch, it has become increasingly important to forge autonomous space for the arts, possibly by inhabiting and transforming those omnivorous structures.[69] If the admittedly reductive survey I have presented above is correct, it is not surprising that the U.S. National Endowment for the Arts (NEA) was cutting funds at a time of unprecedented economic prosperity in the 1990s. Perhaps the stake in the individual freedom of abstract modernist art has withered in the wake of the falling Iron Curtain a decade ago. Perhaps, too, the waning of academic modernist music in elite institutions in recent years is to be expected. The compositional output of students at Columbia and Princeton Universities, once bastions of high modernist music, has become considerably more eclectic, hybrid, even tonal, in recent years—possibly a sign that its composers have had increasingly to negotiate the dynamics of the marketplace.

In terms of music research in the universities, the recent interest in writing ethnomusicological critiques of serious music institutions seems to have arrived too late. For example, Georgina Born writes in her anthropological study of the *Institut de Recherche et de Coordination Acoustique/Musique* (IRCAM) in Paris, "IRCAM . . . represents both the increased autonomization of art and its opposite: an intensified subsumption—institutional, bureaucratic, scientific, technological—of the aesthetic."[70] The problem with such criticism today is that the rhetorical affinity between a modernist musical aesthetic and centralized power is, in fact, lodged within an outmoded high art/low art opposition and its supporting apparatus. The critic thereby turns a blind eye to the new configurations of power. IRCAM no longer holds the alleged "current dominant position, in the absence of great public or industrial success," that it once did; nor are the "mechanisms of legitimation of high culture" what they once were.[71] Born, in charging IRCAM's "universalizing" of "scientific and technological discourses" with arbitrariness and ideology, implies a contrast with the localized and spontaneous discourse of rock and popular music.[72] But the censorious dimension of popular music, as well as its investment in postmodern capital, is left uninterrogated—even though the mediating layers of its production, engineering, marketing, and styling today are more than a match for any IRCAM-like hegemony. In any event, it is likely, given the enthusiasm for the study of music in new historical, hermeneutic, and anthropological terms today, that what is required for a genuine critical praxis is a dialectical return of the repressed dimension of aesthetic autonomy—rather than an increasingly irrelevant and outdated critique of it. Let me explain.

The principle of aesthetic autonomy was originally tied to a progressive and dynamic model involving creative nature and inspiration. The modernists recognized this.[73] Even if a description of music proposes a mythical autonomy from language and the world, one cannot reduce to mere hermetic indifference what was also an aversion to and disagreement with the status quo. It could not be abbreviated in worldly terms, in other words, because the autonomous musical work insisted on the interpreter's utmost attention to its own hidden detailed singularity, and so demanded that the interpreter focus its absolutely unexpected field of operation. Felix Mendelssohn Bartholdy, in connection with his *Songs without Words*, declared that music expressed "thoughts not too *indefinite* for words, but rather too *definite*."[74] Mendelssohn's proposed non-identical relation between music and words was testimony to the failure of ordinary discourse, which, for Mendelssohn, was ensnared in brute vagueness. Thus the interpreter could rest on no assured position. Only when music became wholly lost to description—raised to the upper reaches, where not even the highest-flying birds of imagination could reach it—only then were the inadequacies of the political world brought into vivid focus. This is not to say that the romantic version of autonomy is still valid or constructive today. But modernists such as Benjamin had anticipated the postmodern objection in sophisticated ways. So, for Benjamin, history's autonomous monadic aspect had the potential to blast mankind out of the illusion of ordinary historical time. And Benjamin wrote regarding the specific autonomy of art, "[I]f . . . one resolves to open up th[e] romantic dummy [of art for art's sake], one finds something useful inside. One finds the cult of evil as a political device, however romantic, to disinfect and isolate against all moral dilettantism."[75] Indeed, it may be time to guard against the moral dilettantism/correct consciousness of a non-political anti-formalism and of a non-evil "resistance to the aesthetic." After all, one implication of Adorno's critique of Enlightenment has an uncanny resonance in the postmodern age: in a context that subscribes to the myth that all claims to truth are mythical, subjective agency becomes paradoxically limited to strategically harnessing various illusions of the past. It may be time to probe Benjamin's dummy.

I am not saying that any kind of musical formalism or belief in autonomy necessarily eludes the hold of instrumental reason or opens political horizons. As Adorno argues in his *Introduction to the Sociology of Music,* autonomous music is always perilously close to becoming engulfed in commodification. Its antithetical character even risks becoming the ultimate commodity.[76] Also in terms of logic, formalism's conspicuously narrow calculus produces certain unthought zones peculiar to it. But this may be the very point. By rigorously pursuing its own binary logic to its extremes, that which cannot be captured by that logic is revealed. In other words, when the literal closedmindedness of formalism is taken to its limits, its exclusions become marked for consciousness. This is no "new musicological" method. In fact, it is the oldest method available to us, the blindest, the one most ready-to-hand in our all-too-worldly world. But, it is a blindness alert to its antipodes. Like a kind of ultra-Enlightenment that produces the unassured darkness of negotiable knowledge, such formalism would reveal what Mendelssohn might consider the vagrant vagueness of commonsense faith by which we live. Its obstinate focus on the radically insulated particular would flush out those unacknowledged beliefs and secrets that we are habitually in on.[77] Like Black Consciousness movements, or lesbian separatism, such dissociated formalism would challenge the limits of mainstream political and cultural discourse. After all, musical culture does not develop evenly with the political and economic realms. Its relative autonomy is its relative advantage. Perhaps musical formalism announces the twilight of the extramusical idols by producing narrow words without songs. But perhaps it also announces their dawn, beyond intra- and extramusical, by producing a presentiment of new songs without words (yet).

It is only once we encounter the undecidable ground, upon which the music to which we turn our ears rests, that we can do it the injustice, turn to it the wordly blind eye, that is our ethical and political imperative.

Notes

For their insightful comments about my work in recent years, I would like to express my grateful thanks to Andreas Huyssen, Joseph Dubiel, Edward Said, Lydia Goehr, Arved Ashby, Joe Auner, and Ralph Locke. This essay is considerably indebted to their writing and thought. All errors are mine.

1. The concept of aesthetic autonomy is vague and variable over historical time. Its exact meanings cannot be given in preliminary definitions but only in the course of analysis, as will be seen.

2. A small sample of such writings includes Ruth Solie, ed., *Musicology and Difference* (Berkeley and Los Angeles: University of California Press, 1993); Lawrence Kramer, *Classical Music and Postmodern Knowledge* (Berkeley: University of California Press, 1995); David Schwarz, *Listening Subjects: Music, Psychoanalysis, Culture* (Durham, N.C.: Duke University Press, 1997); and Gary Tomlinson, *Music in Renaissance Magic: Toward a Historiography of Others* (Chicago: University of Chicago Press, 1993).

3. See Adam Krims, ed., *Music/Ideology: Resisting the Aesthetic* (Amsterdam: G + B Arts International, 1998) or Rose Rosengard Subotnik, *Deconstructive Variations: Music and Reason in Western Society* (Minneapolis: University of Minnesota Press, 1996).

4. Linda Goehr, *The Quest for Voice: Music, Politics, and the Limits of Philosophy* (Berkeley, Los Angeles, London: University of California Press, 1998), 37–47.

5. Daniel Albright, "Series Editor's Foreword," in *Political and Religious Ideas in the Works of Arnold Schoenberg*, ed. Charlotte M. Cross and Russell A. Berman (New York and London: Garland Publishing, 2000), viii.

6. My primary focus is on Schoenberg through the critical lens of Adorno, but the argument applies equally to Hindemith through the critical lens of Heidegger. To make the general claims about dialectics, I will discuss a large roster of critical writers on modernism. In choosing to focus on musical works as well as their critical elaboration, I am following in a certain tradition of aesthetic thought—from Immanuel Kant, via G. W. F. Hegel, Karl Marx, Friedrich Nietzsche, Siegmund Freud, Georg Lukács, Heidegger, and Adorno, to Roland Barthes, Gilles Deleuze, Félix Guattari, and Jacques Derrida—that attempts to philosophize about the role of art in society. Adorno's dictum that because musical "signs and the music which they signify are never directly one and the same thing . . . an interpretative act is always necessary" is pertinent here (Adorno, "Paul Hindemith," in *Gesammelte Schriften* [Frankfurt a.M.: Suhrkamp, 1982] 17:172). In short, in order to expand the realm of its social meanings, music needs criticism.

7. Albrecht Wellmer, *The Persistence of Modernity*, trans. David Midgley (Cambridge, Mass.: MIT Press, 1993), 38.

8. Eric Hobsbawm, *The Age of Extremes: A History of the World, 1914–1991* (New York: Vintage Books, 1994), 19.

9. Albright, "Series Editor's Foreword," ix.

10. Walter Benjamin, *Illuminations*, trans. Harry Zorn (New York: Schocken Books, 1968), 241.

11. Walter Benjamin, "Conversations with Brecht," in *Aesthetics and Politics*, ed. and trans. Ronald Taylor (London: Verso, 1977), 168–208.

12. Theodor Adorno, "Commitment," trans. Francis McDonagh, in *Aesthetics and Politics*, ed. Ronald Taylor, 190.

13. Ibid., 190.

14. Theodor Adorno, *Philosophy of Modern Music*, trans. Anne G. Mitchell and Wesley V. Blomster (New York: Continuum, 1973), 32.

15. Adorno, "Commitment," 191.

16. Walter Benjamin, "Conversations with Brecht," in, *Aesthetics and Politics*, ed. and trans. Ronald Taylor, 90.

17. Walter Benjamin, *Reflections*, trans. Edmund Jephcott (New York: Schocken, 1978), 221.

18. Walter Benjamin, *Illuminations*, trans. Harry Zorn (New York: Schocken, 1968), 155–200.

19. Ibid., 217–51.

20. Ibid., 188, 175. Even in its earlier formulation, Benjamin figured the aura in the context of the negative dialectics with which Adorno was well acquainted.

21. Theodor Adorno, "On the Problem of Musical Analysis," *Music* Analysis 1 (1982): 175.

22. Benjamin, *Illuminations*, 262–63.

23. Ibid., 263.

24. Gottfried Wilhelm Leibniz, *Philosophical Writings* (London: J. M. Dent, 1934), 3–4.

25. Benjamin, "Conversations with Brecht," 72.

26. Ibid., 83.

27. Ibid., 82.

28. Paddison, *Adorno's Aesthetics of Music* (Cambridge: Cambridge University Press, 1993), 18.

29. Adorno, "Commitment," 188.

30. Albright, "Series Editor's Foreword," ix.

31. Ernst Bloch, "Discussing Expressionism," in *Aesthetics and Politics*, ed, and trans. Ronald Taylor, 22.

32. Siegfried Kracauer, *The Mass Ornament: Weimar Essays*, trans. Thomas Y. Levin (Cambridge, Mass. and London: Harvard University Press, 1995), 75.

33. In addition to Adorno's 1934 essay "Der dialektische Komponist," see, for example, Hermann Danuser, "Schoenberg's Concept of Art in Twentieth-Century Music History," in *Constructive Dissonance: Arnold Schoenberg and the Transformations of Twentieth-Century Culture*, ed. Juliane Brand and Christopher Hailey (Berkeley, Los Angeles, and London: University of California Press, 1997), 179–87.

34. Adorno, *Philosophy of Modern Music*, 39.

35. Ibid., 70.

36. Ibid., 54, 59, 63.

37. Ibid., 64.

38. Ibid., 64, 66.

39. Ibid., 61–67.

40. Ibid., 68.

41. Ibid., 62.

42. Schoenberg's polemical writings included the essays "About Music Criticism," "Problems in Teaching Art," "A Legal Question," and "The Music Critic" (found in *Style and Idea*, ed. Leonard Stein, trans. Leo Black [Berkeley and Los Angeles: University of California Press, 1975]) as well as the 1911 *Harmonielehre*. For an account of Schoenberg's place in the critique of culture in fin de siècle Vienna, see Leon Botstein, "Music and the Critique of Culture," in *Constructive Dissonance*, ed. Brand and Hailey.

43. Cited in Patricia Carpenter and Severine Neff, "Schoenberg's Philosophy of Composition: Thoughts on the 'Musical Idea and Its Presentation,'" in *Constructive Dissonance*, ed. Brand and Hailey, 157.

44. Schoenberg, *Style and Idea*, 123.

45. Danuser, "Schoenberg's Concept of Art in Twentieth-Century Music History," in *Constructive Dissonance*, ed. Brand and Hailey, 181.

46. I am indebted to Ethan Haimo's brilliant analysis of Schoenberg's twelve-tone practice in *Schoenberg's Serial Odyssey: The Evolution of His Twelve-Tone Method* (Oxford: Oxford University Press, 1990).

47. I would like to thank Joseph Dubiel for prompting the thought that Schoenberg's *Variations* begin by expressing relationships in terms of pitch and then abstracts them to relationships in terms of pitch-class.

48. The fact that Schoenberg's music is frequently associated with philosophical dialectics should not obscure the central place of dialectical thinking in the music of modernism at large. While I cannot argue the point in the context of this essay, even modernist music driven by criteria that were antithetical to those of twelve-tone music frequently had dialectical aspirations.

49. Compiled in *Postmodernism: A Reader*, ed. Thomas Docherty (New York: Columbia University Press, 1993), 180–83, 185–92, 38–46, 62–92.

50. What I am saying is that if the commodification of the culture industry wholly determines a kind of "psychoanalysis in reverse," to adapt a phrase from Leo Löwenthal, Adorno's argument becomes overdrawn. It leaves no room for resistance and mistakenly treats all sectors of commodified culture as equivalently co-opted.

51. Terry Eagleton, *Literary Theory: An Introduction* (Oxford: Basil Blackwell, 1983), 217. The death of modernist music is frequently tolled in its media representations as well. Kyle Gann's articles for the *Village Voice* in New York City, for example, are repeatedly run on an assured distinction between bad high modernism and good postmodernism. In his article "Ding! Dong! The Witch Is Dead!" Gann writes, "At the start of this new, still-promising century, let us reiterate some eternal truths that the [modernist] 20th century lost sight of: There is nothing wrong with simplicity. . . . The value of music is not proportional to the quantity or intricacy of its technical apparatus. . . . To do nothing but [write 'ostentatiously technical pieces'] . . . is to pretend that composers have no obligation to society, and by extension that neither do doctors, politicians, generals, or any other profession." (2000, 19) The

moral? Fully assured by the clarity of our professional eternal musical truths, the dead modernist witch allows us to live responsibly ever after. The problem is that this post-modern moral needs its modern Other to be what it is. But, can such necrophilia not become the *ne plus ultra* to engagement with real social conditions? When "Ding! Dong! The Witch is Dead!" is sung in *The Wizard of Oz*, there is in fact still another witch who turns out to be far worse than the one the house fell on—significantly, perhaps, the Wicked Witch of the West.

52. Cited in Willi Reich, *Schoenberg: A Critical Biography*, trans. Leo Black (London: Longman, 1968), 117.

53. One reason that Schoenberg and Adorno could still maintain the utopian notion of partial autonomy, whereby not all of the arts were sucked into the commodity machine, was their relative historical proximity to non-commodified artistic practices. For example, various nineteenth-century traditions of classical music-making, such as piano playing in the bourgeois home, were not already united under the sign of "commodity."

54. Guilbaut, *How New York Stole the Idea of Modern Art: Abstract Expressionism, Freedom, and the Cold War*, trans. Arthur Goldhammer (Chicago and London: University of Chicago Press, 1983), 204.

55. The process of showing the "artificiality" of the process of reconstructing images owed its origin specifically to the cubist movement. This kind of formal self-consciousness and montage was a reaction to the pretensions of mimetic art and was extensively deployed by anti-capitalists like Brecht.

56. The funding by the United States Information Agency (USIA) of arts and music expeditions to third-world countries then and now should be analyzed in this context as well. There is a danger, of course, in magnifying the role of the CIA. It casts a kind of enchanting legendary veil over the interpretation of these artworks. Not only does such revelation empower the (secret) scope and control of this banal bureaucracy, but it muzzles the recalcitrant autonomous dimensions of these artworks.

57. Glenn Watkins, *Pyramids at the Louvre: Music, Culture, and Collage from Stravinsky to the Postmodernists* (Cambridge, Mass. and London: Harvard University Press, 1994), 398–476.

58. For a study of the deconstructive aspects of Mahler's Seventh Symphony, see my "The Finale of Mahler's Seventh Symphony: A Deconstructive Reading," *Music Analysis* 14 (1995): 69–88.

59. Theodor Adorno, "On the Fetish-Character of Music and the Regression of Listening," in *The Essential Frankfurt School Reader*, ed. Andrew Arato and Heike Gebhardt (New York: Continuum, 1982), 298.

60. The same kind of argument can be made about the music, once radically experimental, that is deployed for visual effects in mainstream film and television. Relatedly, MTV's average pop video is practically a showcase of early twentieth-century avant-garde visual techniques.

61. Kracauer, *The Mass Ornament*, 324.

62. Horkheimer and Adorno, *Dialectic of Enlightenment*, trans. John Cumming (New York: Continuum, 1997), 81–119.

63. Benjamin, "Conversations with Brecht," 82.

64. Italics mine. Judith Butler, *The Psychic Life of Power: Theories in Subjection* (Stanford, Calif.: Stanford University Press, 1997), 10, 86.

65. The current welfare debate in the U.S. is instructive in this respect. Those who own the means of production tend to have an autonomous hand, while those who do not are encouraged to adopt a kind of renunciation-ethic. As Kracauer might say, life is an invention of the "haves" that the "have-nots" must imitate to the best of their ability.

66. Georg Lukács, *History and Class Consciousness: A Study in Marxist Dialectics*, trans. Rodney Livingstone (Cambridge, Mass.: MIT Press, 1994), 83–110.

67. For example, in Margaret Duckett, "Compulsory Licensing—What Does It Mean? Will It Improve Access to Essential Drugs for People Living with HIV/AIDS?" (paper presented at Columbia University, July 1999), 3.

68. Cited in Christopher Lasch, "The Cultural Cold War," *The Nation* 205, no. 4 (11 September, 1967): 204. While the AIDS crisis dramatizes the point, phenomena like the explosive boom in the automobile industry since the 1970s—which reflects the capital interest much more than, say, considerations of ecology—are equally pertinent. Because of developments such as these, the delinking of ethics and truth from reason was a primary concern in the formation of Columbia University's new Center for the Humanities, which has allied its philosophical work to economic analysis.

69. Time Warner owns the following classical record labels as well: Erato, Teldec, Finlandia, EMI, Virgin, and Nonesuch (which has based its reputation on recording cutting-edge music of various kinds). A recent report on the EMI/Time Warner merger in *Gramophone* reads, "Warner/EMI music, boasting an 8 billion pound turnover, will have the strongest music catalogue in the business as well as the ability to sell it on the Internet, thanks to the recent merger with AOL" (*Gramophone* 78, no.4 [April 2000]: 132). As can be seen, the production and selling of "serious" music falls within the orbit of that of "popular" music, further underscoring the erosion of the distinction in these times.

70. Born, *Rationalizing Culture: IRCAM, Boulez, and the Institutionalization of the Musical Avant-Garde* (Berkeley, Los Angeles, and London: University of California Press, 1995), 30.

71. Ibid., 4, 29.

72. Ibid., 20–21.

73. Antonin Artaud, for instance, felt that only when the theater recognized itself as an "autonomous and independent art," would it free itself from the iron collar of language and its abuse by power. Artaud, *The Theater and Its Double*, trans. Mary Caroline Richards (New York: Grove Press, 1958), 106.

74. Felix Mendelssohn Bartholdy, "An Exchange of Letters"; in Leo Treitler, ed., *Source Readings in Music History*, revised ed. (New York and London: W.W. Norton, 1998), p. 1201.

75. Benjamin, *Reflections*, trans. Edmund Jephcott (New York: Schocken, 1978), 187.

76. Adorno, "Avant-Garde," in his *Introduction to the Sociology of Music*, trans. E. B. Ashton (New York: Seabury Press, 1976), 178–93. The truth of Adorno's observation has been borne out in cultural spheres of relative autonomy and social resistance of "high" and "low" art alike. Not entirely unlike the Society for Private Musical Performance of the Schoenberg circle, the concerts at CBGBs in New York City's lower east side in the mid-1970s (music by the New York Dolls, Patti Smith, Iggy Pop, etc.) engendered a punk rock movement in England radically disdainful

of the economically bloated rock scene prevalent at the time (with artists like Peter Frampton, Electric Light Orchestra, and The Captain and Tenille). But it took only a few years before Malcolm McClary's brazen business interest in the Sex Pistols undid all vestiges of the music's non-conformity and implied social critique. While the Sex Pistols self-destructed shortly after their only U.S. tour, their success spawned a new ("non-") sound that, in general, supplied an impetus to a flagging rock 'n' roll scene. This, in turn, created a new niche market. McClary's exploitative use of African artists on his hit *Double Dutch* in the early 1980s proved, yet again, the pattern of this logic. I am not saying that all music in commodity form is entirely lost to social causes. Prince, for example, anonymously contributes large amounts of his profits to projects geared toward social upliftment. Likewise, not all of capital's profit circulates in the same way.

77. For the early Wittgenstein, this secret should remain sequestered: "Whereof one cannot speak, thereof one must be silent." (Ludwig Wittgenstein, *Tractatus Logico-Philosophicus,* trans. C. K. Ogden [London and New York: Routledge, 1990], 189.) But, for Adorno, whereof the musician cannot speak, thereof the music analyst must speak. Again and again. (Adorno, "On the Problem of Musical Analysis," 177.)

Part Two

Metaphors for Modernism

5

Twentieth-Century Tonality, or, Breaking Up Is Hard to Do

LLOYD WHITESELL

In 1910, Thomas Beecham produced Richard Strauss's new opera, *Elektra*, in London. Audiences were impressed and the season was extended; but, as Beecham recalls,

> so far as I could ascertain, musicians did not like the piece at all. One eminent British composer on leaving the theater was asked what he thought of it. "Words fail me," he replied, "and I'm going home at once to play the chord of C major twenty times over to satisfy myself that it exists." The curious thing about this little piece of criticism is that *Elektra* actually finishes with the chord in question, thundered out several times in repetition on the full ensemble.[1]

Apparently, Strauss's modernist dislocation of tonal language led to a confusion in the mind of our anonymous listener, who could not recognize the cadence for what it was. But the passion of his reaction suggests that more than cognitive transparency was at stake. His express fear was that C major, the icon of diatonic, centric, functional tonality, might no longer exist. Strauss's expressionistic chromaticism represented a threat to linguistic innocence.

This anecdote, in the style of a compact, ironic fanfare, announces several of the themes I want to develop. First is the array of possible hearings prompted by a given work or idiom, displayed here by the satisfied concertgoers, the outraged expert, and the conductor himself. Second is the idea that musical apprehension is inseparable from deeply rooted ideologies of music's proper function, style, and relation to history. Ideological positions of this sort—casually or passionately embraced, consciously or subconsciously elaborated—condition how music is heard, resulting in the wildly contradictory responses I will be surveying.[2] Finally, at the heart of many of these musical disagreements lies a divergence in conceptions of history itself. This is the argument on which modernism is based: the belief that the conditions of modern life are so radically at odds with past experience that one must speak of a historical crisis, and thus the necessity of entirely reinventing the forms of cultural expression. It is significant that the reactionary listener quoted above experienced the challenge posed by *Elektra* in historical terms, as the passing away of a paradigm of understanding. To his horrified ears, Strauss had not merely foregone tonality, he had superseded it.

In this paper I will examine the myths and metaphors which have organized people's understanding of both tonal and post-tonal repertoires in the twentieth century. My texts are verbal records of listening experiences or reflections upon music, set down by composers, critics, and music lovers from Austro-German and Anglo-American culture. The common thread is the reception of traditional tonality—to some, an Old World of restricted boundaries, to others a threatened paradise. The cultural symbolism brought to bear on the concept of tonality is extremely telling. As a "common practice" of harmonic conventions, it has the prestige in the minds of many, whether vanguard or conservative, of a repressed, shadow image of modernism. Thus my study of tonality, its so-called decline and rediscovery, will reflect upon the discordant reputations of modernism as well.

We can begin with Arnold Schoenberg, who threw down the gauntlet with his rigorous and dramatic renunciation of tonal syntax. In his writings, he establishes a historical model of inevitable progress:

> I am probably the last of the modern composers who has occupied himself with tonal harmony in the sense of the oldest masters. . . . Those who examine in my First String Quartet or in my *Kammersymphonie* the relation of the keys to each other and to the incident harmony, will get from them some conception of the demands that are made, in the modern sense, on the tonal development of a harmonic idea. Perhaps they would also understand why a step must be taken from thence onwards, which the critics in question would gladly reverse.[3]

According to Schoenberg, his music has responded to a historical imperative, a distinctly modern demand made on the tonal material. He heaps scorn on those who have not perceived the full implications of tonal evolution:

> When I hear these particular tonal pieces in which are avoided all possible tonal non-relationships, or at least those not developed to the end . . . through an F-sharp or C-major triad—according to the mood, then I always think of those savage potentates who wear only a cravat and a top-hat.[4]

He represents these composers as uncomprehending primitives, who don tonal gestures as totems of civilization (Schoenberg uses the term "shibboleths") without awareness of the integral set of values they imply.

Yet it turns out Schoenberg is more liberal regarding the onward march of style than many of his disciples. He leaves room for the use of tonality in the realm of "popular art," and the occasional composition "in the old style."[5] Furthermore, he says, "even standing where I do at the present time, I believe that to use the consonant chords, too, is not out of the question, as soon as someone has found a technical means of either satisfying or paralyzing their formal claims."[6] Schoenberg's belief in the need for formal integrity, however, is moralistic and intense. He reserves his strongest language for those whose foreground tonal gestures have no organic relation to the long-range process.

> Many modern composers believe they are writing tonally if they occasionally introduce a major or minor triad, or a cadence-like turn of phrase, into a series of harmonies that lack, and must lack, any terms of reference. Others hope the use of ostinati and pedal-points will do the same thing for them. Both are acting like believers who buy an indulgence. They betray their God, but remain on good terms with those who call themselves His attorneys. They use accidentals and key-signatures to fit the key that would like to hold sway, as if putting on a Christian-German mantle for loving their neighbor (something they rarely used to wear), to cloak their secret, sinful converse with dissonances.[7]

One marvels at the ferocity of these Biblical cadences, in which he brands composers as sanctimonious and falsehearted according to standards of adherence to technical consistency at all levels.

It will be instructive to compare Schoenberg's words with those of his disciple, T. W. Adorno. Adorno likewise subscribes to a model of irreversible progress in the evolution of harmonic technique (what he calls the "inherent tendency of musical material"). But where Schoenberg postulates a satisfactory use of triads within the new field of harmonic possibility, Adorno rejects such usage out of hand. The "technically trained ear," he claims, recognizes the prohibition against "exhausted" procedures, which

> today excludes even the medium of tonality—that is to say, the means of all traditional music. It is not simply that these sounds are antiquated and untimely, but that they are false. . . . The most progressive level of technical procedures designs tasks before which traditional sounds reveal themselves as impotent clichés.[8]

In Adorno's view of the modernist era, more purist than Schoenberg's, there will never be a syntax to rescue tonality for the present. The material itself is inauthentic. His criteria for the evaluation of music is first of all historical rather than formal. Second, his understanding of tonal usage is complicated by an exactingly materialist critique of culture, as in the following discussion of Stravinsky's *L'Histoire du soldat*:

> The melodic nuclei are now totally devaluated. . . . These nuclei now bear traces of commonplace music—the march, the idiotic fiddle, the antiquated waltz, indeed even of the current dances such as tango and ragtime. . . . Such music—degraded by the market—needs, to be sure, only be made transparent by compositional virtuosos and their rattling skeleton is revealed.[9]

In Adorno's critique, the idioms of mass culture are inevitably compromised by their commodity status. But the conventional idioms of art music, tonality included, are just as deeply implicated in bourgeois ideology. "Since the beginning of the bourgeois era, all great music has founded its sufficiency in the illusion that it has achieved an unbroken unity and justified through its own individuation the conventional universal legality to which it is subject." It is the role of modern music to challenge the illusion of the "abstract universality of musical language" which those conventions have upheld.[10]

The arguments offered in the name of formal consistency, historical validity, and social consciousness give some idea of what is at stake in the period of the emergence of atonality. We will return to the same issues toward the end of the chapter, from the perspective of a period more than fifty years later, when numerous composers of art music undertook an energetic reevaluation of tonality. These two chronological poles—the generations of Strauss, Schoenberg, and Stravinsky on the one hand, and George Rochberg, Steve Reich, and John Adams on the other—will serve as bookends for a more synchronic survey of the polemical discourse.

Underlying the many colorful and outrageous pronouncements concerning the value of tonal language, we can discern a handful of guiding metaphors. The metaphoric concepts to which we now turn have provided the raw material for sloganeering, and compelling images to which one could appeal in the arguments over tonal authenticity in the modern world. But their conceptual power was never subsequent to a purely auditory experience; in their unruly interaction, these diverse fancies have helped set the terms for the meaning, value, and enjoyment of music. I have grouped the metaphors according to their use by the different camps, with those under "Point" generally used by the challengers of tonality, those under "Counter Point" by its defenders. The order of my list does not imply any dichotomous relation between specific groups.

1. Point: Exhaustion/Death

The first set of metaphors conveys the idea that tonality has expired or run its course. Phrased in inorganic terms, the figure evokes an object or tool that has outlived its use, as in the discussion of new musical systems in Thomas Mann's novel *Doctor Faustus,* where characters speak of "wornout," "banal" components such as "consonance, common-chord harmonics, [and] the diminished seventh."[11] Or it evokes a fund of resources which has been used up, as in Copland's consideration of the twelve-tone challenge: "Has the tonal system really been exhausted and should it be abandoned or are there still hidden resources to be tapped?"[12]

In its organic version, the metaphor refers to decay and death. This figure of speech is often so integrated into our thought as to pass unnoticed, as when Webern speaks of "tonality in its last throes";[13] but it also affords a host of highly arresting images. Ernst Krenek, for instance, writes: "There is no doubt that the ornate, fat, jellyfishlike, bloated character of the newer Viennese style is a kind of sickly degeneration resulting from repressed atonality."[14] Aside from the gusto with which Krenek elaborates his conceit here, this passage is remarkable in that it is focused on the sound of the music. His description is both a record of a concrete listening experience, and an interpretive exemplar meant to influence future listening. Of course the concepts of degeneration and decay are perennial darts in the quiver of the righteous. But the theory of cultural decline as a specifically modern pathology had achieved prominence by the end of the nineteenth century through the writings of the physicians Cesare Lombroso and Max Nordau; this theory provided underpinning for the notion that tonality, and the cultural achievement it represented, could die.[15] Accusations of degeneracy have vaguely moral connotations, and do not necessarily pertain to strictly musical matters. Typically ambiguous is *Le Figaro*'s review of Debussy's *La Damoiselle élue* as "a deeply sensual composition, decadent, even a touch rotten." But the image of decay easily lends itself to a harmonic interpretation, as when Roger Nichols finds in the Parisian reviewer's accusation a suspicion of "loosening, even a 'rottenness' in the stays that held traditional syntax together."[16] And what, then, is the treatment for the pervasive tonal decay? Calling Dr. Wagner: "Music reacted to [*Tristan*] as a human body to an injected serum," wrote Hindemith, "which it at first strives to exclude as a poison, and only afterwards learns to accept as necessary and even wholesome."[17]

A practice as old as tonality becomes vulnerable to charges of wear, exhaustion, and mortality. We have already heard Adorno's complaint about rattling skeletons. Elsewhere in Adorno's writing, we find another striking use of the idea of death: "Insofar as surrealist composing makes use of devalued means, it uses these *as* devalued means, and wins its form from the 'scandal' produced when the dead suddenly spring up among the living."[18] Here again, the language suggests a pithy interpretation of concrete musical juxtapositions. A modern listener thinking in such terms will hear tonal forms as archaeological relics, dry bones of the past with no true claim to an animating spirit.[19]

2. Counter Point: Nature

The previous group of examples embodies a sense of historical transience and irreversibility. In contrast there operates a set of metaphors appealing to notions of constancy and endurance. The classic form here is an evocation of the immutable laws of nature. Hindemith, in his theoretical writing, treats this metaphor as his most basic axiom, and spins myriad variations on the pattern: "Tonality is a natural force, like gravity." "The feeling for the purity, the harmonic completeness, and the satisfying effect of the triad . . . is accordingly just as natural to us as the body's sense of space." "The carpenter would not think of disregarding the natural properties of his wood and putting it together any old way without regard to its grain."[20] The unadorned elegance of the concept of natural law was powerful enough that the proponents of non-tonal music felt the need to counter it. A few years before Hindemith's pronouncement, Schoenberg wrote, "Since tonality is no condition imposed by nature, it is meaningless to insist on preserving it because of natural law."[21] Webern also confronted the metaphor, choosing not to refute it but to apply it to his own purpose. In a lecture series in 1933, he based his entire argument on Goethe's organicist thesis concerning "hidden natural laws" of development. In this way he was able to claim that serial music was the "wholly natural outcome of the ages."[22] Judged as rhetoric, however, these verbal sallies are lackluster, and it fell to Pierre Boulez to discover a countermetaphor which could trump the elegance of the original: "Classic tonal thought was founded on a universe defined by gravitation and attraction; serial thought is founded on a universe in perpetual expansion."[23] Boulez's reference to the paradigm shift from Newtonian to Einsteinian physics appeals to a nature whose laws are no longer immutable, but subject to cognitive upheavals. At the same time, he melds the nature metaphor with the metaphor of expansion, which we will take up in a moment.

But my favorite example of this line of rhetoric is a recent embellishment by Austrian composer Kurt Schwertsik. He begins by relating the gravity concept to auditory experience—the "dangerous magic" that the earliest atonal pieces can work on the listener. "For Schoenberg, atonality . . . meant overcoming the force of gravity, a considerable intellectual feat. Atonality: a state of weightlessness! This is how I experienced it very clearly as a young man." What begins as a tribute to Schoenberg's visionary thought, however, is quickly switched for a practical maxim from an age well-versed in space travel.

> Today we know that long periods of weightlessness lead to loss of muscle tone and to intestinal sluggishness. Therefore, anyone wishing to experience weightlessness in body as well as in mind has to train intensively, for sooner or later he must return to earth, even if he has experienced the "air of other planets."[24]

The mundanity of Schwertsik's image wittily deflates the opening rhetoric. Without sacrificing a sense of modernity, his language reminds us that the age-old processes of nature are still in effect.

3. Point: Expansion/Liberation

The next group of metaphors take their form from movements and changes in the geopolitical realm. Stylistic experimentation is compared to a broadening of spatial horizons, or the arrival of pioneers into new territory. In this vein, Schoenberg spoke of the "music of today" as "developing a field which must first appear entirely new to us. . . . The field must first be cultivated. It is virgin soil."[25] A similar figure (mixed with one or two others) occurs in Krenek's writings:

> Though creating in the golden age of tonality, when no signs of the imminent decay were visible, Beethoven was the first to anticipate the new era. His last quartets presaged the discovery of a coast where the vessel of European music would seek a haven a century later.[26]

But by far the most famous metaphor in this group is the explicitly revolutionary concept of "emancipation." Aside from Schoenberg's ringing phrase, the idea appears in a multitude of stock descriptions of freedom from the shackles or fetters of tradition, tonal syntax, or what have you. Again, Schoenberg has provided one of the most memorable versions of the political metaphor in the well-known passage from *Theory of Harmony* where he compares the sovereignty of the tonic to "Napoleon, who installs his relatives and friends on the European thrones"—thus an implicitly outdated and threatened regime.[27] The same political image is employed in the following riff from the felicitous prose of Paul Rosenfeld, music critic for *The Dial* in the 1920s:

> With Wagner the monarchy of the C-major scale is at an end. . . . The old [scale] has had to lose its privilege, to resign itself to becoming simply one of a constantly growing many. . . . And today there are no longer musical rules, forbidden harmonies, dissonances. Siegfried has broken them along with Wotan's spear.[28]

This line of thinking has not gone without riposte. Hindemith, in an ironic hyperbole, combines both the expansionist and the revolutionary version of the metaphor: "Doubtless these composers see in their freedom from tonality a liberty that will lift their art to the infinity of time and space." However, what the non-tonal composers see as healthy rebellion, he sees as "a lapse into complete absence of plan and rule, and finally pure anarchy."[29] The imputation of the threat of anarchy is a common rejoinder to the fervent liberationist rhetoric. Schoenberg, the "musical anarchist from Vienna," was a frequent target of such charges.[30] Finally, the composer Kamran Ince has recently turned the emancipation metaphor unexpectedly back upon itself, in the context of a new anti-tonal dogma:

> As far as atonal sonorities are concerned how can we say that they are completely freed since in the aesthetics of most composers they cannot be freely preceded or followed by tonal sonorities? . . . What excites me most as a composer living today is that all materials at my disposal are emancipated from any prejudice. . . . Tonal sonorities in my music are emancipated as I use them for

their own resonance and beauty, and do not subject them to the hierarchies of functional tonality.[31]

4. Counter Point: Communication/Currency

The metaphor of language is used by both the proponents and detractors of tonality, to very different purposes. One point of contention: how important is it to understand the languages of modern music? Very important to many listeners, judging from the countless outraged accusations of unintelligibility. Here is one English reviewer:

> *Five Orchestral Pieces* by Arnold Schoenberg . . . was like a poem in Tibetan; not one single soul could possibly have understood it. . . . The listener was like a dweller in Flatland straining his mind to understand the ways of that mysterious occupant of three dimensions, man.[32]

Yet, as Robert Morgan explains, many modernist composers gauged the thrust of their aesthetic rebellion precisely by a turn to hermetic or "secret languages."

> The true force and significance of [Schoenberg's prewar] music lies . . . precisely in its determination to speak in an unknown and enigmatic tongue that largely defies rational comprehension. [Schoenberg] attempted to transform musical language from an essentially "public" vehicle, susceptible to comprehension by ordinary people . . . to an essentially "private" one capable of speaking the unspeakable.[33]

The gap between these two premises has led to disagreements over the continuing validity of "common practice"—i.e., whether there still exists a widely shared (tonal) grammar, or whether such common ground is no longer possible. The opposing viewpoints could not be more sharply drawn. For examples, I turn to two recent essays of cultural criticism focusing on the twentieth-century musical situation. The first is by Richard Norton, who is speaking of the "sonic collectivity" of popular music:

> Largely predictable in horizontal progression through time and symmetrical in phrase structure, this harmony . . . creates and preserves a universally understood harmonic object that amateurs everywhere can rapidly acquire for themselves. . . . There is no spoken language on the planet which even begins to compete with the accessibility provided by common-practice tonality as a means of human communication.[34]

In stark opposition are the views of Robert Morgan. The following quotation is preceded by an assertion of the "ultimate demise" of tonality:

> Of course in some sense tonality remained. . . . But once its possibilities were widely perceived as *exhausted*, incapable of further *expansion*, tonality lost the

traditional basis for its expressive force. And without general acceptance, it surrendered . . . its "universality," its status as a common language. . . . The inevitable consequence of the loss of a central musical language is that music speaks in many different tongues. . . . The more of them we know, the less fluently we speak and understand them. More importantly, we no longer have the ability to speak any musical language as natives.[35]

Morgan's alarming conclusion resounds like a knell, but it rests on an unspoken segregation of art music from vernacular experience. Admittedly, tonality may function quite differently within those different realms, but such an exclusion from his musical philology reflects back to the detriment of his premise concerning the "wide," "general" abandonment of tonality.[36] The allure of his position, however, is just as strong as Norton's, in their contrary promotion of music as icon of the century's predicament. For Norton, music represents the matrix of a global *lingua franca*; for Morgan, it stutters the legacy of a Babel-like deracination.

While Norton is sanguine about the socially integrating power of "popular" tonality, he characterizes that power in terms of aesthetic debasement, about which he is curiously unapologetic: "Tonal limitations [in rock music] became quickly fixed at the level of, perhaps, the ten-year-old Chopin, and there they remain." "'Popular' tonality is . . . numbingly collective, and makes no pretense of going anywhere at all. It cannot change as long as it gives a good return for its investors in the market." In this instance we see the metaphor of linguistic exchange slipping into one of monetary exchange. Cultural interaction is made possible by a common exchange rate: "World tonality is economic tonality." Norton acknowledges the regressive effects of imperialist market forces, yet insists that mass tonality is not thereby "contaminated."[37] Such a critical invocation of the economic metaphor seems out of place in the pro-tonal camp; it is more likely to figure in the arsenal of non-tonal composers for whom "selling" is understood as "selling out."[38] As noted earlier, this critique was forcefully mounted by Adorno. He too makes explicit the metaphorical connection between the economies of language and financial interaction: "The idiom of tonality, . . . which circumscribes the traditional stock of music consumed today, is identical with the worldwide musical consumers' language."[39]

5. Point: Devastation

The next set of metaphors thematizes the modernist myth of historical schism. This is most forcefully conveyed through images of violent physical catastrophe, as in Krenek's account: "It cannot be denied that atonality is founded on a decidedly destructive tendency. The first atonal compositions often give one the impression of watching a cataclysm through reversed opera glasses."[40] The aggressive dismantling of technical structures and stylistic frameworks is conceived as the obliteration of physical structures in the blasts of war. "Atonality . . . is the denial of harmony as a structural means. The problem of a composer in a musical world in this state is to supply another structural means, just as in a bombed-out city the opportunity to build again exists."[41] While in this quotation John Cage envisions the promise of renewal, there are many more who use the metaphor pessimistically, looking for a way out from the "field of wreckage" (Krenek), or reduced to patching together a "montage of the debris of that which once was" (Adorno).[42] The whole point of the metaphor of cataclysm is to convey the belief that the ground plan of the past is beyond recuperation, that whole swaths of its edifices lie in ruins. Some, such as Rudolph Reti, prefer to generalize the destructive tendency into a condition of our modern age: "There was never a time so full of promise yet so threatening. Of course . . . the world was always torn by confusion and catastrophes of all kinds. But today this whole state has reached such a peak that our human species is now literally threatened with extinction."[43] Others, however, see it as a localized problem, situated in a particular tradition whose claim to dominance has faded. Consider Steve Reich:

> Stockhausen, Berio, and Boulez were portraying in very honest terms what it was like to pick up the pieces of a bombed-out continent after World War II. But for some Americans in 1948 or 1958 or 1968—in the real context of tailfins [on cars], Chuck Berry, and millions of burgers sold—to pretend that instead we're really going to have the dark-brown angst of Vienna is a lie, a musical lie.[44]

The aftermath of such violent disruption is marked by agonizing uncertainty over how to move forward. "In the musical iconoclasm of our time," writes Reti, "everything which seemed firm and unassailable in the universe of sound appears shaken to the ground."[45] Thus a variation of this metaphor dramatizes not the violence, but the epistemological disorientation. Donald Mitchell writes: "How to go on after *Tristan und Isolde,* that great destabilizing event . . . which permanently modified the musical landscape, whether it was viewed from Paris or Vienna."[46] Or this from George Rochberg: "The period [after] the denouement of the old world . . . was a descent into the maelstrom, a wandering in the desert."[47] Once again there is fierce disagreement over whether the unraveling of cognitive and cultural frameworks is a proper object of musical enterprise. The destructive metaphor is used with great opprobrium in the following wartime review of a Webern quartet, by Olin Downes: "This music . . . is the ultimate of orderly and deliberate disintegration. . . . Is it any wonder that the culture from which it emanates is even now going up in flames?"[48]

6. Counter Point: Vitality

Finally, there are those who champion the continued use of tonality through images of burgeoning life, as we see in the Steve Reich quotation above, with its finger on the pulse of American popular culture. To these listeners, it is the avoidance of tonality which has proven sterile and lifeless. Downes speaks of "Dead Sea fruit, and Dead End music"; Schwertsik of "dingy, grey boredom."[49] Rosenfeld's perspective is similarly desolate: "With [Schoenberg], we seem to be entering the arctic zone of musical art. None of the old beacons, none of the old stars, can guide us longer in these frozen wastes. Strange, menacing forms surround us, and the light is bleak and chill and faint."[50]

Some point to the unimpeded flourishing of tonal idioms in the musical vernacular. Charles Seeger, for instance, discusses how the "jazz boys had hit upon something the academic or fine-art composer had missed," namely by tapping into the fertile roots of folk art:

> This art of music, the folk music of America, had embodied for well over a hundred years the tonal and rhythmic expression of untold millions of rural and even urban Americans. Contrary to our professional beliefs, the American people at large have had plenty to say and ability to say it, so that a rich repertory has been built up.[51]

Or, as composer Paul Moravec puts it: "When some people announced the death of tonality earlier in the century, they apparently forgot to tell the billions of people who have continued to speak it as a living tongue."[52] There is a wry paradox plaguing my project at this very juncture. Should anyone search for memoranda from the reception of popular music in the early century, commenting specifically on the life and health of tonality, there will be little to find. In the context of that living tongue, "tonality" was not a recognizable sub-idiom to be pooh-poohed or enthused over, but the entire range of harmonic possibility. Reflections on the merits of tonality only awaken with the appearance of a rival.

For that reason, I have found the observations clustering thickest around two temporal horizons, as discussed earlier. The first remarks throng like leukocytes around the atonal hemorrhage. The second cluster, beginning in the 1970s, chronicles the overturning of a latter-day dogma within the academic musical world. "We all learned in college that tonality died, somewhere around the same time that Nietzsche's God died. And I believed it. When you make a dogmatic decision like that early in your life, it takes some kind of powerful experience to undo it." This is the composer John Adams speaking of what he calls his "diatonic conversion."[53] One of the earliest such testimonials of struggle against the metaphor-become-dogma of tonality's demise stems from composer George Rochberg. His writings provide thoughtful, succinct formulations of the experience of a "return" to tonality; I will refer to them in order to review the shifting grounds of musical authenticity. Corroborating testimonials, slogans, and affirmations can be found in a special issue of the *Contemporary Music Review,* entitled "New Tonality." Appearing in 1992, this issue brings together fifteen composers associated with neotonal practice.[54]

Beyond Dualities?

As we have seen, in the aesthetic horizon of the atonal challenge as represented by Schoenberg and Adorno, the claim to an authentic musical voice rested on the pursuit of formal integrity, uncompromising modernity, and radical critique of convention. Such ideals engendered the supportive network of images featuring decay, revolution, and catastrophe. In the neotonal horizon as represented by Rochberg and others, these fundamentals are traded for a different hand. For these composers, an authentic formal sense responds to the contradictions and inconsistencies of our time: "Like every other time, ours is a vast mix which refuses to be reduced to neatly packaged verbal categories," writes Rochberg. "To insist on either verbal or aesthetic consistency is to limit the world." The music of today can equally embrace the "narrow, attenuated gestures" of modernism and the "vast continuities, the grander and more serene gestures of tonal music."[55] History, therefore, is not a line of supersession for Rochberg, but "an emergent procession of varieties of parallel, simultaneous patterns," which include the cyclic pattern of "cosmic return" and "remembering our source." "Even if we grant the emergence of new perceptions and sensibilities, it does not follow that authentic values must be cast aside."[56] Finally, music is not a matter of austere, scarifying introspection, appreciated by the few. "There can be no justification for music, ultimately, if it does not convey eloquently and elegantly the passions of the human heart." Mass culture is not dismissed as degraded, but upheld as a model of vitality and involvement. "To be vital, a new work has to have a satisfying connection with one's own time and sense of place. The desire to create more participatory music, I believe, distinguishes the new tonal composer from the modernist."[57]

For Rochberg and his fellow travelers, then, authenticity is based on formal inclusivity, a transitive, continuous sense of history, and bounteous provision of "personal pleasure and satisfaction" (Moravec).[58] Such ideals are supported by metaphors of communication, vitality, and the steadfast cycles of nature. Of course, these metaphors did not spring into being in 1970. All six of the groups surveyed have been in use throughout the century. The ideological positions of Schoenberg and Rochberg I have lightly sketched in by no means represent the full spectrum of aesthetic aims for which the metaphors have been pressed into service. They do, however, represent stylistic junctures of particular urgency and critical mass, whose issues become sharply incised against their immediate background.

Throughout this article I have been less concerned with establishing the facts of tonality's status in the twentieth century than with analyzing the fractious rhetorical energies unleashed in the accompanying discourse. My point is an epistemological one regarding the reception of the music under discussion. I would like to conclude by briefly addressing a few nagging questions in order to clarify my position. The first question has to do with our own historical perspective. Are we still too close to these repertories— the anti-tonal and the über-tonal—to truly hear them? As the years pass and the polemics recede, will it be possible to listen to these works without bias? My answer is that I hardly know what a true, unbiased hearing would be. The fraught ideologies of modernism might fade, but any future hearing of the music will still take place through ideological filters—probably combining a sedimentation of the original polemics with new unforeseen aesthetic ramifications. One aim of my discourse analysis is to make it harder to swallow sedimented metaphors (like the death of tonality) when we encounter them, and to make it easier to recognize persuasion disguised as neutral historical accounts. I could conceptualize my position by saying that music always comes with words: our musical listening is accompanied by a kind of ghostly dialogue track which, just as in the case of the music track in cinema, is often most influential when we barely notice it.

Given this situation, where bias is natural and inevitable, can we say anything objective about tonality's place in the modern period? For "tonality," we now find, seems to have lost its objecthood. I am not referring to the fact of diverse tonal practices among composers as different as Rachmaninov, Britten, and del Tredici. I mean rather that any one of their tonalities can be multiply and contradictorily described according to the added value of its ideological framing: Rachmaninov plus morbidity-value, Rachmaninov plus human-connection-value, Rachmaninov plus commodity-value, etc. This relativizing premise does not prevent us from making statements about tonality, but it does force us to articulate them from some particular perspective: tonality *for whom?* tonality *as so understood.*

By making these claims, I am clearly revealing my own ideological context of late-twentieth-century North American pluralism. From this perspective, the sharply drawn battle lines of the early modernists, over matters of authenticity and fundamental categories of understanding, have managed to resolve themselves into a new array of alternative choices, equally meaningful and accessible. Where does this leave us? Is it possible to achieve a reconciliation of once fierce aesthetic dichotomies? Or should the question be: has tonality won after all? If I have presented the neotonal aesthetic as a refutation of Schoenbergian modernism, that is because it has been so conceived by its promoters: as an answer to the existential, estericist challenge of atonality and serialism. Their appeal to the vaguely euphoric, participatory properties of tonality will not sit well with everyone; other listeners could relate the very potent "personal pleasures" and enchantments they have wrung from non-tonal repertoires. Furthermore, the aesthetics of stylistic pluralism involves a paradox in its epistemological foundations which still provokes theoretical crossfire. This can be seen in the contrasting formulations of Morgan and Rochberg already presented. Both agree that in the postmodern condition, "music speaks in many tongues." But for Morgan, this situation rather precipitously entails the loss of native stylistic competence. In his decentered linguistic universe, it would seem no authentic perspective is possible. Rochberg, however, is still able to relate without distress to a stylistic "source." The emergence of "new sensibilities" does not displace previously "authentic values." For him, it would seem renewed authenticity rests on the acquisition of multilingual competence. The paradox in Rochberg's liberal inclusion of styles, one might argue, is that a modernist substyle that does not make historical demands, an atonal idiom that does not undercut tonality, has become something different altogether. An atonality and tonality equal in authentic value have lost the arrogance and sting that made them authentic in the first place.

In other words, the concept of authenticity has itself been caught in the tug of shifting premises. Rochberg's pluralist authenticity is a different creature from Schoenberg's agonistic authenticity. The neotonal polemicists do not so much oppose the modernist terms of debate as defuse them by resituating them within a different field of meaning, free of moral imperatives. There is something admittedly irresistible in the apparent promise of reconciliation. As long ago as 1929, Charles Seeger made this prediction:

> The tendency for the last thirty years has been toward avoidance of tonality; the effect is good when it is well done. But just as one can weary of too much tonality, so one can weary of too little. It is possible that the time has come when a composer can employ a tonal center or not employ it, as he [or she] wishes.[59]

Such a peaceable kingdom: The Second Viennese lion lying down with the New Romantic lamb. Perhaps from the present perspective, with our opera glasses turned back upon the century's cataclysmic parade, it might be possible to banish tooth and claw from our mongrel panorama. But given the nature of musical meaning as a dialogic practice, and given the historical impermanence of agreement upon terms, we ought to be skeptical of any detente. The storms and fires of verbal contention are part of the very thrill of music, part of its livelihood. The sheltering hush of the concert hall is merely a respite from those campaigns, whose rumors still attend us, like sharp-tongued spirits bending our ear.

Notes

1. Thomas Beecham, *A Mingled Chime* (New York: Da Capo, 1976), 147.

2. Compare Beecham's horrified listener with T. W. Adorno's ostensibly blasé and condescending response to the same opera: "In the entire final section of *Electra* banality is dominant. But . . . in Electra's monologue and in her scene with Klytemnestra, [Strauss's] compositional material declares—as it were—its independence and advances, against its will, to the very boundary of the tonal realm." Adorno, "On The Social Situation of Music" [1932], trans. Wesley Blomster, *Telos* 35 (1978): 128–64; see especially 156–57.

3. Schoenberg, "Tonality and Form" (1925), in his *Style and Idea: Selected Writings,* ed. Leonard Stein, trans. Leo Black (London: Faber & Faber, 1975), 256–57.

4. Ibid., 257.

5. Schoenberg, "Problems of Harmony" (1934; original lecture 1927), in his *Style and Idea,* 286.

6. Schoenberg, "Opinion or Insight?" (1926), in his *Style and Idea,* 263.

7. Ibid., 258–59.

8. Theodor W. Adorno, *Philosophy of Modern Music* (1941, 1948), trans. Anne G. Mitchell and Wesley V. Blomster (New York: Continuum, 1985), 34. Thomas Mann, a friend of Adorno's, mirrors this entire passage very closely in his novel *Doctor Faustus* (1947), trans. H. T. Lowe-Porter (New York: Vintage, 1992), 239.

9. "Thus began the renaissance of tonality." Adorno, *Philosophy of Modern Music,* 180.

10. Ibid., 39.

11. Mann, *Doctor Faustus,* 193.

12. Aaron Copland, "Schönberg and His School" (1949), in *Copland on Music* (Garden City, N.Y:. Doubleday, 1960), 244. See Richard Crocker's discussion of a similar metaphor ("musical materials have to be 'used up,' . . . shredded down to [their] constituent fibers") in *A History of Musical Style* (New York: McGraw-Hill, 1966), 525; as cited in Leo Treitler, "On Historical Criticism," *Musical Quarterly* 53 (1967): 200; and Richard Norton, *Tonality in Western Culture: A Critical and Historical Perspective* (University Park, Penn.: Pennsylvania State University Press, 1984), 15–16.

13. "I want to prove to you that it's really dead. Once that's proved, there's no point in going on dealing with something dead." Anton Webern, *The Path to the New Music* (1933), ed. Willi Reich, trans. Leo Black (Bryn Mawr, Penn.: Theodore Presser, 1963), 47.

14. Krenek, *Music Here and Now* (1939), trans. Barthold Fles (New York: Russell & Russell, 1966), 83. "Those [in Vienna] who did not want to take part in Schoenberg's innovations—and they, under the pressure of public condemnation, were just about everybody—experienced something like a pathological repression."

15. See Michael von der Linn, "Degeneration, Neoclassicism, and the Weimar-Era Music of Hindemith, Krenek, and Weill" (Ph.D. diss., Columbia University, 1998).

16. Henry Fouquier, in *Le Figaro* (1893), quoted in Roger Nichols, *The Life of Debussy* (Cambridge: Cambridge University Press, 1998), 72.

17. Paul Hindemith, *The Craft of Musical Composition* (1937), trans. Arthur Mendel (London: Schott, 1945), 1:50.

18. Adorno, "Reaktion und Fortschritt" (1930), quoted in Max Paddison, *Adorno's Aesthetics of Music* (Cambridge: Cambridge University Press, 1993), 90. Paddison glosses the term "surrealist music" as music which "juxtaposes its historically devalued fragments in a montage-like manner which enables them to yield up new meanings within a new aesthetic unity."

19. Along similar lines, Michael Cherlin claims: "The sonorities of tonality have not fully disappeared [in Schoenberg's music], they have become estranged, evanescent spectres" ("Schoenberg and *Das Unheimliche*: Spectres of Tonality," *Journal of Musicology* 11 [1993]: 357–73; see p. 362).

20. Hindemith, *Craft of Composition*, 1:152, 23, 55. William Thomson's recent book *Schoenberg's Error* (Philadelphia: University of Pennsylvania Press, 1991) is an extreme version of the claim of tonality-as-nature. Thomson also inverts the tonality-as-moribund metaphor, claiming that atonality was a "localized illness . . . that never quite infected the total population, and whose Viennese virulence had pretty well run its course by the end of our sixth decade" ("Communications," *Music Theory Spectrum* 13, no. 1 [1991]: 118).

21. Schoenberg, "Problems of Harmony," 284.

22. Webern, *The Path to the New Music*, 12, 41. "Readers of the English edition of the lectures should note that editor Willi Reich has reversed the [chronological] presentation of the two lecture series in order to point up the assumed 'natural' foundations that the new music sought as a way in which to rationalize its path to social legitimacy" (Norton, *Tonality in Western Culture*, 275).

23. Boulez, "Series" (1961), in *Notes of an Apprenticeship*, trans. Herbert Weinstock (New York: Knopf, 1968), 304. See also Joan Peyser, *Boulez* (New York: Schirmer, 1976), 26.

24. Kurt Schwertsik, "Long Live Tonality!" trans. Margaret Robinson and Paul Moravec, *Contemporary Music Review* 6, no. 2 (1992): 54. Compare the following passage by Schoenberg: "Can one understand sound-combinations if they hang for ever in the air and never settle down; if they never gain a firm footing? I read somewhere of a device by which aeroplanes refuel over the sea without standing firm anywhere. . . . If that is possible, should one not do it?" ("New Music: My Music" [c. 1930], in *Style and Idea*, 101).

25. Schoenberg, "Problems of Harmony," 286.

26. Krenek, *Music Here and Now*, 133.

27. Schoenberg, *Theory of Harmony* (1911), trans. Roy E. Carter (Berkeley and Los Angeles: University of California Press, 1978), 128.

28. Paul Rosenfeld, "Wagner" (1920), in *Musical Impressions: Selections from Paul Rosenfeld's Criticism*, ed. Herbert A. Leibowitz (New York: Hill and Wang, 1969), 10–11.

29. Hindemith, *Craft of Composition*, 1:154, 50.

30. Cincinnati *Enquirer*, October 12, 1913, quoted in Nicolas Slonimsky, *Lexicon of Musical Invective: Critical Assaults on Composers Since Beethoven's Time* (New York: Coleman-Ross, 1953), 155; see 149, 153, 165. Boulez describes Schoenberg's free atonal period as "very rich, but also very anarchic" ("Arnold Schoenberg" [1961], in *Notes of an Apprenticeship*, 362).

31. Kamran Ince, "Emancipation of Tonal Sonorities," *Contemporary Music Review* 6, no. 2 (1992): 49. On the other side of this debate, however, one may cite James Boros: "Much recent minimalist and 'new romantic' music strikes me as

monolithic, simply because, despite the careful application (via spray can) of 'evanescently flashy timbral patinas,' it's essentially *transparent* with regard to the purposefully 'inflexible and authoritarian' qualities that lie at its core." The role of tonality here is not explicit, but certainly implied ("Why Complexity? [Part Two]," *Perspectives of New Music* 32 [1994]: 91–92).

32. London *Times*, September 4, 1912, quoted in Slonimsky, *Lexicon of Musical Invective*, 151.

33. Robert Morgan, "Secret Languages: The Roots of Musical Modernism," *Critical Inquiry* 10 (1984): 458.

34. Norton, *Tonality in Western Culture*, 229–30.

35. Robert Morgan, "Rethinking Musical Culture: Canonic Reformulations in a Post-Tonal Age," in *Disciplining Music: Musicology and Its Canons*, ed. Katherine Bergeron and Philip V. Bohlman (Chicago: University of Chicago Press, 1992), 47, 57; my italics.

36. In fact he admits as much soon after, when he recognizes the "hegemony of a relatively small and limited body of music" (p. 59), though the realization is never integrated into his earlier argument. This points up a split personality in the essay, which expounds a modernist/hierarchic/linear view of history in its opening pages, and a postmodern/relativist/pluralist perspective in its final pages.

37. Norton, *Tonality in Western Culture*, 230, 271.

38. "Composers such as Glass and Adams [have] acquiesced to the culture industry's demand for consumable objects" (Boros, "Why Complexity?" 97).

39. He continues, "People may fail to grasp what was said in that language, the specific content of the musical works, but they are familiar with the works' superficial connections insofar as the traditional idiom links them automatically . . . [in] a sort of analogy with the relationship between communicative speech and the obligatory one of literary works of art and *minted* texts." Adorno, *Introduction to the Sociology of Music* (1962), trans. E. B. Ashton (New York: Continuum, 1989), 39–40; my italics.

40. Krenek, *Music Here and Now*, 158.

41. John Cage, "Forerunners of Modern Music" (1949), in his *Silence: Lectures and Writings* (Middletown, Conn.: Wesleyan University Press, 1973), 63–64.

42. Krenek, *Music Here and Now*, 86; Adorno, "Reaktion und Fortschritt," 91.

43. Rudolph Reti, *Tonality—Atonality—Pantonality: A Study of Some Trends in Twentieth Century Music* (London: Barrie and Rockliff, 1958), 127.

44. Steve Reich, interview with Edward Strickland (1987), quoted in K. Robert Schwarz, *Minimalists* (London: Phaidon, 1996), 56–57. Note the implicitly affirmative use of the economic metaphor.

45. Reti, *Tonality—Atonality—Pantonality*, 129.

46. Donald Mitchell, "Cradles of the New: Paris and Vienna at the Turn of the Century" (1988), in his *Cradles of the New: Writings on Music 1951–1991*, sel. Christopher Palmer, ed. Mervyn Cooke (London: Faber and Faber, 1995), 139.

47. George Rochberg, "Reflections on Schoenberg" (1972), in his *The Aesthetics of Survival: A Composer's View of Twentieth-Century Music*, ed. William Bolcom (Ann Arbor: University of Michigan Press, 1984), 53. Or this, in highly ironic mode: "Tonality, . . . burdened with the sheer weight of its chromatic excesses, fell headlong into the dizzying abyss of atonal consciousness where it remained paralyzed, impotent, and incapable of further human expression" (Norton, *Tonality in Western Culture*, 225).

48. Olin Downes, *New York Times,* May 22, 1941, quoted in Slonimsky, *Lexicon of Musical Invective,* 251.

49. Slonimsky, *Lexicon of Musical Invective,* 251; Schwertsik, "Long Live Tonality!" 55.

50. Rosenfeld, "Schoenberg" (1920), in *Musical Impressions,* 64.

51. Charles Seeger, "Grass Roots for American Composers" (1939), in *Studies in Musicology II, 1929–1979,* ed. Ann M. Pescatello (Berkeley and Los Angeles: University of California Press, 1994), 384.

52. Paul Moravec, "Tonality and Transcendence," *Contemporary Music Review* 6, no. 2 (1992): 41.

53. Quoted in Schwarz, *Minimalists,* 176.

54. On the dogma of the "exhaustion" and "death" of tonality, see Rochberg, *Aesthetics of Survival,* 235, 240; and "New Tonality," ed. Paul Moravec and Robert Beaser, *Contemporary Music Review* 6, no. 2 (1992): 3, 41, 53, 55.

55. Rochberg, "Reflections on the Renewal of Music" (1972), in his *Aesthetics of Survival,* 234, 238.

56. Ibid., 234–35. Regarding the "cosmic return" see Rochberg, "The Avant-Garde and the Aesthetics of Survival" (1969), in his *Aesthetics of Survival,* 216; regarding "remembering our source" see Rochberg, "Can the Arts Survive Modernism? (A Discussion of the Characteristics, History, and Legacy of Modernism)," *Critical Inquiry* 11 (1984): 339; with the phrase "remembering our source," Rochberg is quoting Owen Barfield, "Modern Idolatry," in *History, Guilt and Habit* (Middletown, Conn.: Wesleyan University Press, 1979), 61–62.

57. Rochberg, "Reflections," 236; Larry Bell, "Some Remarks on the New Tonality," *Contemporary Music Review* 6, no. 2 (1992): 44.

58. Moravec, "Tonality," 40.

59. Seeger, "Tradition and Experiment in (the New) Music" (1929), in *Studies in Musicology,* 125.

6

"Tone-Color, Movement, Changing Harmonic Planes": Cognition, Constraints, and Conceptual Blends in Modernist Music

Amy Bauer

1. Ligeti and the "Listenability" of Modernist Music

György Ligeti has discussed his "micropolyphonic" music of the mid-1960s at some length, in an attempt to explain why its composed *structure* seems to bear no relation to its actual *sound*. Although a work like *Lontano* is based on strict canons, the compositional method assumes a listener will "mis-hear" its structure:

> [In the large orchestral work *Lontano*] I composed . . . an extensively branching and yet strictly refined polyphony which, however, veers suddenly into something else. . . . I don't have a name for it and I don't want to create a term for it. A kind of complex of tone-color, movement, changing harmonic planes.
>
> The polyphonic structure does not actually come through, you cannot hear it; it remains hidden in a microscopic, underwater world, to us inaudible. . . . I have retained melodic lines in the process of composition, they are governed by rules as strict as Palestrina's or those of the Flemish school, but the rules of polyphony are worked out by me.
>
> . . . the polyphony is dissolved—like the harmony and the tone-color—to such an extent that it does not manifest itself, and yet it is there, just beneath the threshold.[1]

In the above passages, Ligeti appears to ally himself with modernists such as Boulez and Babbit, composers who use twelve-tone and other methods to systematically organize pitch structure. By composing with "rules as strict as Palestrina's" that paradoxically produce an "inaudible" structure, however, he presumes that the systematic aspects of this structure—by definition—lie below the threshold of conscious perception. Ligeti's sentiment accords with that of the philosopher Roger Scruton, who states baldly that "The order that exists in [serial compositions] is not an order that can be heard, when we hear the sounds as music."[2] Of course the pronounced ideological slant of Scruton's statement is at odds with the illuminating metaphors introduced by Ligeti. Scruton's support for an "order that can be heard . . . as music" references cognitive research that suggests the apparent "unlistenability" of modernist music, music composed outside the eighteenth- and nineteenth-century system of historically based, hierarchically structured tonality.

Without discounting this research, I question Scruton's implication that an "order that can be heard" must serve as a paradigm for listening to music. Fred Lerdahl supports such a view, stating that "Comprehension takes place when the perceiver is able to assign a precise mental representation to what is perceived."[3] I would like to ask why this mental representation necessarily equates with a grasp of the work's compositional grammar. I also question the corresponding implication that reception of a work is deficient if not founded on conscious perception of this structure. Using the example of Ligeti's micropolyphonic music, and its accompanying commentary, I will argue that to "hear the sounds as music" is never restricted to parsing a work's concrete, self-referential details, but relies on the necessary mediation of metaphor. Scruton himself argues as much, noting that our experience of music depends on a temporal order of tones "dissolved and reconstituted as a phenomenal *space*."[4] But the level at which metaphor describes our aural experience varies, and metaphors often transfer to music concepts from more than one area.[5] Any theory of listening to modernist music must rely not only on conceptual mappings from the temporal to the spatial realm, but on metaphoric projections and connections between music and other experiential domains.

Modern Music Is Unlistenable

George Rochberg and Lerdahl argue that modern music is incomprehensible because its imposed compositional structures resist mental representation and intelligible cognition. Rochberg's 1973 essay "The Structure of Time in Music: Traditional and Contemporary Ramifications and Consequences" borrows the serial and parallel processing of information model developed in Von Neumann's *The Computer and the Brain* (1958) to explain the central nervous system and, by extension, our perception of what Rochberg calls "pitch combination and temporal flow."[6] This conceptual framework explains the cognitive success of all music that features repetition of some type, music containing "structural devices and patterns whose fundamental purpose is self-perpetuation."[7] According to Rochberg, contemporary serial, atonal, electronic, and aleatoric musics "overthrow" the temporal structure characteristic of tonality. These works lack perceptible directionality and causality, and promote a "spatialization" of music, where the "sound substance is formed as the primary object of projection and perception." Music without a clear intention or goal will fail to produce a coherent, organic entity, "which is to say," Rochberg asserts firmly, "it cannot be described as art."[8]

Fifteen years later, with a spate of recent research on music perception at his disposal, Lerdahl attempted to reframe the cognitive dilemma of modernist music. "Cognitive Constraints on Compositional Systems" (1988) expands on and generalizes from earlier work that dealt exclusively with the cognition of tonal music.[9] Lerdahl introduces the dual notions of compositional and listening grammars, the latter referring to the unconscious process by which auditors generate mental representations of the music. These complementary theoretical constructs illustrate the discrepancy between the intentional (purposeful) construction of a modernist work (using Boulez's *Le Marteau sans maître* as a benchmark), and the mental representation that "comprises the 'heard structure' of the piece."[10]

Lerdahl's assumptions vary in name only from those comprising Rochberg's critique. Both authors assume that effective listening strategies rely on the perception of hierarchical aspects of musical structure. But Lerdahl's article transcends earlier polemics by presenting a positive program, in the form of three categories of cognitive constraints that enable listeners to generate mental representations of a work:[11]

1) *Restrictions on allowable event sequences*
A musical texture must be resolvable into discrete elements–identified in a series of eight constraints–which can then be organized by hierarchical strategies. These strategies include symmetry, parallelism, meter, and clearly articulated groups of events.

2) *Constraints on underlying materials*
Six constraints ensure that we may comfortably perceive and relate the basic constituents of the musical language. However, they also allow for leaps of cognitive faith, such as the prescription that chromatic subsets satisfy the mathematically-deduced criteria of uniqueness, coherence and simplicity.

3) *Constraints on pitch space . . .*

Three constraints within the third category represent a significant step forward in Lerdahl's evolving theory. His constraints on pitch space not only incorporate the notion of "cognitive distance" (suggested by the multidimensional representation of pitch relations proposed by Roger Shephard, among others), but they also add to that literature by proposing a pitch space based on reductive logic rather than geometric symmetry.

Lerdahl presents these constraints as neither deterministic nor universally limiting, noting that some "seem to me binding, others optional."[12] But as a whole his listening grammar explains why serial and other precompositional structures defy our attempts to perceive them. This creates a situational paradox: although effective *listening* strategies rely on the perception of hierarchy in musical structure, effective *compositional* strategies often locate musical significance in the literal, note-by-note detail of that structure. This fundamental discrepancy marks what Stanley Cavell calls the "burden of modernism," when artistic technique moves beyond our ken: "[T]he procedures and problems it now seems necessary to composers to employ and confront to make a work of art at all *themselves* insure that their work will not be comprehensible to an audience."[13]

The real question posed by "Cognitive Constraints," in an epilogue entitled "Comprehensibility and Value," is no less than the question of whether a modernist music of consequence is possible. What do we make of a music that is absolute in design and function, but denies perceptual constraints on event sequences, underlying materials and pitch space? If Lerdahl has correctly defined the cognitive parameters of a typical auditor, then for whom is modern music designed? Is it music "for the eye only," or is it music for an auditor who requires neither hierarchical structure nor audible intent? What becomes of modernist music, a contestable yet still-evolving body of works that remain a strong presence in the postmodern age?

Lerdahl and Rochberg's theories tacitly present tonal and other hierarchically structured musics as metaphoric models of "normal" cognition, with the implication that atonal and other non-hierarchically structured musics model "abnormal" states of mind. In effect, cognitive constraints function less as a *requirement for,* than a *description of,* ordinary cognition. If modern music lacks all the elements necessary for comprehensibility, then it must describe an altered state of cognition, perhaps even psychosis. Music that flaunts cognitive constraints might even represent a kind of reified madness.

Modern Music Is Mad

Louis A. Sass equates madness with modernism, in a less tendentious manner, by proposing that many works of modern art and literature exhibit a strong affinity with the phenomenological experiences of patients with schizophrenia.[14] The disjunct narratives and surreal images of avant-garde fiction and visual art reflect the disruption of "reality" we know as madness. Despite lucid moments, the psychotic patient often communicates his or her experiences in an incoherent manner. Discourse that lacks a recognizable theme or narrative line, conventional space-time structure, comprehensible causal relations, and a normal regulation of conventional symbol-referent relationships—all of these features distinguish schizophrenia from other cognitive disorders.

I would argue that modern music, including the composers cited by Lerdahl, presents an even starker, more visceral model for the cognitive processes that characterize madness. The desultory and inappropriate speech of schizophrenia—which seems to betray a private language known only to the speaker—parallels the private language of serial and atonal music, which lacks a familiar syntax and clear referential meaning.[15] The fragmentation, lack of contrast (as conventionally defined), and immediacy of a work like *Le Marteau sans maître* might then be explained as an evocation of madness, of the forms of "internal multiplicity and disharmony" characteristic of schizophrenic experience. Lerdahl describes reactions to *Marteau* from listeners who often perceived little more than the sound qualities presented on the surface of the music, making "what sense they could of the piece in ways unrelated to its construction."[16] This perceptual strategy mimics the "concreteness" attributed to schizophrenic discourse, a superficial grasp of reality marked by credulousness, certainty and automatic response.[17]

But what of the mid-60s work of Ligeti, which lies at the other end of the phenomenological spectrum? Unlike *Marteau,* much of Ligeti's music is continuous and marked by strong contrasts of dynamics, register and instrumentation. As an example, I offer the first section of *Lontano,* which begins quietly on a unison A flat (*pppp*), a focal point of clarity joined by clarinet and bassoon (mm. 1–5), followed by French horn, oboe, and trombone (mm. 3–8; shown in figure 6.1).

The neutral timbre, narrow compass, and extremely low dynamic level of this opening gesture give way when a second canonic unit enters in mm. 14–19. During this passage, the dynamic level rises, and a full complement of strings enters to thicken the texture and expand the registral scope. A dense climax occurs in mm. 25–32, where thirty-six strings occupy a range from E4 to D#6 (E4, F#4–C#5, D#5, F#5–C#6, D#6). The gradual but insistent rise in dynamics, tenuto markings, lack of string vibrato, and individual accents in violin and viola seem to focus the music and bring it closer in this passage, as pitches gradually disappear from the mass. (D sharp drops out in m. 32, B drops out in mm. 34–35, and G sharp drops out in m. 36.)

The minute rhythmic subdivisions of each canonic strand, and the prescription to *enter with an imperceptible attack* combine to deny any recognizable rhythmic punctuation or periodicity. The ametric entrance of canonic strands in different instrumental bodies causes a pronounced waver in pitch. This effect—when added to the vibrato implied by the expressive marking (*dolcissimo, sempre espressivo*)—causes acoustic beats that add resonance, and shifts the overtone structure of the canon. There is no harmonic progression in *Lontano*; rather, triads, octave doublings, and stable intervals rise out of the texture and gradually submerge. The only audible formal cues are a registral expansion and contraction that define the first of two large sectional shapes: a second expansion (beginning in the winds at m. 31) is left open, to break off with a sudden change in range and instrumentation (see the registral outline of this section in figure 6.2).

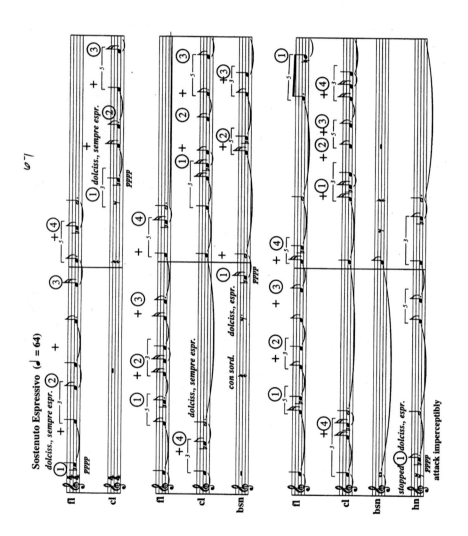

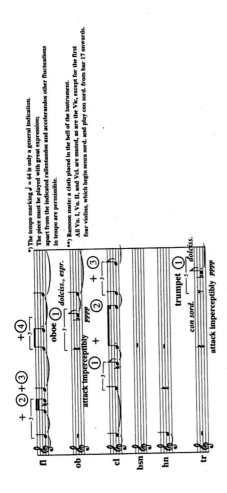

Figure 6.1. Ligeti, *Lontano*. Opening accretion of instruments, mm. 1–7 (circled numbers indicate staggered player entrances, by desk). Schott Music International, Mainz. Used by permission.

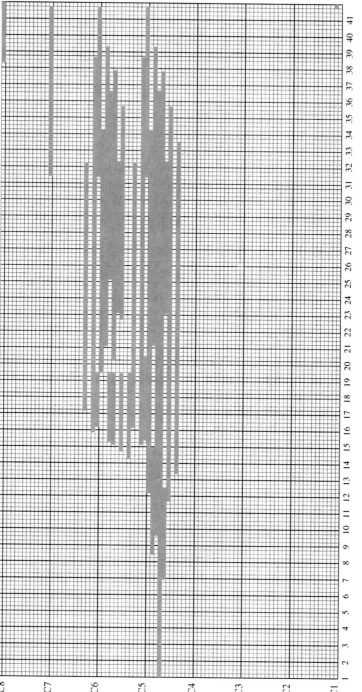

Figure 6.2. Ligeti, *Lontano*. Registral graph of mm. 1–41.

Ligeti has referred to a "new language" in *Lontano;* the work is as far removed from the sound and syntax of Boulez as it is from the music of earlier centuries.[18] This "complex of tone-color, movement, changing harmonic planes" obeys few of Lerdahl's constraints; it resists hierarchical structuring by a listening grammar, and is devoid of the marked transitions that might structure the work on a higher level. In a manifesto of 1988, the composer said, "I favor musical forms that are less process-like and more object-like. Music as frozen time, as an object in an imaginary space that is evoked in our imagination through music itself."[19] Here Ligeti embraces Rochberg's "spatialization" of music, by purposively embracing a compositional style that contrasts with that of the serialists. Paradoxically, Ligeti's music *also* evokes aspects of psychotic experience, invoking what Sass describes as "a universe more dominated by objects rather than by processes or actions."[20] Persons afflicted with schizophrenia often replace the teleological, dynamic, and affective aspects of human experience with expressions and actions that emphasize the immobile, static, and spatial aspects of the world. The author of *Autobiography of a Schizophrenic Girl* presents her reality as an "alien and forbidding world pervaded by a sense of illimitable vastness."[21] She continues in describing

> a country, opposed to Reality, where reigned an implacable light, blinding, leaving no place for shadow; an immense space without boundary, limitless, flat; a mineral, lunar country, cold as the wastes of the North Pole. In this stretching emptiness, all is unchangeable, immobile, congealed, crystallized. Objects are stage trappings, placed here and there, geometric cubes without meaning.[22]

Micropolyphonic works such as *Atmosphères* and *Lontano* evoke a similar "unchangeable, immobile, congealed, crystallized" landscape. In this musical landscape, as in the psychotic experience, time is equated with space, and all that is connected and organic gives way to a discrete, formal isolation, the "infinite present" described by one patient.[23] Ligeti has often compared his music to the paintings of Cézanne's "false" perspective in which time is a field that stretches out in all directions.[24] He describes *Lux Aeterna* (1966) as a "waterfall with a mirror," constantly smoothing and reflecting back on itself, and compares the Cello Concerto of the same year to a landscape.[25]

I find many instructive comparisons between schizophrenic accounts of the "infinite present" and Ligeti's vistas, intended to simulate a "frozen time" full of events, objects and closed forms. The composer states, "from the continuity of time, that lasts indefinitely . . . I show a window, that opens out to particular details in this time-process."[26] *Continuum* for harpsichord (1968) and the second Etude for organ, *Coulée* (1969; the title translates to "flowing" or "streaming"), achieve a sense of stasis through extremely rapid activity, by attempting a kind of *trompe-l'oreille:*

I thought to myself, what about composing a piece that would be a paradoxically continuous sound, something like *Atmosphères*, but that would have to consist of innumerable thin slices of salami? A harpsichord has an easy touch; it can be played very fast, almost fast enough to reach the level of continuum, but not quite (it takes about eighteen separate sounds per second to reach the threshold where you can no longer make out individual notes and the limit set by the mechanism of the harpsichord is about fifteen to sixteen notes a second). As the string is plucked by the plectrum, apart from the tone you also hear quite a loud noise. The entire process is a series of sound impulses in rapid succession which create the impression of continuous sound.[27]

Ligeti's description eerily approximates one schizophrenic patient's reported experience of "an intense cerebral activity in which inner experiences took place at greatly increased speed, so that much more than usual happened per minute of external time. The result was to give an effect of slow motion."[28]

Compositions that exhibit "static form" represent only part of Ligeti's oeuvre; his music resists all categorization, as it resists organization into perceptible hierarchies or easily heard forms. Works such as *Lontano* and the *Requiem* fit comfortably within the contemporary "canon," such as it is, while still representing "an outer extreme of the 20th-century quest for musical otherness."[29] As preeminent examples of modernism in music, they establish a critical, deliberately constructed distance between work and auditor. The aesthetic stance of Ligeti's music parallels the distinction made by Susan Sontag between the invitation to "look" proffered by representational art, and the "stare" provoked by modernist avant-garde art.

A look is voluntary; it is also mobile, rising and falling in intensity as its foci of interest are taken up and then exhausted. A stare has, essentially, the character of a compulsion; it is steady, unmodulated, "fixed." Traditional art invites a look. [Modernist avant-garde art] engenders a stare.[30]

If we replace "a look" with *listening* and "a stare" with *hearing* in Sontag's formulation, we could position contemporary music as a similarly autonomous, self-reflexive art. As the function of modern artworks is bound to the fixed gaze, so the function of modern compositions is bound to their "heard structure."[31] Modernist music offers us nothing to promote active, engaged listening, but demands to be heard, as an object deserving contemplation and analysis.

2. Conceptual Metaphors and Music

My attempt to rehabilitate contemporary music from a listener's perspective has invoked a provocative, if ultimately damning metaphor: modern music as a model for the phenomenology of madness. My cue has been Lerdahl and Rochberg's implication that a hierarchically structured, topically constrained listening grammar models normal cognition. Rochberg's model takes an automated model of information processing and maps its essential aspects onto human cognition. Although Lerdahl's constraints affect a literal description of music perception, they transfer concepts directly from the study of language-processing to that of music. Both theories are grounded in the implicit assumption that there exists an ideal listener whose cognitive processes can—themselves—serve as a metaphor for listening to modernist music.

But as noted in my introduction, to speak of music *at all* is to speak metaphorically, to speak of a world out of reach, populated by phenomenal objects of perception.[32] The history of discourse on music, including analytical discourse, is a history of metaphoric description and elaboration.[33] The most striking uses of analogy and metaphor—such as the "hero's journey" that marked the critical reception of Beethoven's *Eroica* symphony—range far beyond mere description of the "acousmatic" object. As Scott Burnham notes, programmatic accounts embraced not only syntactic and stylistic, but also ethical concerns raised by Beethoven's music.[34]

Metaphor in accounts of music, or of art in general, traditionally address those aspects of aesthetic experience that escape literal description. Marion A. Guck discusses how a figurative description—"portentous" as applied to the C flats that populate m. 53 in the second movement of Mozart's Symphony in G minor, K. 550—"reifies their features and relations in a particularly pungent and insightful way: it makes sense of them in ways not formerly possible."[35] Metaphor indirectly makes expression accessible, by addressing a kind of surplus in the object described.[36] This remainder is intrinsic not only to descriptions of music with programmatic content, but to the historical notion of absolute music as well, which mirrors nature as "perfect form," and which, therefore, serves as a "metaphor for the universe."[37]

This surplus is evident in Ligeti's description of *Lontano* as "an extensively branching and yet strictly refined polyphony which, however, veers suddenly into something else." Metaphors such as these are usually dismissed as program-note platitudes directed at the restless listener, but they actually reveal a sophisticated and coherent use of conceptual metaphor. The linguistic surface invokes an underlying idea, image, or experience of the world, one that links a concrete, visceral realm of experience to an abstract one. The image of "an extensively branching . . . polyphony" relies on a vivid impression of the unchecked, chaotic order of nature as we experience it. The subsequent image of polyphonic structure submerged "in a microscopic underwater world" references a very different encounter with nature. The basic elements of music are "dissolved," an allusion to the vast gulf between the seen and the unseen in nature, between the con-

crete surfaces we experience every day and the infinitely varied life beneath
that surface.

Ligeti's metaphors do not merely transfer concepts from one area to
another; they import the structure of a natural domain to the self-conscious and artificial realm of new music. If polyphony can be mapped to
branches, then a musical work can resemble a tree, or surface embellish-
ments may correspond to leaves. If the polyphonic structure can be submerged, than a musical work is like a body of water, and the shimmer of
tone color may represent its surface.

Conceptual Blending

The same, structure-preserving mapping motivates Lerdahl and Rochberg's
metaphor, which might be termed "Hierarchical Systems of Musical Organization [Tonal Music] Represent Normal Cognition." This multi-leveled
concept rests on an underlying conceptual metaphor, "Mind as Informa-
tion-Processing Device," and its related "Attention as a Filter" metaphors.[38]
That is, a listener uses certain "filters" (constraints on event sequences and
underlying materials) to select objects (musical events) worthy of attention; only these objects can be stored in memory and operated upon later.
This metaphor carries several additional provisos, or entailments: 1) some
information will be discarded in passing through the filter; 2) information
is processed in a serial, rather than parallel, fashion; and 3) attention is a
structure (filter), as opposed to a process or a resource.[39]

I do not question the efficacy of using the "Attention as a Filter" metaphor to describe the listening process. What I question are the assumptions
on which Lerdahl grounds it—that our literal comprehension of music is
the only "comprehension" possible, or that it is, by default, the most desirable. I would argue that musical *understanding* for a competent listener,
not to mention musical *meaning*, is never restricted to parsing a work's
concrete, self-referential details, but relies on conceptual mappings both
from other music and other experiential domains.

A growing body of research in cognitive science suggests that most of
our abstract reasoning and conceptualization is guided by metaphor.[40] These
metaphors are not only linguistic in nature and design, but conceptual as
well. Conceptual metaphors map entities, structures, properties, and relations from a source domain, the domain used as a model, to a target domain, the domain we wish to understand.[41] Most common metaphors—
specific instances of figurative language–spring from a basic, conceptual
metaphor. The conceptual metaphors we use in language can be traced
back, through a kind of recursive mapping process, to "image schemata,"
source domains based on bodily experience and action.[42] We map elements
of our concrete, physical experience of the world onto our abstract, intellectual understanding, as when we label one musical pitch "higher" than

another, or employ kinesthetic notions such as gesture, tension, and release to structure musical experience. At a higher level, detailed experiences of one cognitive domain may be mapped onto elements of a newly discovered or yet unexplored domain, as both Lawrence Zbikowski and Janna K. Saslaw demonstrate.[43] Zbikowksi maps the "Great Chain of Being" and "Atomistic" models of hierarchy to various historical theories of music.[44]

In the "Mind as Machine" metaphor illustrated by Diego Fernandez-Duque and Mark L. Johnson, the machine functions as source and the mind as target. Projection mappings erect correspondences from the source to the target domain, using our knowledge of the source, as in analogy, to structure the target domain. The functions, products, and even shortcomings of the machine are thus directed towards the target; each represents an entity or structure used to construct a specific counterpart in the domain of mental operations (see figure 6.3).[45] Thus the preponderance of expressions such as, "I'm a little rusty today," "Boy, the wheels are turning now," "He suffered a mental breakdown," and "We're cranking out ideas," all rooted in this underlying cross-domain mapping. Outside the context of everyday language, a very specific source domain may be used in a conscious manner to structure a target, as in my own elaboration of the "Mind as Machine" mapping as "Mind as Computer" (see figure 6.4).[46] Fauconnier and Turner stress that, while such a mapping enables us to see the target in new ways, it also constrains our potential knowledge of the target domain. The "Attention as a Filter" metaphor, for instance, maps the filter's property of serial processing onto the target domain of attention, thus eliminating

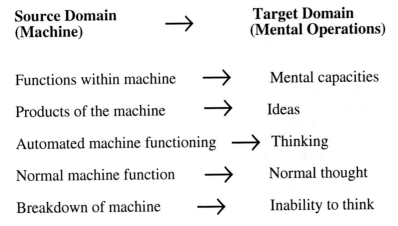

The Mind As Machine Metaphor

Source Domain $\rightarrow$ **Target Domain**
(Machine) **(Mental Operations)**

Functions within machine	$\rightarrow$	Mental capacities
Products of the machine	$\rightarrow$	Ideas
Automated machine functioning	$\rightarrow$	Thinking
Normal machine function	$\rightarrow$	Normal thought
Breakdown of machine	$\rightarrow$	Inability to think

Figure 6.3. Projection mappings in "Mind as Machine" metaphor.

The Mind As Computer

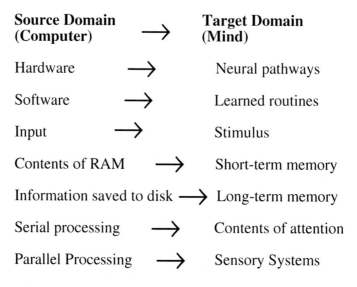

Source Domain (Computer)	→	Target Domain (Mind)
Hardware	→	Neural pathways
Software	→	Learned routines
Input	→	Stimulus
Contents of RAM	→	Short-term memory
Information saved to disk	→	Long-term memory
Serial processing	→	Contents of attention
Parallel Processing	→	Sensory Systems

Figure 6.4. Projection mappings in "Mind as Computer" metaphor.

the possibility that our attention could be divided by the parallel processing of discrete stimuli.[47]

Conceptual metaphors and cognitive mappings are thus not restricted to language use. They structure most of our abstract concepts, and constitute a background mental operation—one that lies below our horizon of conscious observation—that applies within and across domains whenever we think and communicate.[48] Conceptual mappings operate behind the scenes, so to speak, to interpret and provide those inferences necessary to basic cognitive operations.[49] I find the current work of Fauconnier and Turner on the use of conceptual integration, or conceptual blending, in certain linguistic expressions to be of particular relevance to the question of listening to modernism.[50]

Fauconnier and Turner's model of conceptual blending serves to explain how structure is imported from a more stable source domain to structure a more elaborate or complex target domain. A conceptual blend begins with a conceptual mapping between two or more mental spaces (a term Fauconnier and Turner prefer to "conceptual domain"). A mental space is "a (relatively small) conceptual packet built up for purposes of local understanding and action."[51] Blending exploits and develops counterpart connections—elements with corresponding structural roles—between input mental spaces. It differs from simple cross-domain mapping in that the blended space may fuse *any* elements, whether they are counterparts or not. Blending may integrate related events into one conceptual event, develop new structure, reason, draw inferences, or produce humor. The emergent structure may be illogical yet prove efficient at transferring the intended inferences back to the target Input, even if this new structure is never stated explicitly as part of the blend.

The familiar metaphor "digging your own grave" represents just such a conceptual blend.[52] As a warning, this expression is well understood; on the surface, it would seem that the activities that *lead to* failure equate with grave-digging, while failure itself equates with death. It is as foolish to *prepare* one's own failure as it is foolish to prepare one's own burial while still alive, and it is even more foolish *not to realize* that one's actions will lead to failure or death.

Yet a closer inspection of the metaphor "digging your own grave" reveals an apparent mismatch: foolish actions may cause failure, but digging a grave does not cause death. The causal structure of the source domain—death in our everyday experience is followed by grave-digging—is inverted in the target domain—foolish actions (grave-digging) lead to failure (death). In the source domain, the "patient" dies, followed by the "agent" digging the grave in which to bury the "patient." In the target, both actors are fused and the order of events reversed. The conceptual blend inherits the source structure of graves, burial, and digging, and there are some direct correspondences. But the blend inherits causal, intentional, and internal event structure from the target input to create what Fauconnier and Turner call emergent structure: new structure not available in either of the input spaces. Only the blend—the new, emergent structure found in neither source domain—can explain why we have an expression in which the existence of a satisfactory grave causes death.[53] The discordant structure, that death does not usually follow the digging of a grave, does not interfere with the conceptual blend. It does indicate that conceptual blends are not arbitrary, and must have considerable concordant structure—in this case activity pursued towards an irreversible goal—to be successful.

Conceptual Blends in Music

Current research on conceptual metaphor and cognitive mapping extends beyond linguistics and music theory to many other disciplines, guiding basic work in science (including mathematics) and explaining central concepts in the history of philosophy and neuroscience.[54] But to my knowledge, this model has never been applied to music-on-music cross-domain mapping, although Zbikowski has extended Fauconnier and Turner's model to conceptual blending and integration between text and music in song.[55]

Let me suggest one such conceptual scheme—what Fauconnier and Turner term the "multi-space" model—defined by the four mental spaces outlined above: two input spaces, defined by a source and target space, and two middle spaces, a generic space and a blended space. This model proposes that a listener, confronted by the novel experience of hearing a work for the first time, will draw on prior experience to guide him or her. The role of source space is assigned to a work already known by a hypothetical listener (the Familiar Work), and the target space to a previously unheard work (the New Work).

I assume that a hypothetical listener will draw an analogy between the two, mapping information from the already conceptualized source domain (Familiar Work) to the novel target domain (New Work). The source space of our ideal familiar piece may contain a vast amount of information, but for our purposes the Familiar Work will be represented by Lerdahl's seventeen cognitive constraints on compositional grammar. Twelve of these are unique to the Familiar Work; with the other five shared by the source and the target, and thus found in the generic space (see figure 6.5). (I have added a "closed work" stipulation as a sixth property to list in this generic space.) The target space—or New Work—will contain Ligeti's *Lontano*. The two input spaces project structure into two "middle spaces," a generic space and a blended space. The generic space of our model contains elements or structures, along with constraints (such as "the octave is divided into equal parts"), shared by both input spaces: our ideal source piece and the target *Lontano*.[56] The conceptual blend itself is a rich space within which partial structure (elements and functions) from both input spaces is integrated. This generic resemblance will include salient counterparts: both works represent self-contained listening experiences, and may contain information such as instrumentation, genre, or function. However, only five common constraints, Lerdahl's numbers 9 through 13 regarding underlying materials, are imported to the generic space.

Our hypothetical listener recruits structure from each input space to compose the blend, exploiting counterpart connections (such as the role of harmony) between input spaces. For instance, the musical surface of the Familiar Work is capable of being parsed into a sequence of discrete events, whereas in *Lontano*, the musical surface is opaque, and blurs distinctions between events. Nevertheless, the ample concordant structure (those common elements that compose the generic space) encourages the construction of a blended space. The listener combines aspects of Source and Target in order to comprehend *Lontano* as he or she might comprehend a Familiar Work: as exhibiting audible form and structure within a closed aesthetic framework. Emergent structure in the form of a "complex of tone-color, movement, changing harmonic planes" develops in the blended space, and is then available as an input space when the next New Work is encountered.

This account of one possible way in which cross-domain mapping may represent the cognition of new music is necessarily tentative and ill-de-

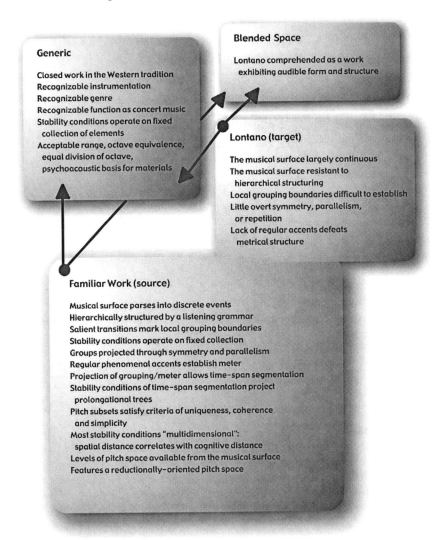

Figure 6.5. Cross-domain mapping, with Ligeti's *Lontano* as New Work (target space).

fined. There are evident difficulties in demonstrating music-to-music mapping across domains, and any discussion of music relies on prior metaphoric blends. Lerdahl's theory of compositional grammar itself relies on several complex but more or less transparent mappings, many of which are found on a master metaphor list compiled by the Berkeley Cognitive Linguistics Group.[57] These include the following, with Lerdahl's renditions given in parentheses:

"Understanding Is Seeing"
("Comprehension takes place when the perceiver is able to assign a precise mental representation to what is perceived.")

"Music Is a Language"
(Music can be described by a grammar, or rule system)

"Reasoning Is Following a Path Through a Landscape
(Map-like diagrams of grammatical systems illustrate Lerdahl's thesis)

Each of these dominant metaphors is structured by fundamental assumptions about the object of investigation and the act of perceiving music. Consider the presupposition that informs the first compositional constraint, "the musical surface breaks down into individual events."[58] This objective definition invokes two foundational metaphors: 1) that "Music Is a Container" (if it has a surface, it must also have an interior), and 2) that "Coherent Is Whole" (smaller, discrete elements come together to compose the musical surface).[59]

The dominant underlying metaphor of Lerdahl's critique, however, is the governing tenet of musical formalism, the rather opaque if sophisticated assumption that "Hearing Is Understanding/Understanding Is Seeing." That is, aural comprehension of musical structure is equivalent to knowledge of that structure, and that knowledge depends on sight. To truly understand Boulez's *Le Marteau sans maître* is to perceive the serial structure revealed by visual analysis of the score. Listeners who do not "even begin to hear its serial organization" do not, in essence, "comprehend" the piece.[60] Although Ligeti's music is not serial, it also challenges this well-worn assumption. By blurring distinctions between musical events, Ligeti's music interferes with the perception (hearing) of composed (visible) structure. As noted, the composer has time and again asserted his intentions to *disguise* compositional structure, to separate his compositional grammar from whatever listening grammar may guide his audience. Once again referring to his micropolyphonic music of the 1960s, Ligeti discussed the relation of intonation to notation, or "seen" structure:

And because of the fact that more and more adjacent pitches are played and because, besides that, the ensemble of strings is divided into many single instruments, the result is small deviations in intonation . . . The small deviations that result in this involuntary manner are here a constructive element in the composition. . . . The music has something artificial about it: it is an illusion. There are many elements in it that don't manifest themselves, but remain subliminal.

I specify many details that are not in themselves audible. But the fact that I have specified these details is essential for the general result—at least, that is what I hope. I think of a large architectural edifice in which many details are not visible.[61]

In these passages Ligeti confirms the importance of "involuntary" deviations and "inaudible" details to the composition as heard. In works like *Lontano*, not only the music but the notation *itself* contains a surplus, "invisible" quirks of intonation and form essential to the aural illusion of the work. Ligeti's suggestion that "A Musical Work Is Like a Building" introduces an alternate metaphor for listening, one which attempts to bridge the gap between our visual knowledge of the score and our aural perception of a micropolyphonic work.

Any discussion of music and, arguably, a great deal of musical appreciation, relies on conceptual mappings from extramusical source domains. Much musical criticism seems to rely on cross-domain mapping, as when the "hero's journey" is combined with structuralist accounts of Beethoven's "Eroica" Symphony.[62] Ludwig Tieck recognized that mixed and inconsistent metaphors let the reader imagine what the hearer of absolute music does: "an experience that overcomes him for an instant, but which cannot be held fast. The musical impression is as fleeting as it is compelling, the poetic paraphrase lingering but insufficient."[63]

Guck has shown the theoretical implications of such a blend, using the image of a "breathing laborer" as an "organizing metaphor" with which to coordinate the "constellation of metaphors" applicable to an analysis of Chopin's B-Minor Prelude.[64] I would argue that the richest music would be that capable of the widest range of associations. Those associations may arise through cross-domain mappings from one work or genre to another, or through conceptual blends that link one area of sensory and intellectual experience to music. In fact, multiple-space mappings would be more directly cognized than mental models which draw from only one source domain (such as "Attention Is a Filter"), and would enlarge our perceptual horizons by establishing a fund of conceptual blends from which to draw in the future. Ligeti relied on just such a conceptual blend when creating his "complex of tone-color, movement, changing harmonic planes." As indicated above, he has evoked painting, vistas, machines, and even food as obvious metaphors for his music. The composer's evocation of visual and tactile referents suggests fresh ways of hearing a music that cannot rely on one standard conceptual scheme—such as that represented by Lerdahl's listening grammar—for its full comprehension.

Ligeti on His Music

As an illustration of what I mean by conceptual blending in modernist music, I will analyze three passages from interviews in which Ligeti discusses *Lontano*. Many critics have employed colorful and elaborate metaphors to describe the sound and visceral appeal of Ligeti's music. I have restricted my illustration to the composer's own extramusical remarks to suggest that—by conditioning the listener's experience of a work—this commentary in effect acts as an extension of the composition.

Each passage appears to rely on one or two central, isolated metaphors, but, in fact, each metaphor has several entailments.[65] Ligeti's comments suggest ten possible input spaces which project partial structure into an eleventh space, the "conceptual blend," as well as a generic space. The elements of the target space are linked to the input spaces in systematic ways, yet are closely integrated to produce their own emergent structure.

Passage 1
1) I rather imagined a vast space of sound in gradual transformation, not through dense chromaticism but through a constantly changing pattern of color like a moiré fabric.
2) Although *Lontano* encompasses the entire chromatic scale, strictly speaking, it is based on a diatonic scale. As I have said, the changes happen in space, the sound of drawing nearer and moving away again.
3) But you are right that there is a second plane on which the music moves in time—quite deliberately.
4) I do not actually quote composers, only allude to nineteenth-century music, evoking late Romantic orchestral effects.[66]

This passage erects four separate source spaces that serve as inputs to the target space "Lontano," listed in figure 6.6. The striking metaphor "*Lontano* Is a Moiré Fabric" is found in the first sentence (1). This metaphor establishes "Moiré Fabric" as an input space, a complex metaphor suggesting that some elements (partial structure) within the "Fabric" space map onto elements in the "Lontano" space. Thus "Musical Scales," "Harmonies," or "Melodic Lines" may be equated with "Threads" or "Colors." A mapping such as "Melodic Lines Are Threads" is a component of the space, but it may also be seen as a specific example of the underlying conceptual metaphors "Change of State Is Change of Shape" and "Sound Is a Solid." These conceptual metaphors are rooted in image schemata, in our experience of change in nature, and our propensity to relate abstract concepts to corporeal objects.

The first sentence tells us that "*Lontano*" is a "vast space" in which changes in pitch move nearer to and farther away from a diatonic scale, as though we were traveling through a landscape (2). The complex metaphor "*Lontano* Is a Landscape We Move Through" conceives of music as not just space but as a space the listener traverses. This input space thus conveys the entailments, or associated metaphors "Change of State Is Change of Location," "Listening Is Following a Path," and "Loud Is Near/Soft Is Far." The third sentence suggests yet a third input space, borrowed from geometry: "Hearing *Lontano* Is Recognizing Two Planes" (3). The concept of geometric planes is a specific instance of the conceptual metaphors "Perception Is Shape Recognition" and "Shapes Are Containers." The final

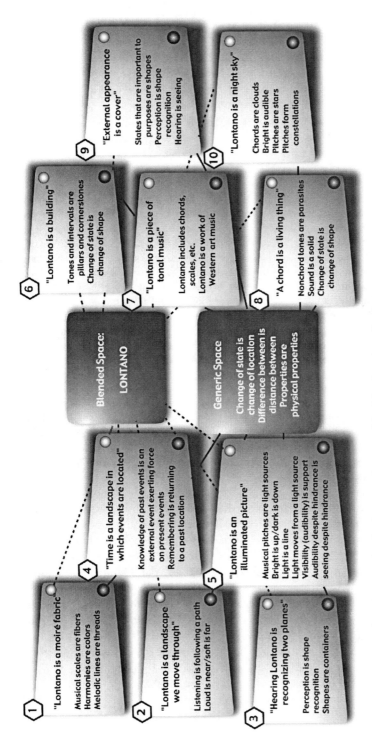

Figure 6.6. Cross-domain mapping in the metaphors used by Ligeti to describe *Lontano*.

sentence of this passage tells us that one of the two "Planes" represents the past. "Lontano" is not a metaphor for nineteenth-century music, since it only "alludes" to Romantic orchestral effects. Rather, the fourth conceptual space evoked here is a metaphor for the past that is referenced. The assertion that "the music moves in time" combined with "[the music evokes] Romantic orchestral effects" leads to the metaphor "Time Is a Landscape in Which Events Are Located" (4). And Ligeti alludes to nineteenth-century music, implying that "Knowledge of Past Events Is an External Event Exerting Force on Present Events."

Passage 2
5) In approximately the last third of [*Lontano*] we get, after a static, very soft plane of sound, formed by a major second and a minor third, a gradual passing into dim, deep regions. . . . Now, this dark progress is suddenly lightened, as if the music had been illuminated from behind. . . . This progress, once it has begun, goes forwards: the violas, cellos and double basses carry on the sequence that has started. All the other instruments, and then the cellos as well, take on a new gesture, something suddenly bright, often not perfectly delineated; it gets continually brighter and the music seems to shine, to be radiant . . . a single note, a D sharp, very high up, emerges and stands there, as if this musical light were at first diffuse, but slowly the diffuseness disappears and there is a single directed beam. . . . At the moment when the high D sharp is there, forming the concentrated pencil of this musical beam, suddenly there yawns an abyss, a huge distancing, a hole piercing through the music. . . . And through this suddenly gaping distance can be heard the sound of horns. . . . Horns coming in like that after a tutti awake in us involuntarily not a direct association perhaps, but an allusion, a reference to certain elements of late romantic music. . . . I can think of a passage in Bruckner's Eighth Symphony, in the coda of the slow movement, where with great tranquility and gentleness the four horns suddenly play a passage that sounds almost like a quotation from Schubert, but seen through Bruckner's eyes.[67]

Several metaphors introduced in Passage 1 above recur in Passage 2, with further elaboration. *Lontano* is equated with an elaborate visual metaphor, through discussions of "dim, deep regions," music "illuminated from behind," "bright" gestures, and a note that serves as a "musical light." This opens up a fifth input space, "Lontano Is an Illuminated Picture" (5), a metaphor with several specific entailments explicitly addressed in the passage. These include "Musical Pitches Are Light Sources," which refers to the conceptual metaphors "Bright Is Up/Dark Is Down"; "Light Is a Line"; and "Light Moves from a Light Source." Added to this musical picture is a musical sequence "carried" by violas, cellos, and double bass, suggesting that "Making Visible (Audible) Is Supporting." The "new gesture . . . often not perfectly delineated" states that "Audibility Despite Hindrance Is Seeing Despite Visual Hindrance."

Comments such as "a gradual passing into dim, deep regions," "illuminated from behind," and "a hole piercing through the music" all support "Difference Between Is Distance Between," a foundational metaphor that is shared by all five input spaces. An even more complex statement recalls input space (4), as the "four horns suddenly play a passage that sounds almost like a quotation from Schubert, but seen through Bruckner's eyes." An earlier composer remembering yet another composer adds one more entailment to "Time Is a Landscape": "Remembering Is Returning to a Past Location."

Passage 3
6) I believe that *Lontano* is the example that demonstrates most purely the crystallization of corner-stones or pillars that are specific intervals or single notes or harmonies. . . . On one level of the work there are tone-color transformations, but there is another, harmonic level which, I would almost say, is behind it: that is also an aspect of *Lontano*, of being distant. . . .
7) There are certain places in which a pitch or an interval or even several intervals—let us use the old-fashioned term "chords"—are clearly to be heard.
8) Then in the middle of a chord the "parasitic" tones gradually sound; they are not ornamental in the sense of the passing notes or auxiliary notes of tonal music, but they do contain a slight allusion to them.
9) The whole tradition of tonal music is present, but always hidden. Now this intervallic or harmonic plane gradually clouds over, and this cloudiness expands more and more, until finally this originally pellucid, clear harmonic structure dissolves into an opaque plane.
10) In the middle of this opaque or neutral plane we then get signs of a new constellation of pitches which by degrees becomes more and more dominant. At first, the constellation is barely audible. Gradually, however, the different parts gather together into the individual intervals which are later revealed in a bright light.[68]

Two new mental spaces are opened by this passage. The "corner-stones or pillars that are specific intervals or single notes or harmonies" summon up "*Lontano* Is a Building" (6). The musical work as a man-made structure is juxtaposed, however, with a discordant notion of "parasitic" tones that disrupt a chord, opening up yet another input space: "A Chord Is a Living Thing" (8), where "Nonchord Tones Are Parasites." In between the contrasting notions of *Lontano* as a "Building" full of "Living Chords," Ligeti returns to the continuing image of "tone-color transformations" on different planes. This image is able to connect all seven input spaces through its implied entailment "Comparison of States in a Dynamic Situation Is Comparison of Distance."

Of course this metaphor is an entailment of conventional metaphors used to discuss music, and Ligeti takes the opportunity to invoke the conceptual space of tonal music through use of the terms "chords" and

"auxiliary notes" (7). Yet the "whole tradition of tonal music" is paradoxically not audible. The "tradition is hidden," an example of the metaphor "External Appearance Is a Cover" (9), which opens up a ninth input
space. "Appearance Is a Cover" shares the entailment "Hearing Is Seeing"
with several other spaces, allowing "parasitic tones" to become "clouds"
that obscure clear intervallic or harmonic "planes." Here Ligeti invokes
the third input space "Hearing *Lontano* Is Recognizing Two Planes" again,
and the conceptual metaphor "States That Are Important to Purposes Are
Shapes." This metaphor informs the final image in Passage 3, the "constellation of pitches," which opens up yet another space, "*Lontano* Is a Night
Sky" (10). This rich metaphor implies that "Pitches Are Stars" and "Bright
Is Audible." The mapping of musical pitches and qualities onto a night sky
could imply other general metaphors, such as "Importance Is Central,"
implied by the convergence of "individual intervals" into a "bright light."

As shown by figure 6.6, Ligeti's comments open ten vastly different but
related mental spaces. The conceptual blend that represents *Lontano* as
experienced inherits partial structure from each space, and exploits counterpart connections among spaces: elements that represent the general metaphors "Change of State Is Change of Location," "Difference Between Is
Distance Between," and "Properties Are Physical Properties." It is thus
highly structured, drawing on both metaphoric connections and conventional connections already part of our listening experience. The target space
inherits chords, intervals, and scales from the space of tonal music, and
those conventions that come with the "listening to music" frame. This rich
blend develops its own emergent structure, which can be recruited for future listening experiences, or for future blends incorporating *Lontano*.

My dissection of the above passages represents more than one or two
alternate hearings of *Lontano*. Ligeti's metaphors enrich our musical experience of the work even as they suggest that conceptual blends are inevitable when confronting a work of art that extends the boundaries of our
experience. The conceptual blend indicates one route the mind may take
towards assimilating new information and complex structures.

3. Listening to Modernism

Modernist music was once simply challenging music. When married to a narrative framework in film, a theatrical spectacle, or a physical art such as dance,
it might momentarily reach beyond a modest, devoted audience. But as an
ongoing enterprise unto itself modernist music has fallen into neglect.[69] When
it was not loved it was at least tolerated by the musical establishment, because—in its unrelenting idealism and purity—it seemed alone among contemporary cultural expressions to have, as Ruth Rosengaard Subotnik put it,
"kept alive the idea of individuality and thus the possibility of art."[70]

Musicologists are infamous for their reluctance to engage in thorny questions of value and meaning: Subotnik could assert as late as 1982 that "Criticism, including the study of criticism, remains an unestablished field of musical scholarship . . . openly deprecated by mainstream musicology as a purely derivative and parasitical enterprise."[71] And they have only recently broken the silence surrounding contemporary music's viability as living culture. The concept of absolute music and its associated ideologies has brought modernist composition under increasing attack from reception and ethnographically oriented scholars, such as Susan McClary, Georgina Born, Allan F. Moore, and Subotnik.[72] Carl Dahlhaus rejects charges of elitism leveled at modern music, citing the "moral and social right" of the avant-garde to be unpopular, a position adopted by several prominent composers.[73] Meanwhile, scattered counterattacks attempt to rehabilitate on an individual basis those provocative and compelling works labeled as modernist.[74]

Yet we can shift the figure of the musical work endlessly on its ideological ground without affecting the object itself, without addressing just what it is that we *do* hear when we listen to modernist music. Lerdahl, Scruton, and Rochberg censure modernist music as a phenomenal object incapable of being cognized. A modernist music that cannot be processed as music undermines the very idea of—to use Subotnik's phrase—an "autonomous significant structure";[75] its rehabilitation lies beyond the appeals of either historical revisionism or political will. Thus, recent cognitive research that would prove the apparent "unlistenability" of modern music comes to take on far-reaching and complex implications.

In a sense, both the compositional and listening "grammars" of *Lontano* critique the idea of an essentialist, formalist music whose structure necessarily determines a particular mental representation. Ligeti's music and its accompanying commentary suggest that modernist music is best approached through a theory that allows for metaphorical and associative leaps, even if those leaps include the input space "Modern Music Is Madness." *Lontano* itself thus serves as a metaphoric solution to the problem of "listening to modernism," with the entailments "A Problem Is a Region in a Landscape" and "The Solution Is Contained in the Problem." To quote Jean-Claude Risset, Ligeti's music is "about composing the sound itself, not merely composing with sounds"; it is a sophisticated critique of modernism, and of the presumptions—both cognitive and historical—that would limit our musical perception.

Notes

1. *György Ligeti in Conversation with Peter Varnai, Josef Häusler, Claude Samuel and Himself* (London: Eulenburg, 1983), 95, 14–15, 99.

2. Scruton, *Aesthetics of Music* (Oxford: Clarendon Press, 1997), 294.

3. Lerdahl, "Cognitive Constraints on Compositional Systems," in *Generative Processes in Music: the Psychology of Performance, Improvisation, and Composition*, ed. John A. Sloboda, 231–59 (Oxford: Clarendon Press, 1988), 232; Lerdahl's essay was reprinted in *Contemporary Music Review* 6, no. 2 (1992): 97–121; subsequent notes refer to the latter publication.

4. Scruton, *Aesthetics of Music*, 75.

5. "What Scruton does not consider in espousing a traditional empiricist view of metaphor . . . is that all language is a product of human cognition and imposes order on the material world, often by transferring words between different realms of experience," Naomi Cumming, "Metaphor in Roger Scruton's Aesthetics of Music," in *Theory, Analysis and Meaning in Music*, ed. Anthony Pople (Cambridge: Cambridge University Press, 1994), 8; see also pp. 9 and 27.

6. Rochberg, "The Structure of Time in Music: Traditional and Contemporary Ramifications and Consequences," in *The Study of Time*, vol. 2, ed. J. T. Fraser and N. Lawrence for the International Society for the Study of Time (New York: Springer-Verlag, 1975), 136–49; a revised and abridged version of this essay appears in Rochberg, *The Aesthetics of Survival: A Composer's View of Twentieth-Century Music*, ed. William Bolcom (Ann Arbor: University of Michigan Press, 1984), 137–47.

7. Rochberg, "The Structure of Time in Music," in *The Study of Time*, 141.

8. Ibid., 146, 141.

9. Lerdahl, "Cognitive Constraints"; : *A Generative Theory of Tonal Music*, which Lerdahl co-authored with linguist Ray Jackendoff (Cambridge, Mass.: MIT Press, 1983), is among the notable studies of tonal music drawn on in "Cognitive Constraints."

10. Judgments of relatedness in tonal music vary as a function of context. Multidimensional scaling techniques position musical elements in a Euclidean space, so that chords (for example) judged as being closely related are near one another, while those judged as being less related are farther apart (e.g., as in J. J. Bharucha and Carol L. Krumhansl, "The Representation of Harmonic Structure in Music: Hierarchies of Stability as a Function of Context," *Cognition* 13 [1983]: 63-102). Lerdahl proposes a hierarchy of pitch relations, with different elements (scale degrees, chords, keys) occupying different levels of tonal space: 1) only the most primitive stability conditions are exempted from multidimensional representation, where spatial distance correlates with cognitive distance; 2) levels of pitch space must be available from musical surfaces to be internalized; and 3) a reductionally oriented pitch space expresses steps and skips that measure cognitive distance and express degrees of melodic completeness. Lerdahl, "Cognitive Constraints," 112–15.

11. The following numbered constraints are taken from Lerdahl, "Cognitive Constraints," 112–13.

12. Ibid., 114.

13. Cavell, "Music Discomposed," in his *Must We Mean What We Say? A Book of Essays* (Cambridge: Cambridge University Press, 1976), 187.

14. Sass, *Madness and Modernism: Insanity in the Light of Modern Art, Literature, and Thought* (New York: Basic Books, 1992).

15. A study by J. David Smith and Jordan N. Witt asked listeners to compare late romantic and serial excerpts by both Webern and Schoenberg. The serial excerpts were rated as more "sensory" than the tonal passages, that is, as pieces em-

phasizing "pure, unanalyzed, sound qua sound." Adjectives used to describe the serial excerpts were grouped under the categories "agitation," "extreme activity," "chaotic motion," "chaotic structure," and "insanity." Smith and Witt, "Spun Steel and Stardust: The Rejection of Contemporary Compositions," *Music Perception* 7, no. 2 (Winter 1989): 169–86. Experiments by Nicola Dibben suggest that any inference of structural stability in atonal music is drawn from events at the musical surface: phenomenal accents, dissonance, and voice-leading. Dibben, "The Perception of Structural Stability in Atonal Music: The Influence of Salience, Stability, Horizontal Motion, Pitch Commonality, and Dissonance," *Music Perception* 16, no. 3 (Spring 1999): 265–94.

16. Lerdahl, "Cognitive Constraints," 97–98.

17. Sass, *Madness and Modernism,* 123.

18. Ligeti, *Ligeti in Conversation,* 126.

19. Ligeti, "On My *Piano Concerto,*" trans. Robert Cogan, *Sonus* 9, no. 1 (1988): 13.

20. Sass, *Madness and Modernism,* 156.

21. Ibid., 47.

22. Renée," from *The Autobiography of a Schizophrenic Girl,* ed. M. Sècheheye (New York: New American Library, 1970), 19; quoted in Sass, *Madness and Modernism,* 47.

23. "Lawrence"; cited in Sass, *Madness and Modernism,* 156. On p. 161, Sass notes the gradual progression toward flatness and "morbid geometricism" visible in schizophrenic commercial artist Louis Wain.

24. Ligeti quoted in Denys Bouliane, "Geronnene Zeit und Narration: György Ligeti im Gespräch," *Neue Zeitschrift für Musik* 149, no. 5 (May 1988): 21. Eva-Maria Houben further discusses this conceit in *Die Aufhebung der Zeit: Zur Utopie unbegrenzter Gegenwart in der Musik des 20. Jahrhunderts* (Stuttgart: Franz Steiner Verlag, 1992), 31–32.

25. Ligeti quoted in Ove Nordwall, *György Ligeti: Eine Monographie* (Mainz: B. Schott's Söhne, 1971), 78–79; Ligeti's reference to the "waterfall with a mirror" is strikingly similar to "Renée's" experience of a world pervaded by the "gloss and smoothness of material things" (*Autobiography of a Schizophrenic Girl,* 19; quoted in Sass, *Madness and Modernism,* 47).

26. Ligeti in conversation with E. Lackner in *Frankfurter Allgemeine Magazin,* 393 (11 September 1987): 20.

27. *Ligeti in Conversation,* 22–23.

28. Sass, *Madness and Modernism,* 160.

29. Alex Ross, "Critic's Notebook: Searching for Music's Outer Limits," *New York Times* (20 March, 1993), 11; see also *Ligeti in Conversation,* 106. Regarding the plurality of styles that comprise musical modernism, see Robert P. Morgan, "Secret Languages: The Roots of Musical Modernism," *Critical Inquiry* 10, no. 3 (March 1984): 443–61.

30. Sontag, "The Aesthetics of Silence," in *Styles of Radical Will* (New York: Dell, 1978), 15–16, quoted in Sass, *Madness and Modernism,* 66.

31. Note the composer's dictum: "I was always a partisan of 'closed' form. Music is not everyday life. Art is artificial, it's an artificial product." Ligeti quoted in *Trackings: Composers Speak with Richard Dufallo,* ed. Dufallo (Oxford: Oxford University Press, 1989), 334.

32. Scruton calls the experience of sound "acousmatic," and describes music as "the intentional object of an experience that only rational beings can have, and only through the exercise of imagination." Scruton, *Aesthetics of Music*, 2–3, 96. Lydia Goehr's paraphrase puts it more succinctly: "the sound world is not a space into which we can enter; it is a world we treat at a distance." Review of Scruton's *Aesthetics of Music* in *Journal of the American Musicological Society* 52, no. 2 (Summer 1999): 402.

33. As noted by Scott Burnham and elaborated upon by Marion A. Guck. Burnham, "Theorists and 'The Music Itself,'" *Music Theory Online* 2, no.2 (March, 1996), http://boethius.music.ucsb.edu/mto/issues/issues.html; Guck, "Two Types of Metaphoric Transfer," in *Metaphor: A Musical Dimension*, ed. Jamie C. Kassler, 1–11 (Sydney: Currency Press, 1991). In "Rehabilitating the Incorrigible," Guck lists a series of well-known contemporary analyses in which figurative language facilitates the detailed progress of a musical work. "Rehabilitating the Incorrigible," in *Theory, Analysis and Meaning in Music*, ed. Anthony Pople (Cambridge: Cambridge University Press, 1994), 68 n. 28.

34. Burnham, *Beethoven Hero* (Princeton, N.J.: Princeton University Press, 1995), 8–9, 16–18.

35. Guck, "Rehabilitating the Incorrigible," 71.

36. Hans-Jost Frey, *Studies in Poetic Discourse: Mallarmé, Baudelaire, Rimbaud, Hölderlin*, trans. William Whobrey (Stanford, Calif.: Stanford University Press, 1996), 29.

37. Carl Dahlhaus, *The Idea of Absolute Music*, trans. Roger Lustig (Chicago and London: University of Chicago Press, 1989), 8, 29.

38. See the discussion of how attention metaphors have guided research on the cognitive psychology of attention and, by extension, circumscribed the nature of what is attended to, in Diego Fernandez-Duque and Mark L. Johnson, "Attention Metaphors: How Metaphors Guide the Cognitive Psychology of Attention," *Cognitive Science* 23/1 (Jan.-March 1999): 83–116. Alan Ruttenberg's discussion of Lerdahl and Jackendoff, 1985 explicitly discusses rules that presume the simple matching processes or face-recognition processes employed by a computer program. Ruttenberg, "Review and Discussion of *A Generative Theory of Tonal Music*" (August 10, 1994), http://alanr.www.media.mit.edu/people/alanr/Jackendoff&Lerda hlFinal.html.

39. Fernandez-Duque and Johnson, "Attention Metaphors," 84–92.

40. Much of this work traces back to George Lakoff and Mark Johnson, *Metaphors We Live By* (Chicago: University of Chicago Press, 1980); see also Lakoff, *Women, Fire, and Dangerous Things: What Categories Reveal about the Mind* (Chicago: University of Chicago Press, 1987); and Lakoff, "The Contemporary Theory of Metaphor," in *Metaphor and Thought*, 2nd ed., ed. Andrew Ortony, 202–51 (Cambridge: Cambridge University Press, 1993).

41. See especially Lakoff and Mark Turner, *More Than Cool Reason: A Field Guide to Poetic Metaphor* (Chicago: University of Chicago Press, 1989); Lakoff and Turner, "Language Is a Virus," *Poetics Today* 13, no. 4 (1992): 725–36; Lakoff and Johnson, *Philosophy in the Flesh: Cognitive Science Brings to Philosophy the Embodied Mind, the Cognitive Unconscious, and Metaphorical Thought* (Chicago: University of Chicago Press, 1999); Turner, *Death Is the Mother of Beauty: Mind, Metaphors, and Criticism* (Chicago: University of Chicago Press, 1987); Turner,

Reading Minds: The Study of English in the Age of Cognitive Science (Princeton, N.J.: Princeton University Press, 1991); and Turner *The Literary Mind* (New Yorkand Oxford: Oxford University Press, 1996).

42. Mark L. Johnson, *The Body in the Mind* (Chicago: University of Chicago Press, 1987) and Turner, *Reading Minds*.

43. Zbikowski, "Conceptual Models and Cross-Domain Mapping: New Perspectives on Theories of Music and Hierarchy," *Journal of Music Theory* 41, no. 2 (Fall 1997): 202–4, and Zbikowski, "Metaphor and Music Theory: Reflections from Cognitive Science," *Music Theory* Online 4, no. 1 (January 1998), http://boethius.music.ucsb.edu/mto/issues/issues.html; see also Saslaw, "Forces, Containers, and Paths: The Role of Body-Derived Image Schemas in the Conceptualization of Music," *Journal of Music Theory* 40, no. 2 (Fall 1996): 217–43. My own essay was completed prior to the publication of Zbikowski's *Conceptualizing Music: Cognitive Structure, Theory, and Analysis*, AMS Studies in Music (New York: Oxford University Press, 2002), which describes the function of categorization, cross-domain mapping, and the use of conceptual models in theories of musical organization.

44. Zbikowski posits the "Atomistic" notion of hierarchy as opposed to the "Great Chain of Being" metaphor in "Conceptual Models and Cross-Domain Mapping," 204–18. The "Great Chain of Being" is explored at length in chapter 4 of Lakoff and Turner, *More Than Cool* Reason, 160–213.

45. Fernandez-Duque and Johnson, "Attention Metaphors," passim.

46. Ibid., 85; see also G. Gigerenzer and D. G. Goldstein, "Mind as Computer: Birth of a Metaphor," *Creativity Research Journal* 9, nos. 2–3 (1996): 131–44.

47. D. Kahneman, *Attention and Effort* (Englewood Cliffs, N.J.: Prentice-Hall, 1973), 121.

48. Gilles Fauconnier, *Mappings in Thought and Language*, 2nd ed. (Cambridge: Cambridge University Press, 1997), p. 1.

49. Mark Turner, "Backstage Cognition in Reason and Choice," in *Elements of Reason: The Science of the Mind and the Limits of Political Rationality*, ed. Andrew Lupia, Mathew McCubbins, and Samuel Popkin (Cambridge: Cambridge University Press, in press); available at www.wam.umd.edu/~mturn/www/backcog/bcframe.html.

50. Fauconnier and Turner, "Conceptual Projection and Middle Spaces," UCSD Cognitive Science Technical Report 9401 (San Diego: University of California, 1994), available from http://www.wam.umd.edu/~mturn; Fauconnier and Turner, "Conceptual Integration and Formal Expression," *Metaphor and Symbolic Activity* 10, no. 3 (1995): 183–203; Fauconnier and Turner, "Blending as a Central Process of Grammar" in *Conceptual Structure, Discourse, and Language*, ed. Adele Goldberg, 113–29 (Stanford, Calif.: Center for the Study of Language and Information, 1996; distributed by Cambridge University Press); and Fauconnier and Turner, "Conceptual Integration Networks," *Cognitive Science* 22, no. 2 (April-June 1998): 133–87.

51. Fauconnier and Turner, "Conceptual Integration and Formal Expression," 1.

52. Ibid., passim.

53. All of the elements necessary for conceptual blending are present in this metaphor: 1) Two input spaces; 2) Selective projection from the input spaces: Input 1 (graves, digging, burial); Input 2 (state of ignorance regarding one's actions); 3) A

Generic space, which contains those properties shared by both Input spaces; 4) A Blended space in which the two Input spaces are composed and elaborated, to become a coherent unit ("Digging your own grave" is foolish, unmindful activity leading to a disastrous end.); and 5) Emergent structure (The deeper you dig your own grave, the closer you are to dying.).

54. A selection of metaphor research in other fields would include Jackson Barry, "Cognitive Science and the Semiotics of Art," *Interdisciplinary Journal for Germanic Linguistics and Semiotic Analysis*, 2, no. 1 (1997): 59–76; Raymond W. Gibbs, Jr., *The Poetics of Mind: Figurative Thought, Language, and Understanding* (Cambridge: Cambridge University Press, 1994); Elizabeth F. Hart, "Cognitive Linguistics: The Experiential Dynamics of Metaphor," *Mosaic* 28, no.1 (1995): 1–23; E. F. Keller, *Refiguring Life: Metaphors of Twentieth-Century Biology* (New York: Columbia University Press, 1995); George Lakoff and R. E. Nunez, "The Metaphorical Structure of Mathematics: Sketching Out Cognitive Foundations for a Mind-Based Mathematics," in *Mathematical Reasoning: Analogies, Metaphors, and Images*, ed. L. English (Hillsdale, NJ: Erlbaum, 1996); and Yeshayahu Shen, "Metaphors and Conceptual Structure," *Poetics* 25, no. 1 (1997); 1–16.

55. Subsequent to the completion of this article, Zbikowski has published *Conceptualizing Music* (see fn 43).

56. Some of Lerdahl's constraints are vague regarding the scope and degree of "local grouping boundaries" (Constraint 3) or "a degree of regularity in the placement of phenomenal accents" (Constraint 5), so textual references to specific musical examples have been used to gauge the applicability of each constraint to the work under consideration. Lerdahl, "Cognitive Constraints," 105–6.

57. "Master Metaphor List," 2nd ed., compiled by George Lakoff, Jane Espenson, and Alan Schwartz, Cognitive Linguistics Group University of California at Berkeley December, 1994, http://cogsci.berkeley.edu/pub/cogling/Metaphor/.

58. Lerdahl, "Cognitive Constraints," 104.

59. Metaphoric entailments to this constraint include "Properties Are Contents" (phenomenal accent, interval, pitch and other salient properties carry structural information to the auditor);"(Bounded) Time Is a Container" (time is marked by a "sequence of discrete events" that are grouped and bounded according to the high-level metaphoric "tree" structures of time-span and prolongational segmentation); and "Logic Is Causation in Control over an Entity Relative to a Location" (time-span and prolongational trees determine a hierarchy of probable events at particular points in a work). These individual metaphors form part of what Lakoff has termed the Event Structure Metaphorical System, a large metaphorical construct that includes notions of attribute, change, and causation conceived in terms of force-dynamic systems; "Master Metaphor List."

60. Donald C. Freeman offers an explanation for the ubiquity of this particular metaphor (Freeman, "Songs of Experience: New Books on Metaphor," *Poetics Today* 12 [1991]: 154):

As an image schema, hearing lacks the structure and components of vision that can be mapped onto understanding: our hearing is much harder to focus and while it can select, it does so with greater difficulty than vision. Both abilities are elements crucial to our understanding. Even the modern locution "I hear ya," meaning roughly "I understand," lacks intellectual conviction and connotes at most a fuzzy emotional sympathy precisely because the faculty of hearing appeals chiefly to intercommunication. Hence the sense of "I hear ya" is almost that of a powerless phatic communion—"I sympathize, but there really isn't much I can do except listen."

61. *Ligeti in Conversation*, 96, 101.

62. "The 'Eroica' served its earlier critics well as an example of music rising to the level of an *Idee*, but not to an exclusive *Idee* from a specifiable source. . . . [T]he type of *Idee* that A. B. Marx had in mind rose above any one exemplar." Burnham, *Beethoven Hero*, 25.

63. Dahlhaus, *The Idea of Absolute Music*, 69.

64. Guck, "Musical Images as Musical Thoughts: The Contribution of Metaphor to Analysis," *In Theory Only* 5, no. 5 (1981): 29–42.

65. Some of these metaphors are explicitly invoked by Ligeti's comments, while others refer implicitly to the basic metaphors catalogued on the "Master Metaphor List" (see note 57).

66. *Ligeti in Conversation*, 56.

67. Ibid., 92.

68. Ibid., 96–97.

69. Witness Michel Foucault's remark, "[T]his music which is so close, so consubstantial with all our culture, how does it happen that we feel it, as it were, projected afar and placed at an almost insurmountable distance?" Foucault and Pierre Boulez, "Contemporary Music and the Public," *Perspectives of New Music* 24, no. 1 (1985): 7. Of course modernist music has received more than its share of outright derision from both professional music critics and composers themselves. These range from rants against the substance of the music itself (Henry Pleasants, *The Agony of Modern Music* [New York: Simon & Schuster, 1955]), to polemics aimed at its institutional and social role (Benjamin Boretz, "Interface Part II: Thoughts in Reply to Boulez/Foucault, 'Contemporary Music and the Public,'" *Perspectives of New Music* 24, nos. 1–2 [1987]: 608–11).

70. Subotnik, "The Challenge of Contemporary Music," in *Developing Variations: Style and Ideology in Western Music* (Minneapolis: University of Minneapolis Press, 1991), p. 275.

71. Subotnik, "Musicology and Criticism," *Musicology in the 1980s: Methods, Goals, Opportunities*, ed. D. Kern Holoman and Claude V. Palisca (New York: Da Capo Press, 1982), 147.

72. See Born, *Rationalizing Culture: IRCAM, Boulez, and the Institutionalization of the Musical Avant-Garde* (Berkeley: University of California Press, 1995); Moore, "Serialism and Its Contradictions," *International Review of the Aesthetics and Sociology of Music* 26, no. 1 (June 1995): 77–95; Moore, "Anachronism, Responsibility and Historical Intention," *Critical Musicology Journal*, http://www.leeds.ac.uk/music/Info/CMJ/Articles/1997/03/01.html; McClary, "Terminal Prestige: The Case of Avant-Garde Music Composition," *Cultural Critique* 12 (1989): 57–81; and Subotnik, "Toward a Deconstruction of Structural Listening: A Critique of Schoenberg, Adorno, and Stravinsky," in *Explorations in Music, The Arts, and Ideas: Essays in Honor of Leonard B. Meyer*, ed. Eugene Narmour and Ruth Solie, 87–122 (Stuyvesant, N.Y.: Pendragon Press, 1988). As Dahlhaus noted, the discipline has divided between music historians who deal with composition and

those who deal with reception. Dahlhaus, "Progress and the Avantgarde," *Schoenberg and the New Music: Essays by Carl Dahlhaus*, trans. Derrick Puffett and Alfred Clayton (Cambridge: Cambridge University Press, 1987), 19.

73. Dahlhaus, "Progress and the Avantgarde," 25. Representative examples of the avant-garde composer's view, from early modernism to the present, include Alban Berg, "Why Is Schoenberg's Music So Hard to Understand?" (1924), in Willi Reich, *Alban Berg*, trans. Cornelius Cardew, 189–204 (New York: Harcourt, Brace, and World, 1965); Arnold Schoenberg, *Style and Idea*, ed. Leonard Stein (Berkeley and Los Angeles: University of California Press, 1984); Milton Babbitt, "Some Aspects of Twelve-Tone Composition," *The Score and I.M.A. Magazine* 12 (1955): 53–61; reprinted in *Sonus* 13, no. 1 (1992): 56–74; Pierre Boulez, *Orientations: Collected Writings by Pierre Boulez*, ed. Jean-Jacques Nattiez, trans. Martin Cooper (Cambridge, Mass.: Harvard University Press, 1986); Roger Sessions, *The Musical Experience* (Princeton, N.J.: Princeton University Press, 1950); and James Boros, "Why Complexity? (Part One)" *Perspectives of New Music* 31, no. 1 (Winter 1993): 6–9; and "A 'New Totality'?" *Perspectives of New Music* 33, no. 3 (1995): 538–53.

74. A select listing of recent analyses that consciously address the "problem" of a work's reception would include Richard Cochrane, "The Ideal Four Minutes and Thirty-Three Seconds: Response to Covach," *Music Theory Online* 1, no. 1 (January, 1995), mto.1.1.cochrane.art; on listening to John Cage; Thomas DeLio, ed., *Contiguous Lines* (Lanham, Md.: University Press of America, 1985) [various composers cited for their use of open form]; Joseph Dubiel, "Three Essays on Milton Babbitt (Part Two)," *Perspectives of New Music* 29, no. 1 (1991): 90–122; Catherine Costello Hirata, "The Sounds of the Sounds Themselves: Analyzing the Early Music of Morton Feldman," *Perspectives of New Music* 34, no. 1 (Winter 1996): 6–27; and Stephen Peles, "Continuity, Reference, and Implication: Remarks on Schoenberg's Proverbial 'Difficulty,'" *Theory and Practice* 17 (1992): 35–58.

75. Subotnik, "The Challenge of Contemporary Music," 266.

7

Sexual and Musical Categories

Fred Everett Maus

*I was called a "seducer of young people," and when a critic once compared
me with Socrates I was not sure whether he intended to honor me or to
suggest that I should be condemned like Socrates and given the cup of poison.*
—Arnold Schoenberg, "How One Becomes Lonely"

1. Musical Museum, Musical Difference, and History

Many people—musicians, music teachers, students, journalists, radio an-
nouncers, casual and serious admirers of classical music—think of early-
twentieth-century musical modernism primarily in terms of stylistic difference, and think of that difference primarily in terms of new ways of organizing pitches. Depending on background, someone might describe the
contrast in terms of consonance and dissonance—"I like classical music,
but only up to the time when it becomes dissonant." The more sophisticated contrast, reflecting greater cultural or educational capital, would be
between tonal and non-tonal music. The opposition between tonal and
non-tonal music figures prominently in music criticism, and academic music theory elaborates the contrast in technical terms.[1] Most of this essay
reflects on the tonal/non-tonal contrast, especially as it appears in postwar
North American music theory. I begin with a broad account of the contexts
of this distinction in concert life and music theory; subsequently, I explore
similarities between these musical categories and contemporary concepts
of sexuality.

The tonal/non-tonal dichotomy categorizes concert music, and also figures in a music-historical narrative. The categories distinguish different
kinds of music, and the narrative describes how one kind, non-tonal, got to
be the way it is. As the story goes, some of the most advanced serious music
came to be non-tonal in the early years of the twentieth century. This was
the final stage in a series of incremental steps away from tonality: chromaticism first decorated, and then increasingly replaced, the scales and
chords that are basic to tonality. In some ways of telling the story, the

change was inevitable. Sometimes, as in Schoenberg's writings, the story is one of progress; but often, the plot combines degeneration and exhaustion (the end of tonality) with an attempt to forge something new. In the second kind of story, non-tonal music figures as a response (successful or not) to the decline of something that previously flourished. Either way, the departure from tonality provides a broad framing narrative for accounts of many individual composers such as Wagner, Debussy, Scriabin, and of course Schoenberg and his students.

This story has some familiar problems: its difficulty in representing or evaluating "belated" tonal composers such as Sibelius or Rachmaninoff, its tendency toward pretentious claims about inevitability, the fierce elitism of its disregard of audience opinion, its emphasis on pitch structure at the expense of other musical attributes. Nonetheless it continues to dominate both academic and popularized thought about musical modernism. Another kind of change, less prominent in most historical accounts but arguably more fundamental, occurred in the late nineteenth and early twentieth centuries. As J. Peter Burkholder emphasizes in "Museum Pieces," that time saw the consolidation of the classical concert as an institution dealing primarily with music of the past.[2] Concerts became occasions to contemplate musical works of lasting value. Works that are central to the concert hall, according to the ideology of the musical museum, have transcended the constraints and contingencies of their original contexts; they are intelligible to concert audiences on the basis of their intrinsic or presented qualities. Observable differences among different compositions, according to this ideology, should be understood as revelations of the individual composer's personality and as manifestations of stylistic options, not primarily as traces of the originating purposes or contexts of the music.

The modern development of museum-like concert institutions set new tasks for living composers. Composers could no longer write in response to a decade or two of recent music; instead, they had to situate themselves in relation to the concert repertory as a whole. New works, new candidates for inclusion in the concert repertory, had to show respect for the values of the established canon. But, since audiences and critics valued compositions for their individuality, new music had to balance respect with innovation. The ideology of the classical music museum, now over a century old, gives a strange, ambivalent role to history.[3] The classical concert has as its central goal the preservation of old music, but it achieves this in a way that seems to disdain historical reflection. A composition in concert performance is not heard primarily as a specimen that gives evidence about another time and place; it is not like an instructive relic in a museum of history or ethnography.[4] Rather, the musical sound itself, in the present moment, is the focus of attention. And the music offers its significance fully to present-day listeners, who should be able to understand and evaluate it just by listening. The museum erases diachronic succession, replacing it with a synchronic assembly of compositions. As bearers of thought and feeling, prized for their individuality, compositions come to resemble people; musical life is somewhat like getting to know an interesting social group, their identities wavering between anthropomorphized compositions and inferred composers.

This anti-historical attitude is clear in the relative importance of musical sound and program notes: the music is not an illustration of the program annotator's lessons, as an artifact in a historical museum might illustrate the history lesson in the tour-guide's lecture. Rather, the program notes are an optional part of the concert experience; they provide historical lore and description, typically in a desultory way, offered as a vague enhancement of the concert experience. The bits of history hover in an obscure relation to the audience's musical experiences, in quiet tension with the belief that listeners can appreciate compositions through a uniform set of listening habits. What the music is, you can hear just by paying proper attention. You might or might not be curious about how the music came into being, and it is not clear what you could do with the information if you had it.

Perhaps some people at concerts do not experience the music in this non-historical, non-contextual way. But it is certainly the way I learned to understand classical music, both as a music student (and child of professional musicians) and as a concert-goer. Schools of music train musicians to play pieces, and concert institutions informally train audiences to listen to them, all in a present-oriented way. The pieces find their interpretive context in the other pieces of the repertory, and their social setting is the present-day world of concert performance.

Burkholder identifies two different early- and mid-twentieth-century strategies by which composers have interpreted their relations to the existing repertory. A composer with a "progressive" ideology thought of the concert repertory in a way that accepts and heightens the paradox of its relation to history. Non-tonal and twelve-tone music are, of course, the central examples of "progressive" music. Schoenberg, who clearly held a progressive ideology, thought of the repertory as a set of exemplary masterpieces from various past times; he accepted the conception of a musical museum. But he also believed that the history of music showed development in the direction of greater sonic complexity and lower redundancy, and he understood his own music as the logical next step in that trajectory. This creates a tension: the progressive ideology, in the context of the museum, seems to assert both that the old pieces are just as good as the new ones, and that the new ones somehow improve on the old ones. It is hard to understand, if the eighteenth- and nineteenth-century masterpieces are perfect, why composers of new music must progress beyond them.

Composers closer to the "emulative" end of the spectrum more fully accepted the anti-historical tendency of the concert hall. Stravinsky, for example, combined eclectic borrowing from music of various periods with a style that seems personal and individualistic; he did not write in order to occupy a position in an unfolding historical narrative. The concert hall, in taking a relatively tolerant attitude toward both progressive and emulative emphases, displays once again the uncertain relation between repertory and history.

But if concert institutions seem to accept both progressive and emulative emphases in new music, this tolerance, from the late nineteenth century to the present, is in the context of a more fundamental neglect or unconcern about new music.[5] The relation between established eighteenth- and nineteenth-century works and the newer compositions that come knocking at the door is hierarchical. Older, established classics are central to concert life; newer compositions are candidates for inclusion at the periphery of the repertory. This sharpens the tension in the status of progressive compositions: in seeking admission to the concert repertory they acknowledge an institution that offers them at best a peripheral position, even while the conception of historical development that shapes their composition positions them quite differently, as the most recent culmination of important trends rather than as marginal. Emulative approaches to composition for the museum seem less conflicted, though also perhaps less exciting.

In the later twentieth and early twenty-first centuries, after many decades of museum-style concert life, the sense of historical progression in musical style, vivid for Schoenberg and his like-minded contemporaries, has become difficult to sustain.[6] By now, music that continues the early-twentieth-century non-tonal traditions seems, from the perspective encouraged by concert institutions, less like a "next step" in some historical development and more like a special category of music, an extreme among the present range of stylistic options. When the association of this music with "progress" becomes unbelievable, it becomes one more kind of music, alongside the other styles (baroque, classical, romantic-programmatic, etc.) in the museum. The difference between progressive and emulative conceptions withers away. Present-day non-tonal composers are specialized emulative composers, drawn to the Schoenberg-Varèse-Ruggles wing of the museum. Nonetheless, despite the increasingly poor match between the ideologies of the musical museum and progressive composition, non-tonal (or twelve-tone) music seems destined to come along with stories about the origin of its style. Non-tonal music seems almost to require a story about how it got that way. In contrast, program annotators and appreciation teachers do not seem obsessed with how tonal music became tonal; historical studies of the development of tonality in the seventeenth century generally remain recondite and academic, of little interest to most practical musicians or concert audiences.[7] The dependence of non-tonal music on a special narrative of origin marks it as different from the self-sufficient, individualized works of tonal music at the center of the repertory.

2. Musical Museum and Music Theory

Burkholder arrived at the views I have summarized as a way of under-standing twentieth-century classical composition. The account is helpful in understanding music theory as well. Indeed, if music history is in an ob-lique relation to the emphases of the musical museum, music theory—that is, the technical theory that is generally regarded as fundamental to musi-cal education—seems to match the ideology of the museum closely.

Tonal theory takes as its subject matter the music at the center of the repertory—the canonized music, predominantly instrumental, of eighteenth- and nineteenth-century Europe.[8] Like the concert hall, it treats the music in terms of characteristics that are observable from performances or scores. In seeking common concepts for the description of all that music, tonal theory proposes a non-historical explanation of how the works that form the central repertory belong together. According to tonal theory, the mu-seum has at its heart a common practice: the central works are all, in im-portant ways, the same. That is why uniform listening strategies can yield understanding of the central works in the repertory. In its match with the core repertory, tonal theory both supports the concert institution, articu-lating a rationale for its main boundaries, and also gains support from the concert institution, since the concert repertory seems to affirm the central-ity and unity of the style that theorists emphasize.

But when attention turns to the twentieth century, tonal theory can no longer account for some new works in the repertory. This raises questions about the status of this new music—questions that music theory attempts to answer in technical terms. To early-twentieth-century theorist Heinrich Schenker, the poor fit with tonal theory just showed that the new composi-tions did not belong in the museum! But generally, theorists have tried to invent ways to describe non-tonal or post-tonal music. In some analytical approaches the techniques of the later music seem to develop out of the earlier; Schoenberg favored this kind of evolutionary, gradualist account. But the approach that has been favored in late-twentieth-century North American theory emphasizes the distinctness of recent music by offering a second theory, a theory of pitch structure in non-tonal music (or, in an alternative tradition, twelve-tone music), as a counterpart to tonal theory. Thus, in the typical style of the musical museum, a chronological succes-sion becomes a non-temporal contrast, an opposition between two rich and valid systems of pitch organization.

While tonal theory generally reproduces the musical judgments embod-ied in the concert repertory, theories of non-tonal music do diverge to some extent from the hierarchies of the museum. That is, while non-tonal music may be permanently marginal to the repertory, non-tonal theory as profes-sionally practiced seems to give it equal standing: the implicit assertion is that non-tonal music is different but just as rewarding. Thus, professional music theory proposes a canon that has somewhat different values from the actual concert repertory.

However, the priorities of the concert hall return strongly in academic music theory curricula, especially at undergraduate levels. (At graduate levels, theory courses begin to reflect the distinctive emphases of professional theory.) Undergraduate music students normally receive several years of required training in tonal theory, after which they may or may not get a few months of theory training for non-tonal music. This plan reproduces perfectly the paradoxical equal-but-subordinate, culminating-but-marginal role of progressive compositions in the museum. The theory curriculum makes a certain conservative sense as training for performers. It can be confusing for young composers, depending on the emphases of their teachers. At many schools, composition students may develop a taste for tonal composition in their beginning theory courses, only to be told subsequently that another range of styles, which might seem foreign and unappealing, represents the styles of our own time. (Of course, the situation varies in different music schools or departments: as I shall explain later, my own experiences as a composition student did not fit this pattern.)

3. Interpreting Musical Oppositions

Naturally, since I am not concerned with normative allegations, I cannot be concerned here with the invocation of the overtone series as a "natural" phenomenon, and that application of equivocation which then would label as "unnatural" (in the sense, it would appear, of morally perverse) music which is not "founded" on it. Now, what music, in what sense, ever has been founded on it?
   —Milton Babbitt, "The Structure and Function of Musical Theory"

The physiology of orgasm and penile erection no more explain a culture's sexual schema than the auditory range of the human ear explains its music.
   —Carole Vance, "Social Construction Theory and Sexuality"

One way to think about the tonal/non-tonal opposition is to compare it with other oppositions that it resembles, seeking parallels between the music theorist's tonal/non-tonal dichotomy and similarly entrenched non-musical concepts.

This approach is familiar in feminist research, which often links oppositions such as nature/culture, body/mind, or intuitive/rational to gender difference. Feminist music scholarship sometimes brings gender into musical contexts by associating a binary opposition in musical thought with gender difference. In such arguments, feminist musicologists associate the two terms of some musical distinction with some construal of masculinity and femininity, and through this association hope to explain something about the musical phenomena. The claim is that gender difference, a socially variable way of conceptualizing many aspects of life (most immediately, sex-linked traits and power relations) extends beyond its most obvious range of applications to include, somehow, aspects of musical life.

Most famously, Susan McClary has insisted that her readers take seriously the traditional gendering of first and second themes in sonata form.[9] According to McClary, historical references of A. B. Marx and others to the masculinity or femininity of themes are not just literary flourishes, but a valuable key to meanings of sonata form. In creating and hearing sonata form movements, composers and their audiences think about the differences between masculinity and femininity, and about relations of power and conflict between men and women. On McClary's account, music, like more obvious examples such as prose fiction or psychology textbooks, is a medium for shared thought about gender relations, and critical response should include a clarification and evaluation of that thought.

In a different way, I have evoked gender difference in writing about the organization of prestige in the present discipline of music theory.[10] I argued that the distinction between "mainstream" and "marginal" approaches in recent North American music theory closely matches the conventional contemporary gendering of discursive styles. Drawing on arguments that some kinds of speech and writing are stereotypically masculine, others feminine, I suggested that these categories help explain the relative prestige or centrality of different texts in music theory. Because of this match, the mostly male scholars in the field tend to feel comfortable with the mainstream, more masculine approaches, and tend to be anxious about using the more feminized alternative styles.

Perhaps someone could attempt to link gender difference to the tonal/non-tonal opposition. But this essay will take another direction, one that I find far more promising. I shall take up two closely related musical distinctions, the contrast between tonal and atonal music along with the more specific contrast between tonal and twelve-tone music, and explore the possibility that these contrasts have sometimes, in some treatments, resembled a difference of sexuality. It is impossible to keep issues of gender and sexuality separate for long, and they will begin to interact later in this essay. But my starting point is a similarity between twentieth-century categories of musical style and of sexual identities, and so my basic comparison differs from the gender-centered interpretations that I have mentioned.

Perhaps it is already easy to see that non-tonal compositions are queers in the concert hall, without any special arguments on my part. To many listeners and performers, they are marginals, oddballs, outsiders, often tolerated rather than loved, sometimes not tolerated at all, products of the degeneration of tonal order, needing a special etiology to explain why they are so peculiar. But, beyond acknowledging this general aura of queerness, I want to develop some comparisons between, specifically, the hetero/homo opposition that dominates present-day thought about sexuality, and the music theorist's oppositions between tonal and non-tonal music. I shall begin by summarizing some widely accepted beliefs about the distinction between homosexuality and heterosexuality as sexual identities, turning later to the music-theoretical phenomena that I find to be analogous.

4. Commonplaces about Sexualities

On the face of it at least, our civilization possesses no ars erotica. *In return, it is undoubtedly the only civilization to practice a* scientia sexualis.
—Michel Foucault, *History of Sexuality: An Introduction*

From the late 1970s on, the influence of Michel Foucault's work on the history of sexuality, along with other work from gay and lesbian research, has discouraged the view of sexuality as a natural force, inhibited by repressive beliefs and institutions, and has encouraged, instead, the constructionist view that practices and discourses create sexualities, in historically diverse forms. Sexuality is not a hard-wired, inflexible biological fact; historical changes in behavior, conceptualization, and institutions amount to changes in sexuality, and the concept "sexuality" itself has a historical origin and development.[11]

The most frequently retold portion of Foucault's history of sexuality concerns the "invention of the homosexual." Late-nineteenth-century sexologists, attempting a scientific study of sexuality, began to think of homosexuality not just in terms of individual same-sex sexual acts but as an underlying personal identity. A homosexual was a kind of person, whose inner, enduring homosexuality served to explain various patterns of behavior. The creation of homosexuality as an identity led to the further, subsequent naming of heterosexuality as the other, commoner sexual identity.

The effects of this invention are pervasive today. Here are some common beliefs that constitute a sort of twentieth-century American and European mainstream of assumptions about sexuality. These are contingent and, in many ways, questionable attitudes; but people who have held these beliefs do not normally identify them as part of an ongoing history of sexuality, rather accepting them as invariant truths about kinds of people, as reliable results of modern medical and psychological study.

An overarching belief is that the categories are coherent and substantial: all homosexual individuals have something basic in common, as do all heterosexuals. There is some important underlying unity to each category, something that might be specified in terms of a particular psychological configuration and perhaps a characteristic etiology. Understanding a person's sexual category provides a basis for understanding many other things about the person. This is especially clear in psychoanalytic traditions, which have often traced apparently non-sexual phenomena, as symptoms, to their sexual causes, but this belief has also become part of common sense for many people.

Sexuality, according to this belief system, is a relatively stable quality of a person, though it might be hidden or misunderstood by oneself as well as others. One's determinate sexuality is there, whether anyone perceives it or not. This makes it very natural to talk of people recognizing or not recognizing, discovering or not discovering, their own sexualities.

There is a presumption of monosexuality, that is, a belief that everyone or almost everyone is determinately homosexual or heterosexual. And consequently, there is an obscurity or puzzlement about the notion of bisexuality. The categories of homosexuality and heterosexuality seem to leave no way of understanding bisexuality except as something "between" the two clearly-defined sexualities. Beliefs in the stability of sexuality and the prevalence of monosexuality invite (though they do not entail) the suspicion that claims to bisexuality reflect deceit or confusion about one's sexual identity. The presumption of monosexuality invites the belief that examples of bisexuality are typically transitional, destined to lead to a stable homosexuality or heterosexuality.

These assumptions about sexuality are familiar; they are also controversial.[12] Now I shall return to the musical categories, focusing on some aspects of North American music theory in order to indicate similarities between the conceptualizations of the sexual and musical categories.

5. Tonal versus Non-Tonal

Criticism does not exist yet on the American music-academic scene, but something does exist which may feel rather like it: theory and analysis.
—Joseph Kerman, "A Profile for American Musicology," 1965

I shall describe two crucial moments in the formation of the contrast between tonal and atonal music, commenting on the ideas of Schenker and Babbitt. Schenker's writings provided the theory of tonal music that has been most influential for North American theorists. Babbitt's work on twelve-tone theory explored one alternative to tonality, and provided the basis for more general theories of atonal music by Allen Forte and others. The combined influences of Schenker and Babbitt form the basis of contemporary North American music theory. In focusing specifically on this theoretical material, I limit my account to one aspect of the broader tonal/non-tonal contrast. It is an important aspect: the assumptions of music theory directly affect the training of classical musicians in North America, and related ideas are fundamental in North American music appreciation, journalism, program notes, liner notes, and so on; similar ideas appear in European settings also. Babbitt is especially important to my account, as the writer who, far more than anyone else, established the tone and content of subsequent North American music theory. His contribution is especially intriguing because of his other role as a leading modernist composer.

Schenker's theory, formulated in the first third of the twentieth century, responded to various contemporary phenomena that, in Schenker's view, showed a poor grasp of the achievements of the greatest composers. In particular, Schenker felt that early twentieth-century composition had broken decisively with the tradition embodied in the masterpieces of the eighteenth and nineteenth centuries, and he wrote to show his readers what they had lost in abandoning that tradition. Schenker believed that the overtone series gave a natural basis for tonal music. He argued that tonal music was in part natural, in part a human invention. Schenker wrote to show the "chord of nature" as the starting point of tonality and also to show how the great composers, through genius, had elaborated this starting point.

Tonality, in Schenker's account, is a crucial common element in all musical masterpieces. Non-tonal music, lacking this shared element, cannot be good; in part this is because it lacks tonality's relation to nature. To Schenker, non-tonal music is unnatural. A Schenkerian analysis of an individual composition shows how, in its individual way, the composition exemplifies the general principles of tonality. Aspects of a piece that may not seem closely related to pitch, such as instrumentation and articulation, can be understood only in relation to its way of being a tonal composition.

Schenker's creation of an elaborate tonal theory in response to post-tonal music resembles, to some extent, sexologists' back-formation of the concept of heterosexuality as a complement to their new concept of homosexuality. In both cases, a conceptualization of the normative or unmarked category follows awareness of an alternative. Schenker's attack on some music as unnatural recalls, of course, similar attacks on homosexuality. Schenker's energy went primarily into the elaboration of his account of tonal music, and that differs from the work of the pioneering sexologists, who focused on the minoritized categories. (For a sexological analogue to Schenker's work, one could imagine an awareness, and dislike, of homosexual activity leading someone to create an elaborate, nature-based psychology of heterosexuality, rather than beginning, as the sexologists did, with an account of marked or stigmatized categories).

Babbitt, whose theoretical publications began in the late 1940s, admired Schenker's work, and his own theoretical thought can be understood partly as a sustained response to Schenker's ideas, through hints about an appropriately revised version of Schenker's theory as well as the articulation of an alternative musical system.

Schenker's argument for the superiority of tonal music had two parts, a claim about a link with nature and a claim about the audible breadth and intricacy that only tonality makes possible. Babbitt offered rebuttals of both claims, denying the link with nature that Schenker and others tried to make, and denying that tonality is uniquely valuable as a musical system. Babbitt insisted on the irrelevance of the overtone series to tonal music, arguing that the chord of nature could not be the basis of any plausible theory of tonality. Babbitt suggested that Schenker's theory be understood, instead, as based on a number of axioms rather than as a natural phenomenon. (Thus Babbitt, from midcentury onward, argued, with regard to musical structure, the position that cultural theorists now call "constructionist.") And, having praised and sketchily reformulated Schenker's theory of tonality, Babbitt offered an explicit account of twelve-tone music as a counterpart, that is, as an alternative system of musical organization, different in many ways but equally intricate and fruitful.[13]

Though Babbitt contradicted many claims dear to Schenker's heart, he accepted one of Schenker's basic assumptions: like Schenker, he often wrote as though the evaluation of music could involve, as an important component, the evaluation of musical systems represented in explicit theories. His defense of twelve-tone music answers Schenker's system with another system, rather than challenging Schenker's belief that a general theory of pitch structure should figure importantly in the praise of individual compositions.[14] In effect, Babbitt practiced a kind of identity politics, redescribing and defending a category of composition that has been rejected, rather than arguing solely from the qualities of individual compositions.

The two systems Babbitt admired did not provide a theory for nontonal, non-twelve-tone music. Allen Forte's work on atonal music drew on Babbitt's representations of pitch-class collections, generalizing that portion of Babbitt's thought beyond twelve-tone music and, in effect, replacing Babbitt's dichotomy with a different pair of theories, one for tonal music, one for atonal (Schenker and sets, as music theorists sometimes jauntily encapsulate this world-view).[15] Like Babbitt, Forte responded to Schenker by describing a second, alternative musical system. Unlike Babbitt, for whom composition has always been primary, Forte and his students undertook the professional project of analyzing many individual pieces in the terms provided by these theories.

Like the conceptions of sexuality I described, these conceptions of music treat the musical category as crucial to the identity of individual compositions. The music theories treat all compositions within a particular category as though they share something basic by virtue of belonging to that category. An analysis of a particular piece will have, as a central task, showing how the piece belongs to its category. Knowledge of the musical category is crucial for understanding other aspects of the piece, and this is especially obvious for the marked category. Knowing that a piece is twelve-tone gives you the starting point for interpreting all its details, as knowing that someone is homosexual might, on some views, give you the starting point for understanding many other things about them, and the same can be said for knowing that a piece is tonal, or a person heterosexual.

As with the presumption of monosexuality, there is a presumption that a composition should belong stably to one musical category. Babbitt's early essay on Bartók's string quartets embodies this presumption in an interesting ambivalence.[16] Babbitt admires the quartets, praising Bartók for the "identification of the personal exigency with the fundamental musical exigency of the epoch"; that is, Bartók's quartets not only show Bartók finding a way to write his next piece, but show him also addressing a compositional problem that is "crucial" for "contemporary musical composition." The problem, though Babbitt does not put it just this way, is where to go if you move away from tonality. In fact, as Babbitt emphasizes, Bartók does not forego tonality but combines it with other methods of organization that are non-tonal and unique to each piece; Bartók attempts to work with "two organizational principles." Babbitt admires the ingenuity of Bartók's solution: Bartók uses the more piece-specific organization for the moment-to-moment thematic elements, the pre-existing tonal system for larger-scale relationships. Still, Babbitt worries that the "highly attenuated tonality" requires extreme non-harmonic means to effect closure: "it is probably true that these thematic means which Bartók is obliged to use to achieve a sense of completeness are symptomatic of a difficulty inherent in an idiom where independent formalism is inhibited by the presence of functional harmony, but where the tonal functionality itself is too rarified and complex to effect unambiguous formal finality." That is, the diminished role of tonality leaves it unable to do its usual structural work, while the presence of the "attenuated tonality" prevents any purely non-tonal organization from taking effect.

Babbitt concludes that "Bartók's solution was a specific one, it cannot be duplicated"; that is, Bartók's engagement with the shared problems of contemporary composition may not have provided a generalizable solution. The essay does not mention twelve-tone music (nor, given its origin as program notes, should it). But it is easy to supply the additional thought that Babbitt elides: as Babbitt's other writings show, he felt that Schoenberg's twelve-tone music, fully abandoning tonality and taking up a different system, came much closer to a generalizable solution to the "exigency of the epoch."

Bartók's quartets fall between the clear-cut alternatives of tonal music and some fully non-tonal option like the twelve-tone system. Like bisexual people, they fall between two clear identities and can be described, in terms of those identities, only as a problematic mixture, a bit of one and a bit of the other. James Baker's book on Scriabin shows a similar approach: Baker identifies a repertory of "transitional" compositions, pieces written during Scriabin's transition from tonality to atonality, and analyzes them using both Schenkerian tonal theory and Forte's atonal set-theory.[17] These dichotomizing theories of sexuality and music yield a third category, or non-category, of mixed, transitional individuals, intelligible only as failed or exceptional instances of both main categories. Of course, given a mismatch between categories and individuals, one might conclude that the individuals render the categories problematic, rather than vice-versa, but that has not been the main tradition in sexual ideology or music theory. It is interesting that music theory, while attempting to defend some of the queer music at the margins of the repertory, should create its own group of misfits. Bisexual activists have made similar claims about some lesbian and gay political thought.[18]

6. Interpreting the Analogies

Music theorists, like sexologists, have pursued a discourse that creates a distinctive subject matter (musical structure, sexuality). A binary opposition dominates in each area, contrasting a marked, marginalized term with an unmarked term, perhaps associated with nature in some valorizing way. In both discourses, polemical defense of the marginalized category has included a constructionist argument that denies the naturalness of the unmarked category.[19] The categories are taken as basic, perhaps essential, for understanding individuals. The exclusiveness of the categories renders intermediate individuals problematic.

While striking analogies exist between the sexual and musical categories, the significance of the pattern is less clear. The identification of a structural "rhyme" between music theory and sexology is not, by itself, an adequate conclusion. To point out that a similar pattern appears in two areas of a culture is only the starting point for interpretation.[20] Certainly it would be hasty to attempt a translation of values from one area to the other. Even if Babbitt's influential conception of music theory resembles constructionist approaches to sexuality, a commitment to anti-homophobic politics has no immediate bearing on one's evaluation of non-tonal music! The very suggestion seems surreal.

Rather than rushing to evaluative conclusions, let me deepen the account. The similarities of sexual and musical categories belong to a larger pattern that constructs sexuality and musicality in similar ways, for me and for others who share my culture. In both the sexual and musical cases, the rigid categories I have described exist in tense interaction with other, more individualized and experiential qualities. Powerful institutions—especially the concert hall and academic music theory for music; medicine, law, and sexology for sexuality—have worked to create a universalized subject matter, an appropriate subject of abstract theoretical knowledge. Meanwhile, vernacular sexual and musical practices have interacted with and responded to the various institutions, without fully falling under their control.[21] The tension between scientistic, categorizing discourses and vernacular practices characterizes modern experiences of musicality and sexuality.[22]

And the vernacular practices of music and sex, like the theoretical inventions I have described, resemble each other closely. Musicality and sexuality both bring meaning and pleasure together in bodily experiences; and we speak of loving music, as we speak of loving another person.[23] In both cases, intensity, unruliness, and privacy characterize the practices. Think of music and sex as sources of intense, individualized pleasure, almost overwhelming and terribly difficult to describe. Think of them as, somehow, very personal but, at the same time, dangerously close to loss of self-control, self-loss. Think of them as realms of individual choice or self-discovery, areas for individual exploration. Think of them as, somehow, especially close to one's identity, so that knowledge of someone's sexual or musical tastes is intimate knowledge. And finally, think of sexuality and musicality as realms where difference can be disturbing: pondering sexual practices, or hearing music, different from what they personally favor, many people have strong, visceral responses of contempt and revulsion. Surely other teachers have had this experience: you play unfamiliar-sounding music, non-tonal perhaps, in the classroom, and some students express, verbally or otherwise, mingled incomprehension, rejection, and a sense of pleasurable superiority, a complex response that resembles some instances of homophobic disgust. In witnessing this musical disgust, I become powerfully aware of students' strongly physical responses to unnatural-seeming music.[24]

In short, not only do the theories about sexual and musical categories resemble each other, but they interact, as official scientific conceptualizations, with similar kinds of lived experience.

The sexual and musical dichotomies present themselves to adolescents and young adults—boys, especially—as crucial, identity-forming choices. (It is still males who are most readily understood, by themselves and by peers and mentors, as agents motivated by strong sexual or compositional desire. As I mentioned before, it is not possible to separate gender and sexuality for long.) I remember, as an undergraduate, feeling that some overwhelming outside force—my culture, I suppose—demanded that I place myself on one side of the street or the other, musically and sexually. I was a composition student, and the musical opposition confronted me directly every time I wanted to write music. In both musical and sexual spheres, it was clear that, as a late adolescent male, I was now expected to start settling into one or the other of two communities. As a composition student, and as a sexual being, I could accept a relatively bland, mainstream identity, respectable and middle-of-the-road, or I could pursue a more controversial, avant-garde way of life associated especially with certain notorious men in coastal cities. (Michael Musto, say; or Milton Babbitt, or Lance Loud.[25]) It was also clear that these decisions were supposed to issue from some kind of introspection, which would somehow tell me where I belonged. Alas, introspection let me down; as far as I could tell, tonal and non-tonal music, like the bodies of men and women, were equally fascinating. Something was wrong and, of course, I felt confused. I am sure many people have felt similar parallel anxieties about their relation to our prevailing musical and sexual dichotomies.

One might ask whether the musical categories are coded in terms of sexuality; that is, whether people who rely on the musical categories are also, inexplicitly, pairing them with specific sexualities. That is the type of claim I made in the essay on gender and music theory that I mentioned before: some styles of talking and writing are coded, stereotyped, as masculine, and mainstream music theory confines itself to those styles, and so it feels comfortable to many theorists as an expression of their masculinity. McClary's reading of sonata form makes a similar claim that aspects of musical style and succession are gender-coded and carry messages about gender relations. Certainly musical styles can carry coded implications of sexuality; think of disco and rock, for instance, long stereotyped as gay and straight.[26] But I doubt that such coding operates in the dichotomies I am discussing here; that is, I do not think that the tonal/non-tonal difference carries definite messages about sexualities. Babbitt denied that tonal music is "natural" and argued for the value of a stigmatized alternative practice. This creates, at an abstract level, a link between twelve-tone music and gayness, as does the role of non-tonal compositions as oddities, their queerness. But the example of Charles Ives's now-famous misogynist and homophobic rants shows the possibility of the other link, between traditional tonal music and homosexuality; Ives wanted to depict his own dissonant music as a healthy masculine response to the effeminacy of concert life.[27] And more generally, modernist innovation has sometimes expressed itself in harshly masculinist language.[28]

One cannot claim that the marginal role of non-tonal music makes it, somehow, the attractive style for homosexual composers. Non-tonal music is certainly not the mark of a gay composer. In fact, the notion that, in North America, non-tonal composers are most often straight, while many twentieth-century tonal composers are gay, circulates as musical gossip, recently elaborated in scholarly mode by Nadine Hubbs.[29] Of course, there is no contradiction if men who belong to a stigmatized sexual category choose a musical identity that is, in musical terms, more central. Indeed, if the sexual and musical categories are parallel in some ways, but some people have formed their identities in ways that cut across the matching categories, that suggests an intriguing, intricate story.

On the other hand, it would be a mistake to link non-tonal music too closely with composers' heterosexuality. Students trained by Milton Babbitt know of his deep respect for the twelve-tone music of Ben Weber, who was homosexual; some other well-publicized twelve-tone or serial composers, both European and North American, are widely assumed to be gay.[30] I heard such rumors about various twelve-tone composers from my adolescence on. Musicians who become seriously involved with twelve-tone music are not likely to associate it with straightness in an exclusive way. My own compositional training, by the way, did nothing to reinforce a link between tonality and homosexuality. My college composition teacher was a middle-aged straight man who wrote tonal music and reminded me a bit of my father (in fact, they had a composition teacher in common). My lessons with him consisted mainly of him trying to talk me out of my recurring twelve-tone tendencies. I felt isolated and misunderstood. I looked around at his straight male graduate students, happily writing tonal music, and wondered, "Am I the only one?"[31]

Of course, some non-tonal composers have gained considerable prestige and social power through their composition, receiving grants, holding significant academic positions, enjoying fine commissions, excellent performances, splendid recordings. The sexual and musical categories, non-tonal and gay, do not match in terms of empowerment. However, it is important not to exaggerate the power attributed to non-tonal and twelve-tone composers; as Joseph Straus has recently shown, the common notion that serial music had some kind of monopoly in post-war new music is wrong.[32]

Further, when non-tonal composers have sought the security of academic positions, this need not be understood simply as an attempt to dominate musical life or reduce musical diversity. When Babbitt has written about the academic institutionalization of modernist music, he depicts it not as an effort to dominate, but as a desperate attempt to survive musically. The well-known essay "The Composer as Specialist" (initially published, to Babbitt's chagrin, under an editor's coarser title, "Who Cares if You Listen?") is often read as an elitist dismissal of mainstream musical audiences, but it is also a plea for separatism or even for a closeting of non-tonal music, an effort to hide it and thereby protect it from uninformed negative judgments.[33] While it is undeniable that Babbitt achieved a position of great privilege for himself, as did some other like-minded composers, I am suggesting that he sought this privilege in part as a shelter for the queer music he wanted to make.

Seeing himself as "a member of a minority within a minority," Babbitt has typically lamented "the problems of a special music in an alien and inapposite world," and despaired of finding a large audience. Instead, he has recommended seclusion: "I dare suggest that the composer would do himself and his music an immediate and eventual service by total, resolute, and voluntary withdrawal from this public world to one of private performance and electronic media, with its very real possibility of complete elimination of the public and social aspects of composition." Just as the metaphor of the sexual "closet" figures secrecy and withdrawal through a closed space, Babbitt is drawn to figures of enclosure. Describing his preference for Schoenberg over Webern, Babbitt says that "Schoenberg was always a much more striking phenomenon for me—the idea of this hermetically sealed music by a hermetically sealed man." Responding to Wallace Berry's suggestion that twelve-tone music might be a cul-de-sac, Babbitt replies that "there are those of us who prefer the relative quiet and solace of the dead-end street to the distractions and annoyances of the crowded thorough-fare." The music itself seems to offer another closed, self-sufficient space, occupying "a five-dimensional musical space determined by pitch-class, register, dynamic, duration, and timbre." An alternative world; a place for us, somewhere over the rainbow. If, in these last passages, the enclosed spaces seem desirable (or at least, desired by Babbitt), in other passages the enclosure has the character of a desperate refuge. Babbitt has said that the survival of serious music depends on "the survival of the university . . . [as] the mightiest of fortresses against the overwhelming, outnumbering forces, both within and without the university, of anti-intellectualism, cultural populism, and passing fashion."[34] Such a passage can be read simply as an expression of elitism. Without denying or endorsing Babbitt's elitism, I want to draw attention to Babbitt's fear of exposure and destruction.

Perhaps, too, the scientific tone of Babbitt's music-theoretical work, broadly influential for North American music theory, can be seen as a kind of closeting. I am now singling out another aspect of Babbitt's thought, different from the aspects—his tonal/twelve-tone dichotomy, his construc-tionist metatheory—that I discussed earlier. The present point concerns Babbitt's recommendation of a scientific approach to theory and analysis. Theory and analysis, as Babbitt practiced them, seek impersonality and objectivity, and while many theorists have followed Babbitt in this, many other people have found such writing to be a bizarre response to music. Rather than taking Babbitt's approach to theory as a complete and accu-rate reflection of his musical world, I think it is promising to interpret the writing pragmatically and as a mark of self-division.

Think of Babbitt as someone who truly loves the strange music he com-poses, who gets from it the intense mental/physical pleasures that most of us, in our shared classical music culture and beyond, seek in music. Hoping to preserve that music, he seeks ways of describing it that meet the norms of mid-century academic discourse; perhaps this will ensure a place in the university, which he regards as "our last hope, our only hope, and ergo our best hope."[35] He finds that, in order to protect the pretty, delicate, odd music he loves, he needs to depict his work, theoretical and compositional, as though it is scientific research, despite the distance between his verbal-izations and musical experience. Not only does the academic setting hide his music from the antagonism of public concert audiences, his attempt to embrace academic norms camouflages and hides his music within the uni-versity. A masterful, masculine theoretical stance hides the vulnerable strangeness of his music. Thus, one important source of the self-alienating masculinity of contemporary music theory may lie in a strategic response to the perceived unnaturalness or queerness of twelve-tone music. The strat-egy has succeeded, on its own dubious terms. Some of the quirkiest, most eccentric music in the world became important to academic canons and curricula—but only on condition that it be depicted primarily through representational techniques that fall somewhere between science and accounting.[36]

The strategy has backfired as well, leading many people to attribute the qualities of Babbitt's writing, and of the theory and analysis he influenced, to the music it depicts, or more precisely, to limit the qualities of Babbitt's music to those denoted and connoted by Babbitt's own words. Hence the common but, to my ears, grossly inaccurate image of Babbitt's music itself, and not just the language he recommended, as having the aggressive butch asceticism of science, math, or logical empiricist philosophy. My interpretative suggestions about Babbitt depend on the possibility of distinguishing between qualities of his music and of his verbal discourse. (My own experiences of listening to Babbitt's music require me to make this distinction. However, in this essay I make the distinction seem rather clean, as though Babbitt's musical and verbal minds have little effect on each other, and that is undoubtedly too simple.)[37] Babbitt himself warned against something like this elision, emphasizing the difference between music and the languages used to describe it.[38] At the same time, he issued terrifying warnings against the kind of impressionistic, subjective, autobiographical discourse that some of us, nonetheless, find crucial in confessing our musical loves, in describing and praising the objects of those loves.

Further consideration of all these issues would have to expand to a richer sense of the various constructed meanings of musicality and sexuality. While I am sure that there have been similarities and associations between the categories of homosexuality and nontonal/twelve-tone music, other patterns complicate the account. For one thing, as I mentioned, the twentieth century has seen many prominent homosexual composers of tonal music. More generally, musicality, in our culture, already has a strange status, both privileged and abnormal. Mainstream tastes and interests, as judged from within the institutions of classical music, are not necessarily mainstream in light of broader social norms; in recent Western society generally, classical music has strong, if vague, associations with effeminacy and homosexuality.[39] These important facts show that the present essay has sketched one part of a rather complex picture. I must end by recommending consideration, in particular lives, of the consequences of the parallels I have described. There is no reason to expect the results to be simple or uniform.[40]

Notes

1. Another contrast, between tonal music and twelve-tone or serial music, sometimes blurs into or replaces the tonal/non-tonal contrast, in both critical writing and music theory. I return to this alternative contrast later.

2. J. Peter Burkholder, "Museum Pieces: The Historicist Mainstream in Music of the Last Hundred Years," *Journal of Musicology* 2, no. 2 (Spring 1983): 115–34. My account of the musical museum depends heavily on Burkholder's, though I have often put things my own way and chosen my own emphases. At a few points, indicated in notes, I am particularly aware of going beyond Burkholder's claims, but there is subtler revision, as well as dependence, throughout. See also Lydia Goehr, *The Imaginary Museum of Musical Works* (New York: Oxford University Press, 1992).

3. This statement simplifies: obviously there is no one uniform ideology of the concert hall. There is a range of practices and ideologies, just as there is a range of conceptions of history and roles for historical thought in present musical experience. Here and throughout, my essay operates at an alarming level of abstraction, working with idealizations for the sake of clear generalization. It is, I think, the only way to do the particular conceptual work I want to do; I end the essay by recommending a return to more concrete, individualized studies.

4. For splendid discussion of issues about this other kind of museum, see Barbara Kirschenblatt-Gimblett, *Destination Culture: Tourism, Museums, and Heritage* (Berkeley: University of California Press, 1998).

5. The exceptions, specialized concert institutions for new music, exist because of this general neglect. In my emphasis on the marginality of new music, I follow Burkholder's essay less strictly than elsewhere. I am indebted to unpublished work by Maura Bosch, who has asked, very reasonably, why women should strive to write music that might enter the musical museum, when the best they can hope for, there, is yet another relation of public subordination to men. Bosch, "The Will to Change," presented at Feminist Theory and Music 4; Charlottesville, Virginia, June 1997.

6. Here again, I move beyond Burkholder's account.

7. However, Susan McClary has recently written about the beginnings of tonality in a more exciting and accessible way. See her *Conventional Wisdom: the Content of Musical Form* (Berkeley: University of California Press, 2000).

8. The match is not quite perfect; the concert repertory and the canon studied by music theorists diverge, with theorists tending toward a high proportion of Germanic absolute music. But, more basic than the discrepancies in work-lists, the theorist's canon and the concert repertory agree in placing tonal music at the center. The compositions in the repertory that theorists typically ignore (for instance, music by Dvořák, Bruch, or Saint-Säens) are still, almost always, tonal music, describable by the theorists' general account of tonality. On the need for separate concepts of repertory and canon, see Joseph Kerman, "A Few Canonic Variations," in his *Write All These Down* (Berkeley: University of California Press, 1994), 33–50.

9. Susan McClary, *Feminine Endings: Music, Gender, and Sexuality* (Minneapolis: University of Minnesota Press, 1991).

10. Maus, "Masculine Discourse in Music Theory," *Perspectives of New Music* 31, no. 2 (Summer 1993): 264–93.

11. Carole Vance's "Social Construction Theory and Sexuality" is an especially clear brief account of constructionist views of sexuality (in *Constructing Masculinity*, ed. Maurice Berger, Brian Wallis, and Simon Watson [New York: Routledge, 1995], 37–48).

12. Recent treatments of bisexuality have offered effective criticism of these

widespread beliefs. Marjorie Garber, *Vice Versa: Bisexuality and the Eroticism of Everyday Life* (New York: Simon and Schuster, 1996) is especially rich and provocative. Good empirical sources include Martin S. Weinberg, Colin J. Williams, and Douglas W. Prior, *Dual Attraction: Understanding Bisexuality* (New York: Oxford University Press, 1994), and Erwin J. Haeberle and Rolf Gindolf, eds., *Bisexualities: The Ideology and Practice of Sexual Contact with Both Men and Women* (New York: Continuum, 1998).

13. These arguments are present in some of Babbitt's earliest publications, a group of very brilliant book reviews published in the *Journal of the American Musicological Society* 3, no. 1 (Spring 1950): 57–60; 3, no. 3 (Fall 1950): 264–67; and 5, no. 3 (Fall 1952): 260–65. *The Collected Essays of Milton Babbitt*, ed. Stephen Peles et al. (Princeton: Princeton University Press, 2003), appeared while the present book was at press. I have not revised my page references to Babbitt's essays, but they may now be found far more conveniently, in the one volume.

14. I think Babbitt's focus on musical systems is clear, though Joseph Dubiel's careful essay "What's the Use of the Twelve-Tone System?" (*Perspectives of New Music* 35, no. 2 [Summer 1997]: 33–51) argues effectively that it is not as exclusive an interest as many have supposed.

15. Allen Forte, *The Structure of Atonal Music* (New Haven, Conn.: Yale University Press, 1973).

16. "The String Quartets of Béla Bartók," in *Musical Quarterly* 35 (1949): 377–85. The statements that I cite in the text are from pp. 377, 378, 388, 384, and 385 of this article.

17. James M. Baker, *The Music of Alexander Scriabin* (New Haven, Conn.: Yale University Press, 1986).

18. The classic anthology of bisexual activism is Loraine Hutchins and Lani Kaahumanu, eds., *Bi Any Other Name: Bisexual People Speak Out* (Boston: Alyson Publications, 1991). For a more recent and more gleeful approach, see Carol Queen and Lawrence Schimel, eds., *Pomosexuals: Challenging Assumptions about Gender and Sexuality* (San Francisco: Cleis Press, 1997). I sometimes find these writers too dismissive of the courage and achievements of lesbian and gay activists; I admire the attempt, in Alan Sinfield, *Gay and After* (London: Serpent's Tail, 1998) to balance respect for activist traditions with recognition that traditional gay politics has excluded many people.

19. The musical argument continues beyond Babbitt, of course: some recent writers have made new attempts to distinguish natural and unnatural music. George Rochberg, in making his famous return to tonality, asked questions like this: "What are the risks facing a composer who runs counter to the natural functions of the central nervous system and literally goes so far as to destroy their correspondence with musical structure?" *The Aesthetics of Survival* (Ann Arbor: University of Michigan Press, 1984), 223. Or see Fred Lerdahl, "Cognitive Constraints on Compositional Systems," in *Generative Processes in Music: The Psychology of Performance, Improvisation, and Composition*, ed. John A. Sloboda (New York: Oxford University Press, 1988), 231–59. Meanwhile, the constructionist side of the debate is not unequivocally affirmative of the marginalized categories. Constructionist accounts of sexuality may, in fact, support the hope that homosexual people can cease to exist, and gay activists sometimes favor arguments for the natural (psychologically or biologically based) status of homosexuality. Schoenberg, of course, defended his

own use of dissonance by appeal to the overtone series. See, for instance, his *Theory of Harmony*, trans. Roy E. Carter (London: Faber and Faber, 1978), 318–22.

20. For discussion of "homology" as a concept in ethnomusicology and cultural studies, see John Shepherd and Peter Wicke, *Music and Cultural Theory* (Cambridge: Polity Press, 1997), 34–55, and Jane C. Sugarman, *Engendering Song: Singing and Subjectivity at Prespa Albanian Weddings* (Chicago: University of Chicago Press, 1997), 24–26.

21. By "vernacular musical practices," I mean everyday musical life, in relation to whatever kind of music a person engages. (I do not mean to evoke the particular musics that are sometimes called "vernacular.") Vernacular practices exist in relation to classical music institutions, often with veiled acknowledgement, if any, in public discourses. See, for instance, Wayne Koestenbaum's treatment of the practices of opera queens: *The Queen's Throat: Opera, Homosexuality, and the Mystery of Desire* (New York: Poseidon Press, 1993).

22. These tensions might encourage the idea of sexuality as a natural force, incompletely mastered by science and powerful social institutions. But I mean to describe the tensions in a constructionist spirit: the vernacular practices, institutions, and scientistic discourses are all historical, contingent phenomena.

23. Musicologists have explored such issues recently. Examples of this work include Philip Brett, "Musicality, Essentialism, and the Closet"; Suzanne G. Cusick, "On a Lesbian Relation with Music: A Serious Attempt Not to Think Straight," both in *Queering the Pitch: The New Gay and Lesbian Musicology*, ed. Brett, Elizabeth Wood, and Gary C. Thomas (New York: Routledge, 1994); Marion A. Guck, "Music Loving, or, the Relationship with the Piece," in *Journal of Musicology* 15, no. 3 (Summer 1997): 343–52; Paul Attinello, "Performance and/or Shame: A Mosaic of Gay (and Other) Perceptions," in *repercussions* 4, no. 2 (Fall 1995): 97–129; and my "Love Stories," in the same issue of *repercussions*, 86–96.

24. It might seem that there is an important contrast: homophobia has crucial elements of fascination and desire. But I do not think these elements are necessarily absent in responses to strange music. In antagonistic reactions to non-tonal music, I often sense a wary fascination and responsiveness, along with a somewhat willful rejection. Nonetheless, my brief remark in this essay leaves much to explore about the phenomenology of these negative responses. I am not, of course, suggesting that negative responses to non-tonal music have anything like the social importance of homophobia, one of our most destructive and most widely tolerated prejudices.

25. Michael Musto's columns in the *Village Voice* have, for years, exported an in-your-face urban homosexual culture across the nation. In one episode of the memorable early-1970s PBS documentary *An American Family*, Lance Loud, the oldest son, took his mother on a tour of gay New York. I, for one, had never seen anything like it; my little jaw dropped.

26. See the contrasts in Richard Dyer's classic essay "In Defense of Disco," in *Only Entertainment* (New York: Routledge, 1992), 149–58; the essay was first published in *Gay Left* in 1979.

27. See Judith Tick, "Charles Ives and Gender Ideology," in *Musicology and Difference: Gender and Sexuality in Music Scholarship*, ed. Ruth Solie (Berkeley: University of California Press, 1993), 83–106, for a discussion of Ives's misogynist and homophobic rhetoric. See below, note 36, for further comment on Tick.

28. Catherine Parsons Smith, "'A Distinguishing Virility': Feminism and Mod-

ernism in American Art Music," in *Cecilia Reclaimed: Feminist Perspectives on Gender and Music,* ed. Susan C. Cook and Judy S. Tsou (Urbana: University of Illinois Press, 1994), pp. 90–106.

29. Nadine Hubbs, "A French Connection: Modernist Codes in the Musical Closet." *GLQ: A Journal of Lesbian and Gay Studies* 6, no. 3 (spring 2000): 399–412. Hubb's splendid book on this subject will appear shortly: *The Queer Composition of America's Sound: Gay Modernists, American Music, and National Identity* (Berkeley: University of California Press, 2004).

30. Paul Attinello, in unpublished work, has been studying the presence of homosexuality in Darmstadt circles. Readers will have noticed that I omit names of composers here. I have no desire to be coy, but I do not know whether these men are open about their sexuality in public, professional settings. So it goes.

31. In the end, these lessons, along with some other experiences, extinguished all my compositional desires, not just the non-tonal ones. I turned with relief to what seemed, at the time, the infinitely saner world of music scholarship.

32. Joseph N. Straus, "The Myth of Serial 'Tyranny' in the 1950s and 1960s," *Musical Quarterly* 83, no. 3 (fall 1999): 301–43.

33. Until the publication of Babbitt's *Collected Essays* (see note 13), this essay was most conveniently available in Elliott Schwartz and Barney Childs, eds., *Contemporary Composers on Contemporary Music* (New York: Holt, Rinehart and Winston, 1967), 243–50. It was originally published in 1958. One of Babbitt's lectures at the University of Wisconsin, Madison, in 1983 constitutes an updated review of the same terrain: "The Unlikely Survival of Serious Music," in Milton Babbitt, *Words about Music,* ed. Stephen Dembski and Joseph N. Straus, (Madison: University of Wisconsin Press, 1987), 163–83.

34. These quotations come from the following sources: "Some Aspects of Twelve-Tone Composition," *The Score and I.M.A. Magazine* 12 (June 1955): 53; "The Composer as Specialist," 249; *Words about Music,* 24; *Sounds and Words: A Critical celebration of Milton Babbitt at 60,* a special double issue of *Perspectives of New Music* 14, no.1 (Spring 1976): 2–15, 22; "The Composer as Specialist," 245; *Words about Music,* 163.

35. *Words about Music,* 183.

36. Joseph Dubiel's superb work on Babbitt has emphasized the importance of describing the music without depending primarily on Babbitt's own descriptive style. See his "Three Essays on Milton Babbitt," in *Perspectives of New Music* 28, no. 2 (Summer 1990): 216–61; 29, no. 1 (Winter 1991): 90–122; and 30, no. 1 (Winter 1992): 82–131. I have written briefly about Babbitt's music (along the same lines as the present essay) in the liner notes for *Milton Babbitt: Piano Music since 1983,* Martin Goldray, piano (CRI CD 746 [1997]). This interpretation of Babbitt's words as a form of closeting draws on my general account of gendered music-theoretical language in "Masculine Discourse in Music Theory" (see note 10). Tick's essay on Ives (see note 27) makes an argument similar to mine: she suggests that the aggressive masculinity of Ives's verbal commentary responds to a perception of powerlessness in relation to established musical institutions. By depicting concert life as effeminate, his own work as masculine, Ives attempts to reverse the power hierarchy. Thus, Ives's rhetoric, rather than simply revealing a masculinism in his music, is in part a defensive response to a sense of (feminizing?) powerlessness. With Tick, I am suggesting that one needs to allow for complexity, in particular for the likelihood of

defensiveness and consequent misrepresentation of musicality, in interpreting masculine discourse about music. Smith (see note 28) seems to take the opposite approach, reading composers' masculinist language as revealing the qualities of their music.

37. A further, very important issue concerns the interaction between performances of Babbitt's music and the common ideologies and images of modernism. Some expert performances seem to strive for the harsh, aggressive qualities that are, for many people, typical modernist traits. Others bring out, much more, the delicate, playful, melodious, sensuous qualities that I value highly. Clear examples would be, for the first style, "Sextets" and "The Joy of More Sextets," performed by Rolf Schulte and Alan Feinberg (New World NW 364-2, 1988); for the second style, Martin Goldray's inspiring performances of Babbitt's piano music (see note 36).

38. "The formal-interpreted theory issue leads immediately to that of the distinction between metalanguage and object language, which arises as soon as a composition (object language) is referred to by a natural or formalized language (metalanguage), or when such a collection of references are themselves discussed in a meta-metalanguage. If this distinction between object language and metalanguage is maintained most vividly by the very difference between the act of composing and the act of talking about composing, the most vulgar and—therefore—most frequently encountered violation of this distinction is that in which a musical composition and—by faulty extension—a body of music are labelled 'mathematical' because an expression containing mathematic terms . . . under suitable interpretation, accurately characterizes some aspect of the musical composition." The passage continues, elaborating the point. "Contemporary Music Composition and Music Theory as Contemporary Intellectual History," in *Perspectives in Musicology*, ed. Barry S. Brook, Edward O. D. Downes, and Sherman van Solkema (New York: W. W. Norton, 1972), 162.

39. This is one emphasis of Brett's essay on essentialism and musicality; see note 23.

40. I presented versions of this essay at the conferences Feminist Theory and Music 5 (London, 1999) and the 1999 Meeting of the Society for Music Theory (in that Society's first session devoted to queer issues). A number of remarkable people read drafts and gave wonderfully helpful comments: Arved Ashby, Joseph Auner, Philip Brett, Mark Butler, Joseph Dubiel, Nadine Hubbs, Martin Scherzinger, and Elizabeth Tolbert. I hesitate to think what the essay would be like without the improvements that their comments made possible. I am also grateful for encouragement from Kevin Clifton, Charles Fisk, Roger Graybill, Marianne Kielian-Gilbert, and Deborah Stein. I am especially indebted to Scherzinger, whose ideas on musical and sexual inversion inspired me to write this essay. See his "Anton Webern and the Concept of Symmetrical Inversion: A Reconsideration on the Terrain of Gender," *repercussions* 6, no.2 (1997): 63–147.

8

Listening to Schizophrenia: The Wozzeck Case

Jeremy Tambling

Since I shall argue that *Wozzeck* may be understood in terms of schizophrenia, I want to use this as a model to approach the modernism of Berg's opera. Since both schizophrenia and modernism foreground a disjunction between the signifier and the signified, so that both work with the breakdown of unitary meaning, I explore in this paper how Berg's opera, which is at the core of modernism, both allows for such disjunctions but also tries to recontain them within a musical unity. In focusing on what is not unified but radically disparate, Berg's opera asks us to listen to schizophrenia as all that there is: this would, of course, be a postmodern reading, deriving from the work of Deleuze and Guattari.[1] In arguing for unity, the opera continues a process of imposition of order whose musical potential does not contradict the tendency in modernism to believe in a truth to be found beyond the fragmentary.

To explore this, I want to work cumulatively, working forwards from Büchner's *Woyzeck*, which I see as proto-modernist in its composition and modernist in the time of its reception: its first performance in 1913, the anniversary of Büchner's birth, its first performance in Vienna in 1914 when Berg saw it, and its production as an opera in 1925.

1. Büchner's *Woyzeck*

Not until 1914, and the researches of Hugo Beiber, was it realized that Büchner's *Woyzeck*, which had until then been published with the name *Wozzeck*, related to the case of a man who had been beheaded in the public square in Leipzig.

On the evening of 3 June 1821, Johann Christian Woyzeck, a barber, stabbed to death the forty-six-year-old widow of a surgeon named Woost in the doorway of her house, using a broken sword-blade. Woyzeck was arrested, and Dr. Clarus, medical adviser to the court, was asked to report after Woyzeck had confessed. His assessment of the prisoner—a virtual postmortem—appeared in September 1821, and the execution was fixed for November 1822. Doubts over Woyzeck's sanity persisted, and a second assessment by Clarus, pronouncing him responsible and therefore fit for execution, appeared in 1823. After the execution, the medical adviser to the Bamberg court raised objections in a pamphlet, "Was the murderer J. C. Woyzeck, executed on 27 August 1824 in Leipzig, responsible for his actions?" Dr. Clarus replied by publishing his two reports in which he showed how he judged Woyzeck to be sane. Büchner's father, who was a doctor, must have read these, and so must his son, for they form source material for *Woyzeck*. So Woyzeck's life emerged after his death. Born in 1780, orphaned at thirteen, he had wandered over Germany looking for work. He had been a mercenary soldier. Demobilized in 1815 he had become a hairdresser in Leipzig, where he had taken up with Frau Woost. Before that, he had fathered a child with another woman but could not marry because his papers were not in order. Maurice Benn, whose account of *Woyzeck* is the most complete in English, shows, however, that Büchner worked from more cases than Woyzeck's: a murder by Daniel Schmolling, who had killed his mistress in 1817, as written up by Dr. Horn in the *Archiv für medizinische Erfahrung* in Berlin in 1830; and from Johann Diess, who stabbed his mistress in 1830. Diess, condemned to life imprisonment, died in prison in 1834, and his body was dissected at Giessen during the very period when Büchner was studying anatomy. Büchner's *Woyzeck* is a composite of these men.[2]

In Büchner's play, Woyzeck is the victim of the Captain, representing the army, and the doctor, representing the court proceedings. Woyzeck cuts the captain's hair, compressing two aspects of Woyzeck's life: army service and barbering. He is the victim of the doctor's crazy medical experiments, while the doctor embodies aspects of Clarus in himself, requiring confession and judging the behavior of Woyzeck like a policeman, and pronouncing on his mental state, as here:

> WOYZECK: Doctor, have you ever seen nature double? When the sun's at noon and it's like the whole world was going up in flames? That's when a terrible voice spoke to me.
> DOCTOR: Woyzeck, you have an *aberratio*. . . . A classic case of *aberratio mentalis partialis* of the second order. Nicely developed too. I shall give you a rise, Woyzeck. Yes, second category: *idée fixe* but otherwise generally rational. . . .[3]

Notions of the *idée fixe* began around 1812 with Dr. Etienne Esquirol (1772–1840) who called an obsession a "monomania"; the Doctor speaks a then-contemporary medical discourse in accounting for Woyzeck as a mono-maniac.[4] He could be quoting Esquirol, who said that "the character of mania is a general delirium whose principle lies in the disorder of the

understanding, a disorder which entails also that of the moral feelings. . . .
For partial delirium we keep the term 'monomania.'"[5] The historic Woyzeck
had told Clarus of his delusions. He had paranoid feelings about the Freemasons; and he had had a dream where "he saw three fiery faces in the sky,
of which the middle one was the largest. He connected these three faces
with the trinity, and the middle one with Christ. . . ." He heard voices:
having encountered his mistress on the dance-floor dancing with another,
"when he was in bed he was full of jealousy, thinking about the church
festival and of his mistress there. And thought he could hear the violins and
basses all mixed together, and imputed the words 'On we go! On we go!'
[*immer zu*] to them." Also he believed that he heard "an invisible voice
admonishing him, 'Stab the Woost-woman (the she-wolf) to death!'"[6] Clarus
had not regarded this as definite proof that Woyzeck was mad, and concluded in his second report that "the only motive for the crime was the
preponderance of passion over reason."[7] The conversations with Clarus in
the condemned cell which were reported to the world at large after Woyzeck's
death are typified by this dialogue with the doctor. But while Clarus might
not believe Woyzeck, the dramatist does, showing it with his references to
the Freemasons (these survive in the opera, Act 1, Scene 2), his vision of
fire in the sky, and above all, in listening to Woyzeck's voices—already
musicalized, before Büchner or Berg gives them attention.

Woyzeck—first published by K. E. Franzos in 1879 and called *Wozzeck*—
is a collection of fragments from four different drafts, and no two editions
agree on an order for its scenes. Franzos's order was altered in 1909 by
Paul Landau's edition, which Berg worked from. The texts of Werner
Lehmann (1967) and of Egon Krause (1969) change this order, making the
play start not with the hairdressing scene, but with what in the opera is
Scene 2: Woyzeck and Andres cutting sticks. In almost his first statement,
Woyzeck speaks of a head rolling—a proleptic utterance in view of his
execution, and giving a sense of the social unconscious of the period, which
is formed by images of the guillotine, and also showing Woyzeck's sense of
himself as the *corps morcelé*, the body in pieces. Woyzeck describes the
head as though it were a hedgehog: hair standing on end, the picture of
horror, of Medusa-like petrification. He feels that the ground below him is
hollow and, related to what he tells the doctor, that the sky is on fire.

On this reading, the play begins with Woyzeck's alienation from "normal" reality. When Marie in the next scene asks him why he looks so bad,
he replies with his vision of the city as Sodom and Gomorrah, quoting
Genesis: "And behold, there was a smoke coming from the land like the
smoke of an oven."[8] The action continues with a fairground scene and
shows Marie with the earrings given by the Drum Major. Only then does it
turn to Woyzeck shaving the Captain, "a parody, not of a soldier, but of a
stupid provincial bourgeois" in his moralistic remarks.[9] After Marie suc-
cumbs to the Drum Major, and Woyzeck confronts her with his knowledge

of it, comes the dialogue between the Doctor and Woyzeck, who has sold his body to be used for the doctor's scientific experiments. This is followed by the Doctor and the Captain together on the street, where the Doctor first reduces the Captain to a state of nerves, and the Captain contemplates what will be said after his death, as it were at the postmortem—"He was a good chap. A good chap."[10] Both then join in teasing Woyzeck.[11] A little later, Wozzeck sees Marie and the Drum Major dancing together in the tavern, Marie saying "Immer zu" as she dances past, to which Woyzeck responds, "Immer zu." "Again, again?"—"Encore, encore!"—it is as though recognizing the machinic power of repetition, life as repetition, as Freud shows in *Beyond the Pleasure Principle,* and so an alienated state which Berg's music responds to. Going out into the open country, Wozzeck hears the voice from the hollow ground:

> On and on, on and on [*immer zu*]. Scrape and squeak—that's the fiddles and flutes. On and on. Ssh. Music. Who's speaking down there? What's that you say? Louder, louder. Stab the she-wolf dead. Stab. The. She-wolf. Dead. Must I? Do I hear it up there too? Is that the wind saying it? I keep on hearing it, on and on. Stab her dead. Dead.[12]

In Scene 13, in the same bed as Andres, Woyzeck tries to tell him about the voices:

> I can't sleep. When I shut my eyes everything spins round and I hear the fiddles. On and on. And then a voice comes out of the wall. Don't you hear anything?[13]

Two scenes later, in this ordering of the action, Woyzeck buys a knife from the Jewish pawnbroker. Scene 16 shows Marie with her child and reading the Bible, the Old Testament, and then two separate places in the New Testament, while Karl the idiot lies on the floor and tells fairy tales. In Scene 17, Woyzeck speaks with total flatness of affect, and signs over his belongings to Andres, as though dead already, as no more than a set of statistics. Everything that will come later, including his killing of Marie and whatever happens to him afterwards, is postmortem.

> Friedrich Johann Franz Woyzeck, rifleman, Four Company, Second battalion, Second Regiment. Born on the feast of the Annunciation, 20th July. I'm thirty years, seven months, and twelve days old today.[14]

In Scene 18, Marie is with the girls at the front door, and the grandmother tells a story of the poor little boy with no father or mother; "everything was dead, and there was nobody left in the whole wide world." When the boy goes to heaven, heaven is dead, and "when he wanted to go back to earth, the earth was an upturned pot."[15] At the end of the scene Woyzeck comes to take Marie, and murders her. Passers-by hear cries, but in Scene

21, Woyzeck is back at the tavern. The children go to see Marie's body; and in the last two scenes Woyzeck returns to the pond, looking for the knife, and goes into the water.

This arrangement of scenes, however, is still forced to leave out fragments from other drafts. In one, Woyzeck is ignored by his son, who is playing with the idiot, Karl. In another, the Court Usher, the Barber, the Doctor, and the Judge appear while the policeman says "A good murder, a real lovely murder. You couldn't wish for a nicer job. We haven't had one like this for years." This might be the prelude to an inquest, or a postmortem or a trial, if it is assumed that Woyzeck does not drown, but stands trial like the historical Woyzeck. To construct *Woyzeck* for stage production, by fixing a linear order, must entail some repression of aspects of the text that do not fit, that differ from others. Its fragmentariness makes it modernist; its non-unified character de-codes it, as Deleuze and Guattari would put it, making it like a schizophrenic text in its resistance to a single structure.

2. Opera and Schizophrenia

At the time of the dispute in Germany whether Woyzeck was mad or not, the word "hallucination" was newly appearing, with a medical sense attached to it. Esquirol first used it in 1817: "A man . . . who has the inward conviction of a presently perceived sensation at a moment when no external object capable of arousing this sensation is within the field of his senses, is in a state of hallucination."[16] Hallucinations became significant in French texts in the 1830s, at the time of Woyzeck.[17] In the history of writing about psychotic states, "schizophrenia" (meaning "a split mind") was first named between 1908 and 1911, by Swiss psychiatrist Eugen Bleuler. The word belongs to the moment of modernism, to the articulation of the split between the signifier and the signified, the basis of the linguistics of Saussure, who died in 1914, and it finds an echo in the first performances of *Woyzeck* (as *Wozzeck*) as a text of schizophrenia. The question whether schizophrenia is a "modernist" condition—Deleuze and Guattari call it "our very own malady"[18]—is asked by Louis A. Sass. He finds "a remarkable similarity between the schizophrenic and the modern condition" in his study of Judge Daniel Paul Schreber and his autobiographical *Memoirs of My Nervous Illness*.[19] Inclining to the view that "there was a significant rise in the incidence of insanity or lunacy in the nineteenth century but that this increase consisted largely of patients with the illness we now call schizophrenia,"[20] his book *Madness and Modernism* shows it with examples from all forms of modern artistic practice, with the exception of music. In this essay, I try to say something where Sass is silent.

Classically, as set forth by K. Schneider in 1957, schizophrenia has four symptoms. The first of the symptoms is auditory hallucinations, which take three forms. Hearing voices that speak your thoughts aloud; hearing voices talk about you; hearing voices carry on a running commentary on you. A second symptom is interference in thinking processes—where the subject loses the sense that his or her thought processes are individual and private. Thoughts are inserted from outside, or thoughts are taken out of the mind, or the subject feels that their thoughts are disseminated amongst others. Third, there are feelings of passivity with regard to the body, where the subject no longer has autonomy over this. Last, there are delusions, which put the subject into the centre of a persecutory universe.[21]

Woyzeck in Büchner's play suffers from most of these symptoms, so that his motivations are beyond what can be accessed by any rationalism. This makes the play necessarily incomplete, necessarily unable to be seen whole, since Woyzeck's actions rest on something outside, which neither he nor we can grasp, though it is also true that his madness comes from irreconcilable demands made upon him by the Captain, the doctor, by his army life, and by his relationship with Marie. The necessity of all these responsibilities is spelled out in the money he gives to Marie in Act 2, Scene 1 of the opera. At the beginning of the opera, the Captain interpellates Wozzeck as an obsessive by the words "Langsam, Wozzeck, langsam, Eins nach dem Andern!" which mean that the Captain wants him to do what he cannot do and go steady, one thing after another, one thing at a time in a sequence that represses.

But before schizophrenia is pathologized too easily in this taxonomy, it should be recalled that hearing voices is basic to opera: Tannhäuser's listening to the voice of the other as he hears Venus's music in the singing contest demonstrates a schizophrenic tendency in a proto-Modernist work; so too Isolde at the end of *Tristan und Isolde* is in an hallucinating state where she asks "Do I alone hear this melody, so wondrously and gently sounding from within him, in bliss lamenting, all-expressing . . . piercing me, soaring aloft, its sweet echoes resounding about me?"[22] And she *is* alone, her experience the definitive one, as Tannhäuser's may also be. Isolde and Tannhäuser are both schizophrenics, which is their heroism and Wagner's modernism, and Wagnerian motifs in relation to hallucinatory states and schizophrenia. Since opera vocalizes thought in a way that embarrasses nineteenth- and twentieth-century drama, and since it adds to that objectification a further "voice" in orchestral sound, it implies an hallucinatory state inherently, whether or not it includes the overt signs of voices speaking to a protagonist. The orchestral sound may be alienating in relation to the emotion on stage, or confirmatory of it—Wagnerian motifs may be either of these things—but the two forms of sound, vocal and orchestral, may be put together as the exterior representation of conscious or unconscious processes.

Since opera-going itself is premised on listening to voices, and audiences may be courting a shizophrenic state in desiring to hear, in opera, the voice of the other, it should be added that schizophrenia cannot be considered in pathological terms only. Deleuze and Guattari, whose topic this is, use "schizoanalysis," which takes issue with psychoanalysis as an attempt to re-code "other" experiences in a way which insists on single truth ("psychoanalysis" assumes in its name the existence of the single psyche: "schizoanalysis" begins with the doubleness, the fragmentariness of psychic processes) to illustrate how alterity becomes pathologized. Modernist culture, as with Freud, recognizes doubleness, signs of the other; but Deleuze and Guattari accuse it and psychoanalysis of returning to a belief in a unitary truth. *Woyzeck* as the text for the opera *Wozzeck* includes accounts of hearing voices, and perhaps it is symptomatic of a "normalizing" tendency in Berg that he should have cut the scene where Woyzeck hears the voice speaking to him—though he still keeps the moment when he tells Andres about it (Act 2, Scene 5 in the opera). The question for this paper is whether Berg could listen, as Büchner could, to schizophrenia. Does *Wozzeck* contain signs of the doubleness that marks Büchner's attention to Woyzeck's fragmented state?

3. Berg, *Woyzeck,* and *Wozzeck*

Critics of Berg's *Wozzeck* do not often concern themselves with the notion of the opera as being double. George Perle, who has been the most authoritative critic of Berg since the 1950s,[23] concludes his volume on *Wozzeck* with reference to "the coherence and unity of the work . . . in terms of the interdependence and interaction of all the structural elements" of the opera that he says his book has identified, along with a further promise of "larger relationships" that he says he has not yet given.[24] Perle's argument assumes autobiographical features in the text: that Berg identified with aspects of Wozzeck, on account of his own history in the Austrian military during the First World War—"there is a bit of me in his character. . . . I have been spending these war years just as dependent on people I hate, have been in chains, sick, captive, resigned, in fact, humiliated."[25] Perle speculates that "an unconscious affinity between the composer and his subject is reflected [in Act 1, Scene 4] in the parallel between Berg's preoccupations with the symbolism of numbers and Wozzeck's preoccupation with the symbolism of the geometrical patterns made by 'the toadstools growing in rings on the ground.'" It sorts with this aligning of Wozzeck and Berg that Douglas Jarman should refer to Berg's "*obsessive* preoccupation with labyrinthine formal designs, intricate symmetries, palindromes and other such 'abstract' and highly organized structural devices."[26] Perle also draws attention to the symphonic interlude, between the death of Wozzeck (Act 3,

Scene 4) and the last scene, which uses motifs related to Wozzeck from the whole opera.[27] He quotes Berg as saying, five years after the opera opened, that this interlude is "the composer's confession, breaking through the framework of the dramatic plot and, likewise, even as an appeal to the audience, which is here meant to represent humanity itself."[28] The conceit of the composer confessing makes this an autobiographical, even romantic text, issuing from a damaged life. If we read Perle's account of *Wozzeck* critically, it would seem that a partial loss of Berg's stability of self, which finds its mirror in Wozzeck's melancholia and despair, has been translated, in an Hegelian *Aufhebung,* into the coherence and stability of the work itself— and that art as so often in opera criticism, redeems life. When Joseph Kerman writes about the symphonic interlude—"Wozzeck is dead, the curtain is down, and the music now connotes a sanity and a relief in warm contrast to the hysterical world of the stage, from which the audience has just been rescued"—he expresses the ideology most clearly.[29] The symphonic interlude flatters the audience that they are normal, i.e. "humanity itself," and that they are able to be confessed to. Kerman, it seems, cannot wait to get back to normal.

In *Lulu,* the composer Alwa, whose construction in the text makes him a figure of Berg's autobiography, says about Lulu, that "it would be interesting to write an opera about her," while the orchestra sounds the opening chords from *Wozzeck.* To write an opera about Lulu has postmortem aspects about it: its aestheticizing objectifies the woman, only less intensely than the way Jack does. The motif from *Wozzeck* proclaims a certain satisfaction with that opera as a completed work of art, even as a conventional work, as perhaps Schoenberg knew when he wrote to his "student," soon after the opera's opening night, that "almost every scene builds to a great orchestral *fff.*"[30] If the opera has within it those elements of conventionality and even of self-satisfaction, they may be symbolized by a detail in Berg's correspondence and in his annotations to a copy of the play. Franzos's spelling of the title and the hero was corrected by Berg before he reverted to the "Wozzeck" spelling.[31] In the change from the letter which makes the dipthong, from *y* to *z,* lies an interesting significance: Berg insists ultimately on the letter which misrepresents the subject, which continues to misname after he is dead. Reading Berg's *Wozzeck* requires noting the splitting which has divided the name from Büchner's name and from history. The name Wozzeck is a like a palimpsest; if we scrape its surface, we find that Berg has re-introduced and then re-excluded Woyzeck. It is Wozzeck, not Woyzeck, with whom Berg identifies. A criticism that aligns Berg with Büchner's Woyzeck, runs a danger of missing the distinction between Woyzeck's lack of privilege and Berg's privilege, and of continuing an aestheticizing of the work that Berg seems to have initiated. Then the question may be returned to—what Berg means when he says that the final interlude is a "confession." What should "the author" be confessing?

Compassion and remorse, on account of "the extreme brutality" that Leo Treitler, for instance, finds in the depiction of Marie's murder (as also Lulu's)?[32] His own implications in the violence of Wozzeck? Perle quotes comments Berg made in 1914 that show he was fascinated by the violence of the war, and saw it as affirming new and important truths, inaccessible in peacetime.[33] Is Berg implying that Wozzeck's stabbing of a woman is identifiable with his own attitudes? Or that Wozzeck's violence towards a woman is forgivable?

Whatever it might imply, whether we can move from attraction to military violence to a more fascist-like violence towards women, Berg's "confession" continues to act as the postmortem process by which Woyzeck is made a more conventionally operatic character, and becomes Wozzeck. If Berg includes himself and his own psychosexuality in the character of Wozzeck, he diminishes the difference between himself and the schizoid hero. If he implies that killing the woman deserves pity, that defense, which in any case takes the privileged place of speaking over Wozzeck's dead body and for him, implies that he has elided what is distinctive about Woyzeck—his fragmented state, so that he speaks from the position of centred composer pronouncing authoritatively on a de-centered subject. It is just that superiority and position of truth that "schizoanalysis" works to overcome. Criticism of *Wozzeck* would need to work in a different direction, expunging the *z* which permits the character not to be allowed to speak, and replacing it with the *y*, which makes no presumption about what is normal, or what it is to be the centered or de-centered subject.

I have noted that Berg's interest in symmetries in the musical structure has been called obsessive, but something should be said about the obsessionalism in the music. Kerman says that "six of the fifteen scenes are built on *ostinato* forms . . . these *are* perceived, and make their unesoteric dramatic effect by providing an overpowering sense of obsession to the action in question." Kerman gives as examples the murder scene (Act 3, scene 2) and its successor, where he says "a superb dramatic point is made by the constant repetition of a single rhythm."[34] The *ostinato* form functions as a way of depicting a man gone mad, and condemned to nothing but repetition, even if repetition is itself a marker of ordinary existence (*immer zu*). For Kerman, the opera "seems to use every available means to refine a unique operatic vision of abnormality," adding that since the events in the opera are looked at through Wozzeck's paranoia, it shows "the dissection of a diseased mind."[35] The critic's superior normality in seeing the opera as a postmortem confirms a tendency in the music: by writing music stressing obsessionalism, a reading of Wozzeck is confirmed that marginalizes and differentiates him. Obsessional motifs set up a narrative that makes inevitable the murder of Marie by Wozzeck, while the musicality of the creation of obsession affirms the superiority of the composer who speaks for Wozzeck and disallows him from speaking for himself. Here too, Woyzeck is confirmed as Wozzeck.

4. Adorno and Cultural Schizophrenia

Nonetheless, the "coherence" Perle finds in Wozzeck runs up against three features of its musical writing which make the operatic text, like the play's, plural: first, its use of *Sprechstimme*, so that there is much sliding between notes. Second, its use of simpler-sounding folk-songs and melodies and set pieces, such as Andres's hunting song (Act 1, Scene 2), Marie's "Soldaten" song (Act 1, Scene 3), her three songs to her child (Act 1, Scene 3; Act 2, Scene 1; Act 3, Scene 1), the soldiers' march, the singing and dancing in the tavern in Act 2, Scene 4 and Act 3, Scene 3, and the children's song in Act 3, Scene 5. Third, there is the music's formal structure, already commented on. In "A Word about *Wozzeck*," Berg outlines the opera's musical forms and adds:

> No one in the audience, no matter how aware he may be of the musical forms contained in the framework of the opera, of the precision and logic with which it has been worked out, no one, from the moment the curtain parts until it closes for the last time, pays any attention to the various fugues, inventions, suites, sonata movements, variations, and passacaglias about which so much has been written. No one gives heed to anything but the vast social implications of the work which by far transcend the personal destiny of Wozzeck.[36]

I will come back to this last sentence in the last section of this essay, but before I do I want to take account of Adorno's reading of the orchestral material that Berg refers to. In *The Philosophy of Modern Music*, he discusses Schoenberg and Stravinsky in terms of structural listening. Schoenberg and Adorno agree, according to Rose Subotnik, in the "goal of reducing music to a condition of what could be called pure structural substance, in which every element justifies its existence through its relation to a governing structural principle." This holds for *Wozzeck*, whose musical structures are justified not in terms of meaning, but as a coherent and consistent musical organization. As Berg says that the structures cannot be detected in performance, so this intellectualism may be said to agree with the "depreciat[ing of] the value of sound" that Subotnik finds in Adorno and Schoenberg.[37] Adorno, writing on Schoenberg's Woodwind Quintet, op. 26, says that it "declares war on color" (i.e., sensuous immediacy) and continues:

> It is easy enough to imagine this late form of Schoenberg's asceticism, the negation of all façades, extending to all musical dimensions. Mature music becomes suspicious of real sound as such. Similarly, with the realization of the "subcutaneous," the end of musical interpretation becomes conceivable. The silent, imaginative reading of music could render actual playing as superfluous as, for instance, speaking is made by the reading of written material. . . .[38]

Schoenberg writes "music for the intellectual ear,"[39] and in Adorno's argument, musical sound partakes of modern alienation. In this, modernism, with its refusal of the immediate and of all that fits bourgeois ideology, gains its justification. The demands of performance or of reproduced sound (for example, the need for balance, or the tendency towards smoothness of sound, or purity of tone, or high resolution in reproduction) are false forms of reconciliation with capitalist reality. They re-unite modernist music with the conditions of bourgeois ideology. The structure that is not detectable, escaping such co-option, becomes an important other and asserts autonomy in a prior recognition of the power of alienation. And it refutes the temptation of, or on, music to become affirmative in performance. We recall Adorno's premise in *Aesthetic Theory* that "in the face of the abnormality into which reality is developing, art's inescapable affirmative essence has become insufferable."[40] A work which seeks for unity or affirmatory wholeness, as opposed to the fragmentary, would express a deep form of alienation. The fragmentary does acknowledge alienation, but to write the whole (in the discourse of modernism) shows how alienated one can be and not know it; it is the condition of reification.

It is relevant that Adorno's reading of *Wozzeck* does not accord any space at all to the idea of schizophrenia. Rather, "Büchner obtained justice [by writing the play] for the tortured, confused Wozzeck, who, in his human, dehumanized state, objectively represents all soldiers. . . ."[41] For Adorno, there is no need to use the discourse of schizophrenia, for Woyzeck is no different from any other soldier, while the soldier is typical of the industrialized worker. If he is schizophrenic, then this schizophrenia is cultural, no more. The music of *Wozzeck* is also not schizophrenic, for instead it tries to engage with humanity. Where Adorno does discuss schizophrenia, it confirms the sense that for him the analysis would not help with *Wozzeck*. He comes to schizophrenia in *The Philosophy of Modern Music* when he discusses Stravinsky. He refers to "hebephrenia," defined as "the indifference of the sick individual towards the external," a lack of "libidinal possession of the objective world."[42] He finds in Stravinsky a failure of "expressivism," a passivity which he also compares to catatonic conditions, meaning that state where the motor system seems to run on independently of the ego, a condition also experienced in people who have been overwhelmed by shock:

> In Stravinsky, there is neither the anticipation of anxiety nor the resisting ego; it is rather assumed that shock cannot be appropriated by the individual for himself. The musical subject makes no attempt to assert itself, and contents itself with the reflexive absorption of the blows. The subject behaves literally like a critically injured victim of an accident which he cannot absorb and which, therefore, he repeats in the hopeless tension of dreams.[43]

Stravinsky's objectivism—where sound is opposed to expression, and is stripped of the possibility of oppositional meaning—suggests schizophrenia.[44] The subject has been alienated, but is unaware of its alienation, hence the failure of expression, which Adorno links with suffering in *Aesthetic Theory*, though not at the level of directly appealing to the subject. For "no work of art, regardless what its maker thinks of it, is directed towards an observer, not even toward a transcendental subject of apperception; no art is to be described or explained in terms of the categories of communication."[45] This fits with Berg's denial that the musical structures of *Wozzeck* can be followed. The modernist musical text is not directed at a centred subject; it assumes, rather, the fractured, deprived auditor; in other words, it assumes as basic the existence of a cultural schizophrenia. Yet, Adorno continues, "expression is the suffering countenance of artworks. They turn this countenance only toward those who return its gaze, even when they are composed in happy tones. . . . If expression were merely the doubling of the subjectively felt, it would be null and void; the artist who condemns a work as being an impression rather than an invention knows this perfectly well."[46] Returning the gaze requires a viewer, or listener who is like Walter Benjamin's allegorist, looking below the surface for the breakdown of the work of art into fragments, ruins,[47] and the justification for Berg's musical structures—which do not merely double what is subjectively felt, or if they do, do so indiscernably—is there in Adorno's word "invention." In this way, Adorno seems to register the existence of schizophrenia, as a problematic condition afflicting both the conditions of writing music within modernism, and listening to it.

In his sympathy with Berg as the artist of a fractured state, Adorno makes the point that *Wozzeck* turns away from the building up of structures, which might lead toward an affirmative art, and instead retracts any such possibilities:

> Berg's compositional niveau proves itself—on a level so high that it is scarcely even perceived today [1968]—precisely in that extremely deliberate syntactical organization, which extends from the movement as a whole to the proper position of every single note, omitting nothing. This music is beautiful in the sense of the Latin concept *formosus*, the concept of the richness of forms. Its formal wealth imbues it with eloquence and with an inherent similarity to language. But Berg possesses a special technique for taking defined thematic shapes and, in the course of developing them, calling them back to nothingness.[48]

As Adorno put it earlier, "the dream of permanent artistic possessions is not only destroyed from the outside by the threatening social condition; the historical tendency present in musical means renounces this dream. [It] questions what many progressives expect of it: structures perfected within themselves which might be exhibited for all time in museums of opera and concert."[49] Musical form, in *Wozzeck*, far from being something reified for a "museum," is taken back in what Adorno calls a "death drive."[50]

The death drive would also be a refusal of narrative, of the one-thing-after-another that the Captain recommended for Wozzeck. The banality of the march-past in Act 1, Scene 3 implies the contempt the operatic text feels both for the military and for the notion of the march of events. The opera disregards a forward narrative by its use of mirror and musical retrograde formations, which, as Adorno says, "are anti-temporal, they organize music as if it were an intrinsic simultaneity . . . they contain an element of indifference towards succession, something like a disposition toward musical saturation of space."[51] The music takes its part alongside the character of Wozzeck in its sense that it cannot work, in linear terms, "langsam." This sympathy is part of what Adorno calls the music's "genuine humanism"—in which it is differentiated from the conventions of grand opera—evidenced in, for instance, its respect for the suffering of the soldiers.

As Adorno puts it, "snores and groans are composed to show that for the unfree even sleep is warped."[52] In their sleep, which is a reminder of how much the war is *Wozzeck*'s displaced subject-matter, Berg shows something entirely new: the colonization of their unconscious, which is not free. Yet the soldiers' regimented sleeping acts as a way to read Wozzeck's state, for he cannot sleep. Their sleeping is at once ironic, comforting, and a measure of how much they have surrendered their freedom to the order of the army. In this presentation the soldiers are not like an affirmative chorus of Verdi-type soldiers in an opera such as *Il Trovatore*; rather they become alienated subjects, the measure of whose alienation is that, like nineteenth-century opera, but also unlike it, they are treated as a chorus.

5. Listening to Schizophrenia

If the unconscious has been colonized, this might be read in operatic terms in ways recalling Wagner on the invisibility of the orchestra—"the music sounds, and what it sounds you see on the stage."[53] If Marie sings "Immer zu," she follows a musical narrative given to her in the whirl of music heard both in the orchestra and in the onstage orchestra; she is not an autonomous agent. The objective patterning of the orchestral score would suggest the impersonality of the Lacanian symbolic order into which the subject is inserted and which creates for the subject its unconscious. Louis Sass, discussing the case of Schreber, whose *Memoirs of My Nervous Illness* recorded his delusions and experiences in mental homes between 1894 and 1902, calls schizophrenia "the most severe form of psychosis."[54] This formal linking of the two terms evokes Lacan, who also makes reference to Schreber in the essay "On A Question Preliminary to Any Possible Treatment of Psychosis." The "defect that gives psychosis its essential condition" is "the foreclosure of the Name of the Father in the place of the Other," and "the failure of the paternal metaphor."[55] The father's authority limits the unbounded relationship between the child and the mother, and in doing so, brings the child into that "signifying chain" Lacan calls the symbolic order, which establishes difference as the principle upon which signification is possible. When this authority is foreclosed, there is left a gap in the field of signification, which sets off "a cascade of reshapings of the signifier"—a rush to try and fill absence by fantasies.[56]

The musical organization could be seen as the power of the symbolic order. The relationship of voices to the score would be suggestive: between *Sprechstimme,* into which characters lapse so often, and the singing voice. An example of the contrast would be Act 1, Scene 2, where Andres sings, and Wozzeck speaks. In *Sprechstimme,* according to Schoenberg, "whereas the sung note *preserves* the pitch, the spoken note gives it at first, but abandons it either by rising or falling immediately after."[57] Arnold Whittall, discussing *Pierrot Lunaire,* says that "the effect is undeniably of song repressed, of the primitive and sophisticated, the impotent and fertile, in conflict." He adds: "Pierrot, too, is talking to the moon; only when he is able to sing, it seems, will other human beings understand and want to listen."[58] There is a certain infantility—remembering that the infant is without speech—implied in *Sprechstimme,* as though this mirrored a state tendentially outside the symbolic order. Whittall compares this *Sprechstimme* with Moses's inability to communicate in *Moses und Aron.* In the case of Moses, who unlike Aron only speaks, inability to sing has to do with his perception of God being outside representation: this places him in a position where he can express nothing to people. *Sprechstimme* would then imply the state of the person who cannot find a place within the symbolic order, who is shut off from discourse. Moses becomes like Wozzeck in his radical severance from the order that Aron and the others embody. Wozzeck's *Sprechstimme* differentiates him from Berg, about whom Adorno said that "he successfully avoided becoming an adult without remaining infantile."[59]

George Perle, however, in contrast to this view of the orchestral music as the constraints of the symbolic order, takes the order of the musical forms as an example of Berg's obsessionalism, as though it represented an utterance that could not be recognized. I think that this view could be supported if we return to the logic of Berg's sentence in his lecture on the opera, already quoted, where he makes a split between the work's "vast social implications" and Wozzeck's "personal destiny." The social implications would be what is visible on the stage, but they would make the point that what there is to be seen on stage is not what there is to see—the events on stage are symptomatic; they evoke another scene, which cannot be represented, because madness is non-representable, except from the standpoint of "normality." Wozzeck's destiny is the subject of the orchestral material, Berg says, but it is impossible to attend to that, as it is also impossible to "know" madness. What prompts Wozzeck's behavior is unknowable, and the way in which the orchestral sound exists both listens to that and refuses to be drawn out into conscious, recognizable articulation.

Listening to schizophrenia—an act of schizoanalysis—would then take the form of attending to a dense and intense structure, for understanding which I return to Louis Sass. Differentiating himself from an anti-psychiatric view of madness as a Dionysian freedom from the social, he agrees with those arguments that see schizoid tendencies in terms of lack of affect (something Büchner noticed in Woyzeck). Sass argues for schizophrenia as a form of "hyperconcentration," "a form of consciousness that is hyperacute, hyper-self-conscious, and highly detached," thinking of things not in a subjective way, as though aware of an inner world, but objectively. In arguing this, he agrees with, or uses, William James, that this way of thinking is "earliest, most instinctive, least developed."[60] We could apply this to both Wozzeck and to Berg. Leo Treitler discusses Wozzeck's condition in terms which suggest that he has built up a set of systematic delusions based upon the Bible, the Book of Revelation specifically. When he sees Marie and the Drum Major dancing together, "it is not an ordinary act of infidelity that he sees, but a symbolic act of depravity. It is, he says, as though the whole world were waltzing about in fornication, and it is the whole world he wants punished at that moment, crying for God to extinguish the sun."[61] Wozzeck is a system-builder, like Schreber, who gave his account of a whole cosmic system operating on him in his *Memoirs of My Nervous Illness,* where he said that he was being transformed into a woman by an intricate system of nerves and rays acting upon him. The solipsism of this is Louis Sass's thesis, which makes him comment that "far from demonstrating an incapacity for concentration or self-monitoring, [Schreber] was unable to perform the most trivial act—such as watching a butterfly flutter past—without obsessively reflecting on his own experience and checking on whether he was really doing what he thought he was doing . . . .his hallucinatory voices were often the expression of this self-consciousness."[62] The belief that everything can be interpreted—itself perhaps solipsistic—makes Wozzeck hyperconscious about the possibility of reading rings of toadstools (Act 1, Scene 4). "Linienkreise, Figuren. . . . Wer das lesen könnte!" he sings, in a truly lyric moment. But Wozzeck does not necessarily think they can be interpreted. He is thus different from his composer, with his attraction to numbers and symmetries. These in the score would also point to a splitting, between what happens on the stage and some other frenetic and knowing organization in the orchestra. While listening to the music from the de-centered position of schizoanalysis would prevent any single reading being given to the musical organization of *Wozzeck,* it would also notice the centring tendency of that music that thinks it can "read" where Wozzeck cannot, and would resist this tendency—a tendency in Modernism—to invest in a truth that can be recovered.

This attraction to order makes Berg one of the composers who went into Thomas Mann's fictional composer Adrian Leverkühn in his novel *Dr. Faustus*. The point does not seem merely incidental. Zeitblom, Leverkühn's imaginary biographer, comments on Leverkühn's and on music's "inborn tendency . . . to superstitious rites and observances, the symbolism of numbers and letters."[63] When Adrian discusses his version of the twelve-tone row, Zeitblom calls this "a magic square,"[64] referring to Dürer's *Melencolia* which depicts such a thing. The force of this combination links music as progressive and modernist with music as atavistic and irrational. Adrian's interest in symmetry is framed within a text which is equally devoted to symmetry within numbers (e.g., at the level of chapter numbers, and what happens within those chapters). Berg's attraction both to writing about a hero defined by obsessionalism and to providing a score whose symmetries make it, like Mann, both progressive and superstitious at once, is repeated in Thomas Mann's text.

The symmetries in Berg's music are symptomatic of a tangle of problems Modernism in music engaged in. They represent an order that the musician is for—and against—which he both works with, and, if Adorno is right, takes away. The order is both unconsciously felt and impossible to be consciously understood. Its impossibility here is both the mark of modernist music's fear of being de-centered, being drawn into the public realm where it will be listened to by people who have no respect for its authenticity, and where its own truth will be misunderstood. In that way, modernist music, as in Berg's opera, protects itself against being seen as schizophrenic. It preserves itself and its truth by its distance and difficulty—and in doing so focuses the weakness within modernism that schizoanalysis points to: its desire not to become fragmented.

Berg and Mann link through their common ground with Adorno, who appears as Herr Kretschmar in *Doctor Faustus* and repeats the stress on modernist music's difficulty when he says that "perhaps it was music's deepest wish not to be heard at all, nor even seen, nor even felt."[65] When Adrian Leverkühn speaks of the twelve-tone row and agrees that people will not hear "the precise realization in detail of the means by which the highest and strictest order is achieved, like the order of the planets, a cosmic order and legality,"[66] Adorno's ideas are being rendered dialogically but it may be said that if Adorno does not register Berg's *Wozzeck* as a text listening to schizophrenia, Mann's text explains why when it posits Adorno as the devil. For Adorno as the devil points to an intellectual retreat in modernism into a private set of fantasies that claim the impossibility of writing—"composing itself has got too hard."[67] While Berg's opera, contra Adorno, does listen to schizophrenia, *Wozzeck* in its own doubleness of response to *Woyzeck* is not utterly different from the demand for order and truth that necessitates schizophrenia as a response.

Notes

1. Gilles Deleuze and Felix Guattari, *Anti-Oedipus: Capitalism and Schizophrenia*, trans. Robert Hurley (New York: Viking Press, 1977).

2. Maurice B. Benn, *The Drama of Revolt: A Critical Study of Georg Büchner* (Cambridge: Cambridge University Press, 1976), 218–20.

3. *Georg Büchner: Danton's Death, Leonce and Lena, Woyzeck*, trans. Victor Price (Oxford: Oxford University Press, 1971), 116. See also Price's Appendix to his translation (133–36). Price follows the scene-ordering of the editions by Georg Witkowski (1920) and Fritz Bergemann (1922) rather than those of Lehmann and Krause. The translation by John Mackendrick, introduction by Michael Patterson (London: Eyre Methuen, 1979) uses the Lehmann ordering, but adds in extra scenes. The translation by John Reddick (*Büchner: Complete Plays, Lenz and Other Writings* [Harmondsworth: Penguin, 1993], 113–38) prints a total of twenty-nine scenes, though basically following the order I have given. On the ordering of scenes and the play generally, see Julian Hilton, *Georg Büchner* (London: Macmillan, 1982), 113–37.

4. On the *idée fixe* and monomania, see Jan Goldstein, *Console and Classify: The French Psychiatric Profession in the Nineteenth Century* (Cambridge: Cambridge University Press 1987), 152–56.

5. Robert Castel, *The Regulation of Madness: The Origins of Incarceration in France*, trans. W. D. Halls (Cambridge: Polity Press, 1988), 145.

6. Hugo Beiber, "Wozzeck und Woyzeck," *Literarisches Echo* 16, no. 1 (June 1914); trans. in Douglas Jarman, *Alban Berg: Wozzeck* (Cambridge: Cambridge University Press, 1989), 129–32; quotations pp. 130, 131.

7. Quoted in Herbert Lindenberger, *Georg Büchner* (Carbondale: Southern Illinois University Press, 1964), 97.

8. Price's translation, 111.

9. Lindenberger, *Georg Büchner*, 106.

10. Price's translation, 117.

11. For good accounts of both the Doctor and the Captain, see Henry J. Schmidt, *Satire, Caricature and Perspectivism in the Works of Georg Büchner* (The Hague: Mouton, 1970), 41–51, 75–87.

12. Price's translation, 122. See p. 111 of Lindenberger, who makes the point about his own translation of this scene, where "scrape and squeak" are simply "Hish! Hash!" that "Büchner depends above all on evocative sound combinations and repetitions of for his effects here." The phrase "bitch of a goat-wolf" is in fact no translation at all, for Büchner's word, *Zickwolfin*, is not a recognizable word, though through its auditory connotations, as Margaret Jacobs has shown, it may suggest a "rapacious she-wolf." Büchner was doubtless struck by the auditory possibilities suggested by a phrase in Clarus's report: "Stich die Frau Woostin tot!"

13. Price's translation, 123.

14. Ibid., 127. Büchner changes Woyzeck's first names (as Marie also gets this name for the first time in Büchner's play), and Woyzeck's age is also changed.

15. Ibid., 128.

16. Quoted in Tony James, *Dream, Creativity and Madness in Nineteenth-Century France* (Oxford: Claremdon Press, 1995), 70.

17. Ibid., 74.

18. Deleuze and Guattari, *Anti-Oedipus*, 130.

19. Louis A. Sass, *The Paradoxes of Delusion: Wittgenstein, Schreber and the Schizophrenic Mind* (Ithaca, N.Y.: Cornell University Press 1994), 156. For me, *Memoirs of My Nervous Illness* is the outstanding unwritten modernist opera libretto and fascinating to imagine as an opera: it would have been even more interesting as a libretto than the one for *Erwartung*.

20. Louis Sass, *Madness and Modernism: Insanity in the Light of Modern Art, Literature and Thought* (New York: Basic Books, 1992), 366.

21. See Philip Thomas, *The Dialectics of Schizophrenia* (London: Free Association Books, 1997), 18–21.

22. On this topic of hearing voices in opera, see Carolyn Abbate, *Unsung Voices: Opera and Musical Narrative in the Nineteenth Century* (Princeton, N.J.: Princeton University Press, 1991), 131.

23. For an overview of Berg scholarship, see Dave Headlam, *The Music of Alban Berg* (New Haven, Conn.: Yale University Press, 1996), 2–4.

24. Perle, *The Operas of Alban Berg*: Vol. 1, *Wozzeck* (Berkeley: University of California Press, 1980), 185.

25. Letter from Berg to his wife, 1918; quoted in Perle, *Wozzeck*, 20 and 129; see also p. 56.

26. Jarman, *Alban Berg: Wozzeck*, 66. My emphasis.

27. Jarman cites these motifs in *The Music of Alban Berg* (London: Faber, 1979), 196.

28. Perle, *Wozzeck*, 129, 88. The text of the lecture of 1929, from which Berg's words are taken, appears in Jarman, *Alban Berg: Wozzeck*, 154–70, see 169.

29. Joseph Kerman, *Opera as Drama* (New York: Knopf, 1956), 231.

30. Letter of 11 January 1926; see *The Berg-Schoenberg Correspondence: Selected Letters*, ed. Julianne Brand, Christopher Hailey, and Donald Harris (London: Macmillan, 1987), 342.

31. See Perle, *Wozzeck*, illustrations nos. 8, 9, 10.

32. Leo Treitler, "The Lulu Character and the Character of *Lulu*," in *Alban Berg: Historical and Analytical Perspectives*, ed. David Gable and Robert P. Morgan (Oxford: Clarendon Press, 1991), pp. 276–77.

33. Perle, *Wozzeck*, 20–21.

34. Kerman, *Opera as Drama*, 226. The ostinato scenes are: Act 1, Scene 4 (Passacaglia), and the five scenes of Act 3: inventions on a theme, a note, a rhythm, a hexachord, and a regular quaver movement. Perle discusses these (Perle, *Wozzeck*, 164–85) and includes discussion on 169–72 of the ostinato heard in Act 2, Scene 4.

35. Kerman, *Opera as Drama*, 227, 229.

36. Alban Berg, in *Modern Music* (November-December 1927), reprinted in Douglas Jarman, *Alban Berg: Wozzeck*, 153.

37. Rose Subotnik, *Deconstructive Variations: Music and Reason in Western Society* (Minneapolis: University of Minnesota Press, 1996), 161.

38. Theodor Adorno, *Prisms* (1967), trans. Samuel and Shierry Weber, (Cambridge, Mass.: MIT Press, 1981), 169.

39. Ibid., 157.

40. Theodor Adorno, *Aesthetic Theory*, trans. Robert Hullot-Kentor (Minneapolis: University of Minnesota Press, 1997), 2.

41. Theodor Adorno, *Alban Berg, Master of the Smallest Link*, trans. Julian Brand and Christopher Hailey (Cambridge: Cambridge University Press, 1991), 84.

42. Theodor Adorno, *Philosophy of Modern Music*, trans. Anne G. Mitchell and Wesley V. Bloomster (London: Sheen and Ward, 1973), 176.

43. Ibid., 156–57.

44. See Max Paddison, *Adorno's Aesthetics of Music* (Cambridge: Cambridge University Press, 1993), 266–70; and Robert W. Witkin, *Adorno on Music* (London: Routledge, 1998), 154–59. For Adorno's views on Berg, see Raymond Geuss, "Berg and Adorno," *The Cambridge Companion to Berg*, ed. Anthony Pople (Cambridge: Cambridge University Press, 1997), 38–50.

45. Adorno, *Aesthetic Theory*, 109. Compare Walter Benjamin, writing in 1924: "no poem is intended for the reader, no picture for the beholder, no symphony for the listener," "The Task of the Translator," in his *Illuminations*, trans. Harry Zohn (London: Jonathan Cape, 1970), 69.

46. Adorno, *Aesthetic Theory*, 111.

47. "In the field of allegorical intuition, the image is a fragment, a rune"; Benjamin, *The Origin of German Tragic Drama*, trans. John Osborne (London: New Left Books, 1977), 176. Adorno's writing shows its debt to Benjamin: alternatively, we could say that shizoanalysis has the task of undoing what seems centred and united.

48. Adorno, *Alban Berg*, 3.

49. Adorno, *Philosophy of Modern Music*, 32.

50. Quoted in Paddison, *Adorno's Aesthetics of Music*, 173; see 171–74 for further discussion of Adorno on Berg.

51. Adorno, *Alban Berg*, 14.

52. Ibid., 6.

53. Quoted in Jeremy Tambling, *Opera and the Culture of Fascism* (Oxford: Clarendon Press, 1996), 43.

54. Sass, *The Paradoxes of Delusion*, 3.

55. Jacques Lacan, *Ecrits: A Selection*, trans. Alan Sheridan (London: Tavistock Press, 1977), 215.

56. Ibid., 217.

57. Quoted in Egon Wellesz, *Arnold Schoenberg: The Formative Years* (1921; London: Galliard, 1971), 139.

58. Arnold Whittall, *Schoenberg Chamber Music* (London: British Broadcasting Corporation, 1972), 29.

59. Adorno, *Alban Berg*, 34.

60. Sass, *The Paradoxes of Delusion*, 39, 40, 41.

61. Leo Treitler, "*Wozzeck* and the Apocalypse: An Essay in Historical Criticism," *Critical Inquiry* 3 (1976): 254.

62. Sass, *The Paradoxes of* Delusion, 37, 38.

63. Thomas Mann, *Doctor Faustus*, trans. H. T. Lowe-Porter, (Harmondsworth: Penguin, 1968), 151.

64. Ibid., 187.

65. Ibid., 63.

66. Ibid., 187

67. Ibid., 231, 232.

Part Three

Writing & Listening

9

The Musician Writes: For the Eyes of the Deaf?

Pierre Boulez
Translated by Robert Samuels

Confronting his text, his translation into writing, what does the composer think? How should he behave? Is he happy to transcribe the musical thoughts which his imagination dictates to him? Is the writing just a dictation brusquely imposed by the concept of a definitive text? Does it take no part in the elaboration of the work? Does it act only as an obstacle to the ideal of the perfect transcription? Or, is it a lever, the strongest there is, with which the imagination has the power to prise open a complex world which could not otherwise be brought to light?

Even more than in poetry, writing is an ambivalent phenomenon in music. It does not obey traditional conventions. It is meant to account statically and quantitatively for phenomena which take place dynamically through time, and which are perceived qualitatively as elements within superimpositions or successions, depending on the context.

In academic teaching, what is the first thing you try to ensure? The correctness and accuracy of certain basic elements of transcription. From this stems the rigorous control of the ability to transmit and receive, through the means of solfège and dictation. The code must be learned: the reality of musical objects corresponds to the signs of graphic notation. More particularly, pitch and duration are specified in this way. This forces the transcription of objects as if they were outside time, as isolated sounds or chords. Moving beyond these fragments of uncontextualized reality produces chord progressions and the combination of voices. Perception is sharpened through reference to the code, since perception of musical reality, and the code governing its transcription, form an essential and unique cycle of identity and identification.

With these reflexes developed, *writing* can be tackled. Indeed, categories of writing . . . You do or don't know how to *write* music. . . . This or that work is a model of *writing*. . . . How often that word is used to sum up musical virtues or strengths. We can no better avoid the mysteries which are found beyond writing. . . . But this one little word is filled with whatever meaning suits the user, unless writing is challenged as being an obsolete phenomenon, no longer capable of representing the reality of today, either in terms of the reality of sonic objects or of the reality of compositional methods. Then again, what are we to make of oral traditions? They can produce "intellectual" music which is complex without needing to be put through the mill of writing: here it would be a superfluous constraint. Moreover, by not producing by means of notation results which are in principle reproducible by anyone who understands the code, one could confine oneself to actions leading to a unique performance; the dissemination of this "product" being assured by the techniques which we possess in abundance for producing duplicates of it. This way the very idea of writing would be short-circuited. Is this true? Does writing need this instantiation in a literal medium in order to exist? Can it be so easy to get rid of an idea which we have symbolized in this way because its direct form is more familiar to us, but which greatly surpasses the basic fact of transcription? This term, "writing," also implies the specificity of the means employed. We speak of "violin writing," of "chamber music writing," of "orchestral writing." We could speak without self-contradiction of "machine-based writing," despite the fact that the reality to which this refers seems irretrievably removed from the preceding. . . . Whether it exists actually or virtually, writing is a system which refers to action. Like all interactive systems, it functions both as a means of transmission and as a mainspring of activity; to such an extent that, if one is not careful, it acquires a certain autonomous status and the job of transmission becomes merely a secondary preoccupation. Writing becomes the object of its own devotion, gaining power and dominion, which may sometimes undermine the very activity it was meant to enrich.

As for oral traditions, are they always immune to being diverted in this way? Do they simply preserve and transmit? A relaying individual cannot function entirely passively: he will fashion the message in his own image, either by accident or on purpose. A mental representation comes into play: a suspended, reserved form of writing, no less corrosive than the explicit form with which we have to deal once a text has been written down. To my mind, there is a difference of degree, or in method, between one form of expression and the other; but the concept of *writing,* in the most general sense, informs every level of artistic invention, whether traditional or not, whether formalized or not.

We will confine ourselves to a limited field, that of the conscious invention transmitting itself by means of a written text, whatever the level of that text may be, from instructions for actions to the recording of results. At first, the establishment of the text derives from intellectual reflection, according to a more or less spontaneous exploration of the possibilities of the text, possibilities for induction and deduction. This is also an exploration of the hold the text exercises on our memory, of the greater or lesser evidence of objects or of forms that it offers to the understanding. However, it can be seen that the composer has not always intended the complete decipherment of his text, and that he may have used a system of symbols—of letters or figures—which will later bring joy to musicological researchers. Nothing can spice up a score like the delight of solving a whodunit.

Here we are talking of what I might call the most visible sort of cryptography. Give me the secret combination, and, like unravelling knitting, I will give you the thread of the work. If the author has not taken enough precautions to hold the sleuth at bay, the latter will be sure he has found the true path; for nothing gives the illusion of uncovering the secret behind artistic creation like decryption. Let us take, close to home, the example of Berg. No-one has used as much as he the ambiguous privileges of writing—what I would term acrostic writing, if that word did not circumscribe too narrowly the activity of tucking away a secret in ambivalent pieces of information which ought to be music, but which, outside of their status as musical symbols, can refer to letters and figures within completely independent languages. Because the German solfège labels the notes with letters of the alphabet, musical onomastics have become enriched through the centuries with many ciphers, some of which have remained famous. These include among others the B-A-C-H "signature" in *The Art of Fugue,* Schumann's A-B-E-G-G variations, and before long the B-A-F-H of the *Lyric Suite,* the three "A"s of the *Kammerkonzert.* . . . Which are better: names or initials? And is one compelled to adopt them? To do so, one language must be favored to the detriment of the other. Thus in order to respect the D-minor tonality, the appendix C sharp–D, which has only a musical function, has to be added to B-A-C-H. . . . Thus too, in order to create the theme of the variations in his *Kammerkonzert,* Berg mutilates Arnold Schoenberg's names to the point that they become unrecognisable if we meet them in their "usable" form: A-D-S-C-H-B-E-G! Need one go further? The *accident* which links various letters of the alphabet to the generic names of pitches goes no further than an epigraph, a dedication, or an acrostic with sentimental connotations.

What is it about numbers, about these symbolic numbers which have been used and abused to organize provisional cosmogonies, from the Trinity to the Golden Section, without forgetting the Horoscope and the Zodiac? Of course, the Trinity—or the principle of it—has been drafted into service time and again, and in the noblest of circumstances: fugue in three subjects or counterpoint in three voices. . . . But the number *three* all but overflows the *Kammerkonzert.* It matters little, moreover, whether we are aware of its symbolic, dedicatory significance, referring to the three "A"s of the Second Viennese School. What we are aware of at once is the division of the instruments into their three families: violin, piano and wind. This is especially so when we are carefully presented with the three combinations two-

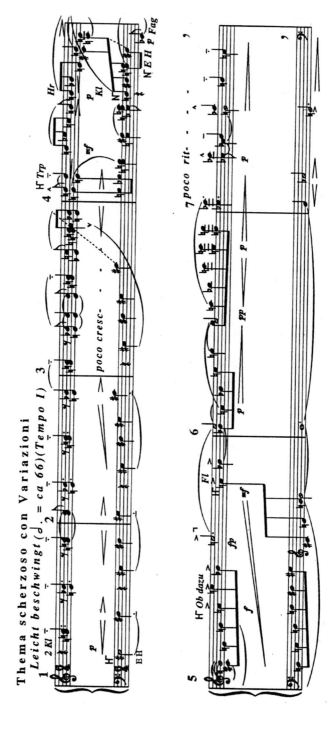

Figure 9.1a. Berg, *Kammerkonzert*. First movement theme (winds), mm. 1–7. Copyright © 1925 by Universal Edition A.G., Wien. Used by permission.

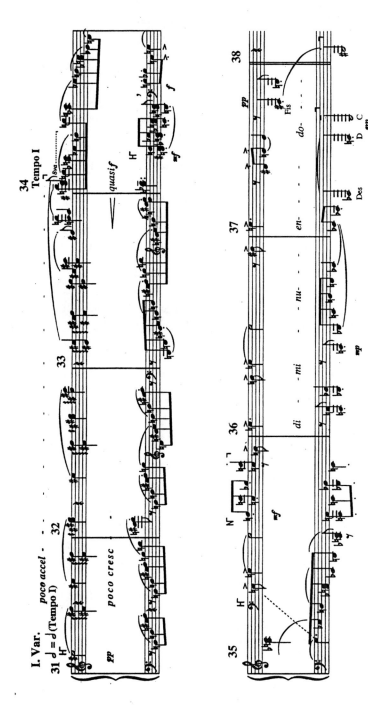

Figure 9.1b. Berg, *Kammerkonzert*. First movement, Variation I (piano), mm. 31–38. Copyright © 1925 by Universal Edition A.G., Wien. Used by permission.

by-two in turn—piano and wind, violin and wind, piano and violin—before we hear all three in combination. One might well quibble that this makes four combinations in total. . . . But in the course of the three movements he wrote, Berg uses the trick of the cadenza—that non-movement *par excellence*—to banish the figure four from the presence of the figure three! Yes, one may well smile. . . . And indeed, I do not think that a surreptitious humor is foreign to these formal tricks; you believe in it, without believing in it too much, while believing in it nonetheless, without absolutely making yourself believe in it. . . . Superstition, subterfuge, mystification? It is a shrewd observer who can distinguish the true from the false, separate exorcism and obsession, identify what is pointless constraint and what is recourse to the omnipotence of number! But beyond this envelope of scoring, whose nature, if not whose meaning, is easily deciphered, what can we hope to perceive as far as concerns this persistence of the number three in certain formal aspects of the work, or in the construction of themes? Of course we will not think of *counting* the number of variations; in fact there are five of them, which, in addition to the theme, gives a six-part form—six, a multiple of three. Can we listen in such a strictly numerical way? Of course not! What interests us is hearing the theme played by the wind, repeated by the piano, in a sort of exposition. [See figure 9.1[1]] After that, we pass through a certain number of variations which divert us from the *Grundgestalt*[2] into a sort of development where piano and wind join together. We then discover the two original expositions superimposed on each other, rather than one following the other. We therefore think of the overall design of sonata form, which is effectively a ternary scheme: exposition, development, recapitulation. How much can even an attentive listener perceive in this development section? Without a doubt, three successive panels essentially characterized outwardly by accelerating tempo, or by greater and greater haste. If the listener becomes a reader, he will quickly become aware, by a *visual* comparison of the three transcriptions of the theme, that this involves first a retrograde, then an inversion, and then a retrograde inversion. In other words, these are the three transformations of an original in traditional counterpoint. For the time being, I do not want to raise the problem of the perception of these forms of contrapuntal variation, especially when they are used on a vast scale. I only want to demonstrate what tricks and dodges Berg has to resort to in order to escape from the number four and come back obstinately to a ternary principle. To sum up the design of this first movement of the *Kammerkonzert* graphically:

Exposition		Development			Recapitulation
Theme	*Variation I*	*Variation II*	*Variation III*	*Variation IV*	*Variation V*
Grundgestalt	Grundgestalt	Retrograde	Inversion	Retrograde	Grundgestalts
1	2			inversion	3 & 4
i	i	ii	iii	iv	i

The four statements of the *Grundgestalt* are condensed to three thanks to their superimposition in the recapitulation. Furthermore, the four contrapuntal forms are separated into the original and the three derivative forms, these three derivative forms occupying the three panels of the development. Looking at the balance of a diagram like this gives a certain satisfaction. Once it has been drawn up in this way and absorbed, can it be projected onto the music at a new hearing? Will it provide genuine illumination of the structure, or will we be trying as best we can to superimpose a hierarchical image on our perception? Is it not a disproportionate thirst for rational knowledge which makes us equate the heard events with their graphic reduction? Is it not an intention to transcend the obligation imposed by temporal succession, in order to refer ourselves to the synthetic vision of a synopsis written virtually in our memory; a synopsis which makes us able, within the listening present, simultaneously to comprehend the past and the future of the known work? Is it not also part of the intention of the composer, or of certain composers at any rate, to give us the formal architecture thanks to which we will be more able to comprehend the evolution of the work, even at the price of agreeing to some artifice; to fix this architecture outside time, so that it is reflected in our listening experience, and better apportions the points when we have to listen more intensely? In this sense, overt reference to schemes which can be visualized would function as a more or less explicit guidebook; moreover, one capable of functioning at very different levels, from simple description of events up to the most abstract formal analysis. That said, we shall see that the composer simultaneously desires and dreads what has to be termed at worst a manipulation and at best a polarization of the attention. The scheme facilitates the encounter with the work, but it is also prone to give rise to many misunderstandings. This may be by excessive simplification, reducing a living organism to a skeleton; or by being unable to account for deeper designs, which the author is moreover unable to explain. In his letter dedicating the *Kammerkonzert* to Schoenberg, Berg wrote:

> The reasons why this analysis has been devoted almost entirely to the predominance of the number three throughout the whole work are: first, this predominance, to the benefit of all the other musical events, would not have been noticed by anyone; and second, it is easier for an author to talk about exterior matters than about internal musical processes. It is obvious that these latter are not lacking in my *Kammerkonzert*, nor in any other of my works.

Nevertheless, he says nothing on the last point, remaining happy with the vaguest suggestions. . . . Just as at the end of an analysis of *Wozzeck*, he earnestly entreats us to forget all these technical details in favor of a naïve listening.

However, since writing is so overloaded with intentions, the question is no longer even, "should we listen naively," but rather, "can we still do so?"

Should we literally ignore the strict methods employed by the author, or leave them in the background of our conscious comprehension; or should we try despite everything to perceive if not all, then at least a part of his intentions and calculations?

To return to the example of the *Kammerkonzert,* if I follow carefully just the theme itself in the first movement, it is by no means certain that I do perceive the "ternary law" dear to the author, wished quite expressly by him to be a strong, constraining feature. Since we have figures, let's set out the figures described by the theme:

First part: fifteen bars, divided into two sections of seven and eight bars respectively.
Second part: nine bars.
Third part: six bars.

These figures confirm in their proportions what I experience at a first hearing and what I feel much more strongly if I try to memorize this theme (it seems to me that memory provides a very relevant and critical faculty for judging the forms actually realized in objects, rather than those described according to intentions). The opening seven bars tend towards the character of an introduction, and I end up with an equal balance between four sections of very similar length (seven, eight, nine, and six bars respectively). On the other hand, this balance between fifteen, nine, and six which is so seductive does not impose itself on me as a reality; still less does the detail that these three numbers are all multiples of three, an observation from which I am persistently drawn away by the melodic structure and the layout. So I am left with my threefold scheme and my fourfold perception of sections on my hands. At the very most I can locate motives here and there whose shape is repeated three times. In the end, even properly tuned in, I have only these slim pickings as far as the generating number goes! ... Hemmed in by other impressions which relate to unique appearances or straightforward repetitions of motives, I can hardly—at a naive glance—favor the number three over one and two. ...

Let's look then at the numbers of bars in this first movement! If I write them out according to the previous diagram, this will describe the length of the sections, remembering that they refer to the same basic tempo:

Theme	Variation I	Variation II	Variation III	Variation IV	Variation V
6/4 x 30 bars	6/4 x 30 bars	3/4 x 60 bars	6/4 x 30 bars	6/8 x 30 bars	3/4 x 60 bars
Leicht beschwingt Schwungvoll	Leicht beschwingt Schwungvoll	Langsames Walzertempo	Kräftig bewegt	Sehr rasch	Leicht beschwingt Schwungvoll

Since thirty bars of 6/4 are exactly equivalent to sixty bars of 3/4, all the segments have equal lengths, except for Variation IV, which is half as long (thirty bars of 6/8 equalling fifteen bars of 6/4). But are you going to experience unadulterated arithmetic impressions, or measure out such proportions so exactly without taking into account the rhythmic density or variation of texture which mark out these bars taken as coherent wholes rather than individually? Of course not! The nature of the musical events, outlined by the various tempo indications (*leicht beschwingt, schwungvoll, langsames Walzertempo, kräftig bewegt, sehr rasch*), and reinforced by the consistent use of lesser or greater subdivisions of the general pulse; this is what will irretrievably distract you from exact counting. At most you will notice that the very rapid Variation IV is in fact much shorter than the others, without thinking overmuch that this half-length in measured time is compensated for by a doubling of the rhythmic density. In any case, the numbers thirty and sixty will remain at the very bottom of your priorities; even if you are absolutely determined to summon them up from their distant burial-place, you will quickly realize the inadequacy of such a measuring tool. What then is the point? Is it something like an action plan, a safeguard, a discipline, even an absurd one, to force the expressive faculty to formalize and so communicate itself? The tethering is linked to a submission: a submission to a higher ordering than the individual pulse. What is the most unquestionable ordering if not that of the absolutely impersonal categories represented by numbers? It is not in the musical realm alone that we see these magical properties of proportion and number deployed. It seems that there is a need to be reassured in this way of the order implicit in the world in comparison to the chaos which we see. In this way, the immersion of the individual will in the secret design of all things implies sacrifice and transcendence. . . . To see oneself justified by a higher order of truth, to protect oneself from the error which our instinct alone does not allow us to avoid; such seems to me to be at root the meaning of this adherence to the mystery of numbers. It appears as a strange obsession with constraint within the instability of the imagination. Humor is not absent from this, even though here it elegantly summons up deep superstitions. . . .

Every composition, faced with its language, feels the tyranny of, or nostalgia for, this ordering—of music, if not of the world—by number. Tyranny, in the sense that expression has to be transmitted through quantifiable elements—which we term pitches, harmonies, rhythms, motives, durations, or whatever. But the quality of expression is in no way subject to the single criterion of quantity. From this stems a nostalgia, whether admitted or not, for the total and inescapable equation of the quality of the result with the quantities of the objects set forth. The "serial" movement in the 1950s was at bottom based on the utopian belief that writing creates the phenomenon; the rigor of the technical apparatus must implicitly guarantee aesthetic validity. One cannot help feeling a certain fascination for this exercise in depersonalizing the language, where a certain number of functions are set into play in a deterministic environment, and the role of the composer is limited to recording the results, a report of the operation. Writing is no longer the intermediary for activity, but its motive force. To follow this line of thought to its conclusion, one would have entirely to bracket the initial choices, the thumbprints left here and there in setting up the processes put into play. But paradoxically this ends in non-writing . . . in chaos! Thanks to this experiment we have, however, lived with great intensity through the antinomy between the will to order and the perception of that order; if not antinomy, then at least the complexity and occasional unforeseeability of the relationships between project and object. In its desire to invent, the mind allows itself to speculate in a parallel field, that of the eye, in the confident hope that the ear can and *must* follow. Out of an irresistible desire to produce unity, the most dissimilar categories are forced to correspond to each other; processes applied to one component part are then applied to another without the slightest change in nature. Up against the extreme naivety of wishful thinking, the world of perception resists and will not let itself be reduced to the systematic combination of a certain number of schemas. Obviously, instinct is a corrective; the rule we had at the beginning has been discarded—but there is still an alternative approach, one rather more aware of certain events which passed unnoticed or were considered to be one-offs. . . .

We will consider several issues: first of all, the identity of the musical object during the transformations to which it can be subjected; then, the concept of an envelope defined purely by an *audible* criterion, that surrounds events which call for a more detailed analysis; then, the additional concept of orientation points or signposts which focus the attention on moments of articulation or transformation; finally, an approach extremely flexible in the manipulation of evidence or its dissolution, of determinism and uncertainty.

The identity, or rather identification, of the musical object through the many modifications to which it may be subject, has hardly ever been in doubt. All composers have made abundant use, in the most traditional of contexts, of the techniques of augmentation and diminution, inversion, retrograding, harmonic displacement—how I could go on! The arsenal is vast and extends back to the very origins of our polyphony. However, was that polyphony not originally a transgression of perception? The cantus firmus presents an extreme stretching in time of a melody meant to be "comprehended"—in both senses of the word—in the more limited bounds of "normal speed"; does it not, by this single fact, make the original object unrecognizable? And this is without contending with the grafting onto it of another melodic line, which will monopolize the attention for several reasons, the first being its speed of statement, which is much easier to grasp!

From these sorts of transgressions pragmatism can be seen to win out over and again in the development both of writing and of inventiveness. The "inventor" seems to display a wish and a need to refer to an initial object. His work, pleasure, even malice often consist of helping or hindering the listener in the recognition and recollection of this initial object through the transformations he imposes on it and the derivative forms he draws from it.

In fact, "perpetual" invention seems to hold no interest within this relationship of the listener and the work. If the listener is always discovering, never recognising, the perspectives of perception undergo no modification capable of holding the attention: interest is dulled by following the discourse. But if we are distanced from or brought closer to a *model,* then and then alone a dialogue can begin; a relationship can be established which goes well beyond formal recognition to illuminate to us the creative thought process itself. So the composer pursues his "object," he *sees* it as much as he *hears* it. And so within him struggle these two impulses to transform it, whether in its visual appearance or in its more specifically auditory properties. It is interesting to note that *improvisatory* writing makes use above all of auditory criteria—in particular, harmonics—whereas *intellectual* writing has made almost immoderate use of visual features—invertible counterpoint and retrogrades, to be specific. The feature which is self-contained, immediate, and harmonic does not need, so to speak, to be visualized; it can pass directly to the perception. The feature which is successive, stratified, and contrapuntal implies a certain visualisation in order to be grasped more clearly. In other words, a phenomenon presented as a simultaneity does not require the same sort of points of orientation as one presented as a succession.

This is what is notable in contemporary practice; memory can be of use here, too, in testifying to those signs which distinguish where perception can operate. For all that, musicians have privileged certain sorts of transformation over others, probably because they seem to them less "abstract," less removed from the original through being auditory phenomena, and therefore more justified in their use. Leaving aside temporal augmentation and diminution, to which I shall return, let us look at the most currently popular manipulations of pitches, which are inversions and retrogrades. What are these if not the musical equivalents of visual transformations in a *mirror?* If the mirror is placed horizontally in relation to the text, we have an inversion; if it is placed vertically, the retrograde appears. It is interesting to observe that these musical techniques appeared and became consolidated at the time that mirror-images played such a big role in painting. Perhaps one need only observe a common obsession with playing with appearances, or creating through illusion!

Up until the Second Viennese School, these manipulations were applied to motives, and their rhythmic profile remained the same. This sameness therefore easily allowed—in the case of inversion—the comparison of the original motive with its transformation: the one appeared as the reflection of the other. If the direction in time is changed, the deduction is much less perceptible. The phrase literally changes in *meaning,* and strongly outstanding features—big differences in intervals or highly contrasting rhythms—are needed for us to be able to latch onto them as unmistakable orientation points. However little traditional academic training he has been through, a musician will be able without hesitation to play the inversion of a given motive; when it comes to the retrograde, the test will be much less conclusive and he will quickly become aware of the effort of mental "visualization" which it demands. He will be able to do it more easily if he does not have to contend with varied rhythmic values—the obstacle of time flowing backwards being thus removed—and if the motive continuously follows a single linear direction, which helps in placing the constituent units; in other words, if the profile of the motive is completely even. There is no need to add that in all cases, the shorter the motive then the easier the task, since the capacity of the memory to parcel up data is not unlimited. . . . These memory tests are, I repeat, invaluable indicators in seeing how our perception reacts and what level of difficulty it can overcome in recognizing the objects presented to it.

However, the composer, who has a position of static visual supremacy in regard to his work, tends to transgress these fundamental ideas which would limit him too far in his means of invention. He transgresses, though, in the hope that this scheme, whose geography is under his control, will at least be glimpsed by his listener—whom he feels obliged to guide with certain spectacular gestures intended to attract his attention. Or again, if he realizes that he has transgressed in a certain realm, he will simplify other elements, precisely so that the attention is not divided, but may forget certain aspects which are easy to grasp in favor of one which is less so, in a system of checks and balances. As a first example of these two attitudes, I will once more turn to Berg's *Kammerkonzert.* The second movement uses its central point as an axis of symmetry, the second half being a retrograde of the first; although the reality is much less simple than this description suggests, given the numerous details which are varied between the original text and the retrograde. In fact, Berg questioned whether, were it not for a sufficiently obvious orientation point, the listener would simply pass on without paying attention to the central moment of the movement, and therefore the central moment of the entire work. So he set up a sort of suspension at this point: the piano, which is excluded from the rest of the movement, enters here surreptitiously—without sounding like a soloist, the author notes—and sounds twelve strokes on a low C sharp before disappearing. . . . "Midnight strikes—the midnight when the die must be cast!" [See figure 9.2.] Making the formal structure emerge through a *gesture* brings to notice if not the entirety of the form, then at least this remarkable moment when it starts to fold back on itself. The truth of these symmetrical layouts, as I have stated, is at best that the motives change their *meaning,* and at worst that they lose it, and that which was conceived according to one directional deployment through time is hard put to support the constraints of returning in reverse. When the motives are already formed with equal rhythmic values and statistical balance between intervals, as is the case in certain parts of the *Allegro Mysterioso* of the *Lyric Suite* or in the Second Act Interlude in *Lulu,* they pass the test without a problem thanks to the ambiguity of the structure in which they are couched; but in this case one tends to forget that one is dealing with a retrograde, precisely because of the apparent identity between the transformed result and the original. It seems to me that one of the most striking and successful examples of the retrograding of a motive is provided by the fugue of Beethoven's Piano Sonata Op. 106, where neutral elements, which are practically unnoticed as reversed, contrast with and balance against sharp-edged rhythms which change radically in outline and accent. But this is notably a fugue subject rather than a whole formal section. [See figure 9.3]

As for Webern, while he constantly employs all the classic "visual" contrapuntal manipulations, it is notable that the further he goes, the more he simultaneously simplifies the elements with which he is working, in both number and nature. In some of his works, the Concerto Op. 24 for one, he strips the thematic material down to a single motive of three sounds, which is the minimal requirement for a feature that can be recognized separately. He does indeed use the transformed versions of this figure to make up the full chromatic complement; but these manipulations are carried out with an object so easy to perceive in its totality that its varied settings do nothing to obliterate the make-up of the original object. Only through this radical simplification can the immediate recognition of the thematic matrix be achieved. There is an immediate communication between sight and hearing, at the necessary expense of the complexity of the *structuring.*

What happens to the relationship between the realization of the work and the faculty of perception when the *structuring* becomes more complex, so that what you can still see with the eye, you are no longer sure that you can perceive by ear? What happens when even the eye has difficulty finding its path through the byways of a deliberately cryptic style of writing? Is it at least left with some remainder whose role and importance it is in a position to judge? Caught between the written reality of his text and the lived reality of his experience, the composer's misgivings sometimes—often?—vanish before a fixed belief in the magic of schemes and numbers. Structures possessed by a mysterious power come to suffuse our knowledge, invade our subconscious, and cause us to participate in their existence in a sort of mystic communion that goes beyond rational justification. Exorcism is going a bit far, but not without a grain of truth. The "required" dimensions of "intellectual" music bring about deviations from accepted musical language; deviations whose origins we perhaps never perceive, unless

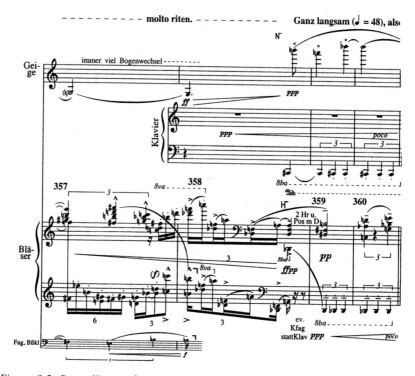

Figure 9.2. Berg, *Kammerkonzert*. Central axis of symmetry, second movement, mm. 357–364. Copyright © 1925 by Universal Edition A.G., Wien. Used by permission.

we keep seeking out and finding their rationale; but whose strangeness we grasp. The requirements of invertible counterpoint bring about the elimination of certain intervals, which are prohibited because they cannot function correctly in two sets of circumstances or under two regimes: that of the original, and that of the inversion of the component parts. So although one is probably not aware of the invertible nature of the counterpoint, one notices the absence of a family of intervals. To connect these two facts with each other implies knowledge of the rules of writing; nevertheless, in ignorance of these rules, your perception will have been directed toward the fact that something is lacking in the prevailing situation. In the same way, in Op. 106, when we meet the strange accentuation in comparison to everything that has preceded it, and the rhythmic figures foreign to Beethoven's usual vocabulary, we are in no sense obliged to relate these to retrograde motion in order to understand that we are dealing with a strict transformation, by which the vocabulary is subjected to such a constraint that it acquires exceptional characteristics. Is it not the result that is important, rather

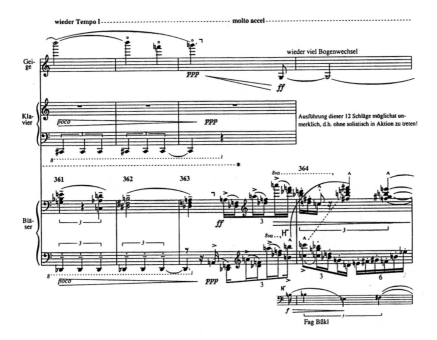

Figure 9.2. *(continued).*

than the intellectual explanation behind the facts? Would the perception alone be incomplete? Would the result only be valid because the perception would be justified by the explanation? It is an unreasonable restriction of the perception's field of operation, to limit it to what can be explained in words. When Berg, at the end of his lecture on *Wozzeck*, advocates that one forget his analyses, it is not simply in order to defend himself against accusations of pedantry, dryness, or excessive cerebration. He does not disavow his constructional processes, but he does declare that if these processes are adequate to the needs of expression, then it is the expression itself which must be investigated, because that way the products of his imagination will be much more reliably *assessed*. In other words, if writing and necessity do not coincide, then all hope of worthwhile results vanishes.

Sometimes, though, does the impression not arise that the means put into play are too complex and unwieldy for the looked-for results? Does it not seem that the perception cannot hold onto more than a tiny part of the design, and that during the varied wanderings, what was intended has evaporated to such a great extent that one might ask whether it was even worth intending it in the first place? One could, of course, put forward the idea of different levels of reading to justify an abundance of things which might, so to speak, be partially useful, usable or used. One could point to the

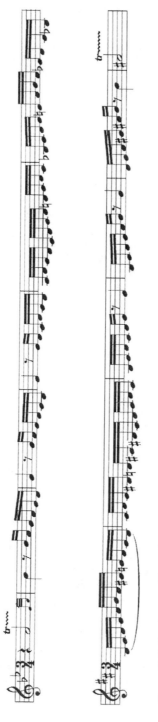

Figure 9.3. Beethoven, Piano Sonata Op. 106, "Hammerklavier." Fugue subject and retrograde in fourth movement (mm. 16–21, mm. 153–158).

progress towards understanding a work achieved by intellectual or non-intellectual endeavour; in other words, the analysis of a specialist or the repeated listening of an amateur. But are there not levels of complexity which no amount of familiarity could make us accept in reality? That is, when it is impossible to align the work and the scheme save by an artificial effort, defeated as soon as realized? Moreover, is there a need to seek out this alignment at any cost? Even if the author's precise wish is for us to have to put his methods out of our mind each time that we come close to the real depths of his work? Is the only approach constantly to shine this unbearable light on what he wants to say and how he tries to express it? That bears a strong resemblance to the electric lamp permanently alight in the cell on death row. . . . Let's leave the joys and sorrows of the labyrinth behind from time to time! The most "readerly" is not necessarily the best. The deep meaning of the result may transcend the technical means which enabled it to crystallize. It brings to mind Claudel: "It is what you don't understand that is the most beautiful, what is the most extended that is the most interesting, and what you don't find amusing that is the funniest."[3]

In any given work, from the most strictly determined piece of working-out to the most apparently disorderly profusion of ideas, we develop our own schematic outline to guide us which is not necessarily that of the author; one that is provisional, tentative, partial, sporadic, maybe false, what does it matter! A work rich in meaning is multiple and ambivalent; it does not dictate one single path. Writing has awoken an infinite number of avenues in addition to a literal approach; all are justified. Sometimes, interpretative misunderstandings are more richly suggestive than a straight reading; the lesson of writing is that it teaches us, paradoxically, to forget and transcend the means themselves, and to see the general idea from which they spring. In truth, would we still study Bach's canons—augmentations, diminutions, inversions, and the rest included—if they did not teach us something profound about space and time? Elemental principles which we may or may not want to appropriate; but if we want to, we will set off in search of the means which have been fashioned to our thought, which will no longer have much if anything in common with what impelled us in the first place. In this way, writing is not a code to be studied in a sterile fashion, but rather, it engenders other codes through a deductive process possible only to a sufficiently powerful imagination. In a work taken as a model, one must of necessity detach the writing from its literal context—by an extension of "naive listening," and sometimes despite it—in order to decipher the universal potential that it possesses, and pass through the mirror to the reality. Every work teaches us by means of its writing, but it is only beyond that writing that we learn.

To consider the work solely as a pedagogical text, however, would be to impose intolerable limitations on it. A work is not fundamentally meant for our edification, whether cultural or professional. Much more than that, it aims to give us a revelation of ourselves, endlessly to open up to us un-suspected vistas. What use is a work of art, if not to enrich both our per-ception and our understanding—of the worth of artistic interchange, and of the strength of the work's power? And how can it do this without conceptualization and writing as intermediaries? We accumulate our fund of personal knowledge piecemeal, in masterpieces of the past where we have patiently searched for it, just as much as in events which suddenly throw it up. And this knowledge undoubtedly lies in understanding the limits of knowledge; in applying it to the extreme flux of events just asone can, in a context which is never entirely foreseeable. Before I even touch on some more specific perspectives, I would affirm that pondering over the concepts behind the music, over the actual make-up of the transcription of those concepts, is instructive because this intellectual reflection, which is somewhat distanced from events, saves one from being ensnared by false ideas. All these categories and methods which seem "self-evident," are they not, really, only a propensity to trust our instincts alone? The creative imagi-nation has at its disposal a number of stock architectonic schemes, whose renewal will not be guaranteed by a few adjustments to intentions. Going forward without the aid of our normal musical instincts, working on the concept directly, brings us by unforeseen short-circuits to new states of language and materials. Did we already have within us this collection of ideas waiting only to be brought to light by suitable methods, or did work-ing on these methods make the ideas if not come into being, then at least crystallize—ideas of which we would never otherwise have suspected the possible existence? This question is of so little importance that it is hardly worth asking. The reciprocal relationship between the organisation of the creative imagination and the organisation of writing is such that one can-not ask which is antecedent and which consequent, hierarchically speak-ing. The step from the *spontaneous* to the *intellectual* does not involve an alteration of essence, but rather a very unstable see-saw. Intellectual reflec-tion can be stimulated by acting on impulse just as much as compositional acts can be revitalized by calculation!

Is it not through acts that we are able to appreciate the calculation: acts by which it is now denoted, now denounced, now denied? The composer thinks according to certain categories which he believes to be important. In the course of his labor, sometimes only when it is over, he will realize that the truly essential categories are not those he thought, but others to which he has probably only accorded secondary attention. By this I do not mean to praise errors in calculation or judgment. These happen, of course, and irritating they are too, indeed intensely so and even in the most trivial de-tails. You only have to misjudge the true value of an instrument's proper-ties, and straight away a single interval is capable of destroying, through its weight and coarseness, the whole polyphonic texture otherwise skilfully realized. The eye can be misled in this sort of assessment, or forget to make it; but the ear remains vigilant and independent; it is concerned not with the method but with the result, and signals the oversight to you at once. No, errors in this first sense of the word are quickly recognized by experience and no longer committed. What I wish to talk about is when one's judgment is caught, pincer-like, by the ambiguity that stems from the relative importance of different concomitant elements.

Consider the starting brief that Webern gives himself in the first movement of the Symphony Op. 21: to write a double canon in four voices disposed as a sonata form movement—exposition, development, recapitulation. This satisfies his idea of a strong hierarchy in the realm of form as much as in that of *writing*; the lines of derivation must be seen to be rigorous in the small as much as at the global level. However, the two canons must be presented in the exposition in a way that distinguishes them from each other, while preserving a static equilibrium. One of them must be primary, eminently readable, and the other a sort of shadow of the first, the persistent fragmentation of its elements greatly reducing its readability. In the development, the four voices have to be clearly of equal weight and importance, the carefully positioned motives being put through four transformations without deviation or exception. In the recapitulation, the necessary variation from the exposition consists of passing that exposition through the prism of the development; in other words, there are no longer two principal, readerly voices and two secondary, more fluid ones, but rather all four are of equal importance. However, in place of the simplification which took place in the development section, here there is ambiguity and complexity in the relationship, emphasized to the full, between one voice and another; from this comes uncertainty in distinguishing the voices at sight.

It is beyond the scope of this study to enter into the compositional details which enable Webern to realize his intentions. So I will pass over this technical aspect in order to point out straight away the interest attaching to such a general description of the form and of the means used to arrive at it. Technical detail is after all *detail,* which we do not have to know in order to perceive the form. What is much more important, even vital, is the phenomenon which I shall call the *envelope* of the musical events, which is the composer's own act.

What is it that actually guides our perception in the first section of this movement by Webern? [See figure 9.4.] Certainly not the four-part writing in itself. First, there is the fact that we have some motives which are clearly recognisable, and others which are less so and remain in the shadow of the first ones: this is the first envelope. Second, we have the fact that the pitches want to remain immobile—all the events take place within a fixed network which disappears for the second section: this is the second envelope, just as powerful as the first for our understanding of the musical discourse. So there are on the one hand phenomena which are linked to the musical

Canons in Webern Symphony Op. 21, mm. 1 - 24

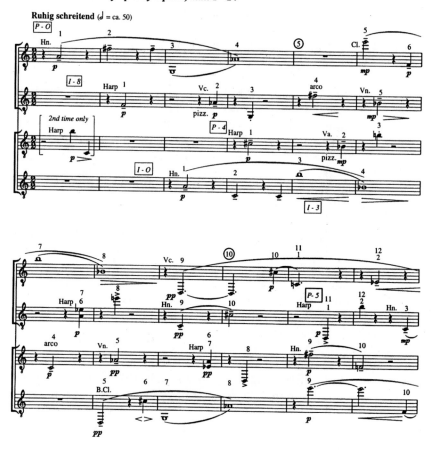

Figure 9.4. Webern, Symphony, Op. 21. Double canon in first movement, mm. 1–24. Copyright © 1929 by Universal Edition A.G., Wien. Used by permission.

content itself—in this case, the double canon in four voices, which gives rise to the structure of the notes; and there are also phenomena which envelop this content and give it a field of action—here, the immobility of the pitches and the readability of the pair of principal voices in relation to the other pair. One can guess what it is that the ear will immediately master in this double plan of action, and that is the envelope; in order to be able to orientate itself in what belongs more to the realm of the eye, that is, the structure of the canonic writing. The phenomenon is not entirely as simple as I have described, since the envelope of fixed pitches does not work only one-way, and I have not mentioned the dividing up of the timbres, which

Figure 9.4. *(continued).*

adds at once clarity and ambiguity, or, explicates and complicates! The fact that principal and secondary voices draw on exactly the same network of pitches does indeed free us from the difficulty of following different tessiturae; the fixed nature of the pitches in a way relieves us of the phenomenon *pitch* and enables us to concentrate on the musical phrases themselves. And it is indeed on these that Webern expends his effort. The principal canon is set forth in regular cells and predominantly in long notes and homogenous timbres; the secondary canon varies the timbre irregularly, in cells of unequal lengths with predominantly short notes. In the first case, we have pairs of statement and response whose symmetry is easy to grasp;

in the second case, while the symmetry is still there, we have much more difficulty in perceiving it, because of the irregularity of division of phrase and timbre. Continuity against discontinuity is how one can crudely sum up the two-against-two voice opposition in this canon. However, in the phrasing which makes up each voice of the principal canon, Webern creates contrasts of timbre which clarify its articulation for us and analyze its symmetry for our ear. So we have the sequence horn–clarinet–cello–clarinet–horn, to which the sequence horn–bass clarinet–viola–bass clarinet–horn responds; each time the same instrument takes the same four notes. From this comes the absolute identity between note, articulation and timbre. Identification functions thanks to this principle, which links the constituent elements of the phrase to the same auditory signals: another envelope. As I said, it explicates and complicates. . . . Indeed, if the phrase had been given on a single instrument, we would not perhaps have grasped its articulation so easily, but we would have been more aware of its continuity. This is how, in producing greater clarity in one respect, one creates obscurity in some other: a shifting relationship between the envelopes, which creates perceptual richness, and causes the text to gain flexibility and variability which keep sensitivity and memory alert.

The game of recognition and the perspectives of hearing: these are the things which constitute the prize and success of a work. They create within us the sense both of an immediate truth of the text, and of a truth buried more deeply, which we cannot be sure we have grasped completely. In the first movement of his Concerto Op. 24, Webern gives us an example of these two states alternating, which goes to define the form effectively. The two extreme states are defined on the one hand by the perfect symmetry of the division into groups of three sounds, and on the other hand by the segmentation of the full chromatic scale into more regular and less regular groups, where the notion of symmetry vanishes. Transitional states allow one to pass from one of these extreme states to the other. So in order for us to be able to assess the form, we have to rely on the succession of these states where our perception makes a to-and-fro movement between strictness and fluidity. These sorts of considerations are infinitely more important to analyse—if one wants to understand the rational basis behind our spontaneous impressions—than the technique of writing, strictly speaking. These phenomena definitively reconcile eye and ear and give meaning to the enunciation and articulation of a text. The creation of perceptible orientation points makes the text rise up to clear definition in the mind, or makes it recede towards regions less defined and less obvious; in this lies the fundamental justification of all "composing-out." There is no need to limit oneself to morphological details to identify these orientation points and to hear them function as signals of lived musical reality; at the very most, the in-depth study of morphology can show us how these signals have been created, and how effectively the means have been used.

In the fugue of Op. 106 discussed above, the shape of the subject in retrograde acts precisely as a signal; it alerts us to the exceptional nature of this transformation in the unfolding of the text. In this way Bartók, in the third movement of the *Music for Strings, Percussion, and Celeste* uses the elements of the fugue theme from the first movement to signal the articulating points of the overall form. In this way Berg signals the hinge-point in his large palindromic movements by a suspension, a dramatic gesture, or the contrast of a non-symmetrical section. There are numerous examples of the "explanation" of a complex category by a simpler one, one which can be invoked instantaneously and gives us information useful in enabling us to find our way in the evolution of the texture, density, or complexity of the work. I would like to cite the example of my own *Rituel,* which is based on the superimposition of denser and denser asynchronous groups. Each of these groups is conducted "in sound" by a percussionist giving a regular pulse. At the opening of the piece, where the oboe plays alone, you pay little attention to the percussion, in order to follow the oboe's melodic line. When two or three groups play together, of course you notice the interference patterns of the different percussion instruments, all the more so because each uses a different timbre; but their role remains in the background, since you are occupied with making out the melodic identity of the different groups, and following the heterophonic game through which they correspond with each other. As the number of groups increases, the density can no longer be perceived analytically, and you latch onto the rhythmic interference patterns of the percussion. The more the perception loses its footing in one realm, the more it latches onto a related realm which it had neglected up till then. The principal phenomena become the secondary, and vice versa.

From determinism to perceptual uncertainty, from definition of events to their dissolution, the eye is there; now to aid the ear, now to mislead it. One is not obliged therefore, in my opinion, to understand writing in order to perceive it. The loss of energy between transmitter and receiver can drive one mad! Certainly, a work's richness of meaning, the fact that it cannot be immediately exhausted, but rather resists inquiry and even reforms its mystery beyond inquiry, its capacity to continue to radiate; these things imply not wastage, but abundance of means, which cannot all—ever—be perceived for sure. The author can even show his propensity for hiding away secrets meant for himself alone, or for giving an esoteric meaning to certain aspects of the work, or for clothing it in cryptic symbols. Hermeticism is not necessarily a measure of quality or superiority; no more is it damnable if understanding can be reached on some other basis. What does counting the bars in the *Lyric Suite* matter to us? If it does show us the author's obsession with *numerological* secrets, it does nothing to guide us concerning the nature of the musical events. It reminds one of the block of marble from which Michelangelo carved his *David.* . . . Does the constraint imposed by these numbers seem absurd to us? We can certainly imagine that the constraint did not work one-way only, and that Berg knew how to manipulate the numbers with such skill and ease that he could make them do whatever he liked. For example, it was not the numbers which dictated the length of his phrases to him, but rather he who imposed on the numbers to make them account for his phrases. In any case it is obvious that he has not *signalled* these numbers as such, but on the contrary has taken them as signals of the articulating points of the form.

The composer may well have no taste for the associated messages; but he will feel the need to make his language rich and dense, to multiply balances and symmetries, to build up the different types of envelope. Is this, too, a waste of effort? Perhaps! It is true that, by forgetting the dynamic nature of relationships and the limits of perception—because the eye which regards the written score is static—the composer will be tempted to create compressed passages whose meaning no longer takes account of the motion laid down by time. Too much meaning means no meaning at all; the memory is incapable of retaining the elements necessary to orientate itself in the midst of constant, excessive change. Is the memory then the principal mediator between the eye and the ear? It certainly seems so. That is what it is—if not exclusively, then at least as the decisive agent. It sets to work at once on the orientation points which you give to it, to take note of signals, in order to give you this information at the required moments, where there is a parallel structure or a similar envelope. It is by means of the memory that the work reveals to you its most immediately striking features. As long as you give it adequate starting materials—arresting moments, dominating proportions, gestures—then it is able to tell you about the stages of the work's development, if not also about the nature of the development itself. If you do not give it such points of purchase, so that it can only register situations that are markedly dissimilar to each other, then information will no longer be transmitted; all the writing will remain a dead letter, at the very most showing itself through chance mishaps, with neither antecedent nor consequent. In fact, the memory is a deductive instrument. When you are unfamiliar with the work to which you are listening, the memory takes a few principal orientation points and gives you no more than very rough deductions. The more often it travels the path mapped out by the work, the more precise and numerous become the orientation points that it registers. They are also assessed with much greater accuracy as far as their position, relative importance and inter-relationships go; in this way the memory's deductions become more and more refined, until eventually they completely cover the besieged territory. Just as it is possible to help or hinder the perception, so it is equally possible to help or hinder the memory; to trick it in regard to its capacity for assessment or deduction, producing a temporary, transient state. For example, an envelope may tell you that a musical event or object belongs to the same family as an earlier event or object; but certain aspects, either internal—the constituent parts themselves—or external—the context—make the memory hesitate over the identification, as similarity and difference balance each other out, preventing a definite recognition.

Evidently, the network which links together the scheme of intentions and the realized texture can give rise to many a reflection, even many a speculation. The pathways implied by this network are of a disconcerting complexity, the fluctuations of which make one unable ever to be sure of grasping them. It is patent that trusting to what one wills to happen leads all too easily to obscurity; the necessary passing of accepted limits threatens to result in non-validity, or equally in absurdity of relationships. Bringing time into play, that dimension essential to all living experience, threatens to carry off and destroy in its wake the best-planned constructions of the static equilibrium of sight. The envelopes risk not observing the hierarchy which one had aimed to give them, if this hierarchy plays fast and loose with certain acoustic facts or perceptual criteria. In short, many things have to be thought about, and it might be as well not to think about all of them at once. The only feasible and reasonable attitude undoubtedly bases its chances on a circumscribed pragmatism and a direct assessment of the events being manipulated. To be systematic, a doctrine would have to be so ramified, and to take account of so many contradictory things, that the effort would be out of all proportion to the results obtained. Assessing and evaluating step by step in accordance with the situation, while taking account of all the factors of the moment, but only of those; considering a localized situation while relating it to the whole of the work by means of strict common lines; this, it seems to me, is the most effective way of proceeding, because it can take account of accidents, momentary deviations, and long-range planning all at once. It does not keep resorting to disproportionately weighty apparatus, but on the contrary allows the importance of methods to be adapted to the expression of needs, and the needs of expression. As far as I can see, it is almost inevitable that, in everything to do with the relationship between eye and ear, between memory and perception, and between expressive power and technical method, absolute dogmatism is hopelessly doomed to failure, since it does not manage to get hold of the many and varied aspects of the problem. The rigidity of the mental attitude causes the creative imagination to wither and die. The creative imagination must still be nourished by a "vision," in the sense that, if the ear is left to itself and is not kept under the watchful guard of the eye, or if the ear is not spurred on by the transgressive power of fantasy, its capacity for invention is too easily diluted in the clichés to which it is then tempted to abandon itself. Here is found the story of improvisers, distant descendants of the "knights of the keyboard" for whom Bach did not demonstrate a great esteem. The ear and the fingers are indeed counsellors not to be ignored; precious antidotes to reflective thought too disengaged from reality; useful helpers in many circumstances. Nevertheless, they do not know how to take charge of the primary tasks of invention and writing, of invention *through* writing, tasks for which the eye remains the principal workman. I repeat again that for me, writing means all methods of transcription; it is not uniquely linked to the one traditional way of transcribing, and it can therefore be virtual, detached from all material support.

Let us then keep ourselves from forgetting whatever may be able to come to our aid from the arsenal provided us by eye and ear. Otherwise, as in the old stories, the fairy who has been forgotten will come to do us mischief! Moreover, why should we complain about the difficulty of having to make sensibility and organisation, scheme and gesture, or plan and accident coincide? Let us then learn to live out the instability of our condition to the full. As common sense teaches us, we are beings steeped in both instinct and reason. . . . I see no advantage in getting rid of the one to benefit the other. That is why I resolutely hold that eye and ear, even when they conflict, must each keep their privileges. It is up to the composer to put up with the discomfort of the situation I propose. Sometimes, cordial relations obtain between the two parties. However, let us not delude ourselves; these cases are the exception in this stormy alliance. And the remainder is purgatory!

Notes

1. [Editorial note: Boulez originally gave this disquisition as a lecture at the Collège de France; it first appeared in print in the journal *Critique,* under the title "L'Ecriture du musicien: le regard du sourd?" and Christian Bourgois published it in the Boulez collection *Jalons (pour une Décennie),* as edited by Jean-Jacques Nattiez (Paris: Christian Bourgois, 1989). The present editor and translator agreed that the essay benefits from insertion of several musical examples, particularly in a collection of this type. As the copyright holder, Bourgois also assented to this change, but the reader is reminded that no examples accompanied the essay when it originally appeared in *Critique* or *Jalons.* We thank Mr. Bourgois for his permission to make this translation.]

2. [Boulez's "original form" (*forme originale*) is translated here as *Grundegestalt*— the less equivocal, Schoenbergian term that Berg used in his own analysis, which Boulez is in part drawing upon.]

3. From Paul Claudel's play *Le Soulier de satin,* 1929, first performed by Jean-Louis Barrault at the Comédie-Française in 1943 and at the Théâtre d'Orsay in 1979.

10

"Are You *Sure* You Can't Hear It?": Some Informal Reflections on Simple Information and Listening

RICHARD TOOP

In the first chapter of his *Introduction to the Sociology of Music*, Adorno establishes a hierarchical list of ways of listening to music. It is undoubtedly elitist, dogmatically pro-modernist and socio-culturally prejudiced, and it has probably won Adorno few admirers outside the Austro-German cultural sphere (some years ago a graduate student of mine, with a distinguished track-record as a big-band 1st trumpet in L.A. and elsewhere, responded to it by exclaiming, "I wouldn't let this guy use my *toilet!*"). Still, by way of preface to what follows, I should like to resuscitate Adorno's two "highest" categories of listening as a basis for suggesting, firstly, that they may be applicable to chronologically much later versions of modernism than Adorno imagined, and secondly, that the option of listening to music in at least the second of these ways, given appropriate information, may be a great deal less exclusivist than he seems to imply. To this end, I shall introduce and discuss some instances of the kind of "expert" information, often quite simple in character, that seems to me to facilitate the hearing of structure and process in many modernist works, just as it frequently does when it occurs in the discussion of Indian classical music, bebop, Eddie van Halen's guitar solos, and much else besides. (The actual term "structural hearing," is one that might seem appropriate here, but it comes loaded with so many associations, especially from Austro-German music theory, that I have been somewhat wary of its use.)

Obviously, I shall make no claim that such listening constitutes an all-embracing experience of music, or that the repertoire in question has a potentially "universal" relevance. (After all, with the possible exception of a tiny time-bracket following the release of Walt Disney's *Fantasia*, relatively complex Western art music has never been a significant part of even a Western population's listening experience.) Nor do I claim that what follows is universally applicable to the kind of repertoire discussed here. My much more modest aim is to indicate possibilities, and perhaps to puncture a few of the assumptions about listening to modernist music that tend to be generated within academic discourse, especially when politicizing the act of listening is the main issue at stake.

Most of the examples I shall refer to are drawn from a post-1945 European modernist repertoire. The primary reason for this is that, of the various contemporary repertoires which are widely held to be problematic in terms of certain kinds of listening, this is the one I am most familiar with, in terms of the music itself and its cultural and conceptual background, and also, perhaps, in terms of its composers' expectations of listeners. Nearly all the works would be regarded as characteristic of the musical avant-gardes of their respective eras, and particularly of what are often regarded as "structuralist" factions, whether serial or stochastic. Naturally the selection of works is determined by the desire to be persuasive rather than all-inclusive, but I would maintain that each work discussed is entirely typical of its composer.

Adorno's highest level of listening is the "expert listener": "He would be the completely conscious listener, who innately misses nothing, and is able to account for what is being heard immediately, at any moment. Anyone who, confronted for the first time with a fluid piece which has disposed of tangible architectonic supports, such as the second movement of Webern's String Trio, is able to name its formal parts, would clearly qualify as this type."[1] No prizes for guessing who Adorno has in mind! Maybe there's also a slightly malicious gibe at Stravinsky here; in his first book of *Conversations with Robert Craft,* published just a couple of years earlier, Stravinsky had described the first (rondo) movement of Webern's trio as "wonderfully interesting but no one hears it as a Rondo."[2]

Stravinsky's claim, it seems to me, is actually open to dispute, at least from a late-twentieth-century perspective. A listener armed only with the word "rondo" might well be in for a degree of puzzlement, if they assume that whatever they hear first will return many times over, as might typically happen in a Mozart rondo. But the wispy, somewhat enigmatic opening bars are only an introduction to the main theme in m. 4, whose "sighing" gesture is quite clear at each recurrence except, perhaps, the last. This having been pointed out, the overall form is immediately clearer, and a couple more sentences will make most other formal turning points audible. It may be, of course, that Stravinsky had something else in mind, namely that at the height of the "post-Webern" era, he and the young avant-garde he was so intrigued by were scarcely looking to Webern for new ways of writing rondos.

Adorno's choice of the String Trio is, in any case, somewhat perverse, since it represents a unique attempt on Webern's part to present inherited formal structures such as sonata and rondo in terms of the expressionist aesthetic of the instrumental works he had been composing fifteen years

earlier. Clearly, the Trio did not satisfy Webern's own increasing requirement for "intelligibility" (*Faßlichkeit*), as witness the complete revision of
agendas in the subsequent instrumental works (starting with the Symphony
Op. 21), in which the composition of clearly perceptible forms is a consistent feature.[3] There are three general criteria for these forms: they are mainly
simple, they are familiar, and they are projected over relatively short time
spans.

The post-war generation of young avant-gardists that adopted Webern
as a patron saint did not necessarily share his passion for formal clarity,
and it certainly didn't share his predilection for traditional forms. When
Stockhausen analyzed the opening of the Concerto Op. 24, there was no
mention of antecedents and consequents, let alone sonata form (of which
more below). Yet some kind of "structural listening" was clearly important to Stockhausen, for a whole series of articles in the 1950s and 1960s,
most of which began life as broadcasts with musical examples, deal directly with matters of auditory perception and propose new criteria for
listening. In a 1954 program, "Von Webern zu Debussy," he applies "statistical" criteria to Debussy's *Jeux*. The following year, in a text subtitled
"Anleitung zum Hören" ("A Guide to Listening"), he presents and discusses his own *Klavierstück I* in terms of "group composition." Neither of
these involves formal analysis (the discussion of *Klavierstück I* only partly
reflects the actual composition process); they are concerned with explaining "how it is possible to listen in on the new musical language."[4] The same
approach holds good for the somewhat later essay "Momentform" (1960),
which begins by referring to "experiences I have had recently in the realms of
musical composition, performance practice, and the practice of listening."[5]

In the context of moment form, Stockhausen's comments are not geared
to the perception of a single, overarching form, for the simple reason that
no such conception of form is present. Rather, they are directed towards
perceiving the criteria for moment to moment differentiation. Later, in the
1970s, that situation changes; in many ways, Stockhausen's "formula composition" from *Mantra* onwards is analogous to cantus firmus composition. Accordingly, Stockhausen's later guides to listening are amplified to
pay greater attention to the audible relation of the part to the whole. But
the emphasis on the moment remains, though its orientation is more obviously tied to tradition. He comments in 1980 that, "there was always much
more to hear in art music than one could hear. It is almost of the essence of
art music that more happens in a work than one can consciously perceive
at the moment of hearing."[6] And in so saying he is essentially echoing the
comments with which William Byrd, almost three centuries earlier, prefaced his *Psalms, Songes and Sonnets* of 1611: "A song that is well and
artificially made cannot be well perceived nor understood at the first hearing, but the oftener you shall hear it, the better cause of liking you will
discover. . . ."

Stockhausen's concerns with new criteria for "structural listening" have not, of course, been universal among the post-war avant-garde. Leaving aside Cage's famous separation of composing, performing, and listening, and Babbitt's editorially mistitled "Who Cares If You Listen?" (I assume that Babbitt is actually extremely concerned about *how* people listen, assuming they choose to do so in the first place), one can take the comments with which Henri Pousseur begins a text from the mid-1960s as characterizing a widespread perception: "For some time, serial music has been regarded as radically asymmetrical, and entirely aperiodic. That's how its audience feels it to be, and that is how it is conceived by its authors, who take every possible step to achieve a maximum of irregularity."[7]

One might reasonably dispute whether, or how broadly, this alleged view was actually true, even for Pousseur. Nevertheless, it has become a virtual shibboleth, and has helped to foster many preconceptions about the latent impenetrability of certain kinds of "new music" over the past half-century. I have no magic wand with which to dispel these, but I shall seek to suggest that in many instances, the capacity of music-lovers to understand what is going on in "modernist works" is considerably greater than they may imagine, or have been led to believe.

Returning to Adorno's listening categories, their author readily concedes that "Anyway, anyone who sought to make all listeners into experts under prevailing social conditions would be acting with inhuman utopianism,"[8] and further, that what is involved is not just a matter of education, but of individual liberty too: an insistence on "expertise" would be tyrannical as well as unrealistic. This leads him to what he (somewhat contentiously) calls the "legitimization" of a rather less utopian category: that of the "good listener." "He too hears more than individual musical details," Adorno writes, "makes spontaneous connections, makes well-founded judgments based not just on categories of prestige or arbitrary taste. But he is not aware of the technical and structural implications, or not fully."[9]

It seems to me that unless one takes Adorno's "not fully" as embracing a vast diversity of experience and capability, then there is a substantial gap between his first and second categories; in effect, a leap from an idealized, immaculate academic expert to the reasonably informed music-lover. Moreover, it seems implicit in his descriptions that by adulthood, perceptual capacities have become frozen in one mold or another. I would not accept such a view. On the contrary, it seems to me that a well-developed adult mind might well welcome new, unsuspected perspectives. After all, the Adorno who polemicized against the impenetrability of the early Darmstadt avant-garde in "Das Altern der neuen Musik" (1954) went on to propose in "Vers une musique informelle" (1963) the transition to a new music in which the kinds of formal connections he had formerly demanded would, by definition, be absent.

It is the changing of definitions—the ability and willingness to accept and apply new criteria in perceiving and evaluating musical form—that is, perhaps, the most crucial issue. The argument advanced by some writers that since innate capacities to recognize form and coherence in certain kinds of music are apparent from a very early age, these form the essential, nature-based template for all future musical perception, is one that I do not find persuasive. At the same age, the vast majority of children will have learned to walk (with some parental encouragement). However, few of them will subsequently be able or permitted to drive a car without lessons, and not all of them will choose to do so! They will also learn to talk, but only as the result of cultural exposure to a world where everyone else seems to talk; moreover, the level of linguistic sophistication they achieve will depend at least partly on environment, and on formal or informal education. A few will show extraordinary speed and aptitude in learning additional languages, but not without having been exposed to them! And the capacity of many young children living in a polylingual environment to converse in several languages is usually lost in a subsequent monolingual environment, unless conscious efforts have been made to sustain it.

Naturally, none of these analogies prove anything in relation to music. However, my own experience as an educator suggests that even a modestly developed musical intelligence can change or modify its perceptual criteria almost instantaneously in the late teens and early twenties, and perhaps at any time, so long as the aural evidence is persuasive. To give this some concrete basis, let's go back for a moment to Webern. Most Sydney Conservatorium undergraduates (including composition majors),[10] listening for the first time to the first movement of the Concerto Op. 24, don't identify it as a sonata form, and are surprised by, or skeptical about, a subsequent proposition that it might be one. In this situation, an instant formalist analysis in sonata terms, though perfectly possible, would be unhelpful, since it would seek to impose a mode of perception that the students do not have at that moment. More profitably, one asks them to set scores aside, and identify by ear alone the points at which the character of the music seems to change significantly.

By general consent, the first such change occurs after 20–25 seconds (depending on the performance). It's clear that, for example, the register, the tempo, the texture, and the combination of instruments has changed. Referring back to the score, and comparing the opening bars (figure 10.1a) with mm. 11–16 (figure 10.1b), one can confirm all these, and in fact highlight ten or more changes, e.g.:

- from fixed octave registers to free ones;
- from a middle/high register to middle/low;
- from a purely motivic texture to melody and accompaniment;
- from a rapid tempo to a slower one;
- from an unstable tempo to a stable one;
- from periodic figures based on different values (sixteenth, triplet eighth, eighth, triplet quarter) to less consistently periodic ones based on quavers;

Figure 10.1a. Webern, Concerto, Op. 24. First movement, mm. 1–5. Copyright ©
1948 by Universal Edition A.G., Wien. Used by permission.

- from 3-note figures which consistently ascend/descend or vice versa
  to mixed forms;
- from mixed articulations weighted towards non legato, to legato/
  tenuto;
- from mainly loud (*f*) to mainly soft (*p*);
- from alternation between winds and piano to a balance between winds,
  piano and strings

Figure 10.1b. Webern, Concerto, Op. 24. First movement, mm. 11–16. Copyright © 1948 by Universal Edition A.G., Wien. Used by permission.

Every one of these changes is aurally verifiable (with the possible exception of the initial *tempo rubato*). Significantly, perhaps, none of them is directly related to the underlying twelve-tone series. Perhaps it's a reminder that the "hunt the row" fetish of earlier times often didn't amount to much more than figuring all the chords and their inversions did in tonal music— perhaps instructive at a didactic level (rather like grammatical parsing), but not always artistically or perceptually enlightening. More positively, it's a reminder of how many other dimensions determine the perception of musical form, and for many student composers, this can be something of an eye- or ear-opener.

Of course, none of this automatically implies a "second subject" or a sonata form! But going through the rest of the movement using the same approach, and eventually supplementing it with "Well, suppose this *were* a sonata form, what might you expect to happen next?" does indeed lead students to the fairly inescapable conclusion that this is what Webern has in mind. For instance, once it's accepted that the passage from m. 17 onwards sounds distinctly like a codetta based on the opening, it might be logical to look out for a development section. So where do the rules of the game change? Does anything "stick out"? Yes indeed—the violin *sff* pizzicato (m. 23), and following that, the longer melodies, and the restricted palette of instruments. Turning again to the score, one sees that from m. 28 at latest, it also *looks* quite different (see figure 10.2).

At one level, this kind of approach soon provides a sense of familiarity where none had been anticipated; by the end, in fact, many students can't suppress an (entirely appropriate) chuckle at the neat little "wrap-up" provided in the final measure. More importantly, though, it rapidly redefines (or greatly expands) familiar criteria for contrast and transitional processes in a way that has great relevance to much post-war music.

In what follows, I shall take the simple and, I hope, uncontroversial view, that listening which is informed by a desire not just to respond instinctively, but also to have some sense of "what is going on," is enhanced by the kind of audibly perceptible characteristics that will be exemplified below. I shall also suggest that the "audibility" or "inaudibility" of structural relationships, in terms of both detail and broad form, are more often the result of individually considered compositional strategies than the automatic outcome of a particular technical method. Going beyond that, I shall suggest that the ability to hear underlying processes in what can loosely be described as avant-garde modernism may be greatly affected by advance verbal information, and that in many cases this information may only need to consist of a few well-chosen phrases.

Part of the reason for my preliminary "educative" excursion is that the comments and assertions that follow rest not only on my personal experience as a "specialist" listener, but above all on my work for over two decades as a tertiary teacher (at the Sydney Conservatorium), working with undergraduates and post-graduates majoring in performance, music education, composition, and musicology. Prior to that, in the mid-1970s, I had spent a couple of years as Stockhausen's teaching assistant at the Musikhochschule in Cologne, working with an unquestionably elite group of international students, some of whom went on to establish significant careers as composers. Though these students were, by any reasonable definition, exceptional, I do not believe that there is any *generic* difference between the way they were able to perceive "new music" and the way my

Figure 10.2. Webern, Concerto, Op. 24. First movement, mm. 23–32. Copyright © 1948 by Universal Edition A.G., Wien. Used by permission.

Australian students do (dealing with cultural artifacts from the other side of the planet). Leaving aside the exceptional talent of the Cologne students, the main differences seem to have been those of experience and commitment.

I should emphasize that my comments below are not the outcome of a validated research strategy, but simply of practice. If the assumptions made concerning the capacity of the full range of tertiary students at the Sydney Conservatorium to aurally identify and intellectually grasp the kinds of features referred to here were false, the courses involved would be a disaster. The failure rate would be unacceptable, student course assessments would be abysmal, and most important of all, the impact on the future musical development of the participating students would be negligible or downright negative. None of these appears to be the case. Naturally, not all students leave the Conservatorium with an enduring passion for the works of Elliott Carter or Iannis Xenakis. Yet a culturally significant number of the performance majors do go on to perform even "radical" new works as a matter of preference (naturally, certain performance staff also play a key role here), and in the music education area, every graduating student has demonstrated a basic ability to deal with key concepts in a repertoire ranging from Stockhausen and Xenakis to Reich and Pärt.[11]

Having invoked Stockhausen so often, let's take him as a first practical exemplar, and begin at his beginning, with the first two characteristic works: *Kreuzspiel* (1951) and *Formel* (1952).[12] Both are early instances of "total serialism," and use essentially the same structural methods. The most obvious difference is that *Kreuzspiel* applies these methods to twelve individualized "points" of sound, whereas *Formel* applies them to "melodies" of 1–12 notes. In both cases, the formal process involves the permutation of basic elements, and their systematic displacement to different octave registers.

The notion of permutation is one that automatically conjures up assumptions of inaudible process, of a sort of random shuffling. In many instances that may be true, but not all; to state the obvious, much depends on what is being permutated, and how. In the first piece of Boulez's *Structures,* one probably wouldn't expect even a suitably informed listener to register much more than the regularly spaced chords which begin each new bundle of series (e.g., at mm. 1, 8, 16), to notice the shift in average density that comes with each, and perhaps to be intrigued by the flicker of repeated notes that arises more or less arbitrarily in the denser sequences as a result of fixed register positions (e.g., at mm. 32ff). But since this is, after all, a deliberately "automated," *tabula rasa* piece, out to erase all traces of the past, the paucity of audible relationships is scarcely surprising.

Although, technically, *Kreuzspiel* operates on a similar permutational basis, both structure and detail are a good deal more tangible. The way that the first movement starts in the extreme registers, then fills out all seven octaves before retreating back to the limits is made doubly clear by the confinement of the piano to the outer octaves, and the two wind instruments to the inner ones. But there's more to it than that: the permutation method used by Stockhausen takes the first and last notes of each series,

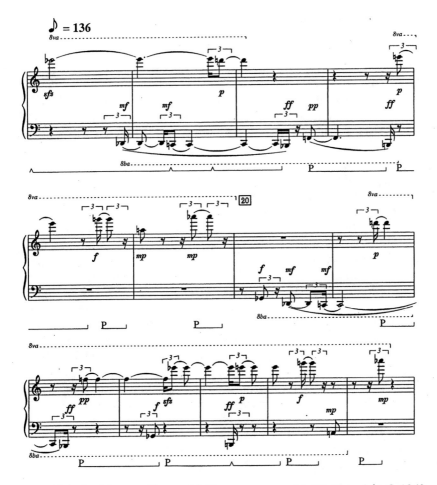

Figure 10.3. Stockhausen, *Kreuzspiel*. Piano part, mm. 14–26. Copyright © 1960 by Universal Edition (London) Ltd., London. Used by permission.

and moves them into the middle. The practical result of this, at least for the first few occurrences, is that much of the series (not just pitches, but register, duration, and dynamics) is repeated literally; as seen in figure 10.3.

These partial repetitions are entirely audible, and especially so at the start of the second section, with its narrow middle-register range (mm. 99ff); they don't require some kind of "super-ear." But I suspect that many people listening to *Kreuzspiel* don't notice them, not because of any difficulty in doing so, but because, since the work is, by repute, "pointillist," "totally serialized," etc., it doesn't occur to them that such relationships are there to be noticed. Here, listening may be not so much a matter of tuning in as switching off. The situation might be compared to certain paintings (early Kandinsky, for example) which seem at first sight to be abstract, but turn out to be obviously "figurative" once certain features have been explained.

In *Formel,* on the other hand, one would have to virtually block one's ears to avoid noticing the constant recycling of the same melodies and accompaniments. But without a few verbal guidelines, one might fail to grasp the logic underlying their succession and transformations, for the simple reason that these don't appear to conform to familiar stereotypes. At one level, as it happens, they do: there is an "exposition" of all twelve melodies, followed by a 'development', in which the melodies and accompaniments are reintroduced in a middle register (in a 1 / 2–1 / 3–2–1 / 4–3–2–1 type of sequence), and gradually transposed to extreme high and low registers; on reaching the extremes, they are eliminated (see figures 10.4 and 10.5). Once one knows what the basic strategy for the development is, the form becomes transparent. This doesn't just mean that one can follow it conscientiously from start to finish; one can "drop in" at any point, assess the situation, and follow the subsequent course of events.

At a broader level, simple formal "pointers" can be found throughout Stockhausen's work in the 1950s. In short, rapid pieces like the second Electronic Study or *Klavierstück VIII,* there's probably barely time to register much more than aural signposts such as the changes of texture and character (e.g., from linear phrases to chords) between each of the Study's five main sections. Yet in such pieces, there's a clear distinction in the compositional process between elements which are "statistical," and serve to keep the basic material circulating in constantly new configurations, and those which are intentionally form-building. The former are not expected to be "heard" in an analytical sense; the latter are. Even at the lightning pace at which David Tudor romps through *Klavierstück VIII,* no special aural acuity is required to register the constant salvos of chords that separate each subdivision of the "main text" (where there is never more than one note struck at a time), or the relatively long, held note that ends each main division of the piece.

At the very least, such information provides an immediate orientation: one may not grasp the total structure of a suburb one is traversing at high speed, but at least one knows when one turns into a new street. Similarly, in the rather more spacious (fifteen-minute) *Zeitmaße,* apart from noting the regular intrusion of relatively flamboyant "indeterminate" passages into a rather more sober basic text, it surely helps to know in advance that the latter falls into three sections, of which the first has a four-part texture, the second three-part, and the last five-part (a fairly evident fact that seems to have eluded most commentators). Once identified, these distinctions are easy enough to hear.

With such serial works, there is at least the theoretical possibility of accounting for every note. With works employing "stochastic" methods,

Figure 10.4. Stockhausen, *Formel (1/6 Formel für Orchester)*, mm. 1–7. Copyright © 1974 by Universal Edition A.G., Wien. Used by permission.

Measure 1: Melody 1; mm. 2–3: Melody 2; mm. 4–6: Melody 3; m. 7: beginning of Melody 4. Melodies are always introduced in the middle octave (4), with accompaniments in octaves 3 or 5. The various instruments are associated with particular octave registers (e.g., the vibraphone plays only in the middle octave).

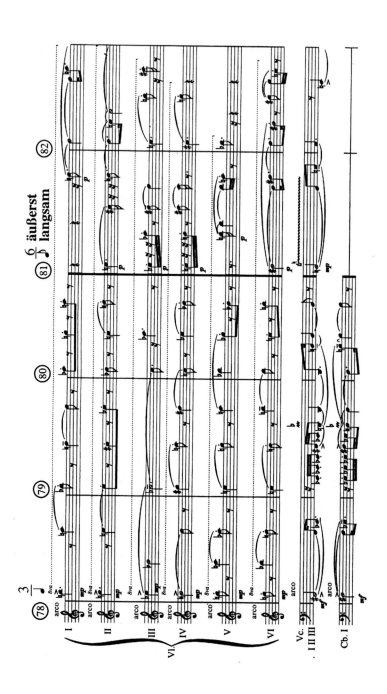

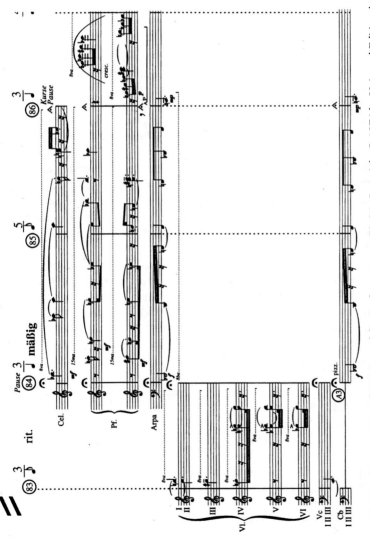

Figure 10.5. Stockhausen, *Formel* (1/6 *Formel für Orchester*), mm. 78–86. Copyright © 1974 by Universal Edition A.G., Wien. Used by permission. Measures 78–80: Melody 4; mm. 81–83: Melody 3; mm. 84–85: Melody 2; m. 86: Melody 1. Melody 1 has reached the extreme octaves, and will now drop out; Melody 2 will make one more appearance; Melody 3 will occur twice more, etc.

such as those of Xenakis, this is evidently not the case, even though the outcome is a fully notated score. But this does not mean that there are no audible formal processes; indeed, it's probably no accident that those early works of Xenakis which are most widely admired (e.g., *Pithoprakta, Eonta* and *Nomos Alpha*) are the ones whose formal processes are most audible, even if relatively few listeners are conscious of what these structures actually are. The Gaussian distributions and Markov chains that figured so prominently in early program notes may be essential to the composition process, but knowledge of them is certainly not necessary to keep track in general terms of what is going on. What is useful is a simple guide to the registral and textural processes of individual passages.

In the opening bars of *Pithoprakta*, for instance, the different degrees of "scatter" of the tapped sounds around a central axis are immediately apparent, as is the gradual incursion of pitched sounds from m. 15 onwards, beginning in the low register and progressively taking over the whole texture. The mass of pizzicati from m. 50 may seem more impenetrable at first, but once one has seen Xenakis's graph paper sketch,[13] the general registral drift is clear enough, and suddenly becomes a great deal more audible (in fact this is an instance where the score itself, with its 46 independent string parts, is almost more of a hindrance to listening than a help). Even in the frantic central episode (mm. 122ff.), which Xenakis describes in terms of nebulae and galaxies, one can at least hear how different types of articulation (e.g., short bowed sounds, pizzicati, and glissandi) momentarily swell up over the prevailing *col legno battuto*. But this is most especially so if it has been pointed out that these shifts of emphasis are there to be heard!

Most works of the immediate post-Webern era were on the short side, or consisted of several short movements (as in *Le Marteau sans maître*). *Pithoprakta* too falls in this category: it lasts about eight minutes. Once the time-scale of avant-garde works started to expand, new problems of orientation arose, as Stockhausen ruefully noted many times over in relation to the unsuccessful premiere of *Kontakte*. As indicated above, his own initial response was the slightly nebulous concept of "moment form." But from 1970 onwards, he was again thinking "architecturally," and from that point onwards, right to the present day, his works are full of almost didactic acoustic markers, intended among other things to clarify the formal structure.

An early example is the orchestral work of about 27 minutes, *Trans* (1971). The piece is not short of unusual features: for a start, it is intended to be performed on a theatre stage, where only the string players are (mistily) visible, behind a purple-lit gauze; the remaining players—wind, brass, and percussion—are gathered in four backstage groups, along with the conductor. Until the final moments of *Trans,* the string parts consist only of very long sustained notes, which change—as does the bow direction—

every time one hears a whip-like sound over stereo loudspeakers (the sound is actually that of a weaving loom). In live performance, this has a decidedly eerie effect—one can imagine the string players doing penance in some kind of purgatory, and at very least, one sees an emblem of the "enslaved orchestra." Now, until Stockhausen DVDs start appearing, home listeners will just have to imagine this. But they will probably notice the changes in the "string curtain," especially as the piece proceeds and the changes (essentially alternations between chromatic clusters and more "transparent" chords) become more drastic. This, though, is a background level of the piece. Let's come back to the foreground.

Each of the four backstage ensembles consists of a bass instrument, and four "treble" instruments which, initially at least, double the bass instrument's melodies in parallel motion (rather like an organ mixture); to be precise, these groups are:

I   bass clarinet + 4 flutes (doubled on amplified celesta)
II   trombone + 4 oboes
III bassoon + 4 clarinets
IV tuba + 4 trumpets with cup mute

In addition, each ensemble has a percussionist whose main function is to mark small-scale formal divisions (somewhat in the manner of gamelan or gagaku). Returning to the tape part, the weaving-loom sounds normally involve a single pass forward and back; on occasion, though, there are double or triple passes. The triple strokes announce all but the first of the work's six main sections, and nos. 2–5 are reinforced by a sequence of "solo scenes" (for viola, cello, violin, and trumpet, respectively), while the last is preceded by a provocatively extended "general pause."[14]

These somewhat unsubtle signals serve to preface something a great deal less obtrusive, but significant (and definitely audible). From the start of the second main section (i.e., after the first triple loom-stroke) individual groups detach from the melody + parallel mixture format, and the upper instruments start playing slow, fragmented descending figures (in free rhythm). The first instruments to be involved are the flutes, who come in one-by-one (at each successive stroke). This is the beginning of an extended process, which may be barely noticeable at first (not least because of the frantic viola solo), but soon becomes audible, and will become increasingly apparent in the course of the work (in each subsequent major section, a further group becomes involved in this relatively aleatoric process). It seems to me that knowing about this secondary process not only inclines one to listen out for something one might otherwise have missed, but affects the way one hears it. There is a difference, surely, between knowing that a new element will be part of an ongoing process, and simply noticing (if at all) that there is something slightly odd going on that wasn't happening earlier.

One more detail: whenever the "string curtain" changes to a chromatic cluster (i.e., at each second loom stroke, with a few exceptions), various other things also change. For a start, the tempo changes, and since *Trans* basically operates with periodic rhythms, these changes are much clearer than in some of Stockhausen's earlier works.

Second, the number and combination of instrumental groups playing changes (this also affects the aleatoric passages, though to a lesser extent), and third, so does the parallel mixture chord over each melody line in the bass. Near the end of each main section, Stockhausen reverts to the full ensemble of four groups, and this is what it signalled by the *double* loom strokes.

Naturally, how much of this detail one *wants* to follow, especially in relation to a "Tibetan Book of the Dead"–inspired work which is intended, among other things, to represent the first music one hears "on the other side," is, of course, a matter of personal choice. After all, on arriving in Purgatory, or the other side of the Styx, or any other limbo, "structural hearing" might not be the first thing on one's mind! The point is, though, that at many levels the form of *Trans* is transparently audible—one might even say it was "acoustically spotlit." Virtually everything visible on the composer's "Form Scheme" (see figure 10.6) is also audible.

The same—perhaps even greater—clarity of formal process is apparent in Boulez's *Rituel in memoriam Maderna*, composed just three years after *Trans*. If *Le marteau sans maître* might seem to embody post-war music at its most enigmatic, *Rituel* presents the opposite situation: a work whose procedures are aurally verifiable at almost every level. Many of these have to do with varied repetition, and follow logically from Boulez's motto for the work:

A perpetual alternation; A sort of verse and response for an imaginary rite;
A ceremony of remembering—hence the numerous returns to the same for-
    mulae, but changing profile and perspective;
A ceremony of extinction, a rite of disappearance and survival: thus do
    images imprint themselves on musical memory as present/absent, in
    doubt.

At the simplest formal level, the antiphony between the two types of music in the first part (which is what I shall concentrate on here), i.e., between massed homophonic gestures and passages where the orchestra is divided into independent melodic ensembles, is obvious to any listener. So, probably, is the general process of growth in both types, and the increasing number of sub-ensembles involved (especially in a concert situation, where one can see this as well as hear it; for CD listening it seems sensible to draw attention to it in advance). Ditto the gradual stripping away of layers in the somewhat briefer second part of the piece. But there are many other things,

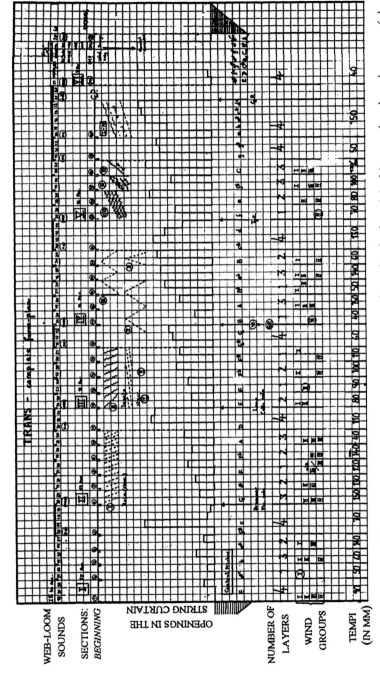

Figure 10.6. Stockhausen, *Trans*. Translated fair copy of the composer's form sketch; the original is reproduced on the cover of the published score, and in the liner notes for the CD recording (both Stockhausen-Verlag).

perhaps less obvious, that only need to be pointed out to become perceptible.

Here, just for once, we might risk the accusation of number fetishism and point out the significant role played by the number seven. At a performance, after all, even before the musicians enter, one can't help noticing the odd way the music stands have been scattered in small groups all over the stage, with a relatively conventional line of stands at the back. Once the performers are onstage, it becomes clear that while all the groups except the one at the back are small, they are of various sizes. If one's curiosity is sufficient to do some simple counting, one will find that in fact each group is of a different size, and comprises between one and seven melody instruments plus a percussionist. The array of brass instruments at the back actually comprises fourteen players, with two percussionists.

One assumes there must be something more than a desire for novelty underlying this arrangement; in any case, by 1974 there's nothing very novel about splitting an orchestra up into spatially separated groups. Once a performance is underway, the rationale becomes clear. The group at the rear (which is the first that one hears) does indeed provide a "backdrop": it is present in all the homophonic (odd-numbered) sections. The first of the alternating melodic (even-numbered) sections involves just the solo oboist (and attendant percussionist), seated at the front right of the stage. In the next homophonic passage (Fig. 3 in the score), the oboe joins in with the brass, and in the following "melodic sequence" the oboe is joined by two clarinets and three flutes (flutes at front left of the stage, clarinets in the center). Each of the three "melody groups" plays at a different tempo, with their respective percussionists audibly providing the basic pulse. At Fig. 4 in the score the new groups too join in with the brass, and so forth.[15] Gradually the acoustic space between front and back of the stage is filled out.

This process, self-evidently, takes fourteen sections (seven homophonic, seven melodic), even though, as indicated above, Boulez doesn't take an absolutely straight-line approach from 1 melody group to 7 (the actual sequence is 1 3 4 2 6 7 5). What does increase steadily is the length of each section, and more specifically, the number of subsections. In the melodic sections, admittedly, one only follows this in broad terms. There are always seven "phrases" per group in each section, but these phrases get ever longer and more elaborate, and once one has, say, four groups playing at four different tempi, one is scarcely going to trace every detail.

With the homophonic sections, the picture is much clearer. In each one, the number of chords increases (from one to seven). Each chord, with the exception of each final one, is prefaced by a grace note, and followed by a measured group of rapid notes (the final chord is always followed by a single E flat). The sequence of "after-notes" is the same for each section, but with a new number added at the front each time. One could represent it as in figure 10.7, with the first number being the grace note and the

Section								0-1
"	1							0-1
"	3						1-3,	0-1
"	5					1-5,	1-3,	0-1
"	7				1-4,	1-5,	1-3,	0-1
"	9			1-7,	1-4,	1-5,	1-3,	0-1*
"	11		1-6,	1-7,	1-4,	1-5,	1-3,	0-1
"	13	1-2,	1-6,	1-7,	1-4,	1-5,	1-3,	0-1

*(See also Figure 10.8)

Figure 10.7. Boulez, *Rituel*. Schema for homophonic sections. (Figure indicates number of grace notes, followed by number of "afternotes" in each measured group of rapid values.)

second the number of "afternotes." As one example of how this schema is played out in Boulez's score, figure 10.8 gives the music from section 9.

I don't assume that listeners will immediately pick up this characteristic procedure. I do say, however, that once it is pointed out, the acumen and concentration required to follow it is no greater than for the many children's rhymes which use the same process.

Even the harmonic and melodic basis of the piece is relatively clear, partly because the basic sound of the main seven-note chord and its inversion which is the source of the entire pitch structure, is so distinctive, and partly because of its obsessive tritone pairings. (If, like one well-known composer of my acquaintance, you have an aversion to tritones, you'd better steer clear of this piece!) Here, I'll just draw attention to one further feature of the chordal sections. *Rituel* begins with the seven-note chord already alluded to; section 3 has a seven-note chord followed by a six-note chord, section 5 has three chords of seven, six, and five notes, respectively, and so forth.

Again, let's be realistic—the difference between a seven-note chord and a six-note one with the same harmonic characteristics is less than earth-shattering, and most people wouldn't register it whether they were informed about it or not. But as the music proceeds, the process of thinning out in the chordal sections does indeed become very perceptible (in stark contrast to the endless proliferation of the melodic ones), and the thirteenth section's remorseless homing in on the final E flat that ends the first part provides as much sense of "arrival" as any tonal cadence.

As an "extreme" case, let's consider a work by the young British composer Richard Barrett: his orchestral composition *Vanity* (1994). Barrett's music is notoriously difficult to play, uses computer algorithms for certain aspects of the composition process, and is broadly associated, rightly or wrongly, with notions of "new complexity." It would therefore be a natural candidate for suspicions about "inaudible processes." Yet in practice, the formal propositions underlying "complex works" are often quite simple, and need to be so, if the working of the surface is going to be intricate. In

Figure 10.8. Boulez, *Rituel.* Page 9 (section 9). Copyright © 1975 by Universal Edition (London) Ltd., London. Used by permission.
The five sustained chords have seven, six, five, four, and three pitches respectively. (NB. Score not in C.)

this work by Barrett, as in many of Ferneyhough's works, the formal "labyrinth" is built from just a few readily identifiable components.

Since *Vanity* is probably familiar to far fewer readers than most other works mentioned here, a few preliminary comments may be useful. The work lasts about twenty-five minutes, and is in three sections, entitled *Sensorium, Memento,* and *Residua* (I shall be focusing on the first). The piece is a "meditation on death," inspired in the first instance by the sixteenth- and seventeenth-century tradition of *vanitas* paintings. In *Sensorium* the orchestra is initially divided into six timbrally distinct ensembles, each with a "lead instrument." There are six sections, each of which is double the length of the preceding one (9", 18", 35", 70", 140", 280"), and the first five ensembles enter successively in each of these, first with a high degree of overlap, and ultimately with long gaps between them. With each entry, the music played by each ensemble becomes more varied and more intricate.

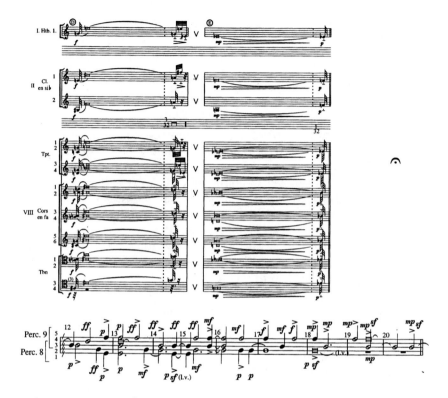

Figure 10.8. *(continued).*

The sixth group—initially keyboards and percussion—enters more unpredictably, and every time it does so, it draws instruments from the other ensembles in its wake, until it has become the predominant force. (The original image was of death gradually siphoning out the essence of the five other groups, representing the five senses, but a literal equivalence between individual groups and senses was abandoned).

So how much of this can one hear without recourse to the score? Just about all of it, I would suggest (with the proviso that one doesn't "hear" a duration of 280 seconds in the same way that one hears an F sharp!), and as the work becomes more familiar, a great more besides (including at least some of the different characteristic musics which form the evolving "repertoire" for each ensemble). In some respects (as with Xenakis), one hears them *better* without the score, since Barrett uses a normal orchestral score format, and the ensembles all employ several instrumental families; what is mixed together on paper stands out in clear profile for the listener. This is not a matter of good luck. It is the result of enormous care and skill on the part of the composer, who has gone out of his way to ensure not only an exceptionally rich and diverse sonic palette, but also a minimization of "masking effects." The latter is actually built into the composition process; in the course of *Sensorium*, each ensemble moves from the initially shared central register to a distinctive one of its own (though naturally there is always some degree of register overlap with other ensembles).

In the wake of such assertions, some clarifications are necessary. First, whatever claims one makes for "audibility" in *Vanity*, it is still an undeniably complex listening experience—the claims concern what can be heard by someone who has appropriate information *and* volition. Second, what I would claim in relation to *Vanity* cannot be assumed to apply to other pieces of similar stylistic persuasions. My contention is that a surprising degree of aural transparency is possible in such works, but is not universally present (for example, I would not make comparable claims for Ferneyhough's *La terre est un homme*—nor, I think, would the composer). Third, the whole question of whether, and to what degree, "audible form" is a measure of aesthetic success is, in my view, an extremely complex one, and it is in no way the focus of this chapter.

If the examples referred to above are drawn primarily from a serial or post-serial repertoire, this is mainly because such works are so often the subject of polemics concerning what can and cannot be heard. However, it would be unfortunate (and quite wrong) if these examples gave readers the impression that the kind of information discussed above was applicable *only* to such a repertoire, and implied some kind of segregated listening. On the contrary, there are any number of other contemporary musics, perhaps with less potentially confronting acoustic surfaces, that use comparable procedures, and for which the same kind of minimal information can enormously facilitate an understanding of what is "going on."

To take just a couple of instances: most commentators, when dealing with Berio's well-known *Sinfonia*, tend to concentrate on the third movement, not only because it represents an extreme instance of 1960s collage technique, but because so long as one has a passing acquaintance with the scherzo from Mahler's *Resurrection Symphony*, one has a prefabricated Ariadne's thread leading through the movement which will make it more "accessible." Yet the second movement (which also has a separate existence as *O King*) has just as audible a thread: a sort of cantus firmus of three related pitch sequences which, if one wished, one could use to whistle or sing along throughout the movement (see figure 10.9). Berio in the karaoke bar?: unlikely, perhaps, but not inconceivable.[16]

The same kind of audible "cantus firmus" procedure is found, on a much broader time-scale, in much of Louis Andriessen's work: one can take *Hadewijch* (from *De Materie*) as an example. Here, clearly, the style of the work is not such as to leave many listeners with a sense of a priori disorientation. But not being innately disconcerted is not the same thing as knowing what's going on, especially over a span of about thirty minutes.

Figure 10.9. Berio, *O King*. Basic pitch sequence.

Yet one only has to know about the underlying "ballad melody," and that the fourteen massive block chords that occur roughly every couple of minutes (and the distances between them) exactly match the fourteen parallel pillars in the Rheims cathedral (one imagines Hadewijch slowly moving from the cathedral door to the altar[17]), to have a quite different engagement with Andriessen's piece—not just in terms of knowing the composer's motivation, but also knowing where one is in the piece.

In fact, the notion of "cantus firmus" composition in its original Renaissance context offers some interesting parallels to issues addressed above. If one's first experience of the cantus firmus mass were something like John Taverner's *Western Wynde* mass, one could probably deduce easily enough what was going on structurally, without a score and without prior information. If, on the other hand, one's initial exposure was to Dufay's *Missa l'homme armé*, let alone something like Obrecht's *Missa Sub Tuum Praesidium*, it might be quite a while before one worked out the underlying compositional processes unless, of course, one had been told to watch or listen out for them. Indeed, some of the more arcane processes in Obrecht might never be accessible to "structural" hearing. The audibility of compositional process is not necessarily an index of aesthetic quality; but where a few words can suddenly make something audible, it seems perverse (to this author) to withhold them.

So why isn't such information more readily available, more regularly communicated, especially within education systems? I sometimes wonder if there isn't a rather dog-in-the-manger-like trait in some music educators which operates along the lines of: "I don't like listening to this music, therefore you shouldn't enjoy it either, and I'll be damned if I'll tell you anything that might enable you to enjoy it more than I do." If so, it's not an attitude to be encouraged. Whatever the ultimate aims of music education may be, they should surely have more to do with disclosure than concealment.

As with any music, such considerations only address limited dimensions of listening, albeit, in my view, important ones. The hermeneutic dimensions of "new music"—the consequences of knowing, for example, that an unexpected rumbling sound in Stockhausen's first Electronic Study celebrates the birth of his first child, that the dynamic profiles of parts of his *Gruppen* are virtual transcriptions of mountain ranges he could see through the window of a hut in Switzerland, that the turbulent masses of sound in Xenakis's early works are a resistance fighter's memories of wartime Athens at night, that the note A has an arcane erotic significance for Bussotti, or that the webs of sound in Ligeti's music may relate to his arachnophobia—are undoubtedly fascinating and greatly neglected, but involve all kinds of cultural problematics outside my present scope, and will have to await attention elsewhere.

Notes

1. Author's translation. "Er wäre der voll bewußte Hörer, dem tendenziell nichts entgeht und der zugleich in jedem Augenblick über das Gehörte Rechenschaft sich ablegt. Wer etwa, zum erstenmal mit einem aufgelösten und handfester architektonischer Stützen entratenden Stück wie den zweiten Satz von WEBERNS Streichtrio konfrontiert, dessen Formteile zu nennen weiß, der würde, fürs erste, diesem Typus genügen." T. W. Adorno, *Einleitung in die Musiksoziologie* (Reinbek b. Hamburg: Rohwolt 1968), 15. E. B. Ashton has translated this work as *Introduction to the Sociology of Music* (New York: Seabury Press, 1976).

2. Igor Stravinsky and Robert Craft, *Conversations with Igor Stravinsky* (London: Faber and Faber, 1959), 126.

3. Cf. Webern's letter to Hildegard Jone on 6 August 1928, a few days after he completed the Symphony: "What I understand by 'art' is the capacity to present an idea in clearest, simplest, that is, 'most intelligible' form." ("Ich verstehe unter 'Kunst' die Fähigkeit, einen Gedanken in die klarste, einfachste, das heißt, 'faßlichste' Form zu bringen.") Anton Webern, *Briefe an Hildegard Jone und Josef Humplik*, ed. Josef Polnauer (Vienna: Universal Edition, 1959), 10.

4. Stockhausen, "Gruppenkomposition: 'Klavierstück I' (Anleitung zum Hören)," in his *Texte zur elektronischen und instrumentalen Musik* (Cologne: M. DuMont Schauberg, 1963), 1:63.

5. Stockhausen, "Momentform: Neue Zusammenhänge zwischen Aufführungsdauer, Werkdauer und Moment," in his *Texte* 1:189.

6. Immer schon gab es in der Kunstmusik viel mehr zu hören, als man hören konnte. Es gehört sogar wesentlich zur Kunstmusik, daß in einem Werk mehr geschieht, als man im Moment des Hörens bewußt wahrnehmen kann." Stockhausen, "Die Kunst, zu hören," in *Texte zur Musik* (Cologne: DuMont, 1989), 5:669.

7. "La musique sérielle a été considérée pendant un certain temps comme radicalement asymétrique, comme intégralement non périodique. C'est ainsi que la ressentait son public, c'est ainsi que l'imaginiaient ses auteurs, qui mettaient tout en oeuvre pour obtenir un maximum d'irrégularité." H. Pousseur, "Pour une périodicité géneralisée," in *Fragments théoriques I: sur la musique expérimentale* (Brussels: Université Libre, 1970), 241.

8. "Wer allerdings aus allen Hörern Experten machen wollte, verhielte unter den obwaltenden gesellschaftlichen Bedingungen sich inhuman utopistisch." Adorno, *Einleitung in die Musiksoziologie*, 16.

9. "Auch er hört übers musikalisch Einzelne hinaus; vollzieht spontan Zusammenhänge, urteilt begründet, nicht bloß nach Prestigekategorien oder geschmacklicher Willkür. Aber er ist der technischen und strukturellen Implikationen nicht oder nicht voll sich bewußt." Ibid., 16.

10. The standard age for these students at Sydney would be about 20, for composition majors a little older (say 23).

11. In Music History 6 (Music from 1950), which is compulsory for under-graduate Composition, Music Education, and Musicology students but also taken as a matter of choice by a substantial majority of Performance majors, the lectures include musical examples from almost 100 works, extending up to the mid-1990s. The associated tutorials examine ten to twelve works; in 1999 these were (in chronological order): Stockhausen: *Kreuzspiel*; Xenakis: *Pithoprakta*; Lutoslawski: *Jeux vénitiens*; Scelsi: *Anahit*; Berio: *Sinfonia*; Andriessen: *De Staat*; Sciarrino: *Che sai guardiano della notte*; Reich: *Tehillim*; Ligeti: Piano Concerto; Pärt: *Berlin Mass*; Carter: Oboe Concerto. Most of the other contemporary works mentioned in this chapter are examined in general electives, or specialist courses for Composition students.

12. All the works discussed in the remainder of this chapter are available in one or more CD recordings: e.g., Stockhausen's *Kreuzspiel* on Stockhausen [Verlag] 1; Stockhausen's *Formel* on Stockhausen [Verlag] 2; Stockhausen's *Klavierstück VIII* on hat ART CD 6142; Xenakis's *Pithoprakta* on Chant du Monde LDC 278 368; Stockhausen's *Trans* on Stockhausen [Verlag] 19; Boulez's *Rituel* on Sony SMK 45839; Barrett's *Vanity* on NMC D041S; Andriessen's *Hadewijch* on Nonesuch 79367–2.

13. In Nouritza Matossian, *Xenakis* (London and New York: Taplinger, 1986), 98. Similar, equally enlightening sketches for mm. 45–50 and 208–250 can be found in various other sources, including Olivier Revault d'Allonnes, *Xenakis / Les Polytopes* (Paris: Balland, 1975), 127, and the liner notes to Erato STU 70526–30 (1969).

14. "Inserts" of this kind are entirely typical of Stockhausen's work. What is unusual about the ones in *Trans* is that they reinforce the basic structure; normally, as in *Mantra* (or indeed *Gruppen*), they create a kind of formal detour.

15. In his Sony recording, made in November 1976, Boulez effectively emphasizes the gradual process of accumulation by staggering the entries of groups on each chord of the odd-numbered sections (e.g., flutes first, then brass, then oboe, and then clarinets). However, this seems to have been an afterthought; it's not indicated in the first publication of the score, and Boulez doesn't do it in the recording of the French premiere in February 1976.

16. I have taken this pitch sequence from P. Altmann, *"Sinfonia" von Luciano Berio: eine analytische Studie* (Vienna: Universal Edition, 1977), 12.

17. See Alcedo Coenen, "Louis Andriessen's 'De Materie,'" *Key Notes* 25 (1988–89): 3–12.

Part Four

Case Study

11

A Fine Madness

Greg Sandow

(The Village Voice, 16 March 1982)

Measured by index space in Paul Griffiths's *Modern Music: The Avant Garde since 1945,* Milton Babbitt is the most important living American nonexperimental composer, and apart from John Cage, the most notable American composer of any kind. But Griffiths can't show nonspecialists why they should care. Babbitt's Second String Quartet, he says, "is based on an all-interval series which is introduced interval by interval, as it were, with each new arrival initiating a development of the interval repertory acquired thus far, each development being argued in terms of derived sets."[1] This comes close to what George Bernard Shaw dismissed as "parsing" and parodied with an "analysis" of "To be or not to be." Shakespeare, as he says, "announces his subject at once in the infinitive, in which mood it is presently repeated after a short connecting passage in which, brief as it is, we recognize the alternative and negative forms on which so much of the significance of repetition depends." Musical parsing is far more defensible now than it was in Shaw's time—styles vary so much that musical grammar can't be taken for granted—but Griffiths does too much of it. He doesn't say how the structures he talks about really work—just how do derived sets "argue" (whatever that means) each new "development"?—and only in passing remarks about the "wit" and "surface rhythmic appeal" of one piece and the "sure musical continuity" of another to tell us how Babbitt's music sounds or how it might make a listener feel.

This isn't entirely his fault, though, because Babbitt talks about music the same way. After some useful thoughts about why Schoenberg's Violin Concerto is hard to perform, he goes on (in liner notes for the Columbia recording) for perhaps one-third the length of this article about its twelve-tone set structure, as if nothing else mattered, adding a few words about a recurring basic form of the set as a sop to "those listeners who depend on surface similitudes . . . to provide continuity and association in the first stages of their acquaintance with a work."[2] Part of his problem is that as a self-described "logical empiricist" he's willing to make only "verifiable" statements about music, which leaves out any necessarily unverifiable reference to the passions that make people want to compose it or hear it. He's like a cryptographer who'll talk about the structure of the Japanese codes but won't tell you whether their planes are in flight toward Pearl Harbor.

Babbitt is both too sensitive and too sensible to pretend that the "unverifiable" things aren't there or that twelve-tone structure in itself could make anything worth hearing, but his unwillingness to talk about what music might mean makes his non-theoretical criticism oddly trivial. (Compare, for example, his bland description of Schoenberg's *Moses und Aron* with David Lewin's essay linking the opera's compositional structure to its dramatic meaning, both reprinted in Norton's *Perspectives on Schoenberg and Stravinsky*.[3]) He values performers not for their verve or inner feeling but for their ability to carry out a composer's precise directions; in *High Fidelity* some time ago he said that they have the same role in music that printers do in literature. In his section of *Soundpieces* (an absorbing collection of interviews with composers just published by the Scarecrow Press) he defines interpretation, which most people regard as a performer's creative work, as nothing more than decisions about compositional elements (details of dynamics in Chopin, for example) that the composer didn't happen to specify.[4] He talks as if composition were the only worthwhile musical activity, or at least as if compositional detail was the only thing worth listening for. (His admirer Michel Phillipot warns against confusing "purely aural pleasure" with music.) All this leads people to call his music "mathematical." He answers that this is a misunderstanding of mathematics, which can only describe things and never be the thing itself, and that mathematical models could be made to describe Bach's or Beethoven's way of composing as well as his own. But that's not the point. People who call his music "mathematical" are using the word metaphorically, to say that human feeling is missing. Instead of rebuking them, Babbitt should speak to the question he surely knows they're asking, and tell them what the human value of his work might be.

Let's look at him now in a different way. In program notes for *Dual*, a piece for cello and piano played by Joel Krosnick and Gilbert Kalish on a Group for Contemporary Music concert presented February 22, Babbitt says, in part:

> The title of this one-movement work is intended to intimate, well beyond the peripheral pertinence of its obvious homophone (in the sense of "dueling ban-jos" and the more gentlemanly, if sanguinary, art) and of the traditional "duet" and "duo," the central and pervasive musical expressions of a duality relation, interpreted variously inter- and intradimensionally. . . . [I]t is just the progression from the local to the global in relational implications which should provide the listener with the means of achieving that cognition of cumulative containment and successive subsumption which human memory in general, and musical memory in particular, requires for a musical work to be entified, eventually, as a unified, closed totality—as an all of a piece of music.

Can anyone doubt that the man who wrote this is—not to mince words—just a little bit mad? He's something of a pedant, obviously, and may well do some pretty profound compositional thinking, but to write English that way Milton Babbitt—Conant Professor of Music at Princeton University, a man of the highest academic and intellectual prestige—has got to be just a little bit mad.

But after reading what he says, wouldn't anyone with a taste for the bizarre, at least, want to know how *Dual* sounds? On third or fourth hearing, those "pervasive musical expressions of a duality relation"—those that depend on "surface similitudes," anyway—begin to be audible. Plucked notes on the cello alternate with bowed notes (so quickly sometimes that even Krosnick, the expert cellist of the Juilliard Quartet, was left gasping); the highest register of the piano alternates with the lowest; insistently repeated single pitches are juxtaposed with disjunct musical lines that leap and squirm; sections mainly for the cello alternate with sections mainly for the piano (the main progress of the piece, in fact, is from piano music with cello commentary to cello music with piano commentary). Two-note phrases—duality—are everywhere, sometimes in one instrument, sometimes divided between both, often nested within each other to produce—and this is just the simplest of numerous possible examples—such phrases as the cello line in mm. 32–33, which (taking both pitch and Babbitt's precisely specified rhythm, dynamics, and articulation into account) I might turn into words as "you too, two! You too, to you (you)." All this turns zany after a while, as if the director of a two-character play had put two of every set piece and prop on stage, and made up each actor with two putty noses. Babbitt's dualities are more pervasive and less obvious than that, of course, and anyone who loves a master of literary wordplay like Vladimir Nabokov, say, should—eventually—be able to enjoy them. But since Babbitt insists that his music can't be understood on first hearing, why did the Group play three pieces on their concert instead of a single piece three times? And I'd suggest that the proper pairing for Babbitt is not Stefan Wolpe, who despite his own formidable complexity comes off bland in comparison, but Mozart, whose equally transparent and unpredictable but less intense music would put Babbitt's in fascinating relief.

In any case, those twisting and squirming lines give plenty of "purely aural pleasure," though you have to listen hard at first to discern them. (People who have trouble following Babbitt should try to imagine themselves singing along with his music as they hear it; for me, at least, that produces a state of mind in which it's easier to log in each event as it happens.) The piano has moments of rarefied repose at the very top of the keyboard, which, thanks to Babbitt's compositional rigor, register not just as intriguing tinkles but as unexpectedly wistful melodic wisps, both carefully planned and intuitively right; but odd still, because they're so high. At the other extreme, cello and piano combine in their lower range to sound

tenebrous and brooding, but still ringing and clear . . . never homogeneous
sludge but instead a precisely calculated interweaving of distinct and as-
tonishing shades of brown. His ensemble writing looks fussy in score but
in performance always sounds lively, pristine, and clear. The notorious complexities of his *Relata* produced the effect, as played last season by the
American Composers Orchestra, of brilliant pinpoints of light.

Milton Babbitt's twelve-tone structures are audible as well, or at least
nearly so, though the effect is rigorous and quirky, rather than ringing and
bright. Serial music is badly misunderstood, dismissed as arbitrary when in
fact it could hardly be—at least in some ways—more coherent. The first
few, isolated cello notes in *Dual* sound as right as they do partly because
each one combines with the piano to complete the same three-note chord.
You may not consciously hear this, but, as Babbitt likes to say, it's also true
that the opening theme of the Eroica symphony is an E-flat major triad
whether you hear that or not. I could turn his analogy against him, of
course, by asking why anybody needs to understand his twelve-tone sets; if
Beethoven's triads mean something to people who don't understand them,
Babbitt's twelve-tone structures might, too. Other details perhaps do have
to be consciously heard to make their effect, though for all I know they too
may have subliminal force. Like any Babbitt piece, *Dual* is a labyrinth of
closely packed information: every detail means something, or—which to
me is the awe and almost the horror of it—could mean something. The F
sharp, E flat, and B natural isolated in the highest register of the piano in
the first two measures return in measure six as the first three notes of a
melodic phrase, accompanied by the B flat, G natural, and C natural that
were the next notes heard in the highest register at the end of measure two
and the start of measure three—and these are just the most obvious connections that could be made between two parts of the pieces chosen almost
at random. Babbitt likes to say that moments in his music can be memories
of what came before, and presentiments of what is to come. Serial technique produces ever-new associations of familiar elements giving everything that happens the power of an omen. Following a Babbitt piece in
close detail is like reading entrails or tea leaves; every rearrangement in
every bar might mean something. So many rearrangements are possible
that you never know what the omens really mean: new developments seem,
if not arbitrary, then at least willful. This is a sort of higher-order zaniness,
something unpredictable and even wild that transcends Babbitt's logic, and
finds its way into something I haven't mentioned yet, which I'll call Babbitt's
mode of musical speech.

This is taken for granted by people who like Babbitt's music and even by
Babbitt himself, but it's likely to be what anyone who's never heard his
music before would notice first. At a lecture-recital sponsored by the New
York University Composers Forum on February 27, Babbitt spoke calmly,
with his usual affable grace, about the structure of the music to come. But

he didn't prepare us for what we actually heard, at least not for the torrents of notes, jumping from one end of the piano to each other, shifting speed every few seconds (though the notated tempos are generally constant: changes in apparent speed are produced by difficult-to-perform and always varying subdivisions of the constant beat); he didn't mention that his music lacks both regularity and any connection to everyday emotional and musical life. It's easy for him to take this for granted because in the past thirty-five years or so it's become commonplace in his circles, but what does it mean? It's easy to see that irregular rhythms serve Babbitt's compositional purposes for a reason suggested by as unlikely a person as John Cage, who complains that regular rhythms cause sounds to be heard not for themselves but as part of a group: if Babbitt used regular rhythms, the pitch relationships that mean more than anything else to him would similarly be submerged in irrelevant rhythmic groupings. He needs irregular rhythms to put those rapidly changing pitch relationships in strong relief.

But what does the irregularity not just of rhythm, but of tempo, timbre, register, and gesture mean culturally and psychologically? Michael Gielen, conductor of the Cincinnati Symphony, is only the latest to say (in a recent "Arts and Leisure" interview in the *New York Times*) that it reflects our current "Age of Anxiety," but that's far too facile.[5] Babbitt suggests a comparison to Joyce, and to modernism in general, but that just passes the buck to art, literature, science, and philosophy (and Joyce, anyway, has a strain of healthy vulgarity you'd have to go far to find in Babbitt, and even further to find in Charles Wuorinen or Elliott Carter). This irregularity of musical speech ought to be the central critical problem for anyone writing about modern music. Any attempt to account for it would be another article as long as this one, so I'll only say that because he's so zany it suits Babbitt more than it suits others; that its most important effect is to distance modern music from everyday life; and that the failure to ask what it means has led to aberrations that are hard not to take as signs that a whole generation of advanced musicians has lost track of the connection between its music and its emotions. One of these signs is George Rochberg's decision—when he wanted to write music with feeling in it—to abandon twelve-tone writing (though not atonality) and develop an intentionally retrogressive style that sounds much of the time like a combination of Mahler and late Beethoven. Another is the puzzling and ultimately sad discrepancy between the profoundly rich twelve-tone score of Roger Sessions's monumental tombstone of an opera, *Montezuma,* and dramatic content simpleminded enough to have come from a 1950s Hollywood epic. Doesn't Sessions know what his own musical language is for? One final sign is that so extreme and eccentric a composer as Milton Babbitt can be such a paragon of academic respectability.

For in the end I do find Babbitt eccentric. He's a superb musical craftsman, and I think, an authentically great composer, though in some ways hard to take, but he's also zany, wild, and—I say this again with admira-tion—more than a little bit mad. His music and the whole school he repre-sents, are products of the 1950s, as much symptoms of the eruption of tumultuous subterranean forces into aboveground life as monster movies, rock and roll, the beat generation, and abstract expressionism. But in Babbitt's case the eruption is controlled, disguised, and unmentioned, the secret nobody will acknowledge or even name. In a videotaped interview with Ann Swartz of Baruch College, Babbitt calls himself "a man of the university," whose music "reflects the life of the academy, in the best sense of the world." That's partly true, of course, but there's much more there. There's no point in thinking that Babbitt should do or think anything but what he does; I wouldn't want to be without his theoretical essays or his often unjustly scorned, often blindly praised, unsettling, provocative, infu-riating, airy, light-hearted, deeply felt, and (on third or fourth hearing) irresistible music. But I can't help thinking that he's sold himself short by trying both to extend the boundaries of his art and to remain academically respectable, and by acknowledging only the verifiable (and therefore trivial) aspects of his amazing work. If—like Joyce, Jackson Pollock, or John Cage—so passionate a man had chosen to define himself as an artist and not as an academic, what might he have achieved?

Notes

1. Griffiths, *Modern Music: The Avant Garde since 1945* (New York: George Braziller, 1981), 94.

2. Milton Babbitt, notes for *The Music of Arnold Schoenberg, Vol. 1* (Columbia M2S679, 1962); reprinted as part of Babbitt's "Three Essays on Schoenberg," in *Perspectives on Schoenberg and Stravinsky*, ed. Benjamin Boretz and Edward T. Cone (New York: W. W. Norton, 1972), 47–50. The statement about "surface si-militudes" appears on p. 50.

3. David Lewin, "Moses und Aron: Some General Remarks and Analytic Notes for Act I, Scene 1," in *Perspectives on Schoenberg and Stravinsky*, 67–77; Babbitt, "Three Essays on Schoenberg," 53–60.

4. Cole Gagne and Tracy Caras, eds., *Soundpieces: Interviews with American Composers*, (Metuchen, N.J.: Scarecrow Press, 1982), 48–49.

5. ". . . what we experience as our world and our existence has, for the younger generation, the basis of Hiroshima and Auschwitz. If music is going to be truthful—I am speaking about composers now—it will have as a main expression anguish, anxiety, fear and uncertainty. And if musical life does not convey this central expe-rience of our time, which is the 'Age of Anxiety,' then it is not a cultural life, but a cultural lie." Quoted in Theodore W. Libbey, Jr., "Is Cincinnati Ready for Michael Gielen?" *New York Times*, 12 February 1982, section 2, p. 17.

12

"One Man's Signal Is Another Man's Noise": Personal Encounters with Post-Tonal Music

Andrew Mead

From the time I began paying attention to music I have been taking as much pleasure from listening to twelve-tone and other non-tonal music as I have from the tonal repertoire; perhaps more so, given that in my own composing I have always been drawn to the sound-world of the total chromatic. My experience of much post-tonal music has always been direct and urgent, as satisfyingly so as my experience of tonal music. I have spent a good deal of time seeking to share my joys in listening to Schoenberg and Carter, Babbitt and Webern (to mention just a few musicians who have thrilled me) in ways that will engage other people's interest. This is not an easy task, and all too often communication fails. Nevertheless, the riches of this repertoire are pleasures I would like to share with my friends, my colleagues, my family.

It is not my task here to try to answer why this music has not become more readily accepted. That is a broad issue, and entails much more than how the music has been talked about. Many factors are involved, from the sounds of the music itself to the enormous changes that have occurred over the past century in the places for music of all kinds in our lives. The advent of electronic recording alone has changed profoundly the ways people encounter music. What I want to consider is how I can be most effective in sharing my love for non-tonal music in the current climate. I have taken my title from a remark I once made to my father in answer to a question from him on the order of, "How can you listen to that stuff?"[1] I have come back to his question to try to formulate a less flip answer, by looking at the ways conversations about music can go awry.

Talk about music (about anything, for that matter) depends not only on what is said, but also on the assumptions shared between the participants.[2] I will examine some of the layers of assumptions we deal with in our conversations about post-tonal and twelve-tone music by chasing a simple remark through a series of different contexts. Let me bring it up as a question between two friends, both composers and fans of such music. The question, "So, what hexachords are you playing with these days?" will make sense if the asker can assume that the listener understands why it might be fun to play with hexachords, what such play might be, and even more basically, what a hexachord is. (Used in this context, the word hexachord is pretty vague, but at the very least would suggest something to do with collections of six different notes. Whether or not they are ordered, how they are distinguished from or related to each other and so forth, would all be tied up in what the two friends knew of each other's work.) Such talk is shorthand, a quick form of exchange resting on a broad foundation of shared assumptions. I don't want to privilege this kind of communication; it is a form of shoptalk, with all the pitfalls and potential for superficiality that such conversations exhibit.

Re-couching the question in somewhat more formal terms produces language that might be more recognizable as a certain type of music-theoretical discourse. The question now becomes one that might be asked rhetorically in an article, or could be part of an analyst's thought processes. (One thing to note here is how quickly the spirit of the word "play" disappears. "Hexachord," on the other hand, becomes more specific, engaging modes of taxonomy and analysis.) Spun out a bit, my question could go, "To what collection-classes do the evident six-note collections I am hearing in this piece belong; which properties of these collections are being projected in the musical surface; and how are those properties employed in generating the musical continuity that I am following?" Each of these questions is based on certain assumptions, or at least definitions, that need be shared between the writer and the reader. For example, there needs to be agreement on the criteria for collection-class membership (the mode of taxonomy), as well as what would make a collection "evident"; there also needs to be a sense of what is meant by "properties," as well as how they might be projected in the musical surface; not to mention a sense of what might be the means by which they generate a musical continuity.

Each of these issues itself becomes an area to be explored, and a considerable part of doing music theory and analysis in the post-tonal and twelve-tone repertoire has involved exactly that. There are numerous articles and books dealing with the properties of pitch collections in the total chromatic. But we can unearth some other assumptions here as well, having to do with the distinction between the manipulation of materials and the perceptual framework within which they are understood. In other words, we might want to ask, "Given that I am hearing six-note collections in the musical surface, am I hearing them in a context of a regular overturn of the total chromatic, or are they parts of scales?" Answering this question can start to dig at some fairly deeply held assumptions about the nature of intervals and how we choose to understand them.

Even this sort of talk is a shorthand. Our tendency to use technical terms as though they referred to *things* can be very handy, but it can mask their origins as terms to describe our *experiences*. Let me offer an example. It is not unusual to hear something like the following: "The Schoenberg Piano Concerto opens with a statement of the row in the right hand." This sort of statement can wipe out all sorts of aspects of our experience of this passage. Turning it around to, "I hear a statement of the row played by the right hand at the beginning of the Schoenberg Piano Concerto," at least focuses our attention to the listener's experience, but it still obliterates much of that experience, by reifying what might be better understood as an abstract conceptual framework. The particularities of the experience of rhythm, register, dynamics, and articulation are subsumed by "the row." More cumbersome, but perhaps a little closer to a statement of experience, might be, "I hear a melody in the right hand at the outset; I hear a wealth of associations and connections within it based on issues of rhythm, register, and so on; one of its attributes is a sequence of intervals from note to note that in whole or in part, and to within various degrees of transformation, chimes with my hearing of lots and lots of the rest of the piece." This still only approximates my experience of the passage, but it shifts the notion of "the row" away from being a thing towards being a possible attribute of what I am hearing.

For much of the tonal repertoire, many people share assumptions about the experiences being invoked by technical terms, even when those terms seem to objectify experience. But even in the realm of the familiar problems can arise. Assumptions about musical experiences change over time, and vary among different repertoires of music. Think of the difference, say, between understanding chords as the by-product of counterpoint, and understanding chords as sounds in themselves with functional implications. These are both vivid musical experiences and not mutually exclusive, but they receive different emphases in different repertoires.[3] It is all too common to find "tonality" referred to as if it were a monolithic form of musical behavior, a "natural language" unchanged from era to era. But think of how an enharmonic pun such as the augmented sixth/minor seventh can go from the rare to unthinkable in Bach, through the gingerly handled in Mozart to the normative practice in Schubert in roughly a century, or how in much jazz what had originated as unresolved neighbor note can replace its resolution to the point that the resolution sounds "wrong." It is frequently useful shorthand to refer to "tonal" and "atonal" music as if they referred to two clearly differentiated, objectifiable worlds, rather than simply being categories imposed on a wide and wild range of musical experience, but doing so can obliterate both broad and fine distinctions of musical experience within and between these repertoires.

Finding language to describe musical experience of any sort is a challenge, especially when there is no intersubjective, mutually agreed-upon shorthand to turn to. One solution is to rely on more figurative language, making connections to the broader range of our shared experiences of everyday life.[4] Let me offer a short example, drawing on the opening of Milton Babbitt's *Philomel,* for soprano, recorded soprano, and synthesized sound. I've chosen a work with a text in part to help make the connection with broader experience.

The composition is a setting of a poem by John Hollander, written expressly for the work. As David Hamilton has observed in his notes for the recording, the poem is based on Ovid's telling of the legend of Procne and Philomela.[5] This is a horrifying narrative of violation and dismemberment. (Philomela is raped by her sister's husband, who then tears out her tongue—in Ovid's treatment, Philomela then metamorphoses into a nightingale.) The poem is placed at the moment of transformation, and bears witness not only to the horror of the event, but to Philomel's survival and transcendence.[6]

A prominent thread in my experience of *Philomel* involves a sense of the voice, of song, of *self,* found in the face of overwhelming trauma, change, and confusion. In the text, this thread unspools not only at the level of narrative, but also in such things as the emergence of words from phonemes at the start of the poem or the slow accretion of various vowel sounds over the first of its three sections. But it also runs through my hearing of the music. The following is best read with a recording of the work handy, but I have added a couple of examples from the score to make it easier to keep track of where we are.

During the first 20 seconds of the piece, we hear the recorded voice surrounded by synthesized sounds (see figure 12.1). Although the voice is

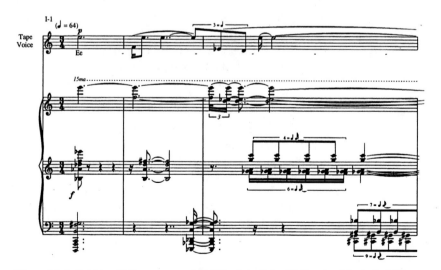

Figure 12.1. Babbitt, *Philomel,* mm. 1–8. Words by John Hollander. Music by Milton Babbitt. Copyright © 1964 (Renewed) by Associated Music Publishers, Inc. (BMI). International Copyright Secured. All Rights Reserved. Reprinted by permission.

on tape, it is still recognizably human—the result of physical efforts I can empathize with—in distinction to the sounds produced by the synthesizer. This is one reason I tend to hear the voice as the focus of the passage. My overall sense of this passage is of a voice first feeling its way into a musical space, then carving out for itself a place to make music, in the process setting in action some additional sounds. The carving is not simple or easy. The voice sounds closed, veiled, almost humming. It sustains a note, but gradually reaches out to more notes, first one, then two, then three, then four, in four little excursions, each of which returns to rest on the initial sustained note. This note is relatively high in the voice's range, an E, and each excursion seems to reach below the ledge of this E to fish for new notes. Furthermore, each fishing expedition retrieves its own notes; there are no repetitions within or among them. By the third and fourth excursion, it does emerge, however, that their melodic shapes are related. While the initial excursion, a single note, leaps a major seventh to the sustained E, the next three all start by dropping a minor second from their initial notes, and the third and fourth trips both continue with a rising major second and a rising minor sixth (followed in the fourth excursion by a rising perfect fifth).

Before continuing with my account of the recorded voice, let me describe my sense of its musical surroundings. The voice's initial sustained E comes into being with a soft but intense attack, a *clink,* of synthesized sounds, pitched across a wide range. The effect is like a short gasp of astonishment, leaving the voice frozen alone in a vast registral space, the top of

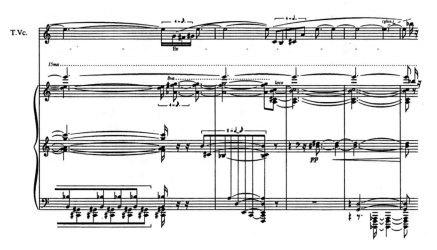

Figure 12.1. *(continued).*

which is a distant E, barely hearable as a pitch, and the bottom of which is a thick, soft sound that fades away. (The sounds heard in the middle register of the opening, aside from the voice, do not sustain beyond the initial attack.) The voice's first excursion—short, swift, tentative, like a single toe stuck in cold water—coincides with a slight thickening of the sound above, and seems to fragment the response in the remaining registers. Instead of the coordinated attack of the opening, we hear a sustained chordlike sound in the middle register followed by another, slightly different, thick and soft sound below. The second excursion thickens the sound above still further, while new sounds in the middle and lower registers are further fragmented. Parts of them pulsate at different rates, and this helps to clarify what they are made of: these middle and lower register sounds are being teased apart into chords of notes. The third excursion takes this further. While the sound above continues to thicken, and continues to have the distantly high E as its top edge, the middle and lower registers are filled by a sequence of notes descending in a moderately quick even rhythm of short sharp attacks. The thick, solid sounds of the outset have been crumbled into a cascade of single notes.

With the voice's fourth excursion, however, the tendency of the top register to accrete sounds is extended all the way down through the lowest register, producing the thickest sustained sound heard so far. This coincides with the voice's longest sustained E. The effect to my ear is of an initial refreezing of the texture, but the voice resists by making a crescendo and sliding upward to a high B flat.[7] Wonderful things happen here. The voice's first steps away from its E were carefully placed and always reaching downward; the high B flat is its first move up, and the crescendo and the glissando allow me to hear its physicality pushing through the musical surface. As if in amazement, the synthesized sounds react with their first rising gesture, a rapid pattering that disperses the thick cloud of sustained sounds in a shimmer of short attacks.

This is the spot where the live voice first enters to inhabit the space opened by the taped voice. Different aspects of the musical fabric vie for my attention in the following passage, leaving me slightly breathless and a little overwhelmed. The live voice enters with short sharp notes, separated in time and register, brightly colored by the vowel "ee." The taped voice, however, also continues, singing long looping phrases that range throughout its available registers. It is no longer humming, but is sounding the same syllable as the live voice. The synthesized sounds also continue, using some of the more active textures set in motion during the opening passage. I am dazzled by their combined effect in this passage, and am eager to follow each of their continuities (see figure 12.2).[8] Although the taped voice does not have the presence of the live voice, its legato phrasing lends it a more immediate sense of continuity than what is available from the live voice's short, separated notes. I am also invested in that voice from the

Figure 12.2. Babbitt, *Philomel*, mm. 8–13. Words by John Hollander. Music by Milton Babbitt. Copyright © 1964 (Renewed) by Associated Music Publishers, Inc. (BMI). International Copyright Secured. All Rights Reserved. Reprinted by permission.

opening, and take heart from its breaking free to swoop and soar and sing openly. But I can't ignore the living presence of the other voice, and I am curious as to how its short bursts will find their own coherence. Over the passage, the bright flashes of the live voice seem to group into their own melodic shapes, dots connected by their very brightness, settling like a splash of highlights on the more continuous spinning of the taped voice. Ultimately the two vocal layers combine to form an image I can liken to blossoms on a twig, or a spray of diamonds on a twist of golden wire.

    The voices are not alone, but are cradled by a skittering and bubbling of synthesized sounds. These terms may seem contradictory, but I am trying

266

Figure 12.3. Babbitt, *Philomel*. Echo of opening (mm. 19–20). Words by John Hollander. Music by Milton Babbitt. Copyright © 1964 (Renewed) by Associated Music Publishers, Inc. (BMI). International Copyright Secured. All Rights Reserved. Reprinted by permission.

to capture my sense of the sounds as both supportive and delicate, enveloping but finely detailed—a woven nest. The passage feels like a headlong rush, a dizzy spill of music erupting, albeit quietly, from the charged stillness of the opening twenty seconds. I find myself rapidly shifting points of view, hoping for a settling of my frame of reference. The passage seems pulled into focus at first by an echo of the taped voice's glissando to its high B flat, the pitch then taken up by the synthesized sound. The gesture is a point of familiarity in all the newness; furthermore, the hand-off of the pitch to the synthesized sounds allows me to follow the B flat as a point of reference, abstracted from the particularities of its production (see figure 12.3). My sense of things stabilizing here continues: the live voice follows shortly with a rising line, more continuous but still staccato, that comes to rest on the initial E of the piece, slipping up, just over and onto the taped voice's ledge (see figure 12.4). Now, for an instant, the live voice seems to perch on the same spot first occupied by the taped voice at the opening, before launching into its first recognizable words on a two-octave leap to the high B flat, "I feel . . ."

And so do I—*feel*—at this moment, feel electrified by what I have heard, feel alive to what will happen next in the piece, brought to this point by the particulars of pitch and rhythm, sound and gesture that I can only clumsily begin to suggest in words, trying to articulate my experience of this music. My words are slow! This whole passage lasts just more than a minute, and I have not mentioned any number of its aspects that are crucial to my hearing: for one, the live voice's staccato rising line forms vividly a reverse

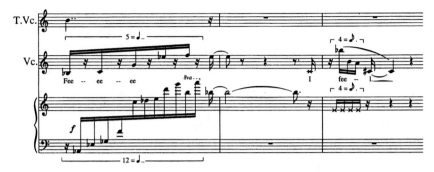

Figure 12.4. Babbitt, *Philomel*. The entrance of words (mm. 23–25). Words by John Hollander. Music by Milton Babbitt. Copyright © 1964 (Renewed) by Associated Music Publishers, Inc. (BMI). International Copyright Secured. All Rights Reserved. Reprinted by permission.

of the sequence of intervals heard gradually compounded in the first section's excursions, now (after a rising major second) a rising perfect fifth, a rising minor sixth, a rising major second, and a falling minor second. The recognizable resonance with the opening is part of what makes me feel better oriented at this spot.[9] This, along with many other factors, helps me sense the complexity of the relationship between the two voices, and between the voices and the rest of the music. The particularity of the details and the ways I can make something out of them allow me to return to this music again and again. The more I hear it, the more I hear my way into it.

This brief opening passage does seem to connect with the thread I mentioned above, finding a music, setting loose a voice in the midst of a welter of sound. Part of my experience of this passage replicates the dramatic location of Hollander's poem in the Philomel narrative, that moment when she is transformed into a nightingale. Just as the live voice seems to alight shocked, dazed and bewildered, finding itself in a state of heightened awareness in the midst of a confusion of sounds and images, so do I find myself seeking sense from the dazzle and glitter of the sounds I am hearing. And, like the voice, I find myself finding my way through this forest of sound, in the process finding my own ear. While I could have used other imagery, the behavior of birds seems a good fit with my experience of the music, and it ties in strongly with the imagery in the poem. This is not to say that the music is "about" birds, but that one way of capturing my sense of the music can chime nicely with what will emerge as verbal meaning in the voice's song.

I don't want to leave the impression that by using figurative language I am distancing myself from or trying to erase what can be said with more technical language. Although I am connecting my hearing of the passage in fairly obvious ways to the imagery of the text, I think I can also connect some of my sense of my musical experience to the language of twelve-tone and atonal theory, even back to my question about hexachords.

My sense of the taped voice's actions in the first twenty seconds is vivid, and I am led by the music to a couple of very specific observations. First, I am always hearing new notes: except for the repeated E, no note or its octave equivalent is repeated in the four excursions, and the high B flat with which the passage ends is also a new pitch-class. Second, those notes are embedded in what is gradually drawn out as the same string of intervals (to within octave compound or complementation). The single rising major seventh of the first excursion is echoed as a falling minor second in the second excursion; the subsequent rising major ninth of the second excursion contracts in the third excursion to a major second. It is heard as part of the string of falling minor second, rising major second, and rising minor sixth; the fourth excursion simply adds a rising perfect fifth to this string. My sense of the voice feeling its way into a musical space depends on both the newness of each note reached from the initial E and a growing familiarity with the interval sequence revealed with each larger excursion (see figure 12.5).

These two criteria severely limit the choices one may make in composing such a passage, and one of the limitations is the choice of underlying hexachord type.[10] With that, I could go back to connect my hearing to the questions of a collection's type, properties, and their handling I raised above; without doing so, I can still intimate that my experience of the passage is connected with some very deft play with hexachords!

With each step I have tried to clarify the set of assumptions I would hope to share with a companion in conversation, whether in shoptalk, professional exchange, teaching, or talking with listeners curious about this music. Part of any such conversation involves seeking common ground; I think a number of problems arise at this stage of the game, either through simple misunderstanding, or more troubling, a desire on the part of the speaker to assert some sort of authority over the listener. The blatant use of a jargon, for example, is all too often a signal that a speaker is trying to position him or herself as an insider in some exclusive club. Alas, this sort

Figure 12.5. Babbitt, *Philomel.* Opening pitch-collections (mm. 1–6).

of behavior is hardly limited to conversations about music, and seems an inevitable part of the political fabric of life. But even with the best will in the world, it is possible to miss finding that shared set of assumptions that will allow a productive exchange.

So far, all of the sets of assumptions I have talked about have been within a context of finding ways to talk about what to listen for. However, these all rest on the assumption that to listen *at all* is itself worth doing. When it comes to the repertoire that I started with, it seems to me that to make this assumption is to put myself on shaky ground, especially as I broaden the circle of people I talk with. The question here is what to do about it. How do I go about persuading someone that the activity is worth doing in the first place? I will return to this question shortly, but first I would like to examine how it hangs on that word, "worth." Many of the old arguments— that this is "high" art, that this is the future of music, that this is somehow "good" for you—are bankrupt, and seemed questionable even when they had some currency. All smack of the coercive, of duty or "historical inevitability."[11]

Alas, this sort of flavor has stuck to a lot of what popular wisdom thinks of as "modern" music, and it is impressive the ways this has seeped into our culture. It has become a commonplace in the public press to draw parallels between the fall of so-called academic serialism and the fall of the Berlin wall. Milton Babbitt is probably better known for the phrase "Who cares if you listen?" than for any of his music, despite having not made it in the first place.[12] The notoriety of the remark has slipped in deeply to musical discussions. In a recent concert review, a contemporary composer was favorably characterized by the phrase, "He cares if you listen," in a context that made no mention of twelve-tone music *at all,* let alone Babbitt. I have no idea if this was an intentionally sly wink on the part of the reviewer, or if it arose unconsciously.

Sometimes things can get pretty funny. I cherish the following, from "TV Pipeline" by Taylor Michaels, in *The Ann Arbor News Television Guide,* for November 1998 (p. 39):

> Q: On "Frasier," I have noticed a framed poster in the back hall of the set with the work "Schoenberg" on it. What is its significance?—Chuck in Port Charlotte, Fla.
> A: It's a nice character touch on the part of the show's set decorators. Arnold Schoenberg was an Austrian composer who created a school of composition called "twelve tone," in which melodies were structured according to a complex formula. Many of his works are dissonant and demanding—in short, exactly the kind of music an intellectual snob like Dr. Frasier Crane would enjoy.

On the other hand, things can get pretty dark, as in a mock news article that circulated on the internet recently in which it was reported that Schoenberg's invention of the twelve-tone method was in fact a code used by Webern to smuggle atomic secrets to the Nazis out of Los Alamos. Disturbing to me was not so much the article, which pretty clearly was a joke, but the number of people who contacted me asking if it could have been true. In this context, simply claiming to like this music is not without a certain amount of risk: does liking Schoenberg or Babbitt make one a Communist sympathizer? A dupe of the Nazis? Or merely an intellectual snob?

To return to my question, "How do you persuade someone that listening to this music is worth doing in the first place," I have had to remember what persuaded me. Ultimately, it was listening to the music itself, of course, but how did I connect with it? Part was chance, and part was opportunity. In those days, the repertoire of post-tonal and twelve-tone compositions was not entirely unavailable on the radio: I can remember hearing Roger Sessions' *Idyll of Theocritus* on our local commercial classical music station one evening and being transfixed by it. But that was after I had already started to pay attention to such works. I think what really got me started was a particular music teacher I had in seventh grade, Harris Poor, who, in addition to directing our glee club, teaching music appreciation, and coaching baseball, was outspoken about his enjoyment of composers like Schoenberg and Ives. It was on his suggestion that I got to know Schoenberg's Violin Concerto, but I am convinced that it was his unmasked pleasure in the music that caused me to go out and buy the recording. This music was not offered as something that was "good" for me, but as something that was wonderful in itself—something that he clearly found thrilling, that he wished to share with others. His teaching, in this case, was teaching by example, and the sense of worth he conveyed about the music was through the evident way that it had enriched him.

This returns me to my father's question, "How can you listen to that stuff?" By trying to answer him directly, I am defeating my purpose. No amount of explanation of twelve-tone composition or aggregate hearing, no matter how deeply I go into the underlying assumptions, will start to answer that question until I can somehow convey to him the answer to the question that lurks just beneath the surface, "*Why* do you listen to that stuff?" And that of course is harder to answer, except by showing the joy such listening gives me. At this point, thrilled and enthralled, I am reduced to saying, "just listen!"[13]

If this is to have any meaning at all, I must believe that simple exposure to the music will be enough to draw a willing listener in, to teach her or him how to hear it, or at least provide a start that conversation can refine. I could simply claim that this is how I learned to hear this music, but I don't think that is enough. I do have some anecdotal evidence that suggests certain crucial distinctions can be picked up without benefit of a theoretical education. By the age of six my daughter had coined the term "daddymusic" to name a category of music that has proven subsequently to be a very specific repertoire, being pretty accurately those pieces that unfold in aggregates. Over the years her musical discrimination (not to mention her terminology) has become more refined, but I have been able to confirm that her initial intuitive distinctions were not so much stylistic or gestural as based on pitch behavior. For example, to her ear *Wozzeck* did not quite fit her intuitions about aggregate music: the ways chords move to chords seemed too much like Mahler (and she knows this from the inside: she has played the *Adagietto* from the Fifth Symphony in her high-school orchestra; thus her comparison). On the other hand, the Schoenberg Violin Concerto *does* belong to this category, despite the fact that many of its gestures are similar to those in the Brahms Violin Concerto. What she has gathered under a single rubric apparently is not just music without pitch-centers, but is music in which the kinds of stepwise voice-leading associated with even highly chromatic triadic music do not serve more than a motivic purpose (contrast the continuous presence of tonal voice-leading lurking in the background of *Wozzeck* with the more motivically based half-steps at the beginning of the Schoenberg Concerto). Furthermore, her category does not distinguish between compositions that are claimed to be twelve-tone or serial and those that are not. While some of Schoenberg's middle-period works and most of his twelve-tone works belong to this category, so does much of the music of Elliott Carter; Babbitt's works belong, but so do those by Ruggles and Varèse. Late Stravinsky, yes; earlier Stravinsky, no. Webern, yes; Berg, well, maybe sort of. What has emerged from my questioning is that there is a pretty good overlap between what she now refers to as the kind of music her father is interested in, and the repertoire of music in which scale-degree differentiation as the basis of functional (or even gestural) discrimination has been replaced with the ways pitch-classes are compositionally disposed within the total chromatic. (As the foregoing should suggest, my daughter's category covers far more than just my own compositions, which have had only the narrowest toehold in her listening experience.)

My daughter's attitude towards this category is fairly neutral: this is simply music that works in a recognizably different way from other musics; different, but enjoyable. Her engagement is rooted in her listening experience, rather than on any kind of training in some sort of generalizable "serial syntax," and her likes and dislikes are based on her reactions to specific pieces, rather than on the acceptance or rejection of some notion of a fixed post-tonal language. Her comfort with post-tonal music is the result of exposure; our conversations about music have always depended on that exposure, and while I may have been able to draw her attention to particular aspects of certain pieces, it was her childhood exposure to Schoenberg, Babbitt, and Carter that gave me the chance to talk with her about what to listen for.

My daughter's exposure was not of her own volition, and it happened young. But I do not think either condition is a necessity for making the initial contact that can allow for productive conversations about post-tonal and twelve-tone music. After years of not getting it, my father, for reasons of his own, undertook an experiment with a part of this repertoire. For a number of weeks he listened repeatedly to a particular work, recycling the recording every time it came to an end, usually while he was occupied with other tasks. He told me that for much of the time he really didn't like what he was hearing, but that one day he noticed that he was able to follow the piece. It made sense to him; he knew where he was in it, and could remember and anticipate what came next. That realization arrived simultaneously with his sense that, in his words, the stuff actually was *music,* and further, he liked it. He then made the next experiment, which was to listen to another piece of the same repertoire, and, no surprise, found it immediately engaging. He had cracked some sort of code: although he didn't have a lot of words for it, this kind of music now makes sense for him—noise had become signal.

I think that the central lesson I have learned in talking with my students, friends, and family is that there really is nothing I can say directly that will help anyone make the connection with this music. All I can do is bear witness to the fact that such connection *can* be made. Once that has happened, though, there is much that can be said to nurture and refine people's hearing, but doing so takes care. Signal can turn to noise if sets of assumptions don't line up; we see examples of that every day when students fail to realize that technical terms are shorthand for musical experiences they have had, or writers use insider's jargon for political purposes. If, however, we are aware of our own assumptions, and have a certain sense of those of our audience, there is much we can share.

Notes

1. Curiously, I learned that my father had been credited with the remark some years before in his own field, respiratory physiology.
2. The complexities of communication about music, and their multiple ramifications both within and amongst musical and other disciplines, are explored to great depths in Kevin Korsyn, *Decentering Music: A Critique of Contemporary Musical Research* (New York: Oxford University Press, 2003).
3. Think, for example of the difference between a suspension understood as the result of the motion of voices in Palestrina and the "sus. chord" of popular music. Add to that the functional significance of a second inversion tonic chord as a dominant in cadential formulations, and you begin to see the variety of ways we reconfigure our experience.
4. I am indebted to Marion Guck for discussions of figurative language and musical experience. She has published pioneering work on metaphor and musical experience; see, for example, her "Metaphors in Musical Discourse: The Contribution of Imagery to Analysis" (Ph.D. diss., University of Michigan, 1981), and more

recently, "Two Types of Metaphoric Transfer," in *Metaphor: A Musical Dimension,* ed. Jamie C. Kassler (Sydney: Currency Press, 1991). It is at her urging that I have essayed my brief remarks about *Philomel.*

5. See David Hamilton's notes to Milton Babbitt, *Philomel* (New World Records 80466, 1995). See also John Hollander's "Notes on the Text of *Philomel,*" *Perspectives of New Music* 4, no. 1 (1967): 134–41.

6. Susan McClary (in her article "Terminal Prestige: The Case of Avant-Garde Music Composition," *Cultural Critique* 12 [1989]: 57–81) brings up this work in a discussion of modernism and misogyny (pp. 74–75). She offers a reading that is sympathetic to the piece as "an *anti-rape* statement" (p. 75), and details how both text and music work from this point of view: "The shattered fragmentation of her human voice . . ., her change from material being into music . . ., and her forging of triumph from violence . . . all serve to acknowledge the horror of the crime and yet the possibility of survival" (p. 75). (The ellipses remove her parenthetical quotations from the poem.) She also mentions the emotional and theatrical impact the piece can make in live performance. All of this matches my hearing of the music, and it was the overwhelming impact of a live performance of this work (in Oberlin in 1972) that drew me to Babbitt's music in the first place. But McClary then turns to questioning this interpretation: "Yet Babbitt's writings discourage one from attempting to unpack his composition along these lines" (p. 75). She continues, "Many of my female students have trouble listening passively to *Philomel* as yet another instance of serial and electronic manipulation: they have difficulty achieving the kind of objective intellectual attitude that would permit them to focus on considerations of sterile compositional technique." I, too, would have trouble taking in the work that way, just as I can't take in the Crucifixus from the B-minor Mass as only an exercise in counterpoint over a ground bass, but then that's not how I ever took in either work in the first place. Furthermore, I don't find McClary's later description resonating with my experience of Babbitt's music as a whole. I certainly don't want Babbitt's writings to limit how I hear his music, and I simply refuse to be discouraged by them!

7. In the score, the crescendo is marked in the center of the tape part, but the crescendo is readily heard in the voice in the recording.

8. It is worth noting that the recorded voice is that of Bethany Beardslee, for whom the work was written. Subtly different senses of the work can emerge whether one is thinking of live performances by Beardslee, live performances by other singers, or recordings of the work, by Beardslee or someone else. The fact that the taped voice is recognizably Beardslee's lends to her performances, live or recorded, possibilities of understanding the relationship between recorded and live voice not available to other singers. As for the recorded performances, the issue of what is "live" and what is recorded becomes a conceit at a certain level. It is readily apparent which is which, from their sound, but they are, of course, *both* recorded. I have heard the work under a number of different circumstances, and each makes for an interesting new sense of the music—the work itself survives, the transformation is not intolerable!

9. Not surprisingly, there is more here. The sequence of pitch-classes, B♭, C, G, E♭, F, and E, reverses the sequence of the sustained note, plus the initial pitch-classes of each of the four excursions, and finally the B flat of the opening.

10. An excellent technical account of the first twenty seconds of the piece may be

found in Richard Swift, "Some Aspects of Aggregate Composition," *Perspectives of New* Music 14, no. 2, and 15, no. 1 (1976): 236–48. The question may well be asked, "Why hexachords?" After all, I haven't been tracking six-note collections. However, one detail that I have not mentioned (and that is treated in Swift) is that the sequence of intervals formed between the sustained note, the initial notes of each excursion, and the high B flat invert the series of intervals gradually being drawn out in the excursions themselves. Making all of this happen depends on the interval-class content and ordering possibilities of the hexachord so formed. This has interesting connections with Igor Stravinsky's twelve-tone practice. See also the discussion in the author's *An Introduction to the Music of Milton Babbitt* (Princeton, N.J.: Princeton University Press, 1995), 126–27.

11. Some would say that during a certain period young composers were coerced into being serialists, if they wanted tenure, prizes, or commissions. However, in this day and age, the opposite could be claimed. I remember receiving a letter describing a composition contest for an ensemble in upstate New York, in which the specifications for entrance included a maximum length for the work, the list of instruments available, and the requirement that "the work must not be serial."

12. This whole sorry story has been told many times; Babbitt's own account may be found in Babbitt's "On Having Been and Still Being an American Composer," *Perspectives of New Music* 27, no. 1 (1989): 106–12.

13. I'm reminded, with a certain amount of irony, of hearing a musical commentator on the radio in Boston when I was a child who often would be reduced simply to saying, in a clearly excited tone, "Listen—listen!" I find it interesting that it was the urgency of his voice more than any particular thing he ever said that I remember.

Part Five

Belated Modernism

13

The "Modernization" of Rock & Roll, 1965–75

Jonathan W. Bernard

There's something happening here . . .

It was January 1968. I was sixteen, going somewhere in the family car, and "Susan," a new song by the Buckinghams, was on the radio. I wasn't expecting much—and so far, this song was sounding a lot like their earlier hits "Kind of a Drag" and "Don't You Care": same adenoidally earnest lead vocals, same predictable harmonic progressions, same hackneyed backing arrangement. . . . I listened half-attentively.

Suddenly my ears perked up. What was this? The song had chugged its way a second time through the bridge—but then, instead of proceeding to a third verse or the out chorus, it suddenly ground to a halt. As the studio-engineered resonance died away, some very different music sprang forth: orchestral, not too loud at first but then swelling in volume, definitely nontonal and restless, after a few seconds overlaid by an electronic track of some sort that quickly brought the passage to a shattering, shrieking climax. It seemed impossible, but I was sure I'd heard the beginning of the first Organized Sound interpolation from Edgard Varèse's *Déserts* in there somewhere. (Later hearings would prove that I was right.) The ultimate appearance of the out chorus barely made an impression; I was too busy feeling astonished, delighted—and also confused. Had the Buckinghams, in those twenty-five seconds or so, just revealed their heretofore secret identity as some far-out, avant-garde group, like the Mothers of Invention? An early interest in Varèse, Bartók, Stravinsky, and other twentieth-century composers had led me, in my adolescent years, to Frank Zappa and the Mothers' album *Freak Out!* not long after its release in 1966, when Zappa began to receive notice as a rock musician who knew something about "serious" music and who particularly revered Varèse. Yet Zappa, as far as I could tell, was a unique figure on the musical scene; the prospect of the Mothers achieving the kind of popularity that would enable them to score hit singles on the charts had seemed reserved, if ever, for some unimaginably distant future. Had that future suddenly and unexpectedly arrived, and were the Buckinghams its unlikely annunciators?

. . . What it is, ain't exactly clear

Well, actually, no—although, as it turned out, the Buckinghams *did* have a "secret identity" of a sort, to be discussed later in this essay. More to the point is that "Susan" was just one manifestation of a phenomenon that, starting in the mid-1960s and continuing well into the 1970s (with some later, vestigial activity), worked on many different fronts to change—in some respects rather obviously, in others more subtly—the face of rock & roll, with effects on everything ranging from harmony, melody, and lyrics, to sonic repertoire more generally construed, to the larger scale of form and format. At the beginning of this period, the nature and scope of the coming change were hardly foreseeable; typical Top Forty Radio consumers, in fact, might have been excused for finding the first two lines of the Buffalo Springfield's song, "For What It's Worth," borrowed for the first two subheadings of this essay, an apt expression of their bewilderment. Today, with some benefit of hindsight, we can see that popular music was experiencing an upheaval in some ways distinctly analogous, in other ways explicitly parallel, to what art music had undergone during the first few decades of the twentieth century: the rise of modernism; the development of an avant garde; the commodification of the musical "product"; and a "backlash" effect that led to the rise of various more or less reactionary alternatives.

Of course, the fact that this upheaval took place in an avidly commercial sphere, in an environment where the dynamics of making money directed events to a far greater extent than they ever had in the Western concert music tradition even at the height of its popularity, meant that the outward effects of change in rock & roll, including its artistic output, were inevitably quite different from those felt several decades earlier in art music. And, it should also be noted, the span of time over which these developments took place in rock & roll was drastically shorter—really a different order of magnitude altogether. Nevertheless, some aspects of the overall shape of events, as they played out starting in the mid-1960s, were remarkably similar in the two cases. So were some of the underlying causes, even though some modernist effects appeared in rock & roll through emulation of art-music models while others developed independently of any such influence.

"Modernization," then, has been placed in quotation marks in the title to signify that the word carries a double meaning in this essay: first, in the common sense of updating, the casting off of old features or conceptions and the appropriation of new ones; second, in a more specialized sense, indicating an engagement with *modernism,* born of an artistic impulse whose influence was, by the mid-1960s, already a venerable part of twentieth-century history. Thus, in the very idea of modernization of rock & roll, a paradox is already embedded. In the art-music culture of that time, "modern music" was not necessarily music that had been composed during the previous week, or even sometime within the last decade. It could be, say, Bartók's Fourth String Quartet, by then nearly forty years old, or Stravinsky's *Rite of Spring,* more than fifty—but in any case music that was still quite youthful by comparison to a core repertoire that remained resolutely centered on the eighteenth and nineteenth centuries. The perpetually marginalized position of most art music composed in the twentieth century, for most of that century's duration, may explain why the first perturbations of musical modernism have continued to seem like relatively recent history—and also why it was possible for popular music in the 1960s and early 1970s, whether consciously or not, to emulate them. Also implicit in the double meaning of "modernization," and perhaps inevitable given the historical distance of the decade 1965–75 from the origins of modernism, is the way in which modernism in rock & roll will be assessed here, by turns, both as arising by analogy to or in direct emulation of modernism in art music and as arising independently, from the same causes but not necessarily out of any awareness on the part of the participants that something similar had already happened in the world of art music.

For the sake of orienting the reader usefully, I have a few more comments—and some accompanying cautions—to voice. Owing to the chronological "telescoping" of rock & roll's encounter with modernism, compared to that of art music, many of the nuances that have generally come to characterize treatments of modernism as a social, political, or cultural/artistic phenomenon are not especially pertinent to the present case. The influences, direct or indirect, that rock & roll received and processed ca. 1965–75 simply came too fast, in too pell-mell and indiscriminate a fashion, for any truly orderly historiographical scheme of categorization to shed much light. However, just because "modern music," in the common parlance, usually embraced *avant-garde* activity among its several aspects, I will use the latter term to identify a quite distinct shade of modernization, one that is of considerable importance in the present context, without attempting in any way to suggest that an avant-garde sensibility was *always* at work (any more, for that matter, than modernism was in general) in rock & roll of the era under discussion; or that the basically "disruptive" tendencies of the avant-garde always preceded the "normalizing" ones of modernism, following the neat order that some have prescribed. In rock & roll, at least, it is not so easy, or in many instances possible at all, to separate the two.

This messiness of rock & roll as subject matter has other ramifications as well. It is notoriously difficult to identify a canon of any sort, or even to pick out representative samples of the many, many different genres and subgenres that have surfaced, however evanescently or persistently, in the course of its scant half-century of history. In fact, to a very considerable extent the repertoire of rock & roll *is* its history. For this reason, I have erred, if at all, on the side of overabundance in the number of examples cited, with songs that everyone knows sharing the stage with relative obscurities. Some of my choices may seem at first glance frivolous, but this strategy of exemplification is necessary precisely to show how widespread the trend toward modernization in rock & roll was at that time, and in how many different ways its effects were registered.

Finally, modernism as a twentieth-century phenomenon reached beyond music into many other areas of human artistic activity. To some extent, aspects of modernism (as well as the avant-garde) in this wider connotation are relevant to the study of rock & roll during the late 1960s and early 1970s, perhaps even more than they are to the art music of the twentieth century usually known as "modern." Such aspects, too, will be treated in what follows.

Some folks call it music; my folks call it noise

"Susan" was not the first odd thing to be heard over the commercial pop airwaves around that time. Earlier, there had been novelty records, with "sound effects" contributing to the (usually) humorous intent;[1] but by the later 1960s they had largely given way to stranger, less readily identifiable sounds quite evidently not played for laughs. One certainly didn't find much to giggle at in the Yardbirds' "Shapes of Things" (early 1966), with its magnificently distorted guitar solo, or the jarring dissonances of the instrumental break in their "Happenings Ten Years' Time Ago" (later the same year). How many listeners must have been baffled at first, or even outraged by the weirdly vibrating feedback that opens the Electric Prunes' "I Had Too Much to Dream (Last Night)" (early 1967), or the even more acerbic guitar feedback at the beginning of Jefferson Airplane's "The Ballad of You & Me & Pooneil" (later 1967)? Hard on their heels came the Jimi Hendrix Experience with "Purple Haze," featuring sounds that few might previously have suspected the electric guitar capable of producing, and a strange mix of mumbled voices during the instrumental break—and then, before 1967 was out, the Beatles' "I Am the Walrus," which supplemented the group's own instruments with horns and eerily sliding strings in a manner more like chamber music than the conventional pop accompaniments of the day, and which made use of bizarre lyrics as well as collage and other sound alteration techniques to produce one of the most compellingly discomfiting records ever issued.

This was entertainment of a different sort, quite a change from the paeans to puppy love (or laments over its loss) and exhortations to join in the latest dance craze that had dominated rock & roll radio since its birth. There was still plenty of such light fare around, but there was also a new seriousness abroad, and the expansion of sonic resources was a big part of this shift in tone. In fact, these new sounds could be regarded as emblematic of a desire to expand the expressive world of rock & roll, beyond the themes and sentiments of the rather banal outward life usually on display and toward a distinctly *inner*, individual sensibility. All five of the examples cited above illustrate this desire in one way or another—even "I Had Too Much to Dream," which retains some overtones of the lost-love song.

Why, though, did such an interest in expanded sonic resources even arise in the first place? There were two principal factors that combined to change the basic sound of rock & roll from the mid-1960s on. The earlier of the two to make its effects felt was the rapid evolution, beginning in the late 1940s, of the guitar from a relatively mild-mannered, at most lightly amplified accompanying instrument to a fully electric, aggressive, heavily amplified solo instrument in the performances and recordings of urban blues musicians such as Muddy Waters, Willie Johnson, Guitar Slim, and Ike Turner. The distortion and feedback that came with these developments was accepted, even embraced and deliberately manipulated as an integral part of the new sound. They led to new playing techniques, as did the introduction of modifications such as the solid-body guitar and the whammy bar; they also forced the development of new recording techniques to capture the exciting qualities of "naturally" loud music.[2] Urban blues, black people's music, had some impact on early American rock & roll. Although the latter was largely the preserve of white performers (and audiences), even in its early years it bore a significantly interracial aspect, as black artists such as Chuck Berry, Little Richard, and Fats Domino succeeded in crossing over. But it took the advent of the British Invasion, with its guitar-based bands whose members had listened closely to both white and black American popular music, to finish the job of bringing American blues, in quantity, into the rock & roll mainstream here in the United States. Within just a few years, guitarists like John Mayall, Eric Clapton, Jeff Beck, Keith Richards, and—especially—Jimi Hendrix (actually a black American who brought his firm grounding in the electric blues-guitar traditions to England, where he formed the Experience with British sidemen), building on what they had absorbed from those earlier blues recordings, had taken some mighty strides toward a thoroughgoing alteration of the sound of rock & roll.[3]

The other major factor in this sonic change was the development of the modern recording studio, with its multitrack capacities and the general capability it afforded for shaping the sound of music to be heard on records. Up until the late 1960s, as rock composer/performer/producer Brian Eno has pointed out, "the recording studio had been a passive transmitter," used to imprint music that already existed, in all or most of its particulars, onto magnetic tape.[4] The change didn't happen all at once, of course; and many of the first sonic alterations accomplished in the studio were mere "effects," as in the novelty records mentioned earlier, grafted onto music that had been conceived independently of any such alterations. By the early 1960s, though, the power of a really good production to enhance the music on a record was already becoming apparent, thanks to new developments like Phil Spector's resonant, quasi-symphonic "wall of sound" approach.[5] Spector's accomplishments inspired Brian Wilson, among others, to aim for even more ambitious goals, as evidenced by his vividly clear and spacious production of the Beach Boys' *Pet Sounds,* released in May 1966. The Beatles soon followed suit with *Revolver* in August of the same year, an album that featured, besides the stellar production of George Martin, a mélange of prerecorded tape loops—each consisting of multiple overdubbed sounds—and John Lennon's singing voice piped through a Leslie speaker on the song "Tomorrow Never Knows."[6] It was this album, together with Wilson's follow-up to *Pet Sounds,* the single "Good Vibrations" (October 1966, discussed elsewhere in this essay), which probably signaled the most strongly at the time that some rock & roll from then on was destined never to be heard in concert performance, and that some popular musicians were shifting the principal focus of their careers to making a more thoughtful and elaborate recorded product than could ever be conveyed live. By fall of 1966, in fact, the Beatles had withdrawn for good from the concert circuit and were concentrating their energies on making a single ("Penny Lane"/ "Strawberry Fields Forever") and an album (*Sgt. Pepper's Lonely Hearts Club Band*) that, ounce for ounce, probably did more than any other two records to change musicians' and audiences' *idea* of popular music in that era, and their aspirations for what it could be.

What both the newly amplified electric guitar and the newly equipped recording studio allowed into popular music was a host of sounds that would formerly have been classified as "noise": that is, undesirable interference, which under the standards that previously applied would have been extirpated as quickly as possible. Certainly a harbinger of this change was the experience of Ike Turner and his band, upon arriving at Sam Phillips's studio in Memphis in 1951 to audition. One of their guitar amplifiers had suffered some damage to its speaker in a mishap en route; as Phillips recounted: "I stuffed a little paper in there where the speaker cone was ruptured, and it sounded good. It sounded like a saxophone. And we decided to go ahead and record."[7] Like all great discoveries, the fuzztone guitar came about from a fortuitous accident. "It sounded good." That remark makes us realize that we are dealing with an engineer of effectively experimentalist sensibilities; Turner and company might not have fared so well at some other studio. These sensibilities proved to be commercially savvy as well: the record that resulted from that recording session, "Rocket 88," became a big hit, and "that fuzzed-out guitar doubling the boogie-bass line was clearly one of its chief selling points." It was something *new*, something that set the record apart from its competition.[8]

Luigi Russolo, for one, would not have been surprised at these developments—and might well have been a little envious at the success enjoyed by these blues guitarists. One of the Italian futurists who burst into notoriety around 1910, Russolo made his principal contributions to the movement by writing a manifesto entitled *The Art of Noises* (1916) and by devising new instruments, "noise-intoners," on which a new kind of music—his own and that of like-minded composer Balilla Pratella—could be performed.[9] In this manifesto, the idea of continuing to distinguish between sound and noise, along the lines set forth by Helmholtz, is dismissed as absurd. "Noise-sound" is championed as the inevitable outcome of the increasing level of dissonance in music over the last several centuries; for Russolo, as a basis for music it offers many advantages, including infinite variety (keeping the ear from becoming bored), greater richness in harmonics, and a capacity for reflecting the aural experience of modern life (including, notably, warfare), in a world inured to noise.

Russolo carried on a struggle throughout the 1920s to organize concerts, both in Italy and abroad, of "networks of noises," as he preferred to call his new compositions, played on instruments whose names described generically the sorts of noises they produced: bursters, cracklers, hummers, hissers, gurglers, and so on. These events provoked a mixture of hilarity, outrage, enthusiasm, and—not infrequently—fisticuffs; the futurists were willing to fight back and even go on the offensive if they thought it useful to do so. A *succès de scandale* they certainly achieved, but not much of a lasting effect upon Western musical culture: their activities eventually ceased for lack of financial support, and none of the actual instruments seem to have survived. Surveying Russolo's and Pratella's experience from a vantage point nearly a century later, one wonders whether one of their problems might have been that their music wasn't *loud* enough. After all, the noise-intoners, non-electrical instruments apparently cranked by hand, would have had only acoustical amplification. Russolo declares at one point in his manifesto: "It cannot be objected that noise is only loud and disagreeable to the ear. It seems to me useless to enumerate all the subtle and delicate noises that produce pleasing sensations."[10] This, in fact, is one of the few passages in *The Art of Noises* that seems out of keeping with the sensibilities of the later twentieth century, at least with respect to rock & roll, or even to the amplified blues that preceded it. Perhaps it is also true, though, that audiences thirty years later, and away from the genteel surroundings of the concert hall, were simply much better prepared to accept noise as a natural part of music. Russolo's manifesto seems otherwise positively prescient in places, in particular his remark to the effect that every noise has a dominant pitch, by means of which that noise can be regulated—exactly what the amplified blues guitarists and their rock & roll descendants would later do.[11]

If, as Russolo said, a kind of "evolution" had taken place to reach this point in the development of musical composition, it was also, paradoxically, a point at which to abjure all that had come before: in Pratella's words, to declare "the liberation of musical sensibility from all imitation or influence of the past," and "to destroy the prejudice for 'well-made' music . . . to proclaim the unique concept of Futurist music, as absolutely different from music to date."[12] Something of the same attitude comes through in remarks by John Cale, a founding member of the Velvet Underground, about the activities of his group in 1966: "Just dig the noise, and you've got our sound. We're putting everything together—lights and film and music—and we're reducing it to its lowest common denominator. We're musical primitives."[13] The Velvet Underground had a stage manner to match their rejection of the conventionally tuneful mid-1960s rock & roll sound, dressing drably in deliberate contrast to "slick midtown [New York] club acts like Joey Dee and the Starlighters who wore matching suits"; they often expressed disdain or at least indifference toward the audience by playing with their backs turned to it.[14] In this demeanor, to the extent that it was meant to be provocative, Russolo surely would have recognized a kindred spirit. And he might have recognized a kindred spirit as well in the approach to noise: initially a deformation, for both the Velvet Underground and the earlier amplified blues, it became a style in its own right.[15]

As for the recording studio, more and more, as its technical range increased, it became a site, not simply for recording and shaping the "normal" sound of a rock & roll band, but also for experimenting with less conventional sounds—some of them familiar from other musical contexts but foreign to rock, some unfamiliar from any context at all. Not all of these sounds were what one might ordinarily classify as "noise." Yet when Beatles John Lennon and Paul McCartney, for example, put down their own instruments and sang to the accompaniment of a double string quartet in "Eleanor Rigby" (1966), it was, under the circumstances, a radical act. Although backing orchestras were often used on pop records, continuing a tradition that had existed long before rock & roll, the quartet on "Eleanor Rigby" was no Nelson Riddle–style arrangement. It was something more akin to art music: strikingly incongruous in that setting (although their audience was almost immediately won over), and therefore, in this very broad sense, *noise*.[16] Even more disorienting, at least initially, were instruments that pop listeners had encountered only rarely, if ever. George Harrison took up the sitar and later brought other Indian instruments into the Beatles' mix; the harpsichord made its appearance in 1965 and became an "exotic" fixture in many recording studios thereafter.[17] Other instruments with ethnic or folk associations—jug, dulcimer, autoharp, caz, oud—were appropriated too.[18] Not only were such disparate instruments combined with rock & roll forces; still others were invented in the studio, such as the distorted human voice—by putting it through a rotating (Leslie) organ speaker, as previously mentioned, as well as subjecting it to phase shifting, echo-delay effects, and processing through the guitar's wah-wah pedal.[19] In short, the studio now put virtuosity of a new and different kind on display—sometimes quite spectacularly, as in Brian Wilson's "Good Vibrations." Using the Beach Boys' voices (including his own) as if they were a set of instruments, Wilson combined them with cello, organ, theremin, and Jew's harp, among numerous others, assembling textures that could not possibly have been performed away from the mixing console of a studio. Effectively, the studio *itself* had become an instrument, which played all the others.

Two further points about the role of the studio need to be emphasized. The first concerns the sheer amount of hard work that the innovations of the Beach Boys, the Beatles, and others required: the sessions that produced records such as "Good Vibrations" and *Sgt. Pepper* were anything but routine events in which everything happened with smooth efficiency. The sense of the struggle necessary to the task, of the difficulties that the height of their aspirations presented, and the feeling of never being quite satisfied, always looking forward to the next potential breakthrough—all this comes through vividly in the first-hand accounts of Wilson and George Martin and suggests a strong analogy with the history of modernism earlier in this century, where there is a prevalent sense of something very difficult being brought to fruition, in turn opening up possibilities for further, even perpetual innovation.[20]

The second point has to do with a *conscious* link that many in rock & roll at that time recognized between what they were doing, or were attempting to do, and what was going on in the world of "serious" art and music. Martin has identified McCartney's connection to that world, which was beginning to develop markedly around the time of *Revolver*, thanks to the encouragement he received from the Ashers, his cultured in-laws; McCartney himself has attributed the idea of the famous orchestral "crazy crescendo" heard twice in "A Day in the Life" (*Sgt. Pepper*) to the influence of "avant-garde composers."[21] Not too much later, Lennon would begin to show an analogous interest in avant-garde art (though it developed in a rather different way from McCartney's), as the result of his relationship with Yoko Ono. The names of John Cage and Karlheinz Stockhausen, two contemporary art-music composers much in the public eye at the time, as well as various others of the twentieth century, both living and dead, were freely bandied about—not only by the Beatles, but also Syd Barrett and Richard Wright of Pink Floyd; John Cale of the Velvet Underground in New York; and Frank Zappa (Mothers of Invention) and Phil Lesh and Tom Constanten (Grateful Dead), all on the American West Coast. One band, Spooky Tooth—otherwise known for rather straightforward and simple hard rock—went so far as to engage an actual art-music composer, *musique concrète* pioneer Pierre Henry, to compose tape-loop accompaniment for their album *Ceremony* (1970).

It is easy to dismiss such claims and activity as name-dropping or self-conscious attempts at "legitimation," to allay the skepticism of lookers-on in either camp—or, perhaps, simply to impress the critics. But such cynicism is not always justified, especially considering that some musicians, at any rate, doggedly pursued their course even after it became obvious that the "novelty" appeal of avant-gardism for many consumers of popular music would extend only so far, and would begin to pall after a while. This would occasionally take on an extreme aspect, as with bands like Red Crayola, whose distortion-filled debut album, *Parable of Arable Land* (1967), and highly abrasive performances at festivals around the same time that even dispensed with any kind of recognizable rock beat, certainly could not have been designed to stimulate massive record sales.[22] To that extent, such musicians can be said to have shunned material success and to have experienced what Renato Poggioli calls "economic alienation" in his account of avant-garde behavior.[23]

One type of avant-garde-inspired activity that did turn out to be immensely popular was the staged rampage of destruction that the British band the Who made a part of its act during the early years of its existence. Like many a future rocker, Pete Townshend had attended art school for a time; and it was there, apparently, that he and others learned of "happenings" and other such events that were taking place in such venues (at that time most schools of music, both in England and America, did not encourage such radical redefinition of musical composition and performance).[24] Fluxus, in particular, a kind of neo-Dadaist movement with a subversive attitude toward the reigning art-music culture, had sprung up in New York around 1960; it later spread to other places (and had imitators everywhere) but never gained what one could call mass appeal. Part music, part visual art, it can be considered a predecessor to performance art, of the type now practiced by Laurie Anderson among others, which has won a wide following.

Among the more notorious activities of Fluxus were some that involved subjecting pianos, those massive icons of Western classical music, to various indignities. Earlier in the century, Henry Cowell had written piano music that directed the performer to reach into the instrument and play the strings directly; and Cage, of course, had "prepared" pianos by inserting metal screws, rubber objects, and other materials between the strings to alter pitch, timbre, and attack/decay characteristics. Such approaches did no harm to the instrument, but pianos that fell into the hands of Fluxus were often not so lucky: foreign substances such as water or glue were poured in, or they might be dropped from a great height, chopped up, or set on fire.

When Townshend, without warning to his bandmates, first smashed his guitar at a Who concert, drummer Keith Moon reciprocated by demolishing his drumset—and the audience, already considerably revved up as Who audiences tended to be by the violent, power-chorded, feedback-laden nature of the music, responded with wild enthusiasm, which encouraged the group to make the destruction sequence a standard finale to all their performances for a while.[25] Jimi Hendrix's practice of guitar-burning, which he took up a few years later (along with occasional ramming/impaling of amplifiers with his guitar) may well have developed in emulation of such routines.[26] The relative obscurity of Fluxus throughout its existence, compared to the huge audiences commanded by the Who and Hendrix, seems to confirm Walter Benjamin's observation that "the greater the decrease in the social significance of an art form, the sharper the distinction between criticism and enjoyment by the public."[27] Both, however, in their physically destructive activities do literally embody the "antagonistic moment" and its hostility toward artistic traditions, and even toward the public, as identified by Poggioli.[28]

Less violent, but probably no less interesting, were the happening-inspired antics of early Pink Floyd concerts. Syd Barrett, their leader, had been to art school too, and he apparently spurred his bandmates on to some of the things Roger Waters, bassist of the group, remembers doing at the Games for May in 1967, such as "chasing clockwork toy cars around the stage with a microphone." He continues: "I can remember spending quite a lot of time moving a bunch of flowers from vase to vase because I couldn't think of anything else to do at the time; I'd run out of potatoes to throw at the gong, . . ."[29] These activities do indeed sound quite Fluxus-like. Pink Floyd was also among the first groups to mount a light show as a supplement to a rock concert, a mixed-media idea that may also have derived from happenings.

Machine dreams

It was probably inevitable that rock & roll, having very quickly developed a heavy dependence upon electricity and the equipment it drives, as well as recording-studio technology ever increasing in sophistication, would eventually develop a fascination with machines and their connotations in highly industrialized Western society: their sleek newness, their repetitive and automated functions—and the threats they posed, actual or potential, to humans. Like the machine music of the 1920s that developed out of more or less intimate contact with Italian futurism—with works like George Antheil's *Ballet mécanique* (1925) featuring airplane propellers, and Alexander Mosolov's *Steel Foundry* (1928) with its relentlessly pounding imitation of factory din—rock & roll in the late 1960s and early 1970s encompassed, among other things, an extensive range of songs, and even group behaviors, directly inspired by contemplation of the role of the machine in modern life.

Some examples from this repertoire are relatively lighthearted, such as the Five Americans' "Western Union" (1967), with its jittery rhythms, unusually high tessitura prominently featuring the electric organ, and a periodically interjected vocalise "imitating" Morse Code. Other songs take a more serious tone, such as "Machines," memorably recorded by Lothar and the Hand People (1968), with its "dystopian" vision of a world of human beings enslaved by their own creations. The clanking percussion, evoking a tireless automaton, effectively "makes" this record. However, the collective persona of the Hand People, a band of folk-rockers who had learned to coexist with theremin, Moog, and taped electronic sounds, was rather more cheerful, not inclined to take itself too seriously. (Lothar is actually the name of the theremin that has "adopted" this band, according to the whimsical liner notes to their debut album, *Presenting Lothar and the Hand People*.) As Poggioli notes, "The avant-garde often loves certain forms and devices of modern life primarily as toys."[30] In a quite different and somewhat more sober style was the Music Machine, whose members dressed identically in black (with one black glove each), dyed their hair an identical black shade in an apparent attempt to blur individual identities, and tuned their instruments down a minor third to give their sound a dense, bass-heavy, "industrial" quality, as on their one single to crack the Top Forty, "Talk Talk" (1966). (Even their record labels were black.)[31] Both of these last two groups seem to respond to the aesthetic of the machine in the ambivalent way of avant-garde art earlier in the century, a response that is also, like that of their earlier counterparts, admixed with a certain amount of humor, black or otherwise.[32]

A later arrival on the rock scene, much more successful than either the Hand People or the Music Machine, was the German synthesizer band Kraftwerk, whose members maintained a preternaturally calm, almost robotic stage presence. Their "Wernher von Braun sartorial aspect," as critic Lester Bangs sarcastically termed it, was intended to emphasize a "scientific" approach to music-making; "they referred to their studio as their 'laboratory.'"[33] Kraftwerk was best known for its long, fixed-tempo, almost monochromatic compositions, like "Autobahn" (1975), which depicts a most prosaic experience: driving on the freeways of Germany—the chant "(Wir) fahr'n fahr'n fahr'n auf der Autobahn," periodically repeated with an almost disembodied lack of inflection, is practically the sole lyric content of the entire 22:42 duration. The music is oddly soothing, despite the occasional distractions provided by other cars zooming past, etc. Listening to this cut recently, I was reminded of American minimalist sculptor Tony Smith's account of driving at night during the early 1950s, illegally, on the (at that time unfinished) New Jersey Turnpike: "The road and much of the landscape was artificial, and yet it couldn't be called a work of art. On the other hand, it did something for me that art had never done. . . . [I]ts effect was to liberate me from many of the views I had had about

Figure 13.1. Kraftwerk, *The Man-Machine*. Copyright © 1978 by Capitol Records, All Rights Reserved. Used by permission.

art."[34] In a similar way, perhaps, freeway driving suggested to the members of Kraftwerk something akin to American minimalist music: not static, in fact quite acutely time-dependent, but almost entirely uniform and predictable (much more so, in fact, than the music of Steve Reich or Philip Glass)— and ultimately, also, both alienating and an expression of alienation.[35]

Kraftwerk's rather chilly product set Bangs to musing upon the role of artifice in popular music, and the ironic outcome of manufacturing synthesizers to exert greater control over sound: "In the music of Kraftwerk, and bands like them present and to come, we see at last the fitting culmination of this revolution, as the machines not merely overpower and play the human beings but *absorb* them, until the scientist and his technology, having developed a higher consciousness of its own, are one and the same."[36] Not for nothing did Walter Benjamin, in his seminal essay, "The Work of Art in the Age of Mechanical Reproduction," quote futurist Filippo Marinetti's phrase, "the dreamt-of metallization of the human body," uttered in the context of a hymn to war, in which mankind establishes dominion over machines by becoming more like them.[37] This is an ambiguous sort of victory to achieve, perhaps not really a victory at all. In fact, Benjamin's discussion of the changes wrought in all the art forms by their reproducibility, tinged as it is with a certain uneasiness about the implications for the future of the arts even as the inevitability of these changes is conceded, has a great deal to say to performers and audiences of popular music in particular, not only because of the machines that are used to make the music, but because of those that are used to copy and disseminate it. With hundreds of thousands, even millions of singles and albums in circulation, reaching far more listeners than could ever attend their concerts—which furthermore began to seem, as the 1960s wore on, rather primitive affairs by comparison to increasingly sophisticated recordings—many groups must have wondered *where*, exactly, their music was, and who was really in control of it.

Even more recent developments in popular music, beyond the proper scope of this paper, show that these issues are hardly dead. From the mid-1970s on, fascination with the machine aesthetic, in varying shades of revulsion and enthusiasm, has if anything been growing: the synthesized drums of disco, which enforced a rigidly unvarying dance tempo, and their later, musically more interesting use by Thomas Dolby and others; Gary Numan's electro-pop; Devo's "devolutionary" robotic pose and the distinctive musical profile that goes with it; and the more recent electronica and techno movements.

Everybody must get stoned

As Poggioli has pointed out, "There originated among romantic and avant-garde artists the illusory hope of being able to attain to aesthetic ecstasy, a mystic state of grace, by means of certain physiological and psychological stimulants . . . those drugs which give easy access to the 'artificial paradises' found in other heavens than that of art."[38] All of Poggioli's examples happen to be writers—probably, among artists at any rate, the most spectacular consumers of mind-altering substances over the past century or so. Composers, in fact, may be a relatively sober lot by comparison to writers and painters. Nevertheless, Poggioli's judgment is accurate in the larger sense—and certainly it brings to mind certain similar activities of rock & roll musicians from the mid-1960s on. Although their extensive use of hallucinogens, amphetamines, and even stronger stuff, including heroin, may not have arisen for the most part in direct emulation of De Quincey or Rimbaud—its more local and telling impetus coming as it did from the Beat poets and from Timothy Leary, who had risen to a fame of sorts as the "LSD guru"—the example of the romantics and early avant-gardists may be judged as a strong secondhand influence. Not coincidentally, at a time when many popular musicians were beginning to find dissonance and sonic distortion mirroring their inner experience under the influence of mind-altering chemicals, they also found it an intensely expressive device, its extensive employment in their music actually stimulated by recourse to drugs. Thus developed the catch-phrase "psychedelic music," which through the usual commercial debasement came to apply to just about any even slightly unusual feature—whether it be instrumentation, style of vocal, subject of the lyrics, form, length of solos, or the more clamorous racket produced by feedback and phase-shifting.[39] In songs tailored for the Top Forty, this connection was usually disguised, obviously so as not to discourage airplay (and so that expressions like "getting high" or "blowing your mind" could be plausibly taken to connote a naturally induced state of euphoria).[40]

One record that made it into the Top Forty, in fact to Number One in December 1966, with sales of well over a million copies, was the Beach Boys' "Good Vibrations," Brian Wilson's first and unquestionably most brilliantly successful work under the heavy influence of drugs. As mentioned earlier, putting this record together was an immensely laborious undertaking: as Wilson himself reports, seventeen sessions in six weeks spread over a total period of three months at five different studios, at a cost of somewhere between fifty and seventy-five thousand dollars, an unprecedented sum to spend on one single at that time. But it is unlikely that "Good Vibrations" would have taken just the form it did without some other, special help. Said Wilson in summer 1966: "I'd written it five months earlier and imagined the grand, Spectorlike production while on the LSD trip I'd described so enthusiastically for Al."[41] "Good Vibrations" is, superficially considered, a love song; and that may well be what the lyricist, Mike Love, originally had in mind. Yet the words, heard in Wilson's musical setting, seem more mystical than romantic, more than hint at another kind of meaning, reinforced by the utterly idiosyncratic studio production, involving all sorts of unusual instruments and combinations, and a striking four-part form compressed into three and a half minutes.[42]

Wilson's LSD experience, according to his own account, ended with his third trip, in summer 1966. Later efforts to "get farther out," in an album that was to be called *Smile,* were not as productive, despite the attempts of Wilson and his lyricist Van Dyke Parks to stoke their creative fires with large quantities of marijuana, hashish, and speed. Although a good deal of material was produced over a period of several months, it never came together in the brilliant "teenage symphony to God" that Wilson had envisioned.[43] Instead, the steady ingestion of drugs combined with a flareup of his long-standing psychological problems induced a series of breakdowns from which Wilson only slowly emerged, and in permanently frailer condition, unable to equal his past achievements.

A far more disastrous outcome—both musical and psychological—awaited Syd Barrett, founding member and first leader of Pink Floyd, when he first began dropping acid. Barrett went on many more than three trips, and over time the size of the doses he took increased alarmingly. In his case, though, it is difficult to maintain any strict separation between the influence of drugs and "purely" musical formative exposures. For one thing, his drug-taking experiences began well before formation of Pink Floyd; for another, there can be no doubt that his abandonment during 1966 of the R&B material that initially served his band as their core repertoire and his embrace of a more "experimental" idiom was inspired in part by the albums of the Mothers of Invention, the Byrds, and the Fugs; the feedback-injected performances of the early Who and the long, frenetic jams, or "rave-ups," favored by the Yardbirds; the jazz-based improvisational collective AMM; and Fluxus and its imitators, as mentioned earlier. Most, if not all of these musical influences can be heard as operative in Pink Floyd's first album, *The Piper at the Gates of Dawn* (1967), for which Barrett wrote most of the material; by the same token, however, some kind of altered state of awareness seems to lie behind the "spacey" character of such long jam-type numbers as "Interstellar Overdrive" (to be addressed again in the next section of this essay, under the influence of science-fictional imagery) and the offbeat, "weird" character of many of the other cuts, including the often jarring shifts of tone and character from one to the next.

Contemporary accounts strongly suggest that for Barrett LSD use went hand in hand with his attraction to innovative, adventurous music, and that as a musician he was opened to avant-garde tendencies by the one just as much as the other.[44] This is as close as we are likely to get to a precise assessment of the impact of drugs on Barrett's work, since Barrett, unlike Wilson, has not published his memoir of those days. He is, in fact, in no position to do so, having retreated some decades ago into an uncommunicative, psychotic state.[45] Pete Townshend has reported that Barrett "was the first person I had seen who was totally 'gone' on stage,"[46] and other observers during this period imply that his drug-taking was both symptom and cause of behavior typical of the frustrated avant-garde artist, a dual role that soon degenerated into a downward spiral.[47] Barrett eventually became unable to direct himself or the group, and his relatively straight bandmates effectively kicked him out in 1968. This event initiated a change in direction for Pink Floyd, an evolution that will receive further attention later in this essay.

If Wilson's and Barrett's experiences with drugs, in the end, seem all too concisely expressed by Poggioli's phrase, "illusory hope," there are at least two American bands of note that managed a sustained output of decidedly original, unusual-sounding music while at times massively under the influence: the Velvet Underground and the Grateful Dead. In contemporary mythology, they represented the two poles of American rock musicians' pharmacopoeial experience: the Velvets in New York, taking stimulants like speed and harder drugs, such as heroin; the Dead in San Francisco, favoring the "softer" intoxicants and hallucinogens, such as pot and acid. This somewhat simplistic distinction actually did contain a grain of truth, which emerged in the radically divergent qualities of the two bands' music.

From the Velvets came edgy material such as "Waiting for the Man," told from the point of view of a white man standing on a street corner in Harlem to make a drug buy; "Heroin," probably the most harrowing song about drugs recorded by anyone during this period, with its extremely graphic lyrics, its form and tempo changes corresponding to the rush and the nod associated with shooting up, and a barrage of feedback and harmonics from John Cale's amplified viola seemingly calculated to convey the brain-frying nature of the experience; and the relentless blast of "Sister Ray," with its endlessly redundant lyrics, in which heroin users are depicted among the transvestites and sailors in an orgiastic scene. Perhaps the most disturbing thing about these songs is Lou Reed's deadpan, almost affectless voice. One is readily persuaded that Reed is not merely posturing, that he really *is* a heroin addict—and, indeed, both he and Cale were addicts for a time.[48]

The Grateful Dead, whose music always came across as much more benign (though, in the final analysis, no less out of an altered state of consciousness) than that of the Velvets, was also brought together by a shared experience with drugs. The Dead didn't really coalesce until their participation in the famous Acid Tests in the Bay Area of California, mass tripping organized by Ken Kesey and His Merry Pranksters toward the end of 1965. As bassist Phil Lesh later noted, the Tests were not a regular gig; this was "the only time our music has had a real sense of proportion in an event."[49] The band played at different times during these events, and not always with all of its members present and accounted for; "sometimes you just couldn't play," being too stoned or too involved in whatever conversation had sprung up with the other partygoers.[50] The almost experimental circumstances of this coming together seem to have set the tone for the entire career of the Dead, which lasted until the death of Garcia in August 1995: not only did improvisation emerge as important in the performance of individual songs, but *every concert as a whole* became an improvised event, by its very nature nonrepeatable. This modus operandi remained in place even as their music gradually evolved away from the more complicatedly structured material of their second and third albums, which did not shift in massive quantities (*Anthem of the Sun*, 1968; *Aoxomoxoa*, 1969), and pieces like "Feedback," an imaginatively improvised nine-minute symphony of screeches (*Live/Dead*, 1970), to a more "accessible," often folk-tinged idiom from *Workingman's Dead* (1970) on. As Garcia put it, the band sustained its energies by having "faith in this form that has no form . . . faith in this structure that has no structure"[51]—a strategy that seems to have translated into remarkable staying power.

For Lesh, the acid experience eclipsed even the previously "most stimulating thing I'd ever encountered in my life," a composition class with Luciano Berio at Mills College.[52] Although his compositional aspirations, quite strong during the early 1960s, gradually withered away as the Dead flourished, it is clear that the trade-off brought a special kind of reward. It is tempting to conclude, in fact, that the Dead lasted as long as they did because they were a latter-day version of the Decadents—not always thought of as avant-garde, usually assigned instead to the romantics, but in Poggioli's terms a movement not that different from futurism, for both decadents and futurists dream of rebirth, even if for one it is rebirth to infancy and for the other to "a new maturity of youth."[53]

Electricity comes from other planets

What could be more futuristic than science fiction? Despite the ready appeal one might think that science-fictional themes would have for composers of a modern bent, such themes attracted little attention in art-music circles earlier in the century (although Edgard Varèse did make an abortive attempt at a "Space Symphony" in the 1930s, which at one point had the working title *Astronomer*). This circumstance is perhaps explained by science fiction's (largely deserved) reputation at the time as a genre for adolescents: cheap escapism and old-fashioned romance tricked out in shiny new metallic garb. By the late 1960s, however, science fiction had branched out from space opera and bug-eyed monsters into more cutting-edge territory.

Some of that territory had been staked out, earlier in the decade, by the so-called New Wave of science fiction in England, headed up by writers like Brian Aldiss, J. G. Ballard, and Michael Moorcock. Ballard, reacting directly against the proclivities of a genre that he and others felt had not progressed very far beyond rocket ships and scantily clad Martian maidens, declared an interest in exploring *inner* space: in keeping the action, not just here on Planet Earth, but within the mysterious workings of the human mind and body: "I'd like to see more psycho-literary ideas, more meta-biological and meta-chemical concepts, private time-systems, synthetic psychologies and space-times, more of the sombre half-worlds one glimpses in the paintings of schizophrenics, all in all a complete speculative poetry and fantasy of science," he wrote in 1962. More than the trappings of any real-life space race, such as the one then in progress between the United States and the Soviet Union, "it is that *inner* space-suit which is still needed, and it is up to science fiction to build it!"[54]

Ballard, it should be emphasized, had conceived of such inner exploration to be the work of the imagination alone, unstimulated by chemical means.[55] Ironically, some of his ideas, in however filtered or distorted a form, would find sympathetic reception among a youth culture inspired by Alexander Trocchi's widely quoted characterization of drug users as "cosmonauts of inner space," and by Timothy Leary's similar pronouncements.[56] It seems beyond mere coincidence that "spaced out" became both a way of describing those under the influence of drugs and a synonym for the psychedelic in music.

Other imagery inspired, at least nominally, by extraterrestrial matters was also thrown into the mix of stimuli. One prominent contributor was Stanley Kubrick's film *2001: A Space Odyssey* (1968), with a musical score that made brilliant use of "textural" orchestral and choral works by György Ligeti. The impact of this film at the time of its release was massive; it was easy to imagine that everyone from their teens up to the age of forty had seen it at least once, with its juxtaposition of images alternately mundane and inscrutable, ranging from the ennobling to the pathetic and back again, and including special effects of a sophistication never before seen in a film on a science-fictional theme. Around the same time, the German composer Karlheinz Stockhausen, already famous in avant-garde art-music circles, began to gain much wider exposure, particularly in youth-oriented media such as *Rolling Stone*. Stockhausen was to the 1960s what Cage had been to the 1950s—that is, he was the avant-garde composer whom those not intimately involved with the avant-garde themselves were most likely to have heard of—and he dressed the part, in hippified costume with long hair. But this public-relations success was in some sense deserved, for what he had to offer was bound to be of genuine interest to a generation raised on amplified music and the manipulations of studio production. Richard Kostelanetz's entry for Stockhausen in his *Dictionary of the Avant-Gardes* shows why: mentioned are live electronic music, studio composition and sound alteration, collage, incorporation of "various radical live human sounds," a serious absorption with world musics, and a penchant for realization of cosmic visions in his compositions—all potential points of contact and influence for the more progressively minded rock musicians.[57] And well in keeping with the cosmic, the titles of some of his works, such as *Setz die Segel zur Sonne* (Set Sail for the Sun, 1968), *Sternklang* (Star-Sound, 1971), and *Sirius* (1975), suggested that he could lay claim to being a "space-music composer" as well.[58]

Many of the most spectacular examples of rock embodying science-fiction imagery come from the British. The early history of Pink Floyd is especially notable for this sort of thing: "Interstellar Overdrive," "Astronomy Domine," "Set the Controls for the Heart of the Sun," and "A Saucerful of Secrets" all date from 1967–68. The first two were composed by Syd Barrett, and have a special manic, unsettling quality, deriving in part from the chromatic motion of the characteristic riffs, that is largely absent from Pink Floyd's work after Barrett left. "Interstellar" is entirely instrumental and lends itself to protracted, "space-jam" treatment, as the several versions available on recordings show. "Astronomy," despite its title and the names of several celestial bodies in the lyrics, does not depict a journey to outer space; it looks inward, and in this sense parallels Ballard's view (not in its druggy overtones, however). "Set the Controls," written by Roger Waters, and "A Saucerful," a group effort (with Dave Gilmour, the guitarist who replaced Barrett), like "Interstellar," are lengthy affairs and become even lengthier in live recordings; both give keyboardist Richard Wright, here at the height of his Stockhausen phase, a good deal of latitude in improvisational passages devoted to eerily swooping and otherwise freaky sounds.[59] As the live material on *Ummagumma* (1969) shows, even in Barrett's absence Pink Floyd continued to embrace "space-rock" enthusiastically—drug-taking was neither necessary nor sufficient to bring it off—although the attributes of space-rock would eventually be absorbed and sublimated in their evolving style.

Both of the first two albums by the Jimi Hendrix Experience include tracks with recognizable science-fictional themes—in both cases seeming to portray Hendrix himself as an alien visitor on the verge of departing from this world or, perhaps, on the verge of destroying it. At the outset of "Third Stone from the Sun" (Planet Earth, in other words, as seen by an outsider), on *Are You Experienced?* (1967), Hendrix's voice is heard greatly slowed down. This remains more or less in the background throughout the cut, fading in and out, supplanted for two brief passages by Hendrix's voice at normal speed, which however is never completely clear: it's as if one were listening to one of the Mercury astronauts speaking through his suit radio to NASA's Mission Control down below. Toward the end of the track, as the accompanying bass and drums lay out, the guitar part suddenly shifts away from its gliding melody into a pyrotechnical cadenza of bursts and screeches that slowly fade away: the space vehicle, whatever it is, pulling away from Earth's orbit.[60]

King Crimson's "21st-Century Schizoid Man" (*The Court of the Crimson King*, 1969) rather explicitly dreads a dystopian future; adding to the effect of the disquieting lyrics, Greg Lake's voice is distorted grotesquely. This, the first song on the first album by a group that would turn out to be a mainstay of the British progressive rock movement, is in its science-fictional allusions atypical of the rest of its album and of much to come in British progressive rock. An appreciable portion of this work touches on themes that fall instead into the category of "high fantasy," a genre often confused with science fiction but actually its flip side, lacking as it does the tendency of science fiction to make an explicit theme of the future, near or remote, as an extrapolation upon present-day reality. Works of high fantasy, by contrast to science fiction, take place in an indeterminate time, as easily far in the past as in the far future, or perhaps even on some completely different plane.[61] Often riddled with pseudo-medieval imagery and myth, they are of the same general literary classification as fairy tales (or "low fantasy"), and are in some ways actually *anti*-modern. The somewhat ambiguous relationship of the prog-rock repertoire to earlier manifestations of modernism in rock will come up for discussion later.[62]

Movie for your ears

It is unsurprising that Kubrick's *2001* should have had such widespread influence, quite apart from the popularity of science fiction and international interest in the real-life "space race"—for by some estimations the visual in Western culture has been steadily increasing in importance since the seventeenth century, and the advent of the motion picture at the beginning of the twentieth may have greatly accelerated this development. These factors, together with the modernist tendency to appropriate ideas from one art in the service of another—another link, of course, to the romantics—made for considerable interest in the visual impact of rock & roll. Some of its ramifications were predictable, such as Pink Floyd's work in film music (*More,* 1969). Some songs, such as the Rolling Stones' ominous "Citadel" (1967), refer to actual, well-known films—in this case, Fritz Lang's futuristic *Metropolis* (1926). Other bands literally combined art forms: the Velvet Underground found its first big success playing as "accompaniment" for Andy Warhol's films and in his multimedia extravaganza, the Exploding Plastic Inevitable, which melded music, dance, visual projections (including films), and a light show. Even more interesting at this point, though, are musical productions that, although exclusively aural, strongly allude to an imaginary visual component. One might wonder, at first glance, what would distinguish such an approach from that of program music in the nineteenth century. The difference lies in the modern ability to make such allusions extremely vivid, thanks to the resources of the recording studio, using sounds that literally evoked images (instead of merely suggesting them) by means of the techniques of montage and collage. Some representative examples are briefly discussed below.

The cinematic aspects of the Byrds' "Draft Morning" (from *The Notorious Byrd Brothers,* 1968) are quite simple, designed as they are to portray an explicit scene. It eventually becomes clear that this gentle, introspective song concerns a young man who, on his way to induction into the army, experiences forebodings of what awaits him—for the instrumental "break" features a battle-call-like trumpet figure, menacingly dissonant against the underlying harmony of the song (which meanwhile is becoming increasingly strident), with the gradually increasing noise of gunfire laid atop it all.

Buffalo Springfield's "Broken Arrow" (from *Buffalo Springfield Again,* 1967) is more involved. The last track on the album, it opens with what is apparently an excerpt from a live performance (complete with screaming audience) of "Mr. Soul," the song that (in studio rendition) opens the album, then "cuts away" to "Broken Arrow" proper, with lyrics describing the band wrapping up its concert and leaving the hall. The transitions (some involving studio-engineered, "dreamlike" sonic distortion) between these and other elements in the song—including, at different points, some unidentified light jazz and what sounds like a steam calliope playing the opening bars of "Take Me Out to the Ball Game"—are strongly reminiscent of the "dissolves" of film.

The short-lived United States of America produced one eponymously titled album (1968) on the central theme of modern life in the U.S., of which it takes a dim view.[63] Two cuts, "The American Metaphysical Circus" and "The American Way of Love" (which effectively frame the album, being the first on Side 1 and the last on Side 2 respectively), are marked by extensive use of collage and montage. "Metaphysical Circus" begins with a calliope that is presently joined by overlapping, clashing band marches, inevitably reminding one of Charles Ives's sound pictures, like "Putnam's Camp" in *Three Places in New England*; "The American Way of Love" ends with a grand montage of excerpts from most of the previous tracks on the album, each fading out as the next fades in, sometimes with overlaps. As in "Broken Arrow," such flashbacks have strong visual affinities, which work in tandem with intimations of a (musical) cyclic structure.[64]

The Buckinghams' album cut "Foreign Policy" (on *Time and Charges*, 1967; also used as the B-side of the single "Susan") makes use of collage/montage techniques in a way that seems cinematic yet is difficult to pin down, cutting back and forth as it does between the song itself—a quiet affair prominently featuring flute and acoustic guitar—and two other elements: the recorded voice of former President John F. Kennedy giving a speech; and stridently dissonant brass textures. Obviously meant as dead-serious sociopolitical commentary (JFK had been assassinated less than four years earlier), "Foreign Policy" represented quite a contrast to the Buckinghams' highly commercial chart hits, all written by non-Buckinghams Gary Beisbier and James Holvay. It was the work of James William Guercio, who had taken over as producer for this second album by the group, and who also produced their third album, *Portraits* (1968)—and who was responsible for the *musique concrète*-style collage in the middle of "Susan."[65]

It is probably not a coincidence that two other American musicians who conceived much of their music in "filmic" terms, Frank Zappa and Jim Morrison, lived and worked in the Los Angeles area, where the influence of Hollywood and the movie culture is even more pervasive than in the rest of the country. The terrifically prolific Zappa spent a good deal of his time on movie projects, and not just on composing music for them. His film *200 Motels* (1971), which he conceived, produced, and co-directed, was preceded by *Uncle Meat* (ca. 1967–68), which as a film remained unfinished, and was followed by *Baby Snakes* (1979) and various other shot-on-videotape efforts. Speaking as a composer and songwriter, Zappa often described his ideas and methods in cinematic terms, referring to the harmonies that open a song as establishing the "harmonic climate," analogously to the establishing shot at the beginning of a film: "It tells you where it's happening. Then the action takes place."[66] This is borne out by Zappa's fondness for "story songs," in which the musical elements are often extremely simple—as in "Billy the Mountain," "Titties 'n' Beer," "The Illinois Enema Bandit," or "Dinah-Moe-Humm"—or otherwise subservient to the largely spoken words that limn the plot, as in "The Adventures of Greggery Peccary."[67] Other Zappa albums that have no explicit script still seem somehow filmlike, such as perhaps his most sustained avant-garde effort, *Lumpy Gravy* (1967), in which passages for the small studio orchestra, ranging in style from Varèse imitations to deliberately cheesy pop, are interspersed with *concrète* noise treatments, improvised dialogue recorded inside an open piano with the dampers off, Cage-inspired monologues about working on cars or in an airplane factory, and—once in a while—some rock & roll.

Jim Morrison's contribution to the music he made with the band he helped form, the Doors, was, by contrast to Zappa's, almost entirely lyric: he was the classic, musically "illiterate" rock & roll singer who had to rely on his bandmates (especially keyboardist Ray Manzarek and guitarist Robby Krieger) to provide the musical setting for his words and, sometimes, melodic ideas.[68] Yet his lyrics alone were often quite striking; obviously aspiring to the status of poetry (though some critics scoffed at such a characterization as pretentious), they were notable for consisting nearly exclusively of series of visual images. Morrison's first career aspirations lay in film; he had dropped out of the filmmaking program at UCLA shortly before teaming up with Manzarek and the others. Casting a spell over the audience, as a really good rock band was capable of doing, became for him the next best thing to making films. In one of his prose poems he once called cinema, approvingly, the "most totalitarian of the arts," a "transforming agent" under whose control "the body exists for the sake of the eyes; it becomes a dry stalk to support these two soft insatiable jewels."[69] Contemporary reports suggest that he wasn't all that interested in other bands, or even in music in general; what really excited him was what could be seen, or alluded to as seen.[70] Morrison's ambitions, however, quickly outran his compositional abilities. His most grandiose idea, a setting of his poem "The Celebration of the Lizard"—which was to be a nearly half-hour tour de force, "a bizarre mixture of Marat/Sade theatricality, erotic rock, and neobeat poetics"—never came close to being fully realized.[71]

The present-day composers refuse to die!

By appropriating this sentence from Edgard Varèse's 1921 manifesto for the International Composers' Guild, altering it (significantly) from plural to singular and reproducing it on the sleeves of several of his early albums, Frank Zappa signaled the degree to which he saw his life in popular music as a struggle for survival. Even as his rock career burgeoned he still thought of himself as a *composer,* modeling himself after the early-twentieth-century figures he regarded as paragons while engaging in a peculiar mix of idealistic and pragmatic behavior to ensure that his music would be heard in some form.[72] He was not alone, however. How have modernistically inclined composers—schooled in art music or not—managed to function within the world of rock & roll without losing their identities, either to rampant commercialism or to the collective personality of a band? This section is devoted to the analysis of a few particularly striking careers.

Don Vliet, Zappa's fellow Californian, in fact his classmate at high school in Lancaster during the mid-1950s, later changed his name to Don Van Vliet and eventually took the stage name Captain Beefheart. Vliet and Zappa shared a passion for rhythm and blues, and also for jazz to a certain extent; but beyond that their paths diverged. Vliet apparently never learned to read musical notation and had no particular interest in the repertoire of twentieth-century art music that held such fascination for Zappa. What he ended up doing instead was something quintessentially avant-garde, resembling not a little the approach of another California composer, Harry Partch: working with musicians who were committed to him alone, and using instruments that he had in part modified, he devised an utterly original compositional and performance practice.

The rock band as cult, essentially cut off from the outside world, was not an entirely new idea in the late 1960s; Vliet, though, deserves recognition for taking it to extremes. Initiates to the Magic Band were forced to accept new names devised by their leader: guitarist Bill Harkleroad became Zoot Horn Rollo, drummer John French became Drumbo. Both Harkleroad and French remember being subjected to a kind of brainwashing experience, when band members would be kept in a room talking for twelve hours or more, and to group meetings at which one band member would be singled out for criticism until he broke down emotionally.[73] Often, when the band went into rehearsals for a new album, or for a tour, the musicians would occupy the same house for weeks on end, getting by on little sleep while Vliet worked obsessively with them on their parts until he felt they'd got everything right.

Sometimes it was hard to tell when this point had been reached. At first, as Vliet composed each band member's part, he would teach it to him by rote. As his ideas became more complicated, without access to notation it became increasingly difficult for him to remember what he had composed. Thus he came to depend more and more on someone else in the band (usually French at first, later others) to take dictation, as Vliet played the music on the piano. This by no means eliminated all problems, though, even for those musicians who were fluent readers. Vliet's rhythmic and pitch ideas often presented formidable challenges: simultaneous different time signatures and polyrhythms in complex proportions were commonplace. What emerged was a kind of music that sounded quite distinctive, for reasons that Harkleroad has identified: "Don didn't really know anything about music in the conventional sense. He was not a composer or arranger, but a very intense conceptualist. So it took a great effort on everyone's behalf to create these 'sculptures' from something that was written in a non-musical way." And: "He adopted more the mentality of a sculptor. His idea was to use sound, bodies and people as the tools . . . our job as his band was to turn [his work] into sounds that were repeatable."[74] Apparently, even after the parts were written down, they could be further revised in rehearsal, until Vliet felt they sounded right—and then they were fixed for good.[75] Sometimes this fierce concern for detail paid handsome dividends: in the recording session for *Trout Mask Replica* (1969), the Magic Band managed a complete set of successful takes in four-and-a-half hours, which would be an astoundingly short time for any double-LP album, let alone one as extraordinarily inventive (and full of fiendishly difficult music to play) as this.[76]

As far as the history of their reception is concerned, however, Vliet and his group resembled all too clearly an avant-garde that courted material success but found popular acceptance elusive, to say the least. As Poggioli points out, "The effect of an avant-garde creation . . . is thus to distinguish the public along the lines of Ortega's formula, not dividing those who know from those who do not know, but those who 'get it' from those who do not."[77] Contemporary accounts suggest that audiences at Vliet's concerts divided into two distinct populations exactly along such lines: a small but fervent fan base who knew the music from records, and a larger group who were "angered or simply baffled" by what they heard.[78] After nearly two decades of sporadic success and more frequent disappointments, Vliet quit the music business in 1982 and turned to full-time pursuit of his first artistic love, painting.

Unlike either Zappa or Vliet, before becoming involved with rock & roll, future Velvet Undergound member John Cale had received some formal musical training, first in his native Wales, then in London. In 1963 he traveled to the United States on a scholarship to study composition at Tanglewood with Iannis Xenakis—some of whose ideas about the relationship between architecture and music he later remembered thinking were "a load of codswallop."[79] Cale, it seems, had already been infected by the Fluxus philosophy in one of its rapidly circulating variants; some of his music, which involved destroying pianos, was specifically interdicted at Tanglewood by Aaron Copland. Cale next moved to New York and joined La Monte Young's Dream Syndicate, where he learned to appreciate drone-based textures. He amplified his viola, then restrung it with guitar strings, "and I got a drone that sounded like a jet-engine!"[80] This bit of technological application would shortly become very important in the band he formed with Lou Reed.

Cale met Reed in the process of checking out, half in fun, the possibility of breaking into the pop music business. Cale and his roommate on the Lower East Side, fellow Syndicate member Tony Conrad, ended up playing and promoting a song that had already been composed and recorded by Reed for Pickwick Records, "The Ostrich." According to Conrad, the people at Pickwick "said, 'Don't worry, it's easy to play because all the strings are tuned to the same note,' which blew our minds because that was what we were doing with La Monte in the Dream Syndicate."[81] This confluence of performance practice was certainly an accidental discovery, but it must have suggested to Cale a link between the avant-garde and rock & roll, one that he became more certain that he wanted to strengthen as he got to know Reed and realized how well their musical ideas complemented one another.

Besides Cale's amplified viola drones, the musical practice of the Velvets was unusual in other ways for rock. When Cale wasn't playing viola, he picked up the bass, an instrument that he immediately made sound different because, as guitarist Sterling Morrison points out, "he didn't know any of the usual riffs"; in rock & roll terms his bass lines were "illogical, inverted" or "totally eccentric."[82] At a time well before long, improvised compositions had become regular fare at rock concerts and on records, the Velvets had begun to do such things, in an attempt (as Cale admits) to get on people's nerves.[83] Cale: "We wanted the Velvet Underground to be a group with a dynamic symphonic flair. The idea was that Lou's lyrical and melodic ability could be combined with some of my musical ideas to create performances where we wouldn't just repeat ourselves."[84] Cale also put the lessons of Young's Syndicate to good use, employing open-string drones (mostly using only his upper two strings) in tunings that approached, even if they didn't quite achieve, just intonation. To accommodate this use of the viola, the rest of the band tuned down as much as a whole step. As Morrison explains, this was done "in deference to what John's viola was built to do. If we played in a normal E tuning, for John to get the pitch that he wanted in an open modal style, he would have to uptune, which would put too much strain on the neck and bridge of the viola." To compensate for the decreased tension, the guitarists used heavy gauge, flat wound strings. In Cale's opinion, tuning down "was better for Lou's voice . . . and better for all the instruments. It gave everything a squelched, slightly squashed sound, creating more sustain."[85] In general, by his own account Cale always tried to slow down Reed's "poppy little songs," make them "slow 'n' sexy," an effort which the lower tuning and increased sustain certainly would have abetted.[86] Reading these accounts and listening to the music, one gets the impression of a practice being built up *ex nihilo*, after every conventional precedent had been torn down. This impression certainly harks back to Cale's earlier quoted remark about the Velvets being "musical primitives," and reminds us that primitivism (or neoprimitivism) is also one of the ma-

Figure 13.2. John Cale at Warhol's Factory, 1967, beneath *Elvis 1 & 2*. Photo by Stephen Shore. Copyright © Stephen Shore, All Rights Reserved. Used by permission.

jor currents of the avant-garde as well as one of its links to earlier romanticism.[87]

Cale's remarks about a "dynamic symphonic flair" have an affinity with the "wall of sound" famously engineered by Phil Spector—a producer highly esteemed by Cale—and show what he and his bandmates were aiming at with their other major sonic innovation, ear-splitting volume. The Velvets may have been the first *really* loud band, and in the opinion of some it was the combination of this feature with the visual bombardment in Warhol's shows that initiated the practice of not dancing at rock performances: audiences were simply too overwhelmed to do more than sit and passively take it in.[88] This was not sensory overload through variety of experience, but rather its opposite: sensory impoverishment from a tremendous dose of just one experience. In this way, the Velvets became a part of what has been called Warhol's reductivist aesthetic, "the same exact thing" over and over again to achieve a "better and emptier" feeling.[89] Perhaps the Velvets did not share Warhol's aesthetic regarding all of their music, but something of it comes through in their longer pieces, like "European Son" on the first album, or "Sister Ray" on the second. How much of it came from Cale specifically? Of course, it is true that the Velvet experience had a lasting impact on him—its influence is evident in everything he has done since as a solo songwriter, performer, and arranger.[90] But his impact on the Velvets as a composer is perhaps best assessed by noting how completely different the band sounded on its final two albums, once Cale had left.

Like Cale, Yoko Ono did not begin to develop as a composer until she moved from her native Japan to New York and came into contact with Fluxus and its offshoots; unlike Cale, she had reached her first creative maturity before her activities began to impinge upon, and then shift into, the world of popular music. After studying composition at nearby Sarah Lawrence College, Ono set out on her own in New York in 1957, well before Fluxus began to come together; the large loft on Chambers Street in which she took up residence in 1960 served as the site for several of the first programs by artists and composers who would later be known collectively by that name. Her own art at that time was as much visual as aural—as that of many among the Fluxus group tended to be, such as La Monte Young and George Brecht. Like Brecht, Ono preferred to call some of her works "events," to distinguish them from the better-known *happenings*: "Event, to me, is not an assimilation of all the other arts as Happening seems to be, but an extrication from the various sensory perceptions. It is not a 'get togetherness' as most happenings are, but a dealing with oneself," she wrote in 1966.[91] The "score" for an event usually consists of a set of simple directions, by means of which an activity of some sort (possibly quite mundane) may be set in motion. "Painting To Be Stepped On" (winter 1960) reads: "Leave a piece of canvas or finished painting on the floor or in the street."[92] "Toilet Piece/Unknown," the sound of which is included on her album *Fly* (1971), is both the sound of a single flush, from the manipulation of the flush lever to the final glug of water in the bowl, and the human-initiated act of flushing itself.

As is well known and abundantly documented, Lennon's encounter with Ono changed him considerably—as a musician, as well as in other ways. Ono, already an internationally recognized artist in her own right, was changed too: musically as much by Lennon as by her abrupt introduction to the world of popular music. This at first had some startling results. The vocal techniques that she has talked of employing as early as her solo recital at Carnegie Recital Hall in 1961 metamorphosed into a repertoire of shouting, screaming, and ululating, apparently out of a need to make herself heard over the amplified Plastic Ono Band.[93] But the work of an explicitly avant-garde, experimental bent that Ono and Lennon did together early on—such as "Revolution 9" on the Beatles' so-called White Album and the two discs of *Unfinished Music*[94]—and much of Ono's two albums with the Plastic Ono Band, *Yoko Ono/Plastic Ono Band* (1970) and *Fly* eventually gave way to a practice more resembling pop songwriting. Ono has never quite abandoned her special vocal techniques—they make occasional reappearances on her later records (witness "Kiss Kiss Kiss," on *Double Fantasy* [1980], for example)—or, for that matter, her original attitude about making art. Nevertheless, by *Approximately Infinite Universe* (1973) the overtly avant-garde approach has nearly disappeared, replaced by songs of a simple tonal design, sung in a more "normal" pop or rock & roll style, often with highly didactic lyrics on social-protest and/or feminist themes. It's almost as if Ono, feeling that she was not being taken particularly seriously, in fact hardly tolerated by the rock audiences Lennon had brought her to, concluded that she had to change her style to something more accessible, with a readily comprehensible "message"—a style which has indeed proven to have a wider appeal.

Brian Eno, like both Cale and Ono, came to rock & roll by way of the avant-garde—but unlike them without any musical training to speak of. As it had for several other future English rockers, art college (Eno attended Winchester) proved a stimulating place to be in the mid-to-late 1960s for the progressively minded artist who had any interest in analogous developments in music. Eno's musical interests, however, evolved out of a growing frustration with the visual arts: painting, for instance, began to strike him as too solitary, too slow, and too product-oriented. He looked to music as an art that was more collaborative, more immediate—and more an art of process, one that made use of time by consciously structuring it.[95] Since he couldn't play any instrument, he began experimenting with the manipulation of sound using tape recorders. After college, living in London and playing occasionally with Cornelius Cardew's Scratch Orchestra and the Portsmouth Sinfonia—ensembles in which nonmusicians had a role—he became engrossed in the challenge of importing avant-garde musical ideas into rock music, circumventing the "antiphysical" aspects of the former and the anti-intellectual aspects of the latter and ending up, if possible, with the best of both worlds.[96] Eno's stint with Bryan Ferry's band, Roxy Music, in 1971–73 probably marked the first time that anyone had held down a rock & roll job playing nothing but synthesizer and tapes. But there can be no question that his contribution was crucial: the futuristic lounge music that became the hallmark of Roxy's sound would likely never have developed otherwise.

Eno continued making rock albums on his own after parting ways with Ferry; the brittle edginess of much of his work has had a substantial influence, as has its carryover into the wide range of production work he has done for others. Some of the musicians he has engaged for his own projects must have wondered whether they were part of some perverse sociological experiment, for Eno has spoken of deliberately assembling musicians who are incompatible, both with one another and with himself, just to see what will happen—a predilection that may well partly explain the edgy qualities of the recorded result.[97] One collaborative relationship that seems, contrariwise, to have been quite amicable is the one with Robert Fripp; in their records from the 1970s and later, Eno develops drones and quasi-minimalist grooves out of tape loops and synthesizer routines, which serve as a foil for Fripp's idiosyncratically modified guitar sound. Also highly influential has been Eno's work in the development of "ambient music," which he initiated in 1975 with *Discreet Music*. The title cut, half an hour in duration, is meant to be listened to "at comparatively low levels, even to the extent that it frequently falls below the threshold of audibility"—not focused upon directly, in other words, but allowed to permeate, in almost subliminal fashion, whatever else one is doing.[98] The genre now known as New Age is an obvious outgrowth of such ideas. Finally, Eno has continued to hold his position as the thinking man's rocker by writing about newer non-rock music, especially that of his British contemporaries: pieces by Cardew, Michael Nyman, and Gavin Bryars are covered in one article published in the mid-1970s—with special attention, not surprisingly, to the ways in which *process* in these pieces both produces and limits the variety of outcomes in performance.[99]

Aftermath and afterthoughts

A curious thing happened, back in January 1968, after the first few times I heard "Susan" on the radio. The local Top Forty station started playing a different version, with the interlude of "electronic collage" excised. I had been half expecting this; the interlude was just a little too strange for WTRY 980, and the song did sound smoother and less contrived without it, even if its underlying mediocrity was now unmistakable. Yet somehow I felt as though I'd been dealt a sucker punch. Was this kind of bowdlerization now going to be perpetrated on *any* single that came on the radio with interestingly dissonant sounds in it?[100] Was there any chance that rock & roll, on which I had for a while been pinning increasingly high hopes, would ever get beyond its endless parade of boring crap like Herb Alpert & the Tijuana Brass, the Monkees, Bobby Goldsboro—or, for that matter, the Buckinghams?

As usual for me at that age, I was overdramatizing. Even within my relatively brief experience with popular music, there had been many interesting songs on the radio, songs with unusual harmonies in them, or rhythms, or timbres—and there seemed to be more of them all the time, even if altogether they constituted only a small percentage of what actually got played. Not only that, but it was already obvious that albums, not singles, were the wave of the future: not just *Sgt. Pepper,* but records like Cream's *Disraeli Gears* or the Blues Project's *Projections* or Hendrix's *Are You Experienced?* contained all kinds of great stuff that AM radio was never going to play—and what did it matter? It wasn't long afterward that I discovered an AOR (album-oriented rock) station on the FM dial, out of Boston—it must have been one of the first anywhere—and tuned out Top Forty entirely.

Still, though, there was something about that summary removal of the "Susan" interlude from the airwaves, inconsequential though it might have appeared in the larger scheme of things to any dispassionate observer, that I couldn't quite get out of my mind—something which now leads me to suggest that this episode could be taken as a harbinger of the eventual outcome of rock & roll's encounter with modernism, hastened by the exigencies of the popular music business. As far as concert promoters, record-company executives, press flacks, and record retailers were concerned, experimentation was all very well and good, and was even to be encouraged as long as it had novelty appeal for the teenage consumer. But no novelty appeals, on the basis of novelty alone, for very long—and once this appeal had faded, it was inevitable that a lot of intriguingly weird records would suddenly disappear from stores, that many groups whose proclivity for strange sounds had previously made them eagerly sought after would suddenly find themselves dropped from their labels, and that other groups would abruptly revise their sound to a more conservative alternative in order to survive.

These developments, which had pretty much run their course by late 1970, brought what we could call the first phase of the modernization of rock & roll to an end. To this extent, Theodor Adorno's pessimistic assessment, some thirty years earlier, of popular music in general can be taken as an accurate forecast: the vicious circle of stimulation and boredom that controls the ascent to and descent from popularity for a given song or style; the masochistic behavior of fans who suddenly "would like to ridicule and destroy what yesterday they were intoxicated with"; the role of radio in wearing out music by overexposing it.[101] And since "repetition now constitutes the very threshold of music's social audibility," as one contemporary critic has pointed out,[102] once music of an experimental tinge had fallen out of heavy rotation on Top Forty radio, and below acceptable profit margins for record companies, it was *gone*—at least until fairly recently, with the massive rerelease on CD of much of this older popular repertoire, marketed to aging baby-boomers anxious (supposedly) to recover their past.

Would an Adornoesque judgment upon the "psychedelic" style of the late 1960s also be appropriate—to the effect that this allegedly new style, like all its predecessors, simply provided "trademarks of identification," not true differentiation from what had come before? Was the only reason for the success of ostensibly "far-out" or experimental music in a popular context that it simply applied a veneer of novelty to a reassuringly familiar framework—resulting in a "pseudo-individualization" that "hears for the listener"?[103] Perhaps this would be a fair conclusion to draw about the work of bands like Strawberry Alarm Clock and the Blues Magoos; but one would be on shakier ground making such claims about Jimi Hendrix or later (post-1966) Beatles. Some of what was done, musically speaking, in the late 1960s has turned out to be of more enduring value than the rest. Judgments of this kind are easier to make as time goes on, in part because we also have a better perspective on what happened next in popular music. The avant-garde impulse wasn't in fact completely swallowed up or nullified by the next big trend to come along. But it was redirected quite considerably.

To begin assessing the dimensions of this change, some instructive examples are provided by the histories of three different British bands in the early 1970s that got their start in the late 1960s. After the eclecticism, mild experimentation, and classical aspirations evident in their first four albums, Deep Purple embarked determinedly on a stylistic makeover, declining to issue Jon Lord's second rock-band-with-orchestra piece, the *Gemini Suite,* under the band's name, simplifying and hardening their approach to yield the musical profile for which they are now best known and with which, at the time, they became much more popular than before, starting with *Deep Purple in Rock* (1970). The Soft Machine, after two albums full of decidedly odd music—built out of abrupt shifts of direction, very short cuts often segueing into quite long ones, wispy vocals projecting sometimes whimsical lyrics (such as the alphabet recited in reverse), and a certain eclectically jazzy feeling—adopted a much more consistent approach from *Third* (1970) on, a jazz-rock "fusion" style that carried them well into the decade and that is now considered to be their definitive sound. And Pink Floyd, whose first album, *The Piper at the Gates of Dawn* (1967), was a quirky and stylish hodgepodge of compositional ideas revolving mostly around the mercurial, increasingly unstable personality of Syd Barrett, began an odyssey after Barrett's departure that took in space jams, epic-orchestral collaborations, and pastoral musings to arrive, in *Dark Side of the Moon* (1973), at a markedly simple, conservative style that subsumes many of these elements but no longer seems at all experimental—the last traces of Barrett's weirdness having disappeared—and that brought them far larger audiences and record sales than ever before.

Stylistic consolidation and retrenchment, then, if not outright retreat from the avant-garde, were what characterized the activity of many already established bands at the outset of the 1970s. These artistic approaches were also characteristic, in a somewhat different way, of a large category of British groups that had barely existed, if at all, in the 1960s, such as Curved Air, Emerson Lake & Palmer, Genesis, Gentle Giant, King Crimson, Van der Graaf Generator, and Yes, among others. Their music, usually referred to collectively as progressive rock, was melodically, harmonically, and rhythmically intricate, with often deeply philosophical and oblique lyrics that signaled complete seriousness of purpose, and often sounded as though the customary improvisational freedom of popular musical practice had been greatly curtailed, with most elements appearing quite specifically *composed* from beginning to end. Called "progressive," perhaps, in emulation of progressive jazz of about a decade earlier, it was certainly progressive by comparison to much else heard on the rock & roll scene during the 1970s—especially, of course, on the singles charts and in the disco palaces. But it was not avant-garde either; and although stylistically it did range from the relatively conservative (Emerson Lake & Palmer) to the relatively adventurous (Gentle Giant), its general stylistic outlines were, almost from the start, remarkably consistent and fluent. Actually it was a kind of synthesis, owing as much to British folk traditions and the rock that had come out of them—one thinks particularly of Pentangle and Jethro Tull, also of Traffic in its "John Barleycorn Must Die" phase—as it did to the psychedelic period, to British art music of earlier in the century, and to sacred music of the Anglican tradition, in which many members of these bands had had early experience.[104] Its modernism was thus akin to that of neoclassical Stravinsky by comparison, say, to Viennese atonal music of the 1910s and American experimental music of the 1920s: in some ways looking ahead, in other ways looking—and rather self-consciously at that—behind.[105]

During the late 1960s and early 1970s, rock & roll finally proved, in case there had been any doubt, that it was no passing phenomenon. Once it had lasted long enough to have at least the beginnings of a history, it also became more self-conscious and self-critical—and potentially more avant-garde too, since this quality goes hand in hand with historical self-contemplation, as Bontempelli pointed out[106]—while also continuing to change very fast, as any commercially oriented product does. The striving for *something more*, something beyond what had come to seem (in certain quarters) trivial pop, was generated by this self-consciousness, while the speed of change practically guaranteed that the modernistic flowering would be brief, provoking a relatively prompt reaction against the intricately, consciously unusual and offbeat and leading to a streamlined simplicity that took no chances as the 1970s got under way. What couldn't have been predicted by a simple cyclic model, though—one that would dismiss the avant-garde 1960s in rock as a mere aberration—was the rise of progressive rock: a kind of streamlined modernism (as, actually, Stravinskyan neoclassicism was felt to be by its adherents at the time). Nor might one have expected to witness the persistence, if only in subdued or scattered fashion, of a few of the leading lights of the avant-garde 1960s, a type of survival which also has its parallel in the fate of the art-music avant-garde during the 1930s and 1940s. This kind of persistence is, however, exactly what one might expect if popular music were following the avant-garde model: submitting to fashion, out of necessity, while attempting simultaneously to transcend it, "to win for itself . . . the sanction of its own classics."[107]

I wonder what Adorno would have said, faced with the vast quantity of recent CD rereleases of rock & roll ca. 1965–75, a good many of which have placed a heavy claim on my waking hours for the past several months. Would he have attributed both the motivation of record companies in issuing them and their appeal to forty- and fifty-somethings to the mass commodification of nostalgia? Maybe. Or might he have been willing to admit, however grudgingly, that they could be taken as evidence of some enduring value to their contents? Maybe not: after all, by Adorno's lights, classical music can be commodified too. Certainly, the *intent* to commodify cannot be denied: rock & roll has always been a commodity to just about everyone connected with it (including the musicians), and the prospect of making new money off old recordings has obviously proved alluring to many of the parties involved.

In the end, however, we must recognize that Adorno's world is not ours, that the universality of recorded media has changed everyone's musical experience, in the West at any rate, rather drastically since the early 1940s, and that music, rather than having suffered irrevocable degradation as a result, may actually have become inured to the more toxic effects of packaging and mass commodification that were once considered so dangerous. Anecdotal evidence, at least, does suggest that many people are buying these CD rereleases because they wish they still had their old LPs, or have worn them out—or even because they are too young to have heard anything from the late 1960s or early 1970s the first time around and are curious about it: in other words, because of the music's appeal *as music,* not as some sort of soundtrack to the wistful yearnings of the middle-aged to recapture their long-lost youth, or (for the youth of today) some arcane initiation into the mysteries of the past. To follow this line of thought just a little further, and then stop: If recordings have become, in some sense, the new universal musical standard, then this development may have made it a lot easier, in cases where there is other, independent evidence to support them, to make assertions about commonalities between art and popular music, such as those that I have advanced in this essay.

Appendix: Discography

NOTE: All catalogue numbers refer to most recent issues on CD, unless otherwise noted. All dates (in parentheses) refer to year of original issue; in a few cases, there is a slash followed by a second, more recent year, which refers to a CD reissue that is significantly altered in some way from the original LP, usually by addition of bonus tracks.

Beach Boys, "Good Vibrations" (1966). Capitol 5676 (45rpm)

———, *Good Vibrations: Thirty Years of the Beach Boys* (1993): includes several cuts originally destined for the album *Smile*. Capitol 81294 (5 CDs)

———, *Pet Sounds* (1966). Capitol 48421

Beatles, *The Beatles* (1968) [a.k.a. "The White Album"]: "Revolution 9." Capitol 46443 (2 CDs)

———, *Magical Mystery Tour* (1967): "I Am the Walrus," "Penny Lane," "Strawberry Fields Forever." Capitol 48062

———, "Rain" (1966). Capitol 5651 (45rpm)

———, *Revolver* (1966): "Eleanor Rigby," "Love You To," "Tomorrow Never Knows." Capitol 46441

———, *Rubber Soul* (1965): "Norwegian Wood." Capitol 46440

———, *Sgt. Pepper's Lonely Hearts Club Band* (1967): "A Day in the Life," "Within You Without You." Capitol 46442

Blues Magoos, "Pipe Dream" (1967). Mercury 72660 (45rpm)

Blues Project, *Projections* (1966). Verve FTS-3008 (LP)

Buchanan & Goodman, "The Flying Saucer" (1956). Luniverse 101 (45rpm)

Buckinghams, "Kind of a Drag" (1967). U.S.A. 860 (45rpm)

———, *Portraits* (1968): "Susan." Columbia CS-9598 (LP)

———, "Susan" (1967). Columbia 44378 (45rpm) (also on *Portraits*)

———, *Time and Charges* (1967): "Don't You Care," "Foreign Policy." Columbia CS-9469 (LP)

Buffalo Springfield, *Buffalo Springfield Again* (1967): "Broken Arrow." Atlantic 33226

———, "For What It's Worth" (1967). Atco 6459 (45rpm)

Byrds, *Fifth Dimension* (1966): "Eight Miles High," "Mr. Spaceman." Columbia 64847

———, *The Notorious Byrd Brothers* (1968): "Draft Morning," "Space Odyssey." Columbia 65151

———, *Younger than Yesterday* (1967): "C.T.A.–102." Columbia 64848

Cale, John, *The Academy in Peril* (1972). Warner Bros. 2079

———, *Church of Anthrax*, with Terry Riley (1971). Columbia 474604

———, *Paris 1919* (1973). Warner Bros. 2131
———, *Vintage Violence* (1970). Columbia 1037
Captain Beefheart, *Grow Fins: Rarities, 1965–1982* (1999). Revenant 210 (5 CDs)
———, *Trout Mask Replica* (1969). Warner Bros. 2027
Chambers Brothers, "Time Has Come Today" (1968). Columbia 44414 (45rpm)
Cream, *Disraeli Gears* (1967). Polydor 531811
Deep Purple, *The Book of Taliesyn* (1968). PID 438332
———, *Concerto for Group and Orchestra* (1970). PID 438352
———, *Deep Purple* (1969). PID 438342
———, *Deep Purple in Rock* (1970). Warner Bros. 1877
———, *The Gemini Suite* (1998). Deep Purple Pyramid CLP-0234
———, *Shades of Deep Purple* (1968). PID 438322
See also Lord, Jon
Doors, *The Doors* (1967): "Light My Fire." Elektra 74007
———, *In Concert* (1991): "The Celebration of the Lizard." Elektra 61082
———, *Waiting for the Sun* (1968): "Not to Touch the Earth." Elektra 74024
Electric Prunes, "I Had Too Much to Dream (Last Night)" (1967). Reprise 0532 (45rpm)
Emerson Lake & Palmer, *Tarkus* (1971). Rhino 72224
Eno, Brian, *Discreet Music* (1975): title cut. Editions EG 23
———, *Here Come the Warm Jets* (1973). EG 11
———, *Taking Tiger Mountain by Strategy* (1974). EG 17
See also Fripp, Robert, and Eno, Brian; Roxy Music
Fever Tree, "San Francisco Girls" (1968). Uni 55060 (45rpm)
Five Americans, "Western Union" (1967). Abnak 118 (45rpm)
Fripp, Robert, and Eno, Brian, *Evening Star* (1975). Editions EG 3
———, *(No Pussyfooting)* (1973). Editions EG 2
See also Eno, Brian
Genesis, *Nursery Cryme* (1971). Atlantic 82673
Grateful Dead, *Anthem of the Sun* (1968). Warner Bros. 1749
———, *Aoxomoxoa* (1969). Warner Bros. 1790
———, *Live/Dead* (1970): "Feedback." Warner Bros. 1830
———, *Workingman's Dead* (1970). Warner Bros. 1869
Hendrix, Jimi, Experience, *Are You Experienced?* (1967/1993): "Third Stone from the Sun." MCA 10893
———, *Axis: Bold as Love* (1967): "EXP." MCA 10894
———, *Electric Ladyland* (1968): "1983 . . . . (A Merman I Should Turn to Be)." MCA 10895
Jefferson Airplane, "The Ballad of You & Me & Pooneil" (1967) RCA 9297 (45rpm)
Kaleidoscope, *A Beacon from Mars* (1967). Edsel 532
———, *Incredible Kaleidoscope* (1969). Edsel 533
King Crimson, *In the Court of the Crimson King* (1969): "21st-Century Schizoid Man." EG 1
———, *Lizard* (1970). EG 4
Kraftwerk, *Autobahn* (1975): title cut. EMI 46153
Lennon, John, and Ono, Yoko, *Double Fantasy* (1980): "Kiss Kiss Kiss." Capitol 91425
———, *Unfinished Music No. 1: Two Virgins* (1968). Rykodisc 10411

———, *Unfinished Music No. 2: Life with the Lions* (1969). Rykodisc 10412

See also Beatles; Ono, Yoko

Lord, Jon, *The Gemini Suite* (1971). Line 900122

See also Deep Purple

Lothar and the Hand People, *Presenting Lothar and the Hand People* (1968): "Machines." One Way 17960

Love, *Da Capo* (1966): "The Castle," "Revelation." Elektra 74005

Moody Blues, *Days of Future Passed* (1967). Deram 4767

Mothers of Invention, *Freak Out!* (1966). Rykodisc 10501

———, *Just Another Band from L.A.* (1972): "Billy the Mountain." Rykodisc 10515

See also Zappa, Frank

Music Machine, "Talk Talk" (1966). Original Sound 61 (45rpm)

Napoleon XIV, "They're Coming to Take Me Away, Ha-Haaa!" (1966). Warner Bros. 5831 (45rpm)

Nervous Norvus, "Transfusion" (1956). Dot 15470 (45rpm)

Nice, *Five Bridges* (1970): "Five Bridges Suite." Mercury SR-61295 (LP)

Nico, *Desertshore* (1971). Warner Bros. 6424

———, *The End* (1974). Island 314518892

———, *The Marble Index* (1969). Elektra 74029

Ono, Yoko, *Approximately Infinite Universe* (1973). Rykodisc 10417/18 (2 CDs)

———, *Fly* (1971): "Toilet Piece / Unknown." Rykodisc 10415/16 (2CDs)

———, *Onobox* (1992). Rykodisc 10224/29 (6 CDs)

———, *Yoko Ono/Plastic Ono Band* (1970): "AOS." Rykodisc 10414

See also Beatles; Lennon, John, and Ono, Yoko

Pink Floyd, *Atom Heart Mother* (1970): title cut. Capitol 46381

———, *Dark Side of the Moon* (1973). Capitol 46001

———, *More* (1969). Capitol 46386

———, *The Piper at the Gates of Dawn* (1967): "Astronomy Domine," "Interstellar Overdrive." Capitol 46384

———, *A Saucerful of Secrets* (1968): title cut, "Set the Controls for the Heart of the Sun." Capitol 46383

———, *Ummagumma* (1969): live versions of "Astronomy Domine," "A Saucerful of Secrets," and "Set the Controls for the Heart of the Sun." Capitol 46404

Procol Harum, *Procol Harum Live* (1972). A&M SP-4335 (LP)

Red Crayola, *Parable of Arable Land* (1967). Collectables 0551

———, *Red Crayola Live 1967* (1998). Drag City 92 (2 CDs)

Rolling Stones, *Aftermath* (1966): "Lady Jane," "Paint It Black." Abkco 7476

———, *Their Satanic Majesties Request* (1967): "Citadel." Abkco 8002

Roxy Music, *Roxy Music* (1972). Warner Bros. 26039

———, *For Your Pleasure* (1973). Warner Bros. 26040

See also Eno, Brian

Seville, David, "The Chipmunk Song" (1958). Liberty 55168 (45rpm)

———, "Alvin's Harmonica" (1959). Liberty 55179 (45rpm)

Shangri-Las, "Leader of the Pack" (1964). Red Bird 014 (45rpm)

Sly and the Family Stone, *Stand!* (1969): "Don't Call Me Nigger, Whitey," "Sex Machine." Epic 26456

Small Faces, "Itchycoo Park" (1968). Immediate 501 (45rpm)

Soft Machine, *The Soft Machine* (1968). One Way 22064

————, *Volume Two* (1969). One Way 22065
————, *Third* (1970). Columbia G-30339 (2 LPs)
Spooky Tooth (with Pierre Henry), *Ceremony* (1970). Edsel 565
Strawberry Alarm Clock, "Incense and Peppermints" (1967). Uni 55018 (45rpm)
Thirteenth Floor Elevators, *The Psychedelic Sounds of the Thirteenth Floor Elevators* (1967). Collectables 550
Traffic, *John Barleycorn Must Die* (1970): title cut. Polygram 842780
————, *Mr. Fantasy* (1967): "Dear Mr. Fantasy." Polygram 842783
United States of America, *United States of America* (1968): "The American Metaphysical Circus," "The American Way of Love." Edsel 541
Velvet Underground, *Peel Slowly and See* (1995). Polydor 31452 7887-2 (5 CDs)
————, *The Velvet Underground and Nico* (1967): "European Son," "Heroin," "Waiting for the Man." Polydor 1250
————, *White Light/White Heat* (1968): "Sister Ray." Polydor 1251
Wooley, Sheb, "The Purple People Eater" (1958). MGM 12651 (45rpm)
Yardbirds, "For Your Love" (1965). Epic 9790 (45rpm)
————, *For Your Love* (1965/1999): "Heart Full of Soul" (sitar version). Repertoire 4757
————, "Happenings Ten Years' Time Ago" (1966). Epic 10094 (45rpm)
————, "Shapes of Things" (1966). Epic 10006 (45rpm)
Zappa, Frank, *Chunga's Revenge* (1970). Rykodisc 10511
————, *Hot Rats* (1969). Rykodisc 10508
————, *Lumpy Gravy* (1967). Rykodisc 10504
————, *Overnite Sensation* (1973): "Dinah-Moe-Humm." Rykodisc 10518
————, *Studio Tan* (1978): "The Adventures of Greggery Peccary." Rykodisc 10526
————, *200 Motels* (1971/1997). Rykodisc 10513/14 (2 CDs)
————, *Zappa in New York* (1976/1991): "The Illinois Enema Bandit," "Titties 'n' Beer." Rykodisc 10524/25 (2 CDs)
See also Mothers of Invention

Notes

Research for this essay was partially supported by a grant from the Royalty Research Fund of the University of Washington. Many thanks to John Covach, Shannon Dudley, Larry Starr, and Richard Will for their close reading and useful comments; to John Hanford and Tim Hughes for helpful repertorial suggestions; and to Walt Everett for all of the above, as well as an extensive and stimulating e-mail correspondence on this topic over a period of several months and a number of highly interesting cassette dubs.

1. Some examples: Buchanan & Goodman's "The Flying Saucer" (1956); the double-speed voices of David Seville's series of Chipmunks records (1958–62); the double-speed voice and sax on Sheb Wooley's "The Purple People Eater" (1958); many examples of car and motorcycle effects, among them Nervous Norvus's "Transfusion" (1956) and the Shangri-Las' "Leader of the Pack" (1964); and the peerlessly silly "They're Coming to Take Me Away, Ha-Haaa!" (1966) by Napoleon XIV, with its chanting voice gradually modulating upwards in pitch and attenuating in

timbre to simulate, in a cartoonish way, encroaching madness. (The B-side of this single [Warner Brothers 5831] offered another novelty: it was simply the A-side recorded in reverse, and its label was a mirror image of its counterpart on the A-side.) For this and all other recordings mentioned in this essay, see the appended discography.

2. See Robert Palmer, "The Church of the Sonic Guitar," *South Atlantic Quarterly* 90 (1991): 649–73, for an excellent account of these developments.

3. The catalog of Hendrix's guitar innovations is stunning, not only for the remarkable power of imagination and breadth of invention that it evinced, but also for the fact that it was developed over such a short period of time: wrist vibrato, employment of the thumb for chording, unusual objects applied to the strings for sliding effects, nonstandard tunings (sometimes even retuning while playing), virtuoso volume and tone control effects, switching pickups in the middle of sustained notes, tapping on the fingerboard or behind the neck of the instrument, and a vast range of feedback techniques, among a host of other things, were all parts of his arsenal. Most of these are mentioned, with further useful details, in Don Menn, "Jimi's Favorite Guitar Techniques," in *The Jimi Hendrix Companion: Three Decades of Commentary*, ed. Chris Potash, 83–88 (New York: Schirmer Books, 1996).

4. Brian Eno, Foreword to Mark Cunningham, *Good Vibrations: A History of Record Production* (Chessington, UK: Castle Communications, 1996), 7.

5. See Cunnningham, *Good Vibrations*, 53–59.

6. For a full account of the production of this song, see George Martin (with William Pearson), *With a Little Help from My Friends* (Boston: Little, Brown, 1994), 79–82. Recorded around the same time as "Tomorrow Never Knows" but released only as a single shortly before *Revolver* was "Rain," with its outro featuring Lennon's voice singing a phrase from earlier in the song in reversed playback. (*With a Little Help from My Friends*, 78–79.)

7. Quoted in Palmer, "The Church of the Sonic Guitar," 658.

8. Palmer, "The Church of the Sonic Guitar," 660. There are any number of later reports of rock musicians taking a razor blade to their speaker cones to produce similarly distorted sounds; the early Kinks surely must have been among them. The experimentalist search for "virgin new forms" (in this case, sounds) is one of the telltale signs of the specifically *avant-garde* sensibility as well, as Renato Poggioli notes in *The Theory of the Avant-Garde*, trans. Gerald Fitzgerald (Cambridge, Mass.: Harvard University Press, 1968), 57.

9. Luigi Russolo, *The Art of Noises*, trans. and ed. Barclay Brown (New York: Pendragon, 1986). See also Balilla Pratella, "Manifesto of Futurist Musicians" (1910), trans. Caroline Tisdall, in *Futurist Manifestos*, ed. Umbro Apollonio, 31–38 (New York: Viking, 1973).

10. Russolo, *The Art of Noises*, 25.

11. Ibid., 27. Theodore Gracyk also discusses this point in *Rhythm and Noise: An Aesthetics of Rock* (Durham, N.C.: Duke University Press, 1996), 115.

12. Russolo, *The Art of Noises*, 24; Pratella, "Manifesto of Futurist Musicians," 37.

13. John Cale quoted by Richard Goldstein in "A Quiet Night at Balloon Farm" (1966), repr. in *The Penguin Book of Rock & Roll Writing*, ed. Clinton Heylin, 216–20 (London: Viking, 1992).

14. Sterling Morrison (member of the Velvet Underground), quoted in Victor

Bockris and Gerard Malanga, *Up-Tight: The Velvet Underground Story* (New York: Quill/Omnibus Press, 1983), 20; John Cale, quoted in Lynne Tillman and Stephen Shore, *The Velvet Years: Warhol's Factory 1965–67* (New York: Thunder's Mouth Press, 1995), 64.

15. Poggioli discusses this process of transformation as it played out in the history of the avant-garde in *Theory of the Avant-Garde*, pp.178-79.

16. This I take to be one of the many meanings ascribed to the word "noise" in Jacques Attali, *Noise: The Political Economy of Music*, trans. Brian Massumi (Minneapolis: University of Minnesota Press, 1985).

17. Harrison was first heard on sitar in "Norwegian Wood" (*Rubber Soul*, late 1965), and then again in "Love You To" (*Revolver*, 1966); he imported performers on the tamboura, tabla, and dilruba for "Within You Without You" (*Sgt. Pepper*). The exotic appeal of the sitar spawned a host of imitators, such as Brian Jones in his very successful outing on the Rolling Stones' "Paint It Black" (1966)—and, for those unable or unwilling to learn to play the real thing, devices were soon marketed that would lend the guitar a sitar-like sound. Interestingly, Jeff Beck may have been the first to record his guitar with a fuzzbox attachment that produced such an effect, as on a demo alternate version of the Yardbirds' "Heart Full of Soul," recorded sometime in 1965 but unreleased until very recently. For early uses of the harpsichord, see the Yardbirds' "For Your Love" (1965) and the Rolling Stones' "Lady Jane" (1966), as well as "The Castle" and "Revelation" on *Da Capo* (1966), the second album by the Los Angeles group Love.

18. The jug was played as a very distinctive kind of percussion instrument on records made by the Texas band Thirteenth Floor Elevators. The caz and oud, Near Eastern instruments, were heard on several albums by Kaleidoscope in the later 1960s.

19. Traffic's "Dear Mr. Fantasy" (1967); the Small Faces' "Itchycoo Park" (1968); Sly and the Family Stone's "Don't Call Me Nigger, Whitey" and "Sex Machine" (both 1969); and the remarkable "Time Has Come Today" (1968) by the Chambers Brothers, with its repeatedly shouted "Time!" gradually slowed down and subjected to echo/delay. Some of these songs have psychedelic or other kinds of overtones, to be discussed later.

20. Brian Wilson (with Todd Gold), *Wouldn't It Be Nice: My Own Story* (New York: Harper Collins, 1991), 145; George Martin (with Jeremy Hornsby), *All You Need Is Ears* (New York: St. Martin's Press, 1979), passim; Martin, *With a Little Help from My Friends,* passim. Irving Howe's essay, "The Idea of the Modern," offers a clear characterization of modernism since the late nineteenth century—mostly with reference to literature, although his ideas apply readily to music. See Howe, *Selected Writings, 1950–1990* (New York: Harcourt Brace Jovanovich, 1990), 140–66.

21. Martin, *With a Little Help from My Friends,* 79–80; McCartney quoted in Derek Taylor, *It Was Twenty Years Ago Today: An Anniversary Celebration of 1967* (New York: Simon and Schuster, 1987), 28.

22. See Richie Unterberger, *Unknown Legends of Rock & Roll* (San Francisco: Miller Freeman, 1998), 389–94, for an essay on this group.

23. Poggioli, *Theory of the Avant-Garde*, 112–14.

24. Don Menn has attested to the art-school influence on Townshend in this respect in "Jimi's Favorite Guitar Techniques," 84. Other attendees who went on to

notable rock & roll careers were Ray Davies (the Kinks), John Lennon, Keith Richards (the Rolling Stones), and Syd Barrett (Pink Floyd). Art school has been called "the traditional English sanctuary for bright young misfits who couldn't cut it at the more rigorously academic institutions" (Nicholas Schaffner, *Saucerful of Secrets: The Pink Floyd Odyssey* [New York: Harmony Books, 1991], 5).

25. Timothy White, "Pete Townshend," in *Rock Lives: Profiles and Interviews* (New York: Henry Holt, 1990), 215. In relating this account, White suggests that Townshend's guitar demolition was a delayed reaction to the violent domestic surroundings of his upbringing, "a Shepherd's Bush household where frying pans were always airborne and crockery forever being smashed" (214). This is a little too psychobiographical for me; the art-school connection to happenings is more compelling.

26. Another British band of the late 1960s, the Move, at one point also became notorious for object-smashing at their shows: sometimes their instruments, sometimes television sets, even on one occasion a car brought on stage especially for the purpose. Contemporary accounts suggest, however, that these were stunts, carried out at the instigation of the Move's manager (who may well have been aping the Who), and must soon have ceased, since they would have seemed incongruous in the context of the Move's relatively "poppy" material.

27. Walter Benjamin, "The Work of Art in the Age of Mechanical Reproduction" (1936), in *Illuminations*, ed. and introd. Hannah Arendt, trans. Harry Zohn, 217–51 (New York: Schocken, 1969).

28. Poggioli, *Theory of the Avant-Garde*, 25–26.

29. Roger Waters quoted in Julian Palacios, *Lost in the Woods: Syd Barrett and the Pink Floyd* (London: Boxtree, 1998), 147. Palacios makes an explicit connection between Fluxus and even earlier Pink Floyd performances, at the Spontaneous Underground in London (see 65–66).

30. Poggioli, *Theory of the Avant-Garde*, 25–26.

31. Unterberger, *Unknown Legends of Rock & Roll*, 56–62, contains a fascinating essay on this relatively obscure group.

32. Poggioli, *Theory of the Avant-Garde*, 140–41.

33. Lester Bangs, "Kraftwerkfeature," in *Psychotic Reactions and Carburetor Dung*, ed. Greil Marcus, 154–60 (New York: Vintage, 1988). Experimentalism or scientificism is, of course, a hallmark of the twentieth-century avant-garde in general, and it seems especially typical of the German "take" on these matters. (Poggioli, *Theory of the Avant-Garde*, 136.)

34. Samuel Wagstaff, Jr., "Talking with Tony Smith" (1967), in *Minimal Art: A Critical Anthology*, ed. Gregory Battcock, 381–86 (New York: E. P. Dutton, 1968).

35. This impression is certainly confirmed by accounts of the visuals in Kraftwerk's stage shows, which, according to one observer "deliver a deadpan celebration of technological utopia, a deadly efficient parody and confirmation of Germanic efficiency." (David Toop, *Ocean of Sound: Aether Talk, Ambient Sound and Imaginary Worlds* [London: Serpent's Tail, 1995], 203.) Apart from the minimalist overtones, I've wondered whether there might not also be overtones of *neue Sachlichkeit* (the "new objectivity") of 1920s German art, which sought "to give classical rigor and materialistic solidity to a fleeting and fluid modernity" (Poggioli, *Theory of the Avant-Garde*, 229).

36. Bangs, "Kraftwerkfeature," 156.

37. Benjamin, "The Work of Art in the Age of Mechanical Reproduction," 241.

38. Poggioli, *Theory of the Avant-Garde*, 194–95.

39. For an extended and thoughtful treatment of psychedelic music in the 1960s, see Michael Hicks, *Sixties Rock: Garage, Psychedelic, and Other Satisfactions* (Urbana and Chicago: University of Illinois Press, 1999), 58–74.

40. Some examples: Byrds, "Eight Miles High" (1966, "raga-style" twelve-string guitar); Strawberry Alarm Clock, "Incense and Peppermints" (1967, ensemble including high electric organ and sonically altered guitar); Blues Magoos, "Pipe Dream" (1967, ditto); Fever Tree, "San Francisco Girls" (1968, ditto, with special emphasis on the guitar); Small Faces, "Itchycoo Park" (1968, phase shifting including vocals). The same sort of tactic was also employed for group names: some of those cited above are rather "trippy"-sounding, though not overtly so. Another kind of example is Blue Cheer, which held title for a time to being the loudest band in existence, and which favored an extremely freaked-out, distorted sound. Some people no doubt wondered why a rock group would name itself after a well-known brand of laundry detergent—but "blue cheer" was also the street name for a particularly potent variety of LSD. Another form of disguised reference, notably employed by the Blues Magoos, lay in the acronyms of song titles: "Love Seems Doomed" and "Albert Common Is Dead," for example.

41. Wilson refers here to producer Phil Spector, whom he practically idolized, and fellow Beach Boy Al Jardine.

42. Daniel Harrison agrees, noting that the song's "prominent images are not surf 'n' sun but sensory stimuli of near psychedelic intensity." See Harrison's fine analysis of "Good Vibrations" in "After Sundown: The Beach Boys' Experimental Music," in *Understanding Rock: Essays in Musical Analysis*, ed. John Covach and Graeme M. Boone, 33–57 (New York and Oxford: Oxford University Press, 1997).

43. See Wilson, *Wouldn't It Be Nice*, 144–69 passim. Larry Starr, in his article "The Shadow of a *Smile*: The Beach Boys Album that Refused to Die," *Journal of Popular Music Studies* 6 (1994): 38–57, recounts the sad story of *Smile*'s demise and the mythology that subsequently grew up around it, and speculates as to how the recently released fragments of this album-that-never-was might be pieced together to form something like the originally planned complete work.

44. See Palacios, *Lost in the Woods*, 61–78 for further details of Barrett's musical influences.

45. There is some disagreement among those who knew Barrett well as to whether drugs, LSD prominent among them, actually caused his psychosis or simply exacerbated an underlying condition that would have surfaced sooner or later anyway. See Kris DiLorenzo, "Syd Barrett: Careening through Life . . . from the Floyd to the Void," *Trouser Press* 5/2 (February 1978): 26–32.

46. Townshend quoted in Mike Watkinson and Pete Anderson, *Crazy Diamond: Syd Barrett and the Dawn of Pink Floyd* (London: Omnibus, 1991), 58.

47. As one such observer put it: "Barrett was incapable of performing for its own sake. He wanted to achieve something indefinable each time he set out to play, and frequently this Olympian vision prevented Syd from producing anything at all for fear it not be perfect, brilliant, and innovative." (DiLorenzo, "Syd Barrett: Careening through Life," 28.) This description, in its evocation of a certain Romantic image, reminds us again of the connecting thread of drug use between the romantics and the moderns. Barrett really partook of both.

48. Drug use created a bond between Reed and Cale, and may go some way toward explaining how these two very different men, from very different backgrounds, were able to work together so effectively for several years: how the classically trained Cale was able to reconcile himself to rock, in which he had had no experience prior to meeting Reed and about which he clearly felt somewhat skeptical at first, and how Reed, who knew more about literature from a formal standpoint than music and whose musical background was strictly confined to rock & roll when the Velvets first started up, was able to adjust to the avant-garde elements that Cale brought to their mix. (See Victor Bockris, *Transformer: The Lou Reed Story* [New York: Da Capo, 1997], 85.)

49. Phil Lesh, 5 February 1983; in David Gans, *Conversations with the Dead: The Grateful Dead Interview Book* (New York: Citadel Press, 1995), 206.

50. Ibid., 206.

51. Jerry Garcia and Phil Lesh, 24 February 1983; in Gans, *Conversations with the Dead*, 209.

52. Lesh, 30 July 1981; in Gans, *Conversations with the Dead*, 104. Other members of this class included Lesh's roommate Tom Constanten, later a member (briefly) of the Dead; Steve Reich; and John Chowning.

53. Poggioli, *Theory of the Avant-Garde*, 74–76. As the Dead aged, their resemblance to the Decadents strengthened: the world of their concert tours, sustained by a base of fans that traveled with them in a haze of marijuana smoke, was largely self-enclosed, as if the 1960s had never ended—perpetually childlike despite the growing abundance of gray hair.

54. J. G. Ballard, "Which Way to Inner Space?" (1962), repr. in his *A User's Guide to the Millennium: Essays and Reviews*, 195–98 (New York: Picador USA, 1996). This essay is the *locus classicus* for the phrase "inner space."

55. Ballard himself confessed to having tried LSD once, in 1967 or 1968; he had the classic "bad trip," and as a result even swore off marijuana. See Andrea Juno and Vale, "Interview with JGB," in *J. G. Ballard*, Re/Search No. 8/9 (San Francisco: Re/Search Publishing, 1984), 24–25.

56. Palacios, *Lost in the Woods*, 145.

57. This dictionary entry is reprinted, tellingly, in *Dead Reckonings: The Life and Times of the Grateful Dead*, ed. John Rocco, 219–20 (New York: Schirmer Books, 1999).

58. The force of these various developments engineered a huge shift in attitude for popular music, decidedly away from the comic, novelty use made of UFOs and aliens starting in the late 1950s (in records like "Flying Saucer" and "The Purple People Eater," mentioned earlier), and away too from the sensibilities of countless records from the early 1960s seeking to cash in on public fascination with (the romance of) space exploration, with titles like *Strings for a Space Age* and *The In Sound from Way Out!* (For more about such novelty and space-impressionistic records, see the interviews with composers and record collectors compiled in *Incredibly Strange Music*, vols. 1 and 2, Re/Search Nos. 14 and 15 [San Francisco: Re/Search Publishing, 1993, 1994].) Humorous songs on science-fictional subjects did not die out entirely—note, for example, the Byrds' "Mr. Spaceman" (1966) and "C.T.A.–102" (1967)—but the Byrds also recorded "Space Odyssey" (1968), which with its solemn, almost hymnlike tempo and harmonized voices—and, of course, its allusion to the Kubrick film—is quite clearly of serious intent.

59. Wright's interest in Stockhausen is mentioned in Schaffner, *Saucerful of Secrets*, 25, 27. The title "Set the Controls for the Heart of the Sun" is reputedly taken from a novel by William S. Burroughs, an American writer with ties to the Beats. Some of Burroughs's work, with its hallucinatory science-fiction-derived imagery, would certainly fit the criteria of inner-space exploration suggested by Ballard—and, furthermore, brings drugs explicitly into the process.

60. "EXP," on *Axis: Bold as Love* (1967), makes use of a similar device to suggest the ascending trajectory of a "Mr. Paul Caruso" (Hendrix), who has just been asked by a radio interviewer, his voice dripping with sarcasm, about the existence of "space people" and has decided to reveal that he is, in fact, one of them. By the time of *Electric Ladyland* (1968), Hendrix seems to have become more interested in laying down long, meditative tracks, often involving water imagery, that probe the depths of (his) inner space; certainly, there is nothing overtly science-fictional about them, except perhaps for the futuristic hint in the title "1983 . . . (A Merman I Should Turn to Be)."

61. Such a setting might be called a "parallel universe" if it were to unfold in real science-fictional terms, but without the real world as a reference point (or plane), there is nothing for it to be parallel to. I follow here the distinction between science fiction and high fantasy drawn by David Ketterer in his book, *New Worlds for Old* (Garden City, N.Y.: Anchor, 1974).

62. Some examples of progressive-rock albums largely or wholly constructed around themes of high fantasy are: King Crimson, *Lizard* (1970); Genesis, *Nursery Cryme* (1971); Emerson Lake & Palmer, *Tarkus* (1971). Of course, there is much in progressive rock that is neither science-fictional nor fantastic; another strong tendency in this genre is toward the mystical and introspective. But one symptom of prog rock's affinity for both kinds of themes is also its attraction to the symphonic, a trend which can be said to have started with several late-1960s British rock groups, some of them predecessors to prog bands. At this stage, to do an album with an actual, full-size symphony orchestra—usually in a recognizably English late-romantic or neoromantic/pastoral style—became something to try at least once: the Moody Blues (1967), Pink Floyd (1970), the Nice (1970), Deep Purple (1970), and Procol Harum (1972) all did. The apparent aspiration to "classical" legitimacy embodied in such efforts, even if combined syncretically with rock textures, seems largely anti-modern in intent.

63. See Unterberger, *Unknown Legends of Rock & Roll*, 365–70, for an interesting essay detailing the brief career of this group.

64. The cyclic feature of this album finale, combined with a duration well in excess of the standard pop three-minute single, together exemplify another development tangentially related to modernism: the so-called concept album. Here we find aspirations to the established, "legitimate" status of classical music, if often rather naively expressed, often intertwined with the high seriousness of modernism—sometimes with an avant-garde tinge, as is the case here.

65. Guercio, for a very brief time, had been a member of the Mothers of Invention and had perhaps acquired a taste for dissonant "modern" sounds from his contact with Frank Zappa, the Mothers' leader. He supplied encouragement to the Buckinghams—acted upon in *Portraits*—to write some of their own material, to which he continued to add a certain amount of modernistic seasoning.

66. Zappa quoted in Tim Schneckloth, "Frank Zappa: Garni du jour, Lizard

King Poetry, and Slime," *Down Beat*, 18 May 1978, 15–17, 44–46. Zappa referred to his album *Hot Rats* (1969) in the liner notes as a "movie for your ears"; *Chunga's Revenge* (1970) was accompanied by an elaborate scenario.

67. This aspect of Zappa's work, and its implications for his musical structures, is discussed in Jonathan W. Bernard, "Listening to Zappa," *Contemporary Music Review* 18, no. 4 (2000): 63–103 (esp. 89–91). I note, in passing, that at least two of the song titles mentioned above more than hint at Zappa's penchant for another well-known avant-garde activity, *épater les bourgeois*.

68. See the accounts of Morrison's collaboration with the other Doors in Ray Manzarek, *Light My Fire: My Life with the Doors* (New York: Putnam, 1998), especially the composition of "Light My Fire," 149–51.

69. Jim Morrison, "Cinema Is Most Totalitarian of the Arts," in *The Doors Companion: Four Decades of Commentary*, ed. John Rocco (New York: Schirmer Books, 1997), 66.

70. Bruce Harris, "Film Sensibility Set the Doors Apart," in *The Doors Companion*, 66–68.

71. James Riordan and Jerry Prochnicky, *Break on Through: The Life and Death of Jim Morrison* (New York: Quill/William Morrow, 1991), 214–24. Originally intended to occupy one entire side of the Doors' third LP, *Waiting for the Sun* (1968), "Celebration" never came together coherently enough to persuade the other band members to put it on the album, save for one section, "Not to Touch the Earth." Under pressure to supply some kind of setting for his text, a 133-line poem, Morrison began drinking ever more heavily, effectively putting himself out of commission at least as far as this project was concerned. Eventually, "Celebration" did achieve a live performance which was issued commercially, but the work remains a pitiful skeleton compared to what had been envisioned, consisting as it does mostly of Morrison declaiming his poem with extremely minimal accompaniment from the rest of the band; at 14:28, it is much shorter than the originally projected length. Only the section previously recorded as "Not to Touch the Earth" sounds truly finished. (The entire poem did appear on the gatefold of the sleeve for *Waiting for the Sun.*)

72. For extensive discussion and analysis of Zappa's work, particularly in the orchestral medium, see: Arved Ashby, "Frank Zappa and the Anti-Fetishist Orchestra," *Musical Quarterly* 83 (1999): 557–606; Bernard, "Listening to Zappa"; Bernard, "The Musical World(s?) of Frank Zappa: Some Observations of His 'Crossover' Pieces," in *Expression in Pop-Rock Music*, ed. Walter Everett, 157–210 (New York: Garland Publishing, 2000).

73. See Bill Harkleroad (with Billy James), *Lunar Notes: Zoot Horn Rollo's Captain Beefheart Experience* (Wembley, Middlesex, UK: SAF Publishing Ltd., 1998); John French, "There Ain't No Santa Claus on the Evenin' Stage," in booklet accompanying Captain Beefheart and His Magic Band, *Grow Fins: Rarities 1965–1982* (Revenant 210, 5-CD box set, 1999), 12–91.

74. Harkleroad, *Lunar Notes*, 37, 34.

75. Eric Drew Feldman (pianist for the Magic Band in the late 1970s) emphasizes this fixity in remarks quoted by Stuart Nicholson, *Jazz-Rock: A History* (New York: Schirmer Books, 1998), 265.

76. French, "There Ain't No Santa Claus," 59.

77. Poggioli, *Theory of the Avant-Garde*, 114, 92.

78. Langdon Winner, "In Search of America: Captain Beefheart and the Smithsonian Institute Blues," *Rolling Stone*, 1 April 1971, 40–43, 56.

79. John Cale (1981), quoted in Dave Thompson, *Beyond the Velvet Underground* (London: Omnibus, 1989), 12. More recent reminiscences by Cale of his early (pre-Velvets) musical experiences are to be found in Victor Bockris and John Cale, *What's Welsh for Zen: The Autobiography of John Cale* (New York and London: Bloomsbury Press, 2000).

80. Bockris and Malanga, *Up-Tight*, 13.

81. Ibid., 17.

82. Sterling Morrison quoted in Victor Bockris, *Transformer: The Lou Reed Story* (New York: Da Capo, 1997), 92.

83. Bockris, *Transformer*, 89.

84. Bockris and Malanga, *Up-Tight*, 22.

85. Morrison and Cale quoted in David Fricke, booklet essay for Velvet Underground, *Peel Slowly and See* (Polydor 31452 7887–2, 5 CDs, 1995), 30–33.

86. Cale quoted in Bockris, *Transformer*, 128.

87. Poggioli, *Theory of the Avant-Garde*, 49–50, 55.

88. Bockris, *Transformer*, 122. Another reason for the transformation of rock performances from music for dancing to actual *concerts* was evidently the increasing use of meters other than the simple or compound duple for which the dance styles of the post-ballroom era were designed. But triple, mixed or irregular, even simultaneous different meters were more than a disincentive to dance; they embodied an intricacy that encouraged audiences to sit and listen, passively or actively.

89. Donald Lyons speaks of Warhol's art as embodying "a lot of reductivist contempt for the structures of popular culture" (in Tillman and Shore, *The Velvet Years*, 77); Warhol himself writes that "the more you look at the same exact thing, the more the meaning goes away, and the better and emptier you feel" (Andy Warhol and Pat Hackett, *POPism: The Warhol '60s* [New York: Harcourt Brace Jovanovich, 1980], 50).

90. Some of Cale's work since 1968 is still experimental, some of it conservatively lyrical in a folk-tinged way—the latter the product, one would guess, of the lessons he drew from collaboration with Reed and from his own earlier musical background. This dichotomy fairly neatly classifies his first few post-Velvets projects: *The Academy in Peril* (1972) and his collaboration with minimalist composer Terry Riley, *Church of Anthrax* (1971), are relatively daring, *Vintage Violence* (1970) and *Paris 1919* (1973) much less so. Somewhere in the middle (or partaking of both sides of his musical personality) are his arrangements for Nico's albums *The Marble Index* (1969), *Desertshore* (1971), and *The End* (1974).

91. Yoko Ono, "To the Wesleyan People (who attended the meeting)—a Footnote to My Lecture of January 13th, 1966," in *Ubi Fluxus ibi motus 1990–1962*, ed. Achille Bonito Oliva (Milan: Mazzotta, 1990), 235–39.

92. Yoko Ono, "To the Wesleyan People," 239.

93. Yoko Ono" (interview, November 1984), in *The Guests Go In to Supper*, ed. Melody Summer, Kathleen Burch, and Michael Summer, 169–213 (Oakland and San Francisco: Burning Books, 1986). These techniques are already on display in Ono's "AOS," recorded with Ornette Coleman and other members of his quartet in 1968 and included on *Yoko Ono/Plastic Ono Band* (1970). (A transcription of the opening of "AOS" appears in Everett, *The Beatles as Musicians: "Revolver" through*

the "Anthology" [New York and Oxford: Oxford University Press, 1999], 162.)

94. "Revolution 9" (1968) is credited to Lennon and McCartney on the album sleeve and label, owing to standing contractual arrangements, but was really composed by Ono and Lennon, as Lennon later claimed. The recording history and the sound sources for this essentially *concrète* composition are given in great detail in Everett, *The Beatles as Musicians*, 174–78. The descriptor "unfinished" in the titles *Unfinished Music No. 1: Two Virgins* (1968) and *Unfinished Music No. 2: Life with the Lions* (1969) came from the composers' "conceptual" attitude about *No. 1*: that "much of the album's music was not pressed into the grooves but was to be created in the mind of the listener" (Everett, *The Beatles as Musicians*, 161).

95. Paul Rambali, "Brain Waves from Eno," *Trouser Press* 4/2 (June-July 1977): 15–19.

96. Cynthia Dagnal, "Eno and the Jets: Controlled Chaos," *Rolling Stone*, 12 September 1974, 16, 21.

97. Dagnal, "Eno and the Jets: Controlled Chaos," 21. See also Eric Tamm, *Brian Eno: His Music and the Vertical Color of Sound* (Boston and London: Faber & Faber, 1989), 99–100.

98. Brian Eno, liner notes to *Discreet Music* (EG Records Ltd., 1975), currently available as Editions EG 23 (CD).

99. Eno, "Generating and Organizing Variety in the Arts" (1976), repr. in *Breaking the Sound Barrier: A Critical Anthology of the New Music*, ed. Gregory Battcock, 129–41 (New York: E. P. Dutton, 1981).

100. "Paranoia strikes deep . . ." One reason why the possibility of censorship had crossed my mind was that I had no idea who had decided to delete that interlude. Knowing a little more now, three decades later, I can make an educated guess as to the responsible parties. The new version almost certainly did not come from the record company (Columbia); new edits of this kind, once a single has been released for radio play, are practically never issued, as Walter Everett assures me— and, indeed, the stock single for sale to the public continued to include the interlude. It is therefore highly likely that the radio station in question (or several stations independently) made its own edit, perhaps after gaining permission from Columbia to do so. After all (so the reasoning might have gone), the interlude seemed to be an insertion in the first place, so to take it out would actually *improve* the "product"; its dissonant sounds probably bothered some listeners, and those who didn't care one way or the other would hardly notice the change; and (undoubtedly the most compelling argument of all) removal of these twenty-five seconds would bring the playing time for "Susan" down from 2:48 to 2:23, leaving more time for other songs—or more commercials.

101. Theodor W. Adorno, "On Popular Music" (1941), in *On Record: Rock, Pop, and the Written Word*, ed. Simon Frith and Andrew Goodwin, 301–14 (New York: Pantheon, 1990); Adorno, "On the Fetish-Character in Music and the Regression of Listening" (1938), in *The Essential Frankfurt School Reader*, ed. Andrew Arato and Eike Gebhardt, 270–99 (New York: Continuum, 1982).

102. John Mowitt, "The Sound of Music in the Era of Its Electronic Reproducibility," in *Music and Society: The Politics of Composition, Performance, and Reception*, ed. Richard Leppert and Susan McClary, 173–97 (Cambridge: Cambridge University Press, 1987).

103. Adorno, "On Popular Music," 307–9.

104. Edward Macan has discussed the harmonic debt of progressive rock to earlier twentieth-century British art music in "'The Spirit of Albion' in Twentieth-Century English Popular Music: Vaughan Williams, Holst, and the Progressive Rock Movement," *Music Review* 53 (1992): 100–125. Macan also discusses the influence of Anglican church music in his book, *Rocking the Classics: English Progressive Rock and the Counterculture* (New York and Oxford: Oxford University Press, 1997), 148–51.

105. For a somewhat different view of progressive rock and its significance, see John Covach's important article, "Progressive Rock, 'Close to the Edge,' and the Boundaries of Style," in *Understanding Rock: Essays in Musical Analysis*, ed. John Covach and Graeme M. Boone, 3–31 (New York and Oxford: Oxford University Press, 1997).

106. Cited in Poggioli, *Theory of the Avant-Garde*, 14.

107. Poggioli, *Theory of the Avant-Garde*, 84.

14

Refiguring the Modernist Program for Hearing: Steve Reich and George Rochberg

JUDY LOCHHEAD

In the mid-1960s both Steve Reich and George Rochberg offered a critique of the modernist practices of both the serialists and experimentalists, largely on grounds of the apprehensibility of the music as sounding presence.[1] Focused on issues of hearing and its possibilities in human terms, their critiques of modernist practices served as both an impetus and justification for the new compositional directions that each composer explored. Their particular concern for issues of hearing is significant for prefiguring an aesthetic change that would be more fully realized in later years. Specifically, this particular focus on hearing is a marker of the turn from modern to postmodern practices of musical creation. In initiating this turn toward a postmodern aesthetic, Reich and Rochberg not only articulate a transformation of how hearing engages the musical object but further reveal an implicit modernist program for hearing.

Contrary to the occasional assertion that modernist composers of mid-century had no concern for the listener, both the serialists and experimentalists recognized hearing as a necessary function of music.[2] The hearing entailed by the modernist aesthetic is prescribed by a composer's intended compositional design; and the intended design then constitutes a kind of program.[3] A programmed hearing of this sort is grounded in a belief about the structural nature of the musical object: the object's intended structure determines its proper hearing.[4] The turn away from modernist and toward postmodern musical practices may be traced through the operative conception of the musical object and its relation to hearing. While Reich and Rochberg did offer critique of their predecessors, they did not question the underlying belief about the structural nature of the musical object. Rather, they focus on the apprehensibility of the intended structural design. However, their concern for what the listener may or may not hear gives voice to an alternate assumption about the nature of the musical object and how it engages acts of hearing.

While issues of hearing do not typically figure in discussions of musical postmodernism, they can illuminate the turn away from modernism and toward postmodernism in the arena of musical sound.[5] Rather than focusing on the stylistic signs of musical postmodernism, I have chosen here to trace how hearing is figured in the musical practices of post–World War II modernism and then the refiguring of hearing at this crucial moment of aesthetic transformation.

My project begins with an account of the critique Reich and Rochberg articulate of modernist practices and of the reception of their music in the critical domain. The following discussion establishes the kind of hearing that is prescribed by the structuring processes of compositional design for both the experimentalists and the serialists, taking the music and rhetoric of John Cage as an exemplar of the former and of Milton Babbitt for the latter. The project concludes by demonstrating that the music and rhetoric of Reich and Rochberg from the mid-1960s and early 1970s both replicates the underlying modernist concerns for structural design and hearing and refigures the role of the listener in relation to musical design. My larger point has two components: first, Reich and Rochberg opened a pathway into postmodern musical practices through not only a rhetoric of hearing but also a musical design that embraces hearing in a new way; and second, their music does not bear out the sense of revolution that surrounded it, demonstrating instead many of the structural concerns of modernist practices.

1. Reich and Rochberg: A Critique and Reception

Steve Reich's earliest explorations of musical minimalism in the late-1960s and 70s were accompanied by a rhetoric critical of, on one hand, the precompositional processes of "experimental" music, and on the other hand, the processes of structural design pivotal to integral serialism. In his well-known "Music as a Gradual Process" from 1968, Reich distinguishes compositional from musical processes and argues that the compositional processes espoused by the two dominant approaches to musical creation at that time can not be heard. Reich claims that both the chance procedures of John Cage and the serial procedures of the Europeans and Americans have no aural presence for listeners and function as "secrets of structure that you can't hear."[6] In response, Reich conceives processes for his own music that are "perceptible" and "determine all the note-to-note (sound-to-sound) details and the overall form simultaneously."[7]

George Rochberg similarly levels a critique of the two approaches to musical creation during the middle years of the twentieth century, asserting that music of the "avant-garde" contradicts *a priori* structures of "musical time" which are rooted in human memory and "our biological structure."[8]

Like Reich, Rochberg identifies the possibilities of hearing as the focus of his critique and proposes an approach to musical creation that restores the hearability of musical design. He conceives a music that is premised on the causality and directionality of music's temporal relations and a plurality of stylistic options envisaged in the idea of stylistic collage, drawing on various past musical traditions in an *ars combinatoria*.[9]

The reception of Reich's and Rochberg's music was etched in black and white: commentary by other musicians and critics in the mid-1960s and early 1970s was either scathing or adulatory. Those reacting negatively to Reich's music observed a "simplistic" and "monotonous" music. Those reacting positively often claimed the emerging style constituted a "revolutionary" coup, dethroning the two dominant strands. The "revolutionary" claims for Reich's music in the mid-1960s and early 1970s were advanced by those who, riding the crest of radical social change in the late 1960s, advocated a "new" and oppositional music. For instance, John Rockwell, writing in 1973, describes Reich's music as "fresh and new"—the "first music in a long time that has the power to shock and outrage." Further, he contends that Reich's music gives "renewed hope that Western music can be revivified."[10]

Reception of Rochberg's music was similarly diverse but without such a sense of ardor for its redemptive characteristics. For instance, John Rockwell praised the "heightened sense of historical awareness" in Rochberg's *ars combinatoria* works; and Jay Reise deemed his compositional technique "progressive" in the sense of Brahms and Michael Linton called the music a "radical rejection of the whole philosophical foundation of the postwar avant garde."[11] But others, such as reviewer Andrew Porter, deemed the music "insignificant" and "almost irrelevant."[12]

The composers themselves played a role in shaping reception through their own prose which included commentary about their aesthetic and technique. Reich's was more aphoristic and tended more toward manifesto, as evidenced in his haiku-like program notes from the late 1960s and 1970s. They include such statements as: "Obviously music should put all within listening range into a state of ecstasy" or "This music is not the expression of the momentary state of mind of the performers while playing. Rather, the momentary state of mind of the performers while playing is largely determined by the ongoing composed slowly changing music."[13] But Rochberg mapped out a more complex aesthetic terrain for his music, one that sometimes contradicted those who championed his music as revolutionary. In a series of articles, Rochberg recounts his embrace and ultimate rejection of the postwar avant-garde.[14] In place of what he considered an expressively bankrupt aesthetic built on the back of cultural scientism, Rochberg proposes a reconnection with pre-modernist musical practices which had been abandoned in the modernist zeal for progress and originality. Themes of reconnection, renewal, and rebirth were advanced rather than the manifestoes of "radical" change that were characteristic of modernist practices.

The rhetoric that circulated both by and about Reich and Rochberg concerning their divergence from postwar high modernism could be understood by two categories of postmodernism that Hal Foster articulated in 1983. In the preface to a collection of articles that was an early entry into the "postmodern debate," he identifies two strands: a postmodernism of resistance which "seeks to deconstruct modernism and resist the status quo" and a postmodernism of reaction which "repudiates [modernism] to celebrate the [status quo]."[15] Through this critical lens, Rochberg's music could be understood as a reactionary retreat into the pre-modern, and Reich's as a resistance that reinstates the modern penchant for originary aesthetic creation. However, from the temporal perspective of the first years of the twenty-first century, this taxonomy of diverging postmodern strategies no longer has a viable explanatory power and must itself be understood as both provisional and a kind of critical call to arms. What I propose here is a more textured understanding of the kind of musical response to postwar modernism offered by Rochberg and Reich, one that focuses on the notion of musical "hearing" that circulated in the 1960s and another that emerged as a consequence of this hearing.

On one hand, both Reich and Rochberg articulate aesthetic positions and create music that defies the originary aesthetic of modernism, but on the other, their music and thought embody a fascination with structure.[16] This fascination is matched, however, by a concern for the "hearability" of structure and hence with listeners and the role that they play in the constitution of musical meaning. It is on this issue of the constitution of musical meaning that the difference between modern and postmodern practices in music may be drawn.

2. Two Branches of Postwar Modernism: The Experimentalists and the Serialists

Reich's and Rochberg's critiques of postwar musical practices in the 1950s and 1960s position the experimental and serial branches as foils for advancing an alternative aesthetic stance. And while these two branches are often posed as anithetical, both Reich and Rochberg address them from a single vantage: composers in both the serial and experimental camps inscribe structural processes in their music which are not directly audible for listeners. This linking of the experimentalists with the integral serialists is justified since each approach is grounded in modernist principles that assume an objective musical sound whose properties as such are the source of an abstract musical meaning. The compositional assertion of an "objective" musical structure and its attendant musical meaning has particular ramifications for the role of the listener and for hearing generally. In each branch of modernism—experimental and serial—the listener's role is apprehension of objectively existing sonic properties.

John Cage and the Experimental Tradition

Recognizing that Cage's overall career resists reduction to a single set of issues, I focus here on his musical production in the late 1950s and 1960s since it was most influential on Reich and Rochberg. In a series of writings in his first collection of essays, *Silence,* Cage articulates his particular version of an aesthetic of objectivity.[17] For instance, in a 1959 article, "The History of Experimental Music in the United States," he writes: "sounds are to come into their own, rather than being exploited to express sentiments or ideas of order."[18] In order to achieve such an objective sound, Cage devises chance and indeterminate compositional procedures which would effectively remove compositional personality—"sentiment" or "order"—from musical production and hence allow "sound as sound" to emerge.

Cage's "Variations II," composed in 1961, exemplifies an indeterminate compositional process, one of the means by which composers can "remove themselves" from the musical product.[19] The score indicates a work for any number of performers playing any instruments and provides instructions and materials with which performers determine what sounds will occur in any particular performance. It consists of six transparent sheets with lines and five transparent sheets with dots. Cage instructs performers to superimpose the sheets, partially or wholly, "to drop perpendiculars from the points to the lines . . . [and to] measure the perpendiculars by means of any rule, obtaining readings thereby for 1) frequency, 2) amplitude, 3) timbre, 4) duration, 5) point of occurrence in an established period of time, and 6) structure of event."[20]

Expecting that performances will differ, Cage frees himself from control of the sound as music and loosens the identification of "piece" with a particular sound configuration. While this compositional process may allow "sound as sound" to emerge for the composer, the process as such has no way to assure that performers or listeners will embrace musical sounds in such objective terms. Rather, compositional process entails the expectation that performers and listeners alike will engage "sound as sound." In other words, compositional intent provides a "program" for hearing that applies to both performers and listeners.

Cage's well-known recounting of his aural experience as a listener clarifies the listener role in experimental music. Upon entering an anechoic chamber—a totally soundless room—Cage reports that "one hears two sounds of one's own unintentional making (nerve's systematic operation, blood's circulation)" and he notes that "the situation one is clearly in is not objective (sound-silence), but rather subjective (sounds only), those intended and those others (so-called silence) not intended."[21] His observation of silence and sound as equally intentional does not lead to an assertion that sentiment and order are also intentional and hence meaningful, rather it leads him to a notion that without such dualities as silence/sound, subject/object, intended/non-intended, sound has only *"its frequency, its loudness, its length, its overtone structure, the precise morphology of these and of itself."*[22] In other words, sound has only its "objective" features and the listener is positioned by this aesthetic to hear these sentiment- and order-less features.

Operating from within a modernist aesthetic, Cage emphasizes the originality of his musical production for both composer and listener: "New music: new listening. Not an attempt to understand something that is being said, for, if something were being said, the sounds would be given the shapes of words. Just an attention to the activity of sounds"[23] In this aesthetic stance, the "new" music—the "sounds as themselves" without history, sentiment, or order—entails its own proper hearing.

Milton Babbitt and the Serial Tradition

In a series of articles written in the late 1950s and early 1960s, Babbitt articulates how the "twelve-tone system is genuinely 'revolutionary' in its nature and implications."[24] The system, itself a new development of the twentieth century, provides for the creation of "musical compositions . . . [which] possess a high degree of contextuality and autonomy."[25] In other words, the modernist aesthetic of originality extends not only to the system itself but to another level of compositional design which assures that each piece expresses a unique structural context.[26]

For Babbitt, the systematic and formal aspects of serial procedures are not fully separable from the music as such. The twelve-tone system is not a technique allowing a musical expression of something other than that technique. Babbitt's defense of the possibility of a non-empirical theory that precedes practice demonstrates this continuity between system and music. His defense is predicated on the possibility of a kind of compositional research and theorizing which results in "musical interpretations of the logical entailments of the formal system."[27] In other words, the logic of the system takes on sounding form through the theoretical and compositional activities of the composer.

This continuity between music and compositional system ". . . imposes new demands of perception and conception upon composer and listener."[28] Babbitt asserts that the "new" music employs a "more efficient," less "redundant" tonal vocabulary than music of the past and defines the listener's new role with respect to this efficiency.[29] Conceiving of each "musical event . . . [as] located in a five-dimensional musical space determined by pitch-class, register, dynamic, duration, and timbre," he then maintains that over "the course of the work the successive values of each component create an individually coherent structure. . . ." A listener's "[i]nability to perceive and remember precisely the values of any of these components results in . . . a falsification of the composition's total structure."[30] The program for hearing then is apprehension of the contextually defined aspects of the system which through compositional action have been bestowed with sounding form.

Philomel, Babbitt's 1964 work for soprano and tape setting poetry of John Hollander, demonstrates this continuity between system and work. The tape part was realized with the RCA Mark II synthesizer, which in the early 1960s allowed certain historically unique complexities of conception and motivated further compositionally oriented theorizing. The piece serializes pitch and rhythm alike, the latter with a time-point system which Babbitt had articulated in a prior article, "Twelve-Tone Rhythmic Structure and the Electronic Medium," from 1962. There Babbitt claims not that the listener's role is apprehension of the systematically-derived structure as such but rather that "musical structure . . . address[es] itself to the ear." Invoking the epistemological problem of the Cartesian mind-body split, Babbitt maintains that the objectively existing structure can only "provide the possibility of coherence."[31] As with Cage's compositional process, there is no way to assure that a compositionally intended structure will result in listener apprehension of either coherence or structure as such. Nonetheless, such apprehension is set up as the program for hearing largely on the assumption of the ontological force of systematic logic.

The central role that compositional system plays in the modernist musical practices of Cage and Babbitt resonates with contemporary critical accounts of concert music in the 1960s. For instance, in 1967 Richard Kostelanetz writes: "For both Babbitt and Cage . . . the compositional methods become the real subject of the piece."[32] The modernist turn toward compositional process as "subject" carries with it an assumption that a proper or adequate hearing entails apprehension of it. The critiques offered by Reich and Rochberg aim at this modernist program for hearing. They do not question whether hearing structure or coherence is an aesthetically viable perceptual goal but rather whether the structures are themselves hearable.

2. Structuralist Fantasies: Reich and Rochberg

Steve Reich

In his written statements of the late 1960s and 1970s, Reich conceives an objectively existing musical process which makes it possible for listeners and performers to shift "attention away from he and *she* and *you* and *me*

Figure 14.1. Steve Reich, *Violin Phase.* "Melody," m. 1. Copyright © 1979 by Universal Edition (London) Ltd., London / UE 16185. Used by permission.

outwards towards it."[33] This process is not a method employed to inscribe coherence or to assure the absence of personality. Rather Reich intends it as a process of the music that operates at the phenomenal level of human experience. But, through its structure, the process takes listeners, composers, and performers alike "away from intentions" and toward "direct contact with the impersonal."[34]

Unlike his predecessors, Reich conceives his musical processes from the perspective of a possible hearing, posing himself as a listener. He writes: "I want to be able to hear the process happening throughout the sounding music."[35] But like his predecessors, he expects listeners to hear processes in terms of constructive features which constitute an objective structure. This structure, setting the program for hearing, provides the means by which listeners themselves can experience not "me" but "it."

Descriptions of three pieces—two utilizing a phasing process and another based on cycling through a harmonic sequence—exemplify Reich's structuralist program for hearing. In *Violin Phase,* a 1967 work for either four violinists or violinist and pre-recorded tape, two or more statements of a violinistic melody are repeated and played against one another. Figure 14.1 cites measure 1 of the melody. The process is the gradual phasing of the melodic unit by increments of the eighth-note. After initial statements of the melodic unit, one part gradually speeds up, making the eighth-note units out of phase. When the eighth-note beats are again "in phase," but the larger melodic pattern is off-set, the original tempo resumes, letting the newly obtained composite pattern to settle in. This process of going-out-of- and coming-into-phase with respect to the eighth-note unit recurs until a whole cycle has been completed. A few added melodic features enrich the

Figure 14.2. Reich, *Drumming.* Rhythmic pattern.

melodic progress of the piece but the cycle of phasing constitutes its focal process.[36] It is this "musical" process of small- and large-scale phasing that Reich sets up as the perceptible program for hearing.

The 1971 work *Drumming* complicates the intended musical process while retaining the basic phasing concept. A one-and-one-half-hour piece for bongo, marimba, glockenspiel, piccolo, and male and female voices, it has four parts, each with differing orchestration. The phasing figure in *Drumming* is the rhythmic pattern cited in figure 14.2. In his program notes, Reich identifies several new techniques utilized in *Drumming*: gradual changes in timbre, the human voice as a matched timbral component of the instrumental ensemble, and alternation of the rhythmic pattern through addition and subtraction of its constructive elements. The underlying phasing process, here enriched by changes to the pattern itself and by timbral variations, still determines the temporal progress of the piece and the program for hearing.

Music for 18 Musicians, a 1976 work for an instrumental ensemble and four women's voices, marks a significant timbral and structural change.[37] Not a phase piece, its process involves cycling through eleven chords. Sections at the beginning and end of the work state the eleven chords in sequence. Extended statements of each chord then serve as the basis for internal sections. In each the marimbas and pianos present a rhythmic "pulsing" version of the chord while the other instruments and voices build "small pieces" over it. The process of this piece occurs over a large temporal scale only, unlike the phase pieces in which it occurs over long and short time scales. This change challenges the concept of listener apprehension of the musical process, especially in the context of the "pieces" built over the pulsing extensions of each of the eleven chords. Reich articulates this change in his aesthetic assumptions and his expectations for listeners in a 1977 interview with Michael Nyman:

> I'm not as concerned that one hears how the music is made as I was in the past. If some people hear exactly what's going on, good for them, and if other people don't, but they still like the piece, then that's OK too. On the other hand, although the overall sound of my music has been getting richer, it has done so without abandoning the ideas that it has to have structure. . . .[38]

Reich abandons his program for hearing the structural processes of the piece but retains the idea of structure, replicating the compositional concerns of those composers who were the focus of his earlier critique.

George Rochberg

In a 1973 article, "The Structure of Time," Rochberg identifies the musical relationships necessary for a music consonant with the disposition of humanity. As Susan Blaustein has observed, Rochberg assumes an essentialist stance toward aesthetic possibility that is grounded in the natural world.[39] For Rochberg, humans are a "biogenetic reflection of nature's urge toward consciousness," and the characteristics of art must be shaped by the limitations set by nature.[40] A music that has the power to "affect us physiologically [and] engage us emotionally and mentally" must be founded on the natural principles of temporality—most notably directionality and causality.[41] Rochberg identifies the constructive units of varying lengths that should be compositionally deployed to assure the qualities of directionality and causality; they include the analytic categories of beat, motive, phrase, section, and overall form and encompass primarily the parameters of pitch (and harmony), rhythm, timbre, dynamics, and texture. In other words, Rochberg identifies paradigmatic structural categories as the basis for the musical qualities that assure effective physiological, emotional, and mental apprehension. As Rochberg identifies them then, the musical structures dictated by Nature are given in the same kind of terms that music analytic practice uses to reveal structural principles of organic unity and systematic coherence—that is in terms that underlie modernist compositional practices.

The reflexivity between the principles of nature Rochberg observes and existing analytic categories of structure that operate within the context of modernist compositional practices also manifests itself in Rochberg's music. That Rochberg composed within a paradigm of organic unity and systematic coherence may be observed not only in his own prose but also in the degree to which his music admits "structural" analysis of the sort emerging in the 1950s and 1960s.[42] For instance, Jay Reise's analysis of Rochberg's Third String Quartet provides evidence for the reflexivity between compositional technique and aesthetic goal. Reise demonstrates a Schoenbergian unity between melodic and intervallic space in the opening of the quartet. The similarity between melodic and harmonic intervals in the quartet's motto gesture which opens and recurs throughout the first movement establishes not only consistency and memorability of musical design but also the more temporally dynamic features of directionality and causality. Figure 14.3, adapted from one of Reise's, depicts intervallic unity in the quartet's motto gesture.

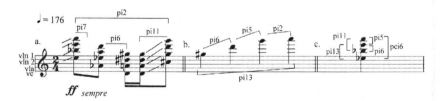

Figure 14.3. Rochberg, String Quartet No. 3. Intervallic unity in the motto gesture. Adapted from Jay Reise, "Rochberg the Progressive," *Perspectives of New Music* 19 (Fall-Winter 1980, Spring-Summer 1981): 398.

Type	A	B	A	B	C	D	C	E	C	E	F	E	F	A
mm.	1	27	40	64	75	81	103	106	109	112	115	118	122	125

Figure 14.4. Rochberg, String Quartet No. 3. Formal recurrences, mm. 1–127. Adapted from Mark Berry, "Music, Postmodernism, and George Rochberg's Third String Quartet," in *Postmodern Music/Postmodern Thought* (New York: Routledge, 2002), p. 242.)

The overtime relations of directionality and causality resist the relatively straightforward kinds of analytic demonstration as the unity of intervallic space, but they may be suggested by observation of overall formal design in the first 127 measures of the quartet. In figure 14.4, based on Mark Berry's analysis of the movement, the schematic depiction of the succession of different formal units during this opening part demonstrates the recurrence of motivic types.[43] The recurrences, which entail a good deal of pitch, rhythmic, and gestural repetition, engender the futural expectations that underlie a temporal directionality. As figure 14.4 suggests, the associations established between recurring musical types give rise to a future-directed sequence of events which over the course of the passage may be interpreted as a causal sequence.

The example only suggests how directionality and causality arise from the web of relations, but the amount of repetition that Rochberg inscribes in the work provides evidence of the kind of assumptions about musical structure that framed his compositional thought in this work. Rochberg's belief that the "central nervous system" of human beings demands musical structures which create the sense of directionality and causality provides the explicit aesthetic basis for his compositional style, but the general outline of the structural model that operates bears a strong similarity to that underlying modernist practices which he criticized. With respect to the issue of hearing structure, however, Rochberg offers a somewhat different model. Rather than assuming that listeners "should" hear the structure inscribed by a composer, he holds up an absolute biological blueprint as the basis for a music structural paradigm: that is, since the "biogenetic" structure of humans dictates what kinds of temporal structures are comprehensible, composers must create within this paradigm of "nature" to assure the "hearability" of their music.[44]

3. A Postmodern Hearing: Associations and Options

Reich's and Rochberg's critiques of a modernist hearing have two results. One is the reconception of the compositional task as the creation of hearable structure, a fine-tuning of the modern program for hearing—not its dismantling. Second is the inclusion of musical features which undermine and refigure the modern program—a refiguring which is an index of the postmodern turn.

Reich retains the assumption that listeners will apprehend structure, but in an act that at once seems superfluous and subversive, he also conceives an ancillary listener function: beyond composer-based intention is the "impersonal, unintended psycho-acoustic by-product of the intended process."[45] This compositional recognition of the agency of the listener and of the indeterminancy of hearing in the context of determinate phasing structures does not fit the modernist program for hearing.[46] Reich gives a concrete example of these "unintended by-products" in the score of *Violin Phase*, in which he composes a sort of "listener part" in one of the violin parts. From the composite of two or three violin parts at specified places in the piece, another live violinist may "pick out alternate resulting patterns which actually exist in the overall combination."[47] At the specified place, the composite pattern and a possible melodic "by-product" are shown in the score in order to exemplify and suggest "musically satisfactory" instances. Figure 14.5 cites one of these passages. The expectation that the listener may "pick out" melodic lines or rhythmic figures implied by the changing musical composites indicates a listener role distinct from that of modernist practice.

The listener Reich articulates in the idea of the "psycho-acoustic by-product" has a degree of agency and as a consequence the musical object, arising through the interaction of sound and hearing, has a degree of indeterminacy from the perspective of apprehension not creation. Listeners may choose to hear melodic or rhythmic patterns as a consequence of their own creative engagements with resultant patterns, and the piece which arises through such engagements has multiple and unpredictable manifestations.[48] This listener

Figure 14.5. Reich, *Violin Phase*. Suggested melodic "by-product" of the melodic composite, m. 11a.

role stands in an uneasy, almost contradictory relation to the listener encompassed by modernist principles. The copresence of both listener roles in Reich's music and thought indicates not so much contradiction as a partial movement away from modernist principles of musical production.[49]

Compositional recognition of listener agency and the correlative indeterminacy of the musical object resonates with ideas that have been characterized as postmodern in the critical literature on cultural change in the mid-1960s and 1970s. Like postmodern approaches to textuality and language which assert a fundamental indeterminacy of meaning, Reich's approach to the musical object assumes an indeterminacy resulting from its enactment by listeners. The two listener roles encompassed by *Violin Phase* mark a change from a modernist to a postmodernist program for hearing.

Rochberg formulates a somewhat more far-reaching version of a postmodern hearing that grows out of his critique of the "scientific temper" of modernist musical practices and his interest in a humanistic music.[50] In fact, the same kind of thinking that grounds a belief in a "biogenetic" blueprint for hearing leads him to human memory and its function in a broad music historical context.

In his 1969 "The Avant-Garde and the Aesthetics of Survival," Rochberg discusses musical structure in relation to "memory functions," showing how musical design "activates memory responses in a listener" through repetition and association at the level of "pitch and/or rhythmic motive" or "large-scale form."[51] While focusing on constructive units such as those operating in the opening of the Third Quartet, Rochberg does articulate a concern for listener apprehension of musical constructs at the phenomenal level of experience; but more significantly, he also amplifies the listener's role through a concept of history. He refutes the modernist aesthetic of originality and the "linear causal progression of human events" it implies and instead bases his aesthetic on a notion of history articulated by Jorge Luís Borges. Borges's understanding of history as "the record of the infinitely varying individual inflections of a universal mind" provides a model for Rochberg in which the musical past may be embraced directly as part of a more comprehensive and inclusive notion of the present.[52] For Rochberg, such a non-teleological sense of history allows the possibility of a music which embodies the "resemblance, replication, and reminiscence" of past music in a continual process of renewal.[53] For the listener, apprehension of a past music in the context of a piece which enacts such renewal "activates memory responses" of a sort different from that occurring at the level of motive and form. In such instances, the past music itself becomes the "subject of the piece" and evocative of associations the listener may make with respect to a passage musically marked as "past." For listeners, a music marked as "past" conjures up a variety of associations through the operation of memory. When a "past" music occurs not simply *as* that music from the past, a whole range of associations will play out for a listener—

only some of which a composer might reasonably assume. Thus, the music itself affords and is premised on listener agency.[54]

The 1965 work for chamber ensemble, *Music for the Magic Theater,* exemplifies Rochberg's compositional figuring of listener agency. The work juxtaposes and combines newly composed and quoted music, and the second movement (or Act) "transcribes" virtually all of the "Adagio" from Mozart's Divertimento K. 287. Figure 14.6 cites a passage from the first

Figure 14.6. Rochberg, *Music for the Magic Theater.* Stylistic allusion and a quick cut (rehearsal nos. 19–20). Copyright © 1972 by Theodore Presser Company. Used by Permission of the Publisher.

movement demonstrating only one of many quick "cuts" in the piece. The listener role implied by this music involves the apprehension not only of musical constructive units at the level of motive and form but also of the associations arising from an individual listener's memory of a past music and from the particular sense a listener will make from the juxtapositions of styles.

As in Reich's case, the listener figured in Rochberg's musical practice has agency which results in a correlative indeterminacy of the musical object—the object no longer simply defined by its structural features. Unlike Reich, however, Rochberg makes the subject of the piece not only the structure in the sense of constructive features but further the stylistic associations with a past music—associations that listeners will realize on an individual basis. This musical and conceptual move more fully connects his music to postmodern thought. Rather than eschewing the past in order to move toward a future, Rochberg embraces the historical past as a recognition of a lived present and this embrace affects his approach to hearing and musical design. In a piece like *Music for the Magic Theater*, references and juxtapositions of music marked as past or present serve as the focus of compositional design, taking on the music structural role. These references and juxtapositions function as units of possible meaning whose significance depends on each listener's particular associations.[55] In this postmodern hearing, listener agency is figured into a concept of musical meaning and the indeterminacy of such meaning enters into compositional design.

4. Concluding Remarks: The Interpretive Turn

The turn away from a modernist and toward a postmodernist program for hearing observable in the middle years of the 1960s entailed a turn from an expectation that listeners should apprehend a composer-intended musical design based in the objectivity of structure or acoustics and toward an expectation that listener agency plays a role in shaping a fundamentally indeterminate musical significance based in listener associations. This turn from musical objectivity and toward listener agency has a parallel in other cultural domains. For instance, writing in 1979 about changes in the social sciences since the early 1960s, Paul Rabinow and William Sullivan identify a similar turn from a structuralist toward an "interpretive or hermeneutic approach to the study of human society."[56] In an introductory essay entitled "The Interpretive Turn" they argue how humanistic studies have repudiated the wish to be "freed" from "passion," the "unconscious," "history," and "tradition through the liberating use of reason" and have embraced instead a new approach that focuses "attention on the concrete varieties of cultural meaning."[57] Instead of assuming that human behavior demonstrates a structure explainable by a rule-based system, such an interpretive approach presumes that meaning is based in the web of cultural understandings that are constituted by subjects in particular historical and social contexts.

Reich's notion of the "psycho-acoustic by-product" of listening and Rochberg's notion of "memory functions" of the listener point toward a similar concept of meaning: musical significance arises for a subject in a particular situation. Compositional conception of the musical object in these instances depends on the essential indeterminacy arising from listener constitution of the musical work,[58] and this figuring of the listener marks the postmodern model for hearing that emerged in the late 60s. The more radical and comprehensive formulation of this program occurs not in Reich's but in Rochberg's musical production, the claims of Reich's revolutionary status notwithstanding. Both composers, however, upheld the structural paradigm that characterized modernist musical practices of both the serial and experimental approaches. Their critique of the program for hearing offered by the composers in both of the approaches led to new compositional designs that refigured the listeners's role, opening the door to a newly conceived postmodern hearing—one that is indeterminate and based in the reflexivity between listener and musical work.

Notes

1. Shortly I will define Babbitt as my exemplar of the "serialists" and Cage of the "experimentalists." But others were essential to defining these two branches of post-World War II modernism: for example, Boulez and Stockhausen for the serialists and Feldman and Brown for the experimentalists.

2. This assertion is typically associated with Milton Babbitt's article, whose provocative title, "Who Cares if You Listen?" has seen all varieties of explanation, apology, and criticism. See Babbitt, "Who Cares if You Listen?" in Contemporary Composers on Contemporary Music, ed. Elliott Schwartz and Barney Childs, 244–50 (New York: Da Capo Press, 1978). The essay was first published in *High Fidelity* 8, no. 2 (Feb. 1958): 38–40, 126–27.

3. I use the term program in the sense of a "program" for a concert or play—a pre-existing plan for the sequence of events, and not in the sense of a specific narrative as is implied by the idea of "program music."

4. I use the term "structural" in its broadest sense, such as "the manner of building, constructing, or organizing" (*Webster's New World Dictionary of the American Language*). Thus, while the experimentalists are not typically identified with "structure" in the same sense as the serialists, their compositional practice did manifest a structural concern in this broadest sense—a point I will argue shortly.

I should also point out a kindred idea from Rose Rosengard Subotnik who writes about the idea of "structural listening" with respect to early twentieth century modernism in her "Toward a Deconstruction of Structural Listening: A Critique of Schoenberg, Adorno, and Stravinsky," in *Explorations in Music, the Arts, and Ideas:*

Essays in Honor of Leonard B. Meyer, ed. Eugene Narmour and Ruth A. Solie, 87–122 (Stuyvesant, N.Y.: Pendragon, 1988). My goal here is not to suggest the limitations of structural listening but rather to demonstrate how such listening is essential to the modernist aesthetic.

5. The assertion of Reich's and Rochberg's music as postmodern needs both scrutiny and qualification. Authors referring to Reich and Rochberg as postmodern include: Jonathan Kramer, "Can Modernism Survive George Rochberg?" *Critical Inquiry* 11, No. 2 (1984): 341–56; and Herman Danuser "Zur Kritik der musikalischen Postmoderne," *Neue Zeitschrift für Musik* 149, no. 12 (1988): 4–9. Some authors conceive of John Cage as "postmodern," largely due to his embrace of "indeterminacy" which has been conceived as a postmodern sign: see Jann Pasler, "Postmodernism, Narrativity, and the Art of Memory," *Contemporary Music Review* 7 (1993): 3–32; and Ihab Hassan, "Toward a Concept of Postmodernism," in *The Postmodern Turn* (Columbus: Ohio State University Press, 1987), 84–96; reprinted in *A Postmodern Reader,* ed. Joseph Natoli and Linda Hutcheon, 273–86 (Albany: SUNY Press, 1993). On the contrary, I consider Cage's music and his larger aesthetic stance as standing clearly within the modernist paradigm.

6. Steve Reich,"Music as Gradual Process (1968)," in his *Writings about Music* (Halifax, Nova Scotia: The Press of the Nova Scotia College of Art and Design, 1974) 10. Robert Morgan has written about the idea of the hidden in his "Secret Languages: The Roots of Musical Modernism," in *Modernism: Challenges and Perspectives* (Urbana: University of Illinois Press, 1986), 33–53.

7. Reich, "Music as Gradual Process (1968)," 9.

8. The terms in quotes occur throughout Rochberg's writings, which have been collected in *The Aesthetics of Survival,* ed. William Bolcom (Ann Arbor: University of Michigan Press, 1984).

9. Rochberg invokes the philosophical ideas of Gottfried Wilhelm Leibniz (1646–1716) who wrote about the "art of combination" as a mode of creativity. Stefan Eckert has explored Leibniz's *ars combinatoria* in the theoretical work of seventeenth-century music theorist Riepel: see Eckert, "Ars Combinatoria, Dialogue Structure, and Musical Practice in Joseph Riepel's *Anfangsgruende zur musicalischen Setzkunst*" (Ph.D. diss., State University of New York at Stony Brook, 2000).

10. John Rockwell, "What's New?" *High Fidelity/Musical America* MA-7 (August 1973): 32. Dean Paul Suzuki gives a good account of both positive and negative reactions to minimalist music generally in his *Minimal Music: Its Evolution As Seen in Works of Philip Glass, Steve Reich, Terry Riley, and La Monte Young* (Ph.D. diss., University of Southern California, 1991).

11. John Rockwell, "What's New?" *High Fidelity/Musical America* MA-10–11 (1974); Jay Reise, "Rochberg the Progressive,"*Perspectives of New Music* 19, no. 2 (1981): 396–407; Michael Linton, Program Notes to *George Rochberg: String Quartets Nos. 3–6,* New World Records 80551–2, 1999.

12. Andrew Porter, "Questions," *Music of Three More Seasons, 1977–80* (New York: Knopf, 1981), 306.

13. Reich, *Writings about Music,* 44.

14. Rochberg's "conversion" to a musical style "steeped in traditional conceptions of causality and directionality" had its catalyst in the death of his son in 1964. Rochberg self-reports this event as the cause of his conversion.

15. Hal Foster, "Postmodernism: A Preface," *The Anti-Aesthetic: Essays on Postmodern Culture* (New York: Free Press, 1998), xii.

16. My position implicitly contradicts that of Jonathan Bernard who, with respect to the music of Philip Glass, claims that it does not invoke "the autonomy of 'modernist' works from earlier in the century." See Bernard, "The Minimalist Aesthetic in the Plastic Arts and in Music," *Perspectives of New Music* 31, no. 1 (Winter 1993): 124. I single out Reich from the other early minimalists—La Monte Young, Terry Riley, and Philip Glass—largely because his musical production and rhetoric demonstrates most distinctly the formalist undercurrents, but these undercurrents are present in the work of these composers as well.

17. One can point to Cage's immersion in Zen practices as a basis for his interest in "selflessness" which in the context of musical sound becomes a concept of sonic objectivity—"sound as sound." Cage's practice of Zen can only offer a partial explanation, however. Since Cage consciously adopted Zen, it makes more sense to explain that adoption by a prior embracing of modernist principles.

18. John Cage, "A History of Experimental Music in the United States" (1959), in *Silence* (Middletown, Conn.: Wesleyan University Press, [1961] 1966), 69.

19. Cage, "Experimental Music: Doctrine" (1955), in *Silence*, 10.

20. Cage, Performance Instructions, *Variations II* (New York: Henmar Press, 1961).

21. Cage, "Experimental Music: Doctrine" (1955), in *Silence*, 13–14.

22. Ibid., 14; italics original.

23. Ibid., 10.

24. Milton Babbitt, "Twelve-Tone Invariants as Compositional Determinants" (1960), in *Problems of Modern Music*, ed. Paul Henry Lang (New York: W.W. Norton, 1962), 108.

25. Babbitt, "Who Cares if You Listen?" 246.

26. Babbitt's point here is not that each piece is a unique representation of the twelve-tone system but rather that the specific structure of a piece's row establishes a unique context that determines musical relationships. Babbitt's position shares some similarities with Cage's indeterminate works in that each composer conceives a musical originality occurring at the level of phenomenal immediacy—in other words, the originality has a transparent aural presence with no prior background system of relationships.

27. Babbitt, "Past and Present Concepts of the Nature and Limits of Music" (1962), reprinted in *Perspectives on Contemporary Music Theory*, ed. Benjamin Boretz and Edward Cone (New York: Norton, 1972), 7.

28. Babbitt, "Twelve-Tone Invariants as Compositional Determinants," 108.

29. Babbitt, "Who Cares if You Listen?" 245.

30. Ibid., 245.

31. Babbitt, "Twelve-Tone Rhythmic Structure and the Electronic Medium" (1962), reprinted in Boretz and Cone, ed., *Perspectives on Contemporary Music Theory*, p.179.

32. Richard Kostelanetz, "Milton Babbitt and John Cage: The Two Extremes of Avant-Garde Music (1967)," in *On Innovative Musicians* (New York: Limelight Editions, 1989), 28.

33. Steve Reich, "Music as Gradual Process," 11. Wim Mertens also takes note of this "objectivity": "American repetitive music is an objective music. . . . The music exists for itself and has nothing to do with the subjectivity of the listener."

Wim Mertens, *American Minimal Music: La Monte Young, Terry Riley, Steve Reich, and Philip Glass,* trans. J. Hautekiet (New York: Alexander Broude, 1983), 90.

34. Reich, "Music as Gradual Process," 10–11.

35. Ibid., 9.

36. These added melodic features are implicated in the ancillary role that Reich articulates. I discuss them more thoroughly at the beginning of Part 3.

37. The instrumentation of *Music for 18 Musicians* is: violin, cello, two clarinets doubling bass clarinet, four women's voices, four pianos, three marimbas, two xylophones and vibraphone (with no motor).

38. Michael Nyman, "Interview with Steve Reich," *Music and Musicians* 25 (January 1977): 18.

39. Susan Blaustein, "The Survival of Aesthetics" (1989), in *Perspectives on Musical Aesthetics,* ed. John Rah (New York: Norton, 1994), 347.

40. Rochberg, "Reflections on the Renewal of Music," in *Aesthetics of Survival,* 235.

41. Rochberg, "The Structure of Time in Music," in *Aesthetics of Survival,* 142.

42. Analysis premised on the existence of organic unity and systematic coherence is typically associated with Schenkerian or "linear" theory and set-theory.

43. Mark Berry, "Music, Postmodernism, and George Rochberg's Third String Quartet," in *Postmodern Music/Postmodern Thought,* ed. Judy Lochhead and Joseph Auner (New York: Routledge, 2002), 242.

44. This position is similar to that espoused by the generative theory of Fred Lerdahl and Ray Jackendoff: see their *A Generative Theory of Tonal Music* (Cambridge, Mass.: MIT Press, 1985). Their work is itself based on the generative linguistics of Noam Chomsky. Recent critique of generative linguistics has called into question some of its biological assumptions. See John Searle, "End of the Revolution" (Review of Chomsky's *New Horizons in the Study of Language and Mind*), *The New York Review of Books,* 49, no. 3 (February 28, 2002).

45. Reich, "Music as Gradual Process," 10.

46. I use the term indeterminacy not in the sense of Cage's "indeterminate" pieces (such as *Variations II* and *Cartridge Music*) but rather in the sense in which it has been used in postmodern or post-structuralist philosophy. For instance, linguistic and conceptual meaning has been theorized as indeterminate—as ultimately non-specifiable in any determinate or universal sense.

47. Reich, Performance Instructions, *Violin Phase*: For Violin and Pre-Recorded Tape or Four Violins (Universal Editions 161851, 1967), iii.

48. Further, the score can no longer serve as representation of the piece as sounding structure. Its function as performance instruction dominates in these instances.

49. Mertens implies the contradiction of the two listener roles by noting that "the listener no longer perceives a finished work but actively participates in its construction" while at the same time asserting that the listeners have been "reduced to a passive role, merely submitting to the process." See Mertens, *American Minimal Music,* 90. Bernard, noting the contradiction implied by Mertens's characterization, understands it as paradoxical and ultimately as a flaw: "By making 'perception' the bottom line, minimal music also reduces the demands made upon the listener." (Bernard, "The Minimalist Aesthetic in the Plastic Arts and in Music," 124.) His criticism is predicated, however, on a modernist hearing in which composer-intended structure sets the program for hearing.

50. George Rochberg, "In Search of Music" (1964), in *The Aesthetics of Survival*, 153.

51. Rochberg, "The Avant-Garde and the Aesthetics of Survival," 224.

52. Rochberg, "Reflections on the Renewal of Music," in *The Aesthetics of Survival*, 232–33.

53. Ibid., 233.

54. This notion of listener agency resonates with that of reader agency that arose with reader response theory in literary theory of the 1970s. As proposed by a number of different authors, the literary work is defined as a "dialogue" between reader and text. See Susan R. Suleiman and Inge Crosman, *The Reader in the Text: Essays on Audience and Interpretation* (Princeton, N.J.: Princeton University Press, 1980) for a collection of representative articles and an astute introduction to the topic by Suleiman.

55. Hal Foster's category of a "postmodernism of reaction" that seeks to "repudiate" the modern in order to celebrate the "status quo" at first seems to apply to the case of Rochberg . (See note 15 above.) But if the listener is taken as the index of cultural orientation, then Rochberg's program for hearing differs significantly from that of the modern program. Rather than eschewing the past in order to move toward a future, Rochberg embraces the historical past as a recognition of a lived present and this embrace affects his approach to hearing and musical design.

56. Paul Rabinow and William M. Sullivan, "The Interpretive Turn: Emergence of an Approach," in *Interpretive Social Science: A Reader*, ed. Paul Rabinow and William M. Sullivan (Berkeley, Los Angeles, and London: University of California Press, 1979), 1.

57. Ibid., 1, 4.

58. It is important to remember here that the indeterminacy involved in Cage's music of the 1960s is composition-based, not listener-based. This distinction is one of the markers between modernist and post-modernist practices.

15

Modernism Goes to the Movies

ARVED ASHBY

Atonality has died and gone to the movies. In America, at least, you are not likely to encounter dissonant, disjunct music in the concert hall, but you may hear painfully amplified homages to Berg, Schoenberg, and Webern blaring away during battle footage, car chases, unfriendly alien encounters, and psychotic flashes, a "gebrauchsmusik" role for discord that Schoenberg predicted in his imaginary film music, Begleitmusik *of 1930.*
—David Schiff, *Times Literary Supplement*, 1999

To the extent that the motion picture in its sensationalism is the heir of the popular horror story and dime novel and remains below the established standards of middle-class art, it is in a position to shatter those standards, precisely through the use of sensation. . . . The fear expressed in the disso-nances of Schönberg's most radical period far surpasses the measure of fear conceivable to the average middle-class individual; it is a historical fear, a fear of impending doom. . . . Naturally the extension of th[e] expressive potentiali-ties [of the new musical resources] is applicable not only to the realm of fear and horror; in the opposite direction, too, that of extreme tenderness, ironic detachment, empty waiting, and unfettered power, the new musical resources can explore fields inaccessible to traditional resources because these latter present themselves as something that has always been known, and therefore are deprived in advance of the power to express the unfamiliar and unex-plored.
—Hanns Eisler and T. W. Adorno, *Composing for the Films*, 1947

In discussing human learning and cognition, recent evolutionary biologists and cultural anthropologists have emphasized the importance of a cumula-tive and collective form of experience they call cultural transmission or "cultural inheritance."[1] Their discussions tend to focus on socially con-structed systems like tools and language. But these so-called sociogenetic factors must also be important in aesthetics and the psychosocial connota-tions of musical gesture, which—as kinds of cognition less inbred than they are instilled through culture—depend likewise on a person modeling his or her behavior on that of others. Psychologists and cognitionists use the term *attitude formation* for this process of learned emotional reactions involving unconscious generalization between two stimuli.[2] In this essay, I explore one particularly powerful means of cultural transmission through which attitudes to modern music have been learned and perpetuated. I am not speaking of the classroom, where aesthetics are minimally transmitted, least of all in classes that take aesthetics as their subject. Still less do I have in mind the concert hall, where aesthetics are not debated but taken as a *fait accompli* before the ostensibly neutral act of playing the music. I am speaking instead of film, a powerful aesthetic forum where reactions to musical styles are learned and passed on, and sometimes rejected.

Perhaps "forum" is not quite the right description. The film theater is less an auditorium than an enlarged Skinner box: the moviegoer is isolated in a controlled environment, where he or she receives pleasure and pain through different senses according to the calculations of director, film composer, editor, and cinematographer. Something like a set of collective aesthetics is laid out, enforced, and reinforced through punishment and reward. (The Skinner box analogy may fail to apply in that systems of aesthetics are more complex than laboratory conditioning, but the two systems differ perhaps more in degree than in kind.) With such means at their disposal, film and the theater are uniquely situated to capitalize upon music's power as, to quote Nicholas Cook, "a bundle of generic attributes in search of an object . . . [or] a structured semantic space, a privileged site for the negotiation of meaning."[3] According to Cook, music proves such a powerful and evocative semantic space that "[p]ure music, it seems, is an aesthetician's (and music theorist's) fiction; the real thing unites itself promiscuously with any other media that are available."[4]

Hollywood film has taken to modernist musical languages with special and unexpected promiscuity. And in doing so, it has created an audience for just the kinds of musical sounds, structures, and gestures that are supposedly alienating in the concert hall. (Among the music I will discuss are Penderecki's *Threnody to the Victims of Hiroshima* and Bernard Herrmann's celebrated music for the shower scene in Hitchcock's *Psycho,* two scores that are as musically similar as their reception histories have been dissimilar.) Both formalists and post-structuralists neglect this popular-culture legacy when they claim modernist music has taken on no meaning apart from compositional-structural meaning. In saying that modernist gestures have indeed taken on *acquired* meaning—or, as Jean Molino and Jean-Jacques Nattiez might describe it, "esthesic" rather than "poietic" meaning[5]—I acknowledge the power the mass media have on the inner sancta where we confer aesthetic value.

With his notion of "agit-cinema," the genre he saw all film aspiring to, Sergei Eisenstein understood the theater as just such a public Skinner box for attitude formation. Indeed, in this type of cinema the aesthetic experience becomes synonymous with attitude-formation or conditioning. In Eisenstein's view, film acts as a kind of conditioning-chain, and therein lies its power as well as its pleasure: "The method of agitation through spectacle consists in the creation of a new chain of conditioned reflexes by associating selected phenomena with the unconditioned reflexes they produce (through the appropriate methods). . . . Bearing this basic situation in mind we should handle the question of played films with great care: they wield such enormous influence that we cannot ignore them."[6] Staged theater, once it has caught sight of this *Gesamtkunstwerk* conditioning-chain, aspires to film rather than the other way around:

> Theater's basic material derives from the audience: the molding of the audience in a desired direction (or mood) is the task of every utilitarian theatre (agitation, advertising, health education, etc.). The instrument of this process consists of all the parts that constitute the apparatus of theatre (Ostuzhev's "chatter" no more than the color of the prima donna's tights, a roll on the drums just as much as Romeo's soliloquy, the cricket on the hearth no less than a salvo under the seats of the auditorium) because, despire their differences, they all lead to one thing— which their presence legitimates—to their common quality of *attraction.*
>
> An attraction (in our diagnosis of theatre) is any aggressive moment in theatre, i.e. any element of it that subjects the audience to emotional or psychological influence, verified by experience and mathematically calculated to produce specific emotional shocks in the spectator in their proper order within the whole. These shocks provide the only opportunity of perceiving the ideological aspect of what is being shown, the final ideological conclusion. (The path to knowledge encapsulated in the phrase, "through the living play of the passions," is specific to theatre.)[7]

In the case of film and popular culture, it needs to be said that the set of aesthetics (or the ideology, to use Eisenstein's word) that theater instills is usually not the filmmakers', but a cumulative set of values: the associations made owe less to the filmmakers' whim than to a larger cultural inheritance propagated through film. In his book *The Cultural Origins of Human Cognition,* Michael Tomasello describes cumulative cultural evolution as a selective process.[8] In his account, the "artifact with accumulating modifications" is modified in each successive instance through individual or collaborative effort, and then passed on through cultural learning to the next generation and their own modifications. Tomasello applies his model to the example of tools. But, in the sense that a glissando or certain kind of dissonance serves the filmmaker as a topos or code or affective tool, Tomasello's model also applies to those musical elements as they enter a film and then through that film make their way into filmmakers' and film composers' parlance more generally.

In addition to reconsidering it as a Skinner box, we could also think of the film theater as a classroom for the very aspects of knowledge and experience that academia and academic discourse have not, until recently, acknowledged. I think it indisputable that film has created a larger,

348 *Belated Modernism*

perpetuating culture around modernist musical gestures and topoi, if not around the works themselves, and it has thereby succeeded where academia has failed. In his 1962 essay "Education on the Nonverbal Level," Aldous Huxley faulted academia for its insistence on the symbolic and the verbal when Western humankind is "multiply amphibious." In other words, the human mind simultaneously inhabits verbal and nonverbal worlds:

> He is at once an animal and a rational intellect; a product of evolution closely related to the apes and a spirit capable of self-transcendence; a sentient being in contact with the brute data of his own nervous system and the physical environment and at the same time the creator of a home-made universe of words and other symbols, in which he lives and moves and has anything from thirty to eighty percent of his being . . . Our amphibiousness is clearly illustrated in the two modes of our awareness of external events. There is a receptive, more or less unconceptualized, aesthetic and "spiritual" mode of perceiving; and there is also a highly conceptualized, stereotyped, utilitarian, and even scientific mode.[9]

According to Huxley, academia and academic discussion have failed to promote and guide the first of these two modes of awareness. Following a similar argument, William Arrowsmith nominated film as the perfect medium for forming and educating—or perhaps conditioning?—people on such an unconceptualized and aesthetic level. In his 1969 essay "Film as Educator," Arrowsmith spoke of "the enormous promise of film" as it stems from an "openness and exemption from the self-consciousness of 'high' culture. . . . [T]he unique situation of film is surely that it comes to us, not as a part of our educationally acquired 'high' culture, but as part of the common culture itself."[10] The mass media and relative concepts of "high" and "popular" art have undergone seismic changes over the past thirty years; and it would be hard to claim nowadays, as Arrowsmith did back then, that most of the "non-expert's" true musical experiences are accompanied by unspoken feelings of fear and inferiority. Still, many of his points remain valid:

> Film itself may be highly self-conscious, but it is surely unique in possessing audiences who take it naturally, who attend to it without fuss or pretense or shame; who for the most part trust its makers and feel unmistakably at ease with its conventions. People go to movies as they go to take a bath or a stroll. . . . By comparison, audiences for poetry, drama, or [concert] music are notoriously unsure, inclined either to dogmatic arrogance or deferential ignorance. The fear of the expert—the academic expert above all—hovers over them.[11]

As Arrowsmith averred, film affects viewers more on non-conceptual levels than on conceptual ones. Because of its short history, means of dissemination, and connections with popular culture, it has become the least academic of art forms. Indeed, this non-conceptuality and non-academicism are the very reasons film has become, at the level of aesthetics and

association, one of the most powerful vehicles—perhaps *the* most powerful vehicle—for meaning in our time. Just as the novel was the prime influence on nineteenth-century ontologies, ours is a video age.

1. Coding and Re-coding Modernist Sounds: *Psycho* and Penderecki

Just what are the non-expert, sociogenetic, or aesthetic connections that are
made in film? Film scholar Claudia Gorbman has one kind of institutionalized film culture in mind when she discusses "cultural musical codes," "cinematic musical codes," and "pure musical codes." By "cultural musical codes"
she refers to such viewer and listener essentialisms as "jazziness = sleaziness,
cheapness, drunkenness" or "Bach fugue = culture, dignity." Her "cinematic
musical codes" are connections the viewer makes according to the structural,
traditional role the music plays in the narrative and structure of the film. The
"pure musical codes" she proposes are carried by the musical structure and
style themselves, independent of any interaction with the visuals.[12]

Searching for an archetypal example of Gorbman's "cultural musical
codes," we could well settle on one of the more notorious comings-to-
gether of sound and film imagery: Bernard Herrmann's famous cue ("The
Murder," figure 15.1) for the scene in Alfred Hitchcock's *Psycho* where
Marion Crane (Janet Leigh) meets a brutal end in a shower at the Bates

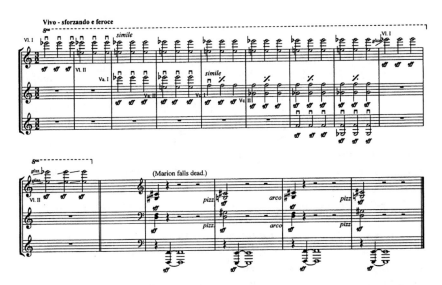

Figure 15.1. *Psycho.* "The Murder," mm. 1–15. From the Paramount Picture
PSYCHO. Music by Bernard Herrmann. Copyright © 1960, 1961 (Renewed 1987,
1988) by Ensign Music Corporation. International Copyright Secured, All Rights
Reserved. Used by permission.

Motel. The chain of musical events is easily recounted: Herrmann's first violins come in on a high E-flat (marked *molto sforzando e feroce*), and then the second violins, violas, cellos, and basses enter on successive lower sevenths (on E-natural, F, F-sharp, and G). The whole series is then repeated, only with the instruments now reaching the notes through split-second upward glissandos. But just what specific aspects of these sounds are coded with which extramusical reactions? A search for "cultural musical codes" would likely focus on pitch, and we can certainly say that Herrmann codes murder as dissonant: by the eighth bar, the composite six-pitch sonority includes two trichord-clusters, centered on A and on F. But if we take the famous "Murder" cue as a reference, a quintessentialization of horror in music, just *how* dissonant is murderousness? This pitch-class collection is not exceptionally unstable or chromatic in and of itself, and so the cue demonstrates that pitch and interval-classes are not the whole story. More important than dissonance per se is the voicing: the intervals are largely sounded as sevenths rather than seconds, and these gaping holes in the voicing are a large part of the horror. Indeed, the vertical diminished octave in m. 2, produced when the second violins enter, is the most devastating event in the whole passage. We should also look at Herrmann's rhythm. These savage downbow strokes give a glimpse into the animalistic impulse of the homicidal brain; this musically enacts an action utterly without thought, muscular contractions beholden to no moral or purpose. Without the terrifyingly single-minded half-note obsessiveness, more a denial than an affirmation of rhythm, the pitch instabilities would come across as far less "murderous." This deprivation is all the more extraordinary after the rhythmic variety and acuity of the rest of the *Psycho* score.

To judge from this key example, then, there is no exclusive, direct, or proportional relation between dissonance and murderousness. It would be better to say that Herrmann provided later composers with a particular aural *Gestalt,* to return to Tomasello: in *Psycho* he codes violent death as dissonant, texturally irregular, harsh in timbre, and rhythmically redundant.[13] Avenues of meaning are two-way streets, and just as the meanings an image is imbued with will spill over into the sound that accompanies the image, the reverse is also true. Because of their collusion into a kind of brilliant synesthesic experience, the sound and the image merge to the point where one inevitably carries the other with it. Any meaning that Hitchcock and Herrmann conferred here has at some level (more unconsciously than consciously, as per the cultural inheritance idea) become part and parcel of the meaning of all repetitious *sforzatissimo* strokes in the higher range of doubled violins. Likewise, shower-taking comes to carry with it (again, at an unconscious level) the hearing of glissandos in high and doubled violins, though perhaps less consistently than the reverse because taking a shower leaves a less precise—more "variable-ridden"—sensory fingerprint than the experience of hearing high violin glissandos in simplistic rhythms.

Judging from this example, only a certain kind of modernist music is coded as horrific and murderous, and such morbid images denote only certain subsets of twentieth-century modernism. Herrmann's particular combination of discord, primal rhythms, and absence of any recognizable voice-leading principles (at least before the "Marion falls dead" passage) is not to be heard in much of the "modern" twentieth-century repertory: neither Schoenberg nor Webern, for example, produced anything really like this. While the repetition and rhythmic simplicity of Herrmann's cue help us code it as "murderous," they also prevent the passage from sounding "modernist" in any Darmstadtian (Boulezian, Stockhausenian) sense: Nor can we really hear much of the Bates Motel in Berio, Carter, Babbitt, Ruth Crawford, Henze, or Rihm. Among the composers who might be more effective in a Hitchcock soundtrack are Xenakis, Birtwistle, and early Nono. The only similar passages in the central modernist repertory are the famous chord repetitions that open the "Glorification of the Chosen One" in Stravinsky's *Sacre du Printemps,* and the "Invention on a Note" that accompanies Marie's murder in Berg's *Wozzeck*: two stage works with their own murderous scenarios.

Some later composers, the ones practicing what I call "phantasmagoric" modernism (see below), more explicitly follow up on Herrmann-type codings and invoke dissonance and harsh timbres as accessories to murder. Early Penderecki is an example, and the opening of his *Threnody to the Victims of Hiroshima (Tren Ofiarom Hiroszimy)* is exceptionally similar to Herrmann's "murder" cue (see figure 15.2). (I am not implying a direct connection between the composers, since the two scores were written at the same time: Penderecki began his composition in 1959 and finished it in 1961, while Herrmann wrote his score between February and March of 1960.) The Penderecki is even as arrhythmic as the Herrmann, though the two contrast in their actual surface rhythms. Penderecki's title acknowledges the "filmic" aspect of *Threnody*'s modernism, and completes the equation of these musical characteristics with murder and vice-versa.[14] His inscription—and thereby also the imagery of charred flesh and radiation sickness—was the result of standing back to ponder while the piece of music functioned as the film does for the film composer: as the point of inspiration for a creative act. For Penderecki originally titled the work *8'37"* according to its timing—that title was a Cagean gesture by the composer's own admission, and presumably the composer also thought his music "contentless" and non-referential in a quasi-Cagean fashion. Penderecki only later concluded that the expressive power of this piece required a very different title: "[I]t existed only in my imagination, in a somewhat abstract way. When Jan Krenz recorded it and I could listen to an actual performance, I was struck with the emotional charge of the work. I though it would be a waste to condemn it to such anonymity, to those 'digits.' I searched for associations and, in the end, I decided to dedicate it to the Hiroshima victims."[15]

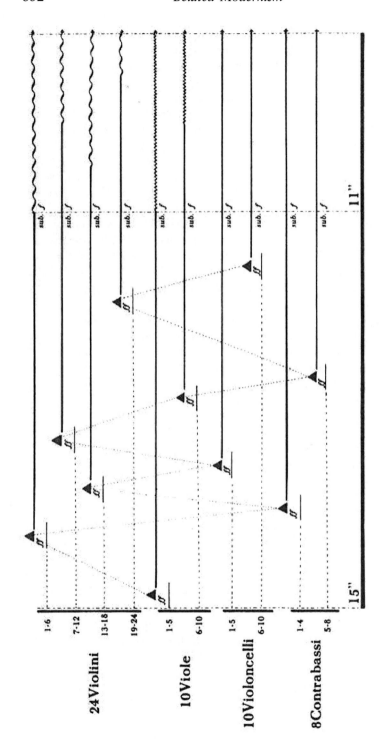

Figure 15.2. Penderecki, *Threnody to the Victims of Hiroshima*. First 26 seconds. Copyright © 1961 (Renewed) EMI Deshon Music, Inc. and PWM Editions. Warner Bros. Publications U.S., Inc., Miami, FL 33014. All Rights Reserved. Used by Permission.

Despite the fact that the title followed completion of the actual composition, associations between nuclear devastation and Penderecki's encyclopedic variety of avant-garde playing techniques (see figure 15.3) prove impossible to shake, much as the unmistakable cognitive thumbprint of Herrmann's *molto sforzando e feroce* violins will forever suggest to a viewer who has seen Hitchcock's *Psycho* sensations of a wet and bloody death. Penderecki's abandonment of definite pitch is similar in effect to Herrmann's quick glissandos to high string registers. Penderecki divides his fifty-two strings into ten parts and these enter—in staggered and canonic fashion, as in the Herrmann—*fortissimo* and at "the highest note of instrument (no definite pitch)."

Penderecki's titling of his composition was truly inspired and the major point of creativity here: for it is really this post-compositional act that was the act of genius, the act that defined the piece and ensured its legacy, and the work could hardly have had such a celebrated public career under its original title. (The orchestral piece *Fluorescences,* written a year after *Threnody,* has not enjoyed similar notoriety.) In this way, the piece owes more to the referential, "inspired," romantic imagination than it does the formalist, avant-garde imagination that purports to be concerned only with sounds—which is to say that *Threnody* is, for all intents and purposes, a romantic piece. Likewise, Penderecki's actual arrangement of notes on the page into a sequence of purely musical events—regardless of titles, original and otherwise—undoubtedly owes something to film and film music. I think specifically of the density of event toward the middle of the piece, where Penderecki divides the strings into twenty-four lines filled with independent *arco, pizzicato,* and *battuto* events—the kind of intentionally opaque cognitive density that seems more visual than innately "musical." Like theater, like film, this music is—despite, or perhaps because of, the aural terrorism at its surface—preoccupied with evocative effect and specificity of impression. If I call this a filmic kind of modernism, that is not meant to impugn music and composer so much as say that Penderecki only acknowledged obvious and inevitable changes in what musical modernism had become by the 1960s. For what cognitive-cultural revolution occurred between Schoenberg and Penderecki? The answer: sound film and its dissemination through the omnipresence of television. Penderecki's *Threnody,* or more specifically his act of titling this composition, shows a composer vicariously learning generalizations between visual and musical stimuli through the medium of film.

2. Modernist Non-Structure: Ligeti and Kubrick's *2001: A Space Odyssey*

We turn now from questions of dissonance and coding to the more complex implications of musical structure and syntax. These are more impor-

Abkürzungen und Symbole
Abbreviations and symbols

Erhöhung um einen Viertelton sharpen a quarter-tone	†
Erhöhung um einen Dreiviertelton sharpen three quarter-tones	‡
Erniedrigung um einen Viertelton flatten a quarter-tone	♭
Erniedrigung um einen Dreiviertelton flatten three quarter-tones	⊲
höchster Ton des Instrumentes (unbestimmte Tonhöhe) highest note of the instrument (no definite pitch)	↟
zwischen Steg und Saitenhalter spielen play between bridge and tailpiece	↑
Arpeggio zwischen Steg und Saitenhalter (4 Saiten) arpeggio on 4 strings behind the bridge	▥
auf dem Saitenhalter spielen (arco), Bogenstrich über den Saiten- halter (in einem Winkel von 90° zu dessen Längsachse) play on the tailpiece (arco) by bowing the tailpiece at an angle of 90° to its longer axis	⊤
auf dem Steg spielen (arco), Bogenstrich über das Holz des Steges senkrecht zu dessen rechter Schmalseite play on the bridge by bowing the wood of the bridge at a right angle at its right side	↑
Schlagzeugeffekt: mit dem Frosch oder mit der Fingerspitze auf die Decke klopfen Percussion effect: strike the upper sounding board of the violin with the nut or the finger-tips	⨍
mehrere unregelmäßige Bogenwechsel several irregular changes of bow	⊓∨
molto vibrato	∿∿
sehr langsames Vibrato mit ¼ Ton-Frequenzdifferenz durch Fingerverschiebung very slow vibrato with a ¼ tone frequency difference produced by sliding the finger	∿
sehr schnelles, nicht rhythmisiertes Tremolo very rapid non rhythmisized tremolo	ⵝ
ordinario	ord.
sul ponticello	s. p.
sul tasto	s. t.
col legno	c. l.
legno battuto	l. batt.

Figure 15.3. Penderecki, *Threnody to the Victims of Hiroshima.* Table of playing techniques. Copyright © 1961 (Renewed) EMI Deshon Music, Inc., and PWM Editions. Warner Bros. Publications U.S., Inc., Miami, FL 33014. All Rights Reserved. Used by Permission.

tant issues, for it is surely the defining aspects of modernist music, the ones responsible for its very openness as a semantic space, that have allowed modernist gestures and syntax to take on their special powers, at least in popular culture: primary among them what Lerdahl and Jackendoff call the non-hierarchical nature of atonal music, the listener's difficulty of assigning "rich structure" to music written with serial, aleatoric, and probabilistic techniques; or what Babbitt has called the "contextuality" as opposed to "communality" of post-tonal music.[16] If room is made for culture in the composer-text-listener equation, the modernist work's cognitive drawbacks become its assets. Taken in the context of film, Lerdahl's hypothesized impediments to "accessibility," ideas formulated on the basis of "detailed attention on the facts of hearing," turn out to be positive boons to their power of evocation and effect: modernist music becomes a kind of Rorschach test.[17]

I have shown how Gorbman's "cultural musical codes" might apply, if heavily nuanced, to Herrmann and Hitchcock (as well as to Penderecki). By contrast, Stanley Kubrick's film style is recognizable by its avoidance of coding: he habitually disclaims familiar narratives and stock associations between emotions, music, and visual images. (I say he disclaimed rather than subverted them, since someone who subverts acknowledges the thing subverted.) If he had filmed Janet Leigh in her fateful shower, he would doubtless have left us far more ambivalent in our responses: Was her death really murder? Did she really die? If it was murder, what was the motive? And these dramatic and visual ambiguities in Kubrick's style have large implications for his choices of music. Kubrick, insofar as he was allergic to cinematic convention, worked to repudiate Gorbman's "cultural musical codes." It thereby becomes all the more difficult to ferret out the meanings he conferred upon the music he uses. (It should be said that subversion and ambiguity do not entail *absence* of meaning. Erwin Panofsky made the statement, even truer now than when he penned it some seven decades ago, that "that which we hear remains, for good or worse, inextricably fused with that which we see."[18] As a corollary to this statement, any musical passage linked with an image must have some association or implication; in short, any moment in any soundtrack must mean something.)

Kubrick's unusual manipulations of visual and auditory meanings became even more complex when he used pre-existing music. *Dr. Strangelove,* Kubrick's black comedy of nuclear apocalypse, gives a sample with its lush but somehow non-ironic arrangements of "Try a Little Tenderness" and "We'll Meet Again." Kubrick's linking Rossini with sex in *A Clockwork Orange* also shows the difficulties of tracing any Kubrickian semiotics between music, visuals, and aesthetics. At one level, the overture to *William Tell* might acknowledge the time-honored genre of porn soundtracks, with their repetitiveness and rhythmic banality. But the additional cultural connotations of galloping horses, Carl Stalling's Looney Tunes cartoon arrangements, and virtuosic orchestration made the equation too complex for later filmmakers to develop. Perhaps he is portraying sex as comic, but any possibility for amusement vanishes with the speeding-up of the film, and such a signification would contradict the sinister implications of sex elsewhere in the movie. And so we come to my chosen example: Kubrick's wonderfully ambiguous use of Ligeti in *2001: A Space Odyssey* is an epochal union, perhaps the most influential bringing-together of film and modernist music, and it will point out some inadequacies in Gorbman's music-film semiotics.

According to Gorbman, classic non-diegetic film music functions to create a certain "bath" or "gel of affect." Film music of such a kind "is like easy-listening, or the hypnotist's voice, in that it rounds off the sharp edges, masks contradictions, and lessens spatial and temporal discontinuities with its own melodic and harmonic continuity. It lessens awareness of the frame; it relaxes the censor, drawing the spectator further into the fantasy-illusion suggested by filmic narration."[19] Familiarity of style, in other words, serves the sense of filmic continuity that is necessary to the fantasy and narrative element of most movies. To function thus, the music must be in an immediately recognizable lingua franca: "A musical idiom must be thoroughly familiar, its connotations virtually reflexive knowledge, for it to serve 'correctly,' invisibly, in classical filmic discourse."[20] Here I imagine Gorbman is thinking of the institutionalized film styles of Max Steiner, John Williams, or Henry Mancini, who was called in by studio executives to re-score Orson Welles's *Touch of Evil* and thereby give it some of the narrative continuity that the great director had been so insolent as to neglect.

Music that is unfamiliar and fails in this function undermines continuity, thereby becoming referential and taking on particular powers of evocation: "music that is noticed, which calls attention to itself, swings away from the imaginary toward the symbolic." Here Gorbman's imaginary-vs.-referential duality matches dualities drawn up by various music cognitionists and theorists, and taken together these suggest a meta-model for the affective and modal differences between modernist and "non-modernist" musics—whether heard in the movie theater or the concert hall. In each of these parallel models, accepted ideas of what Gorbman calls "classical filmic discourse" are confronted by collisions with or escapes from that discourse.[21] Eisler used similar terms in 1947 when he described the ways "the new musical resources" could be useful in film: not because of the increased dissonance per se, but by virtue of their "dissolution of the conventionalized musical idiom" and obstruction of "the institutionalized flow of musical language."[22] Michel Chion describes a similar dichotomy between "internal logic" and "external logic," the first characterized by organicism and continuity and the second by discontinuity and rupturedness. Music semiotician Eero Tarasti, citing a similar duality to the "structure" vs. "idiostructure" opposition described by Eugene Narmour, speaks of a di-

chotomy between "communication" and "signification": the former process encompasses those stylistic structures whereby the composer
"function[s] exclusively according to the ideological and technological
models of the time," and the latter, the locus of aesthetic value, represents
the freer creative space where the composer can escape a certain kind of
socialized speech "and thereby produce some unique signification."[23] In
the writings of Babbitt and Lerdahl, this duality more explicitly approaches
ideas of modern-vs.-non-modern musicality. For Babbitt, contextual music
is music that represents what Tarasti calls "unique signification," while
music marked by communality is music that operates within conventional
and generic structures.

If an unfamiliar musical style proves particularly evocative in film, common practice tonal structures also tend to contradict typical film narratives. Lerdahl and Jackendoff provide with their quasi-Schenkerian tree
diagrams a useful visual representation of the most communicative or com-
munal musical structure imaginable, and the one thereby most resistant to
film. And this analytical perspective helps us understand just how Gorbman's
traditional film composer, the one creating the "bath" or "gel of affect," is
constrained in his or her ability to give the (presumably) tonal music a
hierarchical tonal structure of any size. Lerdahl and Jackendoff describe
the functioning tonal work as an inter-nested pattern of harmonically based
tensing and relaxing that tends to fall into a "normative prolongational
structure," and they offer a series of chords freely based on Schubert's Lied
"Morgengruß" as a miniature paradigm for such structures (see figure 15.4).
Increasing harmonic tension is shown here by a continuing and unbisected

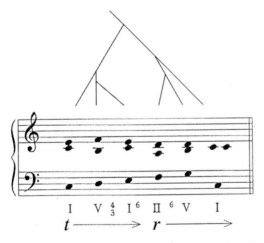

Figure 15.4. Harmonic tension and relaxation in a normal prolongational structure. From Lerdahl and Jackendoff, *A Generative Theory of Tonal Music* (Cambridge, Mass., and London: MIT Press, 1983), p. 195. Used by permission.

line, as traced out in the first half of the example, while increased relaxation (with each chord functionally "subservient" to the next) is shown by the increasing angles of the second half. The example provides in miniature a visualization of the way that a tonal phrase or piece will usually begin in repose, build toward increasing tension, and then relax into a resolving cadence. The minimal branching in the example substantiates the aesthetic impressions of balance and closure given by the progression.

Like a Schenker graph, Lerdahl and Jackendoff's diagram clarifies the point that Western tonal structures tend to be organized around a pattern of (1) a first pitch that leads into a half-pattern of increasing tension and (2) a half-pattern of increasing relaxation that leads to a final sonority, followed perhaps by some prolongation. The diagram also thereby helps visualize the hierarchical structuredness that would make it difficult to pair a pre-existing "normative" piece marked by communicative tonal patterning with an independently produced span of film. Cook analyzes one such pairing, a car commercial that uses the opening of Mozart's overture to *Le Nozze di Figaro,* and finds the producer extending several rests in order to make Mozart's structure fit his or her own.[24] By contrast, Lerdahl and Jackendoff offer three hypothetical—or perhaps incompetently composed—situations that are not marked by balance and closure (see figures 15.5a, 5b, and 5c). Of these three, the first (figure 15.5a) traces uniform and unchanging motion into relaxation, the second (figure 15.5b) an anomalous form of steadily increasing tension, and the third (figure 15.5c) a kind of

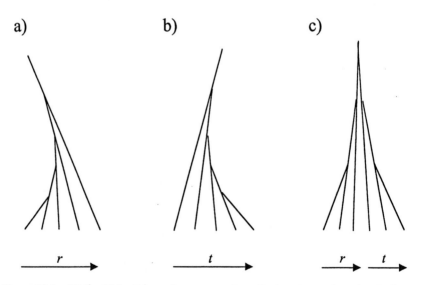

a)   b)   c)

Figure 15.5a, 15.5b, 15.5c. Schematic representation of relaxation and tension in three "non-forms." From Lerdahl and Jackendoff, *A Generative Theory of Tonal Music* (Cambridge, Mass., and London: MIT Press, 1983), p. 198. Used by permission.

inside-out structure that starts with relaxation and ends with increasing tension (compare figure 15.5c with figure 15.4). Tarasti describes significative structures as highly open to narrative interpretation; and Lerdahl and Jackendoff's three imbalanced and non-closed examples, which they describe as having an "open-ended effect" and demonstrating "possibilities uncharacteristic of Western tonality," would certainly qualify.[25]

The three musical "pieces" represented would also suit a film director's wishes and wiles much more than the normative/communicative/hierarchical ones; these could even serve as recipes for writing richly significative, film-friendly music. By virtue of their maximal branching and open-endedness, the first two of these "non-forms" (as I choose to call them) would be infinitely expandable and cuttable, and would thereby be very adaptable when it came to editing. Though not a true example of the increasing-relaxation non-form they discuss (as modeled in figure 15.5a), Bach's Prelude in C Major from Book One of the *Well-Tempered Clavier* gives some idea of how such a piece could sound. The anomalous aspects of this sequence- and suspension-laden piece (see figure 15.6) are its extraordinarily uniform rhythmic and harmonic surface, which in Lerdahl and Jackendoff's words "yields an unusual paucity of evidence for the grouping and metrical analyses."[26] The piece thereby comes close to the uniform and non-hierarchical—slippery—surface that the authors attribute to works written using serial or aleatoric methods. Bach's prolongational structure also turns out to be unusually—yet elegantly—regular, with every harmonic event except the opening tonic chord subsumable into a unit of harmonic prolongation. Moreover, the predominance of left-branching progressions indicates that the piece contains an unusual ratio of local relaxing-patterns—at the middle-ground level, it seems to be constantly and continually resolving.

I offer Kubrick's use of Ligeti's micropolyphonic music in a particular scene in *2001: A Space Odyssey* (1968) as an example of Lerdahl and Jackendoff's third, relaxation-tension non-form (as modeled in figure 15.5c). Kubrick used Ligeti's a cappella choral work *Lux aeterna* and the Kyrie from his Requiem in the scene where Dr. Heywood Floyd's group visits the monolith as it stands excavated on the moon four million years after some extraterrestrial civilization had buried it there. The film pairs sections of these two micropolyphonic works so as to create a single musical mise-en-scène that comes close to the increasing-relaxation-to-increasing-tension non-form; and the example stands out as the only instance where the director had one composition follow directly upon another. The film uses the first twenty-four bars of *Lux aeterna* to accompany the gradual landing of the Moon bus, and then cuts to the opening of Ligeti's Kyrie at the point where the film cuts ahead to the investigating party as they approach the monolith on foot (see figure 15.7). The section of *Lux aeterna* that Kubrick used represents a gradual decrease in harmonic tension, and the Kyrie an

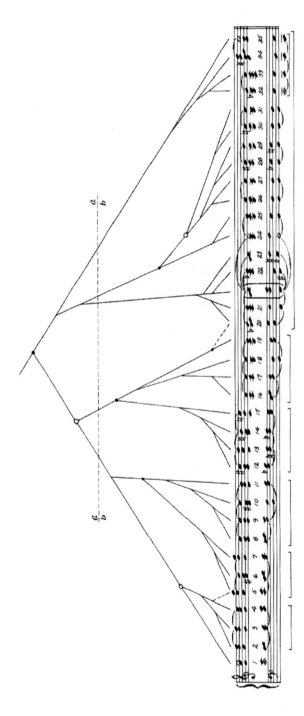

Figure 15.6. J. S. Bach, Prelude in C Major (*Well-Tempered Clavier*, Book 1). Prolongational reduction. From Lerdahl and Jackendoff, *A Generative Theory of Tonal Music* (Cambridge, Mass., and London: MIT Press, 1983), p. 263. Used by permission.

Figure 15.7. *2001: A Space Odyssey.* Approaching the monolith. From 2001: A SPACE ODYSSEY. Copyright © 1968 Turner Entertainment Co., a Warner Bros. Entertainment, Inc. All Rights Reserved. Used by permission.

even more gradual increase in the number of voices and stridency of the sonority. In short, the music works because of Ligeti's Bach-like "paucity of evidence" for any grouping and metrical analyses and Kubrick's skill in piecing together a powerful musical span that turns classical ideas of closed form literally inside-out.

A bit more now on what sections of music Kubrick chose, how he put them together, and what the overall effect is of his final assemblage. First, the fact that the monolith-approach scene opens and ends with Ligeti's instantly distinctive style puts a narrative, diegetic frame around the lunar expedition—forges the section into a single continuous stretch, even with the astronauts' marvelously underplayed lunch-discussion intervening. The opening of *Lux aeterna* is in fact heard twice, once when the Moon bus is first seen taking the investigators toward the monolith, and again (after the sandwich-discussion scene) while the Moon bus makes its final approach toward the landing pad. These first twenty-four measures of the piece are the most seamlessly processual (or "communicative") of the composition— the film cuts *Lux aeterna* off before its first major event, the major point of differentiation in Ligeti's micropolyphonic texture, namely the first sopranos' octave leap to a high A5 (at the pickup to m. 25). Jonathan Bernard's registral graph of this opening section (see figure 15.8) will serve as an analogue to Lerdahl and Jackendoff's prolongational reductions of works in the functional-tonal repertory—no hierarchies are indicated here, but one can easily see from the graph how the "harmonic" sound changes as the piece goes on, and thereby get an idea of Ligeti's own quasi-Lerdahlian, pitch-based patterns of tension and relaxation.

The piece begins with the single pitch F4 doubled in first sopranos and first altos, and it then fills out the registral space (E–G)4 over the first seven measures. Over the eight bars after that (mm. 8–15), more voices enter and this cluster is gradually expanded and "combed out" to a sonority that consists mostly of interval-class-2 (whole-tone) segments. (In Bernard's more precise terminology, the verticalities of mm. 9–15 for the most part represent "[2] striations." In this context Bernard quotes Ligeti's description of another composition where the texture similarly "gets less dense, as if someone went through it with a comb, thinning it out."[27]) The expanding texture is less marked by interval-class-2 striations after m. 15, but more important in the sense of increasing relaxation as we approach m. 25 is the maintained C5 and its separation by ic-2 from the rest of the texture. For acoustic reasons the ear tends to register dissonance most readily when ic-1 (semitone) occlusions occur at the top rather than the bottom of the expanding texture, and the piece exhibits a general relaxation as it moves from the opening (E–G)4 cluster to the ic-2 striations at the top of the texture in mm. 21–25.

The Kyrie from Ligeti's Requiem enacts a different dynamic, as the composer himself mentioned when he described *Lux aeterna* as an attempt to

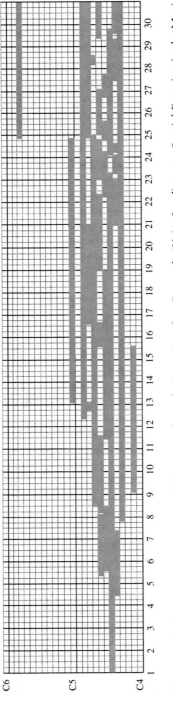

Figure 15.8. Ligeti, *Lux aeterna*, mm. 1–30, registral graph. From Jonathan Bernard, "Voice Leading as a Spatial Function in the Music of Ligeti," *Music Analysis* 13 (1994): 236–37. Used by permission.

avoid the opacity of the Requiem, the piece that it immediately followed in
the composer's chronology.[28] The most obvious factor in the relative thick-
ness of the Requiem is Ligeti's use of twenty voice parts plus orchestra, as
opposed to the sixteen a cappella parts of *Lux aeterna*. Perhaps more important in the Kyrie is the more active canonic subject, which is a kind of
turn figure that constantly expands through chromatic motion and quick-
ens rhythmically to nonuplet sixteenths by m. 13 of the first entry. The
result is a constantly shifting and expanding cluster that fills in a three-
octave span by m. 47. The sonority shrinks in m. 56 to only tenors and
basses, but the passage that follows is marked by climactic tension: the
dynamic has peaked at *fortissimo,* and all eight voice parts are rhythmically very active in pentuplets, sextuplets, octuplets, and nonuplets. The
texture and rhythmic activity stabilize again by m. 61, and Kubrick ends
the scene shortly after this: hit by sunlight for the first time in millions of
years, the monolith is triggered to beam radio frequencies to Jupiter.

The combination of music and imagery becomes even more climactic,
almost unbearably tense, in this last section because the director comes to
coordinate musical events and screen action for the first time—and the
increasing tension of the Kyrie is thereby transferred to the screen images
(see figure 15.9). This is also one of the rare moments in the film where the
editing must have been dictated by the chosen music. (Chion refers to such
a coming-together of film and soundtrack as a "synchretic" moment.[29])
Here Kubrick cuts dramatically to Dr. Floyd as, clearly in awe of the monolith and with a blinding floodlight behind him that resembles images of the
sun itself elsewhere in the movie, he comes around the side of the object.
This "lateral-sunrise" is timed to occur at m. 40 in the Kyrie, a dramatic
structural nexus where the sopranos ascend a sixth and enter on F5 after a
rest. Dr. Floyd then slowly reaches out to touch the object, slowly moves
his hand along the smooth black surface, and then hesitantly pulls his hand
back at m. 54, at the point where Ligeti's texture narrows to the rhythmically and dynamically active passage for tenors and basses that I mention
above. Given the fact that the extraterrestrial beings are never seen in the
movie, there is a particularly overwhelming moment where the lighting
and shadows give the impression of a second hand reaching out from the
monolith to touch Dr. Floyd's fingertips.

I now return to Gorbmann's "cultural musical codes" and the question
of why Ligeti's music proves so seductive and powerful in Kubrick's movie.
It would be a commonplace to say that Ligeti's micropolyphony works so
well in film because of its dissonance, conflicting overtones, and seemingly
chaotic motion—in short, because of the destabilizing effect its surface attributes have on the listener's autonomic nervous system. In applying her
"cultural musical codes," Gorbman would likely say that this music proves
so evocative in film because these foreground properties have been so
strongly coded as anxious and fearful. This interpretation accounts for

Figure 15.9. *2001: A Space Odyssey.* Dr. Floyd touches the monolith. From 2001: A SPACE ODYSSEY. Copyright © 1968 Turner Entertainment Co., a Warner Bros. Entertainment, Inc. All Rights Reserved. Used by permission.

some of the impact of the scene, yet it could only account for individual, synchronic impressions. The moon scene in *2001: A Space Odyssey* has a changing, cumulative visual-musical impact that no purely grammatical or lexical model can hope to explain. Even here, it is not a simple matter of the Kyrie excerpt increasing in complexity and dissonance as the viewer anticipates a dramatic resolution of the monolith mystery: for the scene at the monolith would be distinctly less dramatic without the prefatory spacebus views and the relaxation dynamic of the relevant section of Ligeti's *Lux aeterna.* Kubrick skillfully assembled two post-tonal works into a single non-form, one that would not have been possible in tonal music, and one that serves his scene well. Open-ended or otherwise strange structural dynamics, a defining aspect of modernist or post-tonal music, proved so appropriate to film in this instance that the director worked to make the structural dynamics of his chosen music even more unusual (less "tonal," perhaps). Indeed, this conjoined musical "non-form" replicates the "non-form" of Kubrick's movie, which is in two tenuously connected parts with different casts, sets, and story lines.[30]

Anyone who wishes to cite this scene as evidence that Ligeti's style of this period is culturally coded as anxious and horrific should also consider Kubrick's important dramatic ambiguities, mentioned earlier. If film music is coded according to what happens in the narrative and what we as viewers are supposed to feel, what happens when we don't quite know what's happening onscreen or which emotions the director wishes us to experience at a given moment? Kubrick did not importune his viewers, and habitually refused to manipulate his audience's emotions: critic Alexander Walker spoke of Kubrick's distaste for a director's usual "ingratiating tone of a warm-up man with a studio audience. [Kubrick] operates with the stealth of an infiltrator on the *individual* sensibility."[31] And so it comes as no surprise to find Kubrick undercutting any cinematic equation between musical instability and peril in the *2001* moon scene: the increased dissonance in the soundtrack does not portend death on the screen. No tragedy, or even any particular danger, unfolds. The scene does end in aural pain, causing the characters to stagger and cover their ears in a way that is more slapstick than tragic. But there is no peril otherwise, at least to judge from the screenplay Arthur C. Clarke wrote in collaboration with Kubrick. The novel adapted from the screenplay offers this narrative:

> Floyd was still musing over these thoughts when his helmet speaker suddenly emitted a piercing electronic shriek, like a hideously overloaded and distorted time signal. Involuntarily, he tried to block his ears with his spacesuited hands; then he recovered and groped frantically for the gain control of his receiver. While he was still fumbling four more of the shrieks blasted out of the ether; then there was a merciful silence.[32]

Kubrick foils any affective or emotional associations the viewer might make with Ligeti's music. Remember by way of contrast that the one true, explicit catastrophe of the film, the death of astronaut Poole in the second part of the movie, has no music. Indeed, it has no sound whatsoever, suggesting Kubrick silenced the soundtrack when it was in danger of overinterpreting the visuals. Or perhaps the music is not intended to "interpret" the visuals at all, here or anywhere else in the film.

In the final analysis, a contrast must be drawn between the filmic modernism of Herrmann and Penderecki, and the more elusive (non-formed, less recognizably constructed) modernism of Ligeti's micropolyphony. The former can carry quite specific cultural codings while the Ligeti functions more as a kind of Rorschach test. And it is surely this affective ambiguity that appealed to Kubrick, a director who habitually "undercoded" his films. (Someone might argue that Ligeti's Requiem is no Rorschach test, since it could never inspire pleasurable images, like a garden party or a wedding. But then you could say the same thing of an ink blot, and this is in itself a comment on our preconceived associations between chance and aesthetic displeasure.) A poll of moviegoers would likely reveal a greater variety of responses to the monolith scenes in *2001* than viewers would have after seeing Hitchcock's shower scene: does the monolith inspire wonder? the fear that accompanies the unknown? awe at an unknowable technology? the madness that would follow communication with a higher power? We are not meant to know the answer. Kubrick takes pains to keep the visual narrative of the moon scene free of any particular emotional message. If we play the game of watching the moon scene with other music, including some tonal examples, its significance seems to change completely and

Kubrick and Clarke's ambiguities go unnoticed. Joined to a sweeping, modal, and lushly orchestrated Jerry Goldsmith passage, the scene emulates "classical filmic discourse": the visitation becomes a strange homecoming, an emotional apotheosis.

And yet, the fact that Ligeti's music is highly dissonant is actually irrelevant to the famous scene in *2001*. Given a similar dynamic increase, a-syntactic progressions of consonant sonorities would give many of the same impressions: a Philip Glass soundtrack in the manner of *Koyaanisqatsi* (1982) would be just as ambiguous and just as powerful. Like Ligeti's pieces as Kubrick manipulated them, Glass's works of the 1970s and early 1980s are structural nonentities according to Lerdahl and Jackendoff's criteria. They also disrupt any "institutionalized flow of musical language" and thereby aggrieved many listeners of the time. One could ask if Glass's music still does this, or if it has by way of its increased popularity over the past two decades actually become part of the "institutionalized flow of musical language." But then his soundtrack for the recent film *Naqoyqatsi* (2002), also written and directed by Godfrey Reggio, still provokes the same questions: where is the music going? when will it end? where are the groupings and the hierarchies? is this passage joyful or sad? is it interpreting what's on screen, offering a counterpoint to it, or ignoring the visual aspect altogether?

3. Phantasmagoric Modernism: An "Obvious Desire to Use New Means"

In 1966, Susan Sontag offered a melancholy analysis of film as a nostalgic mechanism whereby "the historical particularity of the reality registered on celluloid is so vivid that practically all films older than four or five years are saturated with pathos."[33] This is false insofar as a film illuminates not only "the beautiful dead," but also the later films that revivify and converse with its gestures (at least to the extent that the original film is not an "infiltrator on the individual sensibility," to return to Walker's description of Kubrick). The "modernist" glissando or tone-cluster inevitably returns as an influence on composers of concert music, whereby a music-film-music circle is completed. Indeed, a later generation of modernist (or pseudo-modernist or post-post-modernist) composers have brought these powerful modernist-filmic associations to bear upon much of the non-film music that comes from their pens. This compositional-cultural process was pioneered by Penderecki and worked through with particular distinction over the past twenty years by John Corigliano—two composers who have purveyed what Adorno might call "commodified" modernism or "phantasmagoria," to use his and Hanns Eisler's phrase for diversionary film music that functioned as a magical "antidote to the picture." (The phrases are typical expressions of Adorno's negative dialectic, in that they do not carry specific value-judgments. I do not use them as criticisms here, rather to acknowledge a simple fact of musical life toward the close of the twentieth century: that just about everything around us has been commodified, including simulacra of aesthetic autonomy.)

When Schoenberg first saw the score of Berg's *Altenberg-Lieder* in 1913, he was disturbed by a "rather too obvious desire to use new means" and added, more as an oblique complaint than an apology: "Perhaps I'll come to understand the organic interrelationship between these means and the requirements of expression."[34] These words could serve as a measure of the aesthetic distance between the formalism of Schoenberg, Webern, and Boulez and the pictorial or "filmic" modernism of early Penderecki. Schoenberg's statement implies that new means must have utility, that their only reason for existence would be to help the artist express new and necessary things, and that they must have an organic relationship with those new things expressed. Schoenberg's points of contention with Berg were primarily timbral, just as his criticisms of *Wozzeck* concerned what he thought were extravagant dynamic changes: in the *Altenberg-Lieder,* his erstwhile student's self-conscious use of *ponticello,* harmonics, *sul tasto,* and so on. It would be easy to imagine Schoenberg appending to his criticisms of Berg something similar to the following passage from Lerdahl and Jackendoff:

> In sum, to the degree that the applicability of these various aspects of musical grammar is attenuated [in contemporary music], the listener will infer less hierarchical structure from the musical surface. As a result, nonhierarchical aspects of musical perception (such as timbre and dynamics) tend to play a greater, compensatory role in musical organization. But this is not compensation in kind; the relative absence of hierarchical dimensions tends to result in a kind of music perceived very locally, often as a sequence of gestures and association. Its complexity often resides in the extreme refinement of individual nuances.[35]

Despite Lerdahl and Jackendoff's apologia, these very reasonable thoughts become nothing less than an attempt to dismiss out-of-hand the claims on value made by entire modernist traditions. ("We believe," they write rather self-righteously in their final sentence on contemporary music, ". . . that our theory is relevant to compositional problems, in that it focuses detailed attention on the facts of hearing. To the extent that a composer cares about his listeners, this is a vital issue."[36]) Still, Schoenberg the formalist and "conscripted revolutionary" would no doubt have approved. As I have suggested above, venerable traditions of film music have been founded upon such a modernist "obvious desire to use new means" (the very term "phantasmagoria" derives from Étienne Gaspar Robert's magic lantern show, which premiered in 1798 under the title *Fantasmagorie*[37]), and it is those non-Schoenbergian situations that I now turn to. It is a fairly motley group of examples, and some might describe it as constituting neither modernism nor a tradition. The first two art-music composers I turn to, Bartók and Messiaen, did in fact wait until more conservative phases of their careers before turning to the particular "obvious desires to use new means" that I discuss.

Adorno used the word "phantasmagoria" to describe a particularly corrupt kind of striving for effect. Adorno's prime example was the "magic delusion" of Wagner's operas, that composer's exploitation of "the outside of the worthless commodity" (as Adorno quotes Schopenhauer). Like Berg's effects—which Schoenberg heard as only so much surface posturing—phantasmagoria cultivates an inorganic relationship between "the means and the requirements of expression"; in like fashion, Adorno heard and saw in Wagner a kind of newness that took on the character of "wares on display."[38] This phantasmagoric brand of modernism relied on novelties to evoke contagion and unwholesomeness rather than to expand the language of music per se: "The conversion of pleasure into sickness is the denunciatory task of phantasmagoria," Adorno writes. It was also a particularly primal kind of moderness: "phantasmagoria comes into being when, under the constraints of its own limitations, modernity's latest products come close to the archaic. Every step forwards is at the same time a step into the remote past. As bourgeois society advances it finds that it needs its own camouflage of illusion simply in order to subsist. For only when so disguised does it venture to look the new in the face."[39]

If there is one twentieth-century score that has been raided again and again by film composers looking for modernist "phantasmagoria," gestures, or aesthetic-musical artifacts, it is the Adagio to Bartók's *Music for Strings, Percussion, and Celesta*. The fact that composers and directors working on far-flung box-office successes like *Rebel Without a Cause* (for which Leonard Rosenman in essence re-composed the Bartók as accompaniment to the planetarium scene), *The Shining*, *Rosemary's Baby*, and *Being John Malkovich* have homed in on a particular composition from 1936 would seem to imply a piece of music that has become particularly rich in cultural meaning. What distinguishes Bartók's Adagio in these films is surely its "obvious desire to use new means," the moments where it moves from communication to signification, where it "swings away from the imaginary toward the symbolic," to return to Gorbman's phrase. Two of these unique and unforgettable sensory fingerprints are Bartók's non-restruck glissandos in the timpani, appearing perhaps for the first time in the literature,[40] and his parallel use of up-and-down muted *pianissimo* glissandos in the violins. Bartók's gestures function on two levels. The fluctuation of pitch is coded as "unease," but the topos is also rooted in impressions of "technology": timpani that tuned more quickly and easily than with the older hand-screws were already in use by the mid-nineteenth century, but Bartók's use of glissandos was predicated on improved pedal instruments.

Accordingly, the valuable effect depends on both sensory and sociogenetic reactions: the physical or sensory impression—the "queasiness" induced by pitch slides, perhaps—and the evocative, "magic" modern commodity that Adorno heard in Wagner.

Messiaen developed a taste for a similarly glissando-capable, phantasmagoric sound: the ondes martenot, one of the first manufactured electronic instruments to have any widespread use. The ondes martenot and its Soviet cousin, the theremin, have had more extensive careers in film than in concert music: the latter accompanied Salvador Dalí's fantastical dream sequence in Hitchcock's *Spellbound,* and numbered *War of the Worlds* (1953), *The Lost Weekend* (1946), and Herrmann's music for *The Day the Earth Stood Still* (1951) among its innumerable soundtrack appearances. The fact that Messiaen was using the ondes martenot in his concert works as early as the 1930s, and that he used it as often to double string parts as he did for soloistic passages, does not make its appearance in his music today any less directly reminiscent of B movies (at least for those who grew up exposed to these precious and ubiquitous mirrors of cold-war American cultural beliefs and social values).[41] One might still ask: what does Miklos Rózsa's music for *Spellbound* have to do with, say, the third of Messiaen's *Petites liturgies de la présence divine,* the movement where the ondes is especially prominent because of the indicated vibrato? By way of an answer, one could go back to Franz Fröhlich's influential early writings on how joy overcomes sorrow in Beethoven's Ninth Symphony, and repeat Nicholas Cook's description of Fröhlich's importance:

> Fröhlich's influential reading became part of a nineteenth-century tradition of interpretation (dominated, incidentally, by Wagner), which not only nuanced the gross emotional properties of the music, but helped to stabilize the reception of a composition that contemporary listeners found problematic. Fröhlich's narrative analysis—and the others that followed—fulfilled the functions that Barthes groups together under the term "anchorage": directing the interpretation of a limitlessly polysemic text, controlling the proliferation of meaning, and easing the transition of sound into discourse. To trace the reception of the Ninth Symphony through responses like Fröhlich's is to see musical meaning in the making.[42]

Along these lines, one might respond with a question to the person doubting any connection between Rózsa and Messiaen: what does Franz Fröhlich's narrative discussion of Beethoven's Ninth in terms of deafness really have to do with that symphony? To question Fröhlich's or Rózsa's legacy is to misunderstand cultural processes, perhaps to deny the existence of culture itself, and to take an unrealistically exclusivist view of where value might reside. To question one place of "anchorage," as Barthes might have it, and not the other is to draw artificial distinctions between high and low culture and to misapprehend how meaning is formed. And to deny the extreme particularity of the ondes martenot's aural thumbprint, which must have been Messiaen's reason for using it in the first place.

Once again, Bernard Herrmann enters the picture—as a particularly passionate practitioner of phantasmagoric modernism, a fervent and "obvious" desirer of "new means." With Herrmann's soundtracks, we find constant experimentation with sounds, a constant search for what Gorbman calls "referential" sounds as a way to pull the viewer or listener into the strange environments he was trying to illustrate. He was quoted a number of times as saying that the possibility for experimentation was one of the main things that drew him back to film music despite his aspirations as a "serious" composer. Ever-shifting orchestrations back up such a statement, and his chilly instrumental colors and obsessive and minimalist motivic writing must have felt like a cool slap in the face for audiences used to the familiar lush strings and melodic themes current in Hollywood music into the 1950s. Herrmann's score for Hitchcock's *Torn Curtain* (1966), which the director rejected, thereby ending their partnership, calls for 16 French horns, 12 flutes, 9 trombones, and no violins. *Beneath the 12-Mile Reef* (1953) used nine harps in its huge orchestra. The composer all but eliminated strings from his score for *Journey to the Center of the Earth* (1959), using instead a large variety of percussion, multiple harps, four electronic organs, a large cathedral organ, and a serpent to convey the special terror of the heroes' confrontation with huge subterranean lizards. In this case, Herrmann himself linked the sociogenetic, conditioned-esthesic "technology" topos with the cultural-musical "fear" topos; in the composer's words, he "wanted to create an atmosphere with absolutely no human contact" for this adaptation of Jules Verne. "This film had no emotion, only terror."[43]

Herrmann outdid himself in his work for Robert Wise's *The Day the Earth Stood Still*. This preceded by several years Louis and Bebe Barron's purely cybernetic soundtrack for Metro-Goldwyn-Mayer's high-budget *Forbidden Planet* (1956), but he managed to come up with a similarly barren soundscape by using electric violin, electric bass, two high and low theremins, four pianos, four harps, and "a very strange section of about 30-odd brass."[44] The theremin is an obvious presence: like Bartók's pedal timpani, this utterly new and at times unidentifiable sound creates an aural topos of technology. The cold-war technology topos was also a fear topos: so often in 1950s science fiction movies (*War of the Worlds*, for example) it was not specifically the alien that was to be feared, but the alien's machine. The deus-ex-machina alien had technological superiority, even to our atomic bomb. In *The Day the Earth Stood Still*, Herrmann linked the theremin specifically with appearances of the extraterrestrial robot-giant Gort, who stands inviolable to all human weapons and has unthinkable destructive capacities, including nuclear capability. Gort is technology anthropomorphized, and his awesome metallic presence (see figure 15.10) required the

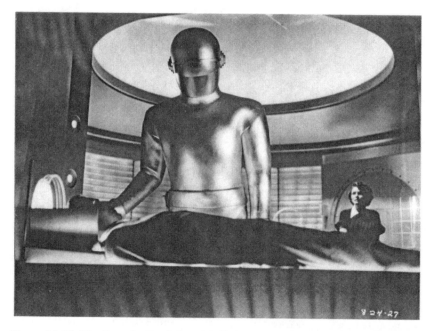

Figure 15.10. *The Day the Earth Stood Still.* Gort resuscitates Klaatu. Copyright ©
1951 20th-Century Fox. All Rights Reserved. Courtesy of the Academy of Motion
Picture Arts and Sciences. Used by permission.

efforts of a costumed seven-foot-tall man as well as models of the head and
time-consuming optical-printing effects for the death-ray. Herrmann specifically introduces the theremin whenever Gort's visor raises and his va-
porizing-ray is activated. Here the sociogenetic codes for the theremin are
in some ways contradictory. What it specifically portrays are the dangers
of technology as threatening Other—the theremin operates entirely in
glissandos without discrete pitches, and thereby introduces an irrationalist
or "ethnic" sound (or, as Adorno might call it, an "archaic" sound).

4. Film as Metaphor: Formalist vs. Phantasmagoric Modernism

I introduce a telling pair of aesthetic contradictions subsumable within wider
conceptions of twentieth-century modernism—a definition of outer modernist boundaries made possible by the medium and cultures of film. Specifically, my opposition sets Schoenberg against John Corigliano, two composers who well represent the formalist-modernist and phantasmagoric-
modernist poles, respectively, that I have sketched above. I will in the context of film contrast Schoenberg's 1930s modernism with the modernist

elements that are such a striking part of Corigliano's unique and powerful order of "postmodernism."[45] The two scores I use to sketch out this opposition are Schoenberg's *Begleitmusik zu einer Lichtspielszene*, Op. 34 (1930) and Corigliano's *Pied Piper Fantasy* for flute and orchestra (1979–82). The compositional circumstances of these pieces immediately present intriguing contrasts. Schoenberg wrote his score as a concert work illustrating no film in particular, but a linear affective sequence ("threatening danger—fear—catastrophe") that the composer gives at the head of the score without cueing any of the three affective designations directly into it. Corigliano's score has no direct connection with film either, although the composer does describe it as "a truly programmatic and theatrical work."[46] However, and here I come to a central point, Schoenberg's "accompaniment to a cinematographic scene" would in fact be inappropriate to anything but the most basic narrative film while Corigliano's concert work is consummately film-like—except, perhaps, in stucture. For instance, Schoenberg's orchestration is almost resolutely non-coloristic, and certainly smaller than his ensemble for the Variations, Op. 31 (1926, 1928): he includes in Op. 34 primarily duple winds, two horns and trumpets, one trombone, and three sporadically active percussionists.

One feels compelled to describe the *Begleitmusik* in negative terms, according to what it is *not*. The piece is not particularly modernist, Schoenbergian, or practical to film narratives, and these observations are interrelated: one gets the sense he was working under the false assumption that film was alien to the basic properties and mechanisms of his own style. (In this respect the *Begleitmusik zu einer Lichtspielszene* contrasts with the Film Music in Berg's *Lulu*, where that composer produced something both characteristic and innovative—and with Weill's typical aplomb in incorporating a 78rpm record of his own "Tango angèle" as the centerpiece in *Der Zar lässt sich photographieren*.) In fact, Schoenberg would seem to have subscribed to a conventional conception of film as an almost mechanical narrative process, and structured his Op. 34 accordingly. First, there is the unusually explicit, almost simplistic narrative frame and structural roundedness of the work. Unusually for him, Schoenberg's piece opens and closes with extended E-flat–G-flat tremolos in cellos and violas (the opening two pitches of the row, also an invariant dyad in the combinatorially related form), thereby imputing a suggestion of E-flat minor to the composition as a whole. More surprising is the sheer length of those opening and closing minor-third tremolos: the introduction stays on this for eight bars of 4/4 at a *Langsam* tempo of quarter = 60, while the epilogue maintains it for 19 bars at the same speed. The second section of the epilogue (mm. 192–219) also repeats specific motives and textural characteristics of the opening, thereby giving the end a kind of recapitulatory feel. (Or, in the words of David Hush, Schoenberg "invites the listener to construe the second part of the Epilogue as a 'composing out' of the pitch materials and textures of Episode I."[47])

	Episode I	(m.1):	$\quad \bullet = 60$
	Episode II	(m.9):	$\bullet = 72$
	Episode III	(m.18):	$\bullet = 96$
	Episode IV	(m.44):	$\partial = 168$
	Episode V	(m.82):	$\partial = 90$
	Episode VI	(m.104):	$\partial = 90$
	Episode VII	(m.117):	$\partial. = 112$
	Episode VIII	(m.123):	$\partial. = 72$
	Episode IX	(m.156):	$\partial. = 100$
Catastrophe	Episode X	(m.170):	$\bullet = 100$
Epilogue	Episode XI	(m.178):	$\bullet = 60$

Figure 15.11. Schoenberg, *Begleitmusik zu einer Lichtspielszene*, Op. 34. Tempo acceleration and deceleration. From David Hush, "Modes of Continuity in Schoenberg's *Begleitungsmusik zu einer Lichtspielscene*," *Journal of the Arnold Schoenberg Institute* suppl. to vol. 8, no. 1 (1984): 4. Used by permission.

More revealing is the likelihood that Schoenberg's middling grasp of film encouraged him to produce an uncharacteristically "communicative" internal structure. The piece is unusual for Schoenberg in that it eschews traditional schematic musical forms; instead, the work is constructed as a sequence of eleven segued "episodes" that demonstrate "different modes of continuity," to use Hush's description (See Figure 11). Generally speaking, the piece represents a series of incremental tempo accelerations (Episodes I–III) followed by a gradual slowing (Episodes IV–VI). Apparently illustrating the motion from danger into fear and finally into catastrophe, the unfolding of pitch-events becomes increasingly compressed—until the catastrophe occurs (m. 170, Episode X) and then the work returns to the original (and slowest) tempo for the epilogue and final reference to the opening pitch constructions. Schoenberg's Op. 34 is thus uncharacteristic in its uninterruptedness, linearity, and overall structural compression of pitch events as the piece progresses. (In this respect, Luigi Rognoni hypothesizes a connection between this work and a later theatrical piece of Schoenberg's, proposing that the *Begleitmusik* was written as a test for "the dramatic-musical dynamic device of paroxysmal crescendo" that he adopted in the "Dance of the Golden Calf" in *Moses und Aron*.[48]) For purposes of contrast, figure 15.12 presents the tempo layout of the Variations for Orchestra, Op. 31, which involves a less processual, less consistent series of tempo changes; note also the doubling of tempo between the start of the work and its conclusion. The inevitable conclusions are that the Variations would be more appropriate to classic narrative filmic discourse and also the more innately Schoenbergian composition, and that Schoenberg's unknowing condescension to the genre (perhaps his belief, to

Introduction	(m.1):	𝅗𝅥 = 60 (♩ = 120)
Theme	(m.34):	♩ = 88
Variation 1	(m.58):	♩ = 72
Variation 2	(m.82):	♩. = 56
Variation 3	(m.106):	♩ = 88
Variation 4	(m.130):	𝅗𝅥 = 90
Variation 5	(m.178):	♩ = 112
Variation 6	(m.202):	♪ = 120, ♩ = 60
Variation 7	(m.238):	♪ = 120
Variation 8	(m.262):	𝅗𝅥 = 100
Variation 9	(m.286):	𝅗𝅥 = 88
Finale	(m.310):	♩ = 120
	(m.344):	♪ = 108
	(m.420)	♩ = 160
	(m.435):	𝅗𝅥 = 120
	(m.502):	♪ = 92
	(m.508):	𝅗𝅥 = 120

Figure 15.12. Schoenberg, Variations for Orchestra, Op. 31. Tempo layout.

quote his pupil Eisler again, that film was "the heir of the popular horror story and dime novel") led him to stifle the very aspects of his style that were most appropriate to film.

As a contrast to Schoenberg's formalist understanding of film, I turn now to Corigliano's phantasmagoric approach. Much of Corigliano's concert work is both film-inspired and phantasmagorically modernist, and the two properties are of course intertwined. The structure of his *Pied Piper Fantasy* is as rounded as Schoenberg's Op. 34, though in inverse fashion: the framing sections are intensely chromatic, dissonant, and coloristic, indeed structurally unstable and "using new means" with obvious and heart-on-sleeve desire. And soon into the piece the listener realizes that the composer is inverting the direct, Lerdahlian tonal correlations between dissonance and structural tension; it quickly becomes clear that he has chosen, to quote Schoenberg again, not to construct an "organic interrelationship between these [new] means and the requirements of expression." The listener also quickly understands that Corigliano uses dissonance in an illustrative and affective, rather than purely musical, way; the piece begins with harmonics in the lower strings and two aluminum rods, tuned a quarter-tone apart, that the percussionists play by stroking them with a rosined hand. The dissonant pitch collections and microtonal affect continue as more instruments enter, including slow glissando harmonics in the strings and a harp played with pitches oscillated via the pedal. The composer describes the opening as "pointillistic night-sounds" and the parallel close of the work as a return of "the lonely sounds" from the opening. This, as so many other parts of the score, is a demonstration *par excellence* of Adorno's phantasmagoria idea; Corigliano's modernism has become a signifier, a commodified vehicle for affective and non-formalist intentions.

When the rats enter the scene, the composer introduces a virtuoso portrait of modernist-phantasmagoric "means"—specifically, what seems to be a striking replication of Lutoslawski. The vermin prove to be as straightforwardly chromatic and non-normative creatures as the human element of the program is diatonic, and their appearance is marked by a catalogue of playing techniques (again, there are similarities with Penderecki): reed squeaks, ponticello, buzz mutes, flutter-tonguing, etc. Corigliano has even pointed to two specific "rat motives" that surface here. The extent of the modernist phantasmagoria warrants quoting the composer's program in some detail. Like Penderecki, Corigliano in his romanticized narrative structure all but anthropomorphizes modernism through the agency of avant-garde sound:

> III. Battle with the Rats—The Piper enters the fray. Clusters of rodents dart about the lower register; he rushes down the scale after them, but they disappear, only to immediately resurface in another spot at higher pitch. The Piper races to that area, but again most of the rats vanish. He tries to scatter the

stragglers with sudden sforzandos, but more and more appear until a sort of *totentanz* ensures, with Piper (flute) and rats (orchestra) locked in angular embrace as the soloist imitates and challenges the rodents with their own musical motives.

IV. War Cadenza—The battle culminates with a gigantic orchestral glissando—and then silence. The soloist explores this sudden quiet, testing the air. He charges up a scale, anticipating flurrying rat-sounds at the top but finding only silence. he savagely attacks a note, expecting the hidden rats to scatter—but once again, silence. He slowly begins to relax and to become more and more lyrical (although sudden short flute outbursts indicate he is still being cautious). But the extended silence finally convinces him. He becomes confident, then joyous, then exultant, singing the same improvisation from the beginning of the work—but with a purer and richer sound.

Just, however, as the Piper is about to relax completely and begin his song again, a soft scraping sound rises from the orchestra. He realizes there are many more rats than he could ever have imagined—millions. They run berserk. Their glissando-motive snarls through the brass, as winds and strings portray their wild scampering. He is overwhelmed.

In the fifth section, "The Piper's Victory," the soloist finally triumphs and the music becomes markedly diatonic. The Piper's Song returns in D-mixolydian, now more lushly harmonized and orchestrated than before. The changes show the transfigured face of melody after it has battled rats, atonality, and noise: in figure 15.13, compare the Piper's Song at rehearsal 4 with its reappearance at the end of the War Cadenza. The tempo is one-third the speed as at the earlier statement, and Corigliano's melodic pause at the D chord at figure 24 becomes pregnant with meaning: it is a loving anticipation of the new B-flat chord and its intimation of an added sixth in the next bar, which itself arrives as a hard-won pleasure.

Corigliano's film scores—he has scored three movies as of this writing, and won an Oscar for his collaboration with François Girard on *The Red Violin*—tend to use latterday sociogenetic codes for phantasmagoria. His music for Ken Russell's *Altered States* (1980) is especially phantasmagoric, with modernist gestures glossing a story about scientists who explore the hallucinatory nether regions of the human mind. Corigliano's main title begins with bass piano strings tuned in quarter tones, and he goes on to use what sound like shawms played in their high registers, and in fact all the expected post-Penderecki avant-garde gestures—even the ghostly serpent that Herrmann had used for *Journey to the Center of the Earth*. Like the rat and battle sequences in the *Pied Piper*, Corigliano's *Altered States* music pays homage to a filmic modernism. The primal quality that Adorno heard in phantasmagoric modernism is particularly brought out by Russell in the final anthropological-regression-delusion sequence, heavily scored by Corigliano, where Emily (Blair Brown) travels to the beyond—Orpheus-like—to bring Eddie Jessup (William Hurt) back to safety (see figure 15.14).

Figure 15.13. Corigliano, *Pied Piper Fantasy*. First and second statements of the Piper's Song. PIED PIPER FANTASY by John Corigliano. Copyright © 1982 by G. Schirmer, Inc. (ASCAP). International Copyright Secured. All rights reserved. Reprinted by permission.

Her motions have a strangely stilted and timeless quality, like folkdance or Martha Graham's choreography, and the two characters devolve right before the end to primal, even embryonic forms. After all this psychedelia, it does not take Franz Fröhlich to hear Corigliano's final return to tonality (at the "Return to Reality" cue) as a hard-won return to the normative.

5. Latterday Modernism as an Escape from the Syntactic?

Syntax entails established rules of grammatical construction, involving a finite set of discrete elements and precepts of combination that yield hierarchical (and perhaps logical) structures. Schoenberg all but accused Berg of

Figure 15.14. *Altered States*. Emily saves Eddie Jessup. ALTERED STATES. Copyright © 1981 Warner Bros. Entertainment, Inc. All rights reserved. Used by permission.

eschewing syntax in the *Altenberg-Lieder*, and in doing so seemed to acknowledge a tendency in nineteenth-century aesthetics that would have struck close to home with him. For there was a precedent for the earthshaking changes I have described in twentieth-century modernist traditions—for the way popular culture latched onto and commodified the film-friendly properties of modernism and thereby changed modernist languages irrevocably between Schoenberg and Corigliano. Leonard Meyer described this precedent when he discussed "declining audience sophistication" over the course of the nineteenth century. Because of the increase in audience size after the industrial revolution, according to Meyer, listeners lost contact with the idea of syntactic constraints, they became unfamiliar with the rules and strategies of style:

> [T]he ability of members of an audience to respond sensitively to the nuances of syntax and the subtleties of form suffered. . . . One of the most important means employed by Romantic composers to compensate for the decline in the ability of many members of the audience to respond sensitively to the subtleties of syntactic process and formal design was the increase in the relative importance of

secondary parameters in shaping musical process and structure—and hence musical experience.[49]

Meyer's primary musical parameters are the syntactic elements, the aspects of music that are hierarchical and described in terms of classlike relationships: antecedent-consequent melody, authentic cadences, anapestic rhythms. As opposed to this conceptualized grouping together of melodic, rhythmic, and harmonic relations, Meyer's secondary parameters are described in terms of amounts, and phrased in statistical and relative terms: sonorities, timbres, dynamic levels, and rates of activity are examples of secondary parameters.[50] And these are the very "phantasmagoric" aspects of the *Altenberg-Lieder* and *Wozzeck* that aroused Schoenberg's suspicions.

Meyer's summary description of trends in Romantic music could also apply to the differences-within-similarity that I have pointed out between Schoenberg and Corigliano in his avant-garde vein: "[T]he syntax of tonal music, like other kinds of syntax, is rule-governed, learned, and conventional," Meyer writes.

> The secondary, statistical parameters, on the other hand, seem able to shape experience with minimal dependence on learned rules and conventions. . . . I do not mean to imply that ordinary listeners did not understand the rudiments of syntax and form. . . . But for many listeners, the power of sheer sound—as music slowly swelled in waves of sonic intensity, culminating in a statistical climax or a plateau of apotheosis, and then quickly declined toward cessation and silence—in a very real sense shaped experience "naturally."[51]

The twentieth century was host to a similar listener-instigated ascendancy of secondary over primary parameters. In this case, the change in listening priorities and abilities is inextricably linked with the development of the mass media, especially film and video. For, just as Eisenstein suggested, the culture-apparatus of film glorifies the non-hierarchical and the conventionally unconventional, and it luxuriates in the sensory world of the relative and statistical. Film is the agent that has usurped Meyer's idea of the musically primary. The dualities that he sketches seem particularly appropriate descriptions of the conflict I hear at the center of Schoenberg's *Begleitmusik*: Schoenberg's form retains the expected "syntactic structuring" but also effects overall structure through the secondary parameter of consistent increase and decrease in tempo. To judge from his description of Ravel's *Bolero,* Meyer would no doubt make similar claims about the *Begleitmusik*: that it requires a relatively "modest degree of musical sophistication" to understand its "culmination processes."[52]

Meyer's explanation, as well as Lendahl's statement that the person listening to non-hierarchical music reverts to "very local"—and therefore superficial—details, should now be appended with two important observations: that (1) "primary characteristics," though important bases for listening, have become decrepit as values and can no longer serve as our criteria for aesthetic significance, and (2) syntactically oriented idioms are doomed as mainstream avenues of meaning because by definition they are limited in the amount of sheer sensory information they can convey. Our stimulus-mad age, under the influence of what Jean Baudrillard calls "the ecstasy of communication,"[53] has less and less time for the hierarchical and innately circumscribed tendencies of what Meyer terms the "musically primary." The success of modernist gestures and sounds in film shows an increasing wish to capitalize upon what Meyer would call the "secondary" attributes of modernist music, and this is a powerful acknowledgment of the flexibility and diverse wealth of this music—much of it, at least.

Brian Ferneyhough came up with the neologism "too-muchness" to describe the New Complexity of recent years, but the phrase is useful for broader descriptions of "difficult" twentieth-century composition. This is a semantic point worth making, for avant-garde music has so often been described as lacking something, as coming up short, in a way that common-practice music does not. McClary and Lerdahl, along with so many others, have faulted modernist music for failing to "communicate" with an audience (Lerdahl basing this on the notion that the modernist composers themselves intended their work to be grammatical), while it is this writer's view that if Xenakis, Schoenberg, Nono, Boulez, and Ligeti have alienated audiences for any one reason, it is that they strove to communicate *too much* in too short a time.[54] And the usefulness of modernist elements in film soundtracks would seem to prove this contention. For the movie-goer is far more open to aural and affective stimulation than the concert-goer, and owes this to the "hot" quality of film, McLuhan's *Understanding Media* description for its surplus of sensory data and its tendency to "do most of the work" for the viewer. The moviegoer owes his or her amenability to the sociogenetic fact that aural stimuli are far more palatable when they are anchored in, linked with, or simply paired with visual images.

To close, I would like to go back to Lerdahl and Jackendoff's tree diagrams and ask the naive question of why these ongoing patterns of functional subservience are not—or cannot be—done with, say, Boulez's *Pli selon Pli*, Xenakis's *Pithoprakta*, or Babbitt's *Transfigured Notes*. The answer must be that there would be so many hierarchies and possibilities to trace. If this surfeit makes modernism non-syntactical, then it is worth noting two things: that (1) this non-syntactical quality reflects the music's tendency to induce sensory saturation rather than deprivation, and (2) there is a general tendency in postmodern cultures, particularly under the influence of media like film, to increasing rootedness in the non-syntactical. The tendency to fault modernist music would seem, then, to stem from interrelated desires to limit the powers of music in general to and prevent it from keeping pace with the sociogenetic, media-related tendencies of recent decades.

It is difficult to avoid describing modernist music as more innately improvisatory, mutable, and syntactically free than common-practice music: in a word, more "emotional" than intellectual in its effect; more emotional, in fact, than the Romantic works we commonly describe with that label. These are certainly the characteristics that film has picked up on and exploited so tellingly, and which it has helped to underline in the original modernist concert repertory. Eisler writes: "While the cinema technique aims essentially at creating extreme tension, traditional music, with the slight dissonances it allows, knows of no equivalent material. But suspense is the essence of modern harmony, which knows no chord without an inherent 'tendency' toward further action, while most of the traditional chords are self-sufficient."[55] Perhaps the issues boil down to the increased primacy of emotion and non-syntactic sensation in postmodernity, and the direct connections, which no one seems willing to acknowledge, between modernist gestures and raw, non-syntactic powers of emotion. In 1925, Kandinsky chose to describe his future abstraction as "the coming Romanticism," and described it as "profound, beautiful (the obsolete term 'beautiful' should be restored to usage), meaningful, joy-giving . . . a block of ice with a burning flame inside. If people perceive only the ice and not the flame, that is just too bad."[56] Postmodernity, and more specifically postmodern qualities of film, have allowed us again to hear the emotion—the flame—in modernism.

Notes

1. See in particular R. Boyd and P. Richerson, *Culture and the Evolutionary Process* (Chicago: University of Chicago Press, 1985); Michael Tomasello, A. C. Kruger, and H. H. Ratner, "Cultural Learning," *Behavioral and Brain Sciences* 16 (1993): 495–552; and Tomasello, *The Cultural Origins of Human Cognition* (Cambridge, Mass., and London: Harvard University Press, 1999).

2. Psychologists have long known that human attitudes, and presumably aesthetics as well, are as manipulatable through classical conditioning as are physical reactions. One such early study is A. W. Staats and C. K. Staats, "Attitudes Established by Classical Conditioning," *Journal of Abnormal and Social Psychology* 57 (1958): 37–40. Emotional reactions to stimuli are also learned in a process called "vicarious conditioning" or "behavioral modeling," even by people who have no access to the original unconditioned stimulus; see, for example, A. Bandura and T. L. Rosenthal, "Vicarious Classical Conditioning as a Function of Arousal Level," *Journal of Personality and Social Psychology* 3 (1966): 54–62. In a recent study, psychologists Marianna Kastner and Robert G. Crowder tested children between the ages of three and twelve and decisively concluded that even pre-schoolers have standard and consistent emotional reactions to major and minor. (The children were asked to point to one of four contrasting face graphics after hearing the same musical example in major or minor.) Invoking Helmholtz, Kastner and Crowder are inclined to account for this with the standard idea that the major third is a more

stable interval than the minor, and also more often heard acoustically. However, they do leave open the possibility—far too grudgingly, it would seem—of acclimation: that American children of the ages they studied are more consistently exposed to major than they are to minor harmonies. See Kastner and Crowder, "Perception of the Major/Minor Distinction: IV, Emotional Connotations in Young Children," *Music Perception* 8, no. 2 (Winter 1990): 189–202.

3. Cook, *Analysing Musical Multimedia* (Oxford: Clarendon Press, and New York: Oxford University Press, 1998), 23.

4. Ibid., 92.

5. See Nattiez, *Music and Discourse: Toward a Semiology of Music*, trans. Carolyn Abbate (Princeton, N.J.: Princeton University Press, 1990), 16–18 and passim.

6. Eisenstein, "The Montage of Film Attractions" (1924), in *The Eisenstein Reader*, ed. Richard Taylor, trans. Taylor and William Powell (London: British Film Institute, 1998), 40.

7. Eisenstein, "The Montage of Attractions" (1923), in *The Eisenstein Reader*, 30. Emphasis in original.

8. Tomasello, *The Cultural Origins of Human Cognition*, 5.

9. Huxley, "Education on the Nonverbal Level," *Daedalus* 91 (Spring 1962): 279.

10. Arrowsmith, "Film as Educator," *Journal of Aesthetic Education* 3, no. 3 (July 1969): 75–83; reprinted in *Perspectives on the Study of Film*, ed. John Stuart Katz (Boston: Little, Brown, and Company, 1971), 30–31.

11. Ibid.

12. Claudia Gorbman, *Unheard Melodies: Narrative Film Music* (Bloomington and Indianapolis: Indiana University Press, 1987), 12–13. Michel Chion, in a volume translated by Gorbman, refers to a similar category of "empathetic music" encodings: "[M]usic can directly express its participation in the feeling of the scene, by taking on the scene's rhythm, tone, and phrasing; obviously such music participates in cultural codes for things like sadness, happiness, and movement. In this case we can speak of *empathetic music*, from the word empathy, the ability to feel the feelings of others." Chion, *Audio-Vision: Sound on Screen*, trans. Claudia Gorbman (New York: Columbia University Press, 1994), 8. Hanns Eisler also refers to something like Gorbman's "cultural musical codes" when he draws attention to the way "music is often brought into play at the very point where *particularly characteristic effects* are sought for the sake of 'atmosphere' or suspense." Eisler (with T. W. Adorno), *Composing for the Films* (New York: Oxford University Press, 1947), 16; emphasis added.

13. Just as Hitchcock became Truffaut's archetypal example of the *auteur*, the single dominating presence in a film, it is worth remembering that Herrmann is exclusively responsible for the musical-visual-theatrical meanings taken on by these high and harsh string entries. Hitchcock originally insisted that the shower scene contain no music, exhortations that Herrmann ignored and which he was finally able to convince Hitchcock were misguided. One study provides a musical-affective control for Herrmann's equation, though as so often the findings are based on a general and therefore almost meaningless division between "tonal" and "atonal" "styles." In perception experiments, J. David Smith and Jordan N. Witt concluded that moderately educated music-lovers tend to associate atonal music with "agitation," "extreme activity," "chaotic motion," "chaotic structure," and "hesitancy and confusion"; while

tonal excerpts are commonly described with such adjectives as "sentimental," "graceful," dreamy," "spiritual," etc. Smith and Witt, "Spun Steel and Stardust: The Rejection of Contemporary Compositions," *Music Perception* 7, no. 2 (Winter 1989): 169–186. I thank Amy Bauer for bringing this study to my attention.

14. Of course, my division between film music and art music is a false dichotomy in both Penderecki's and Herrmann's cases. The composers are mirror images of one another in their straddling of these two enterprises: Herrmann aspired to a career of writing concert music, while the origins of Penderecki's *Threnody* are remarkably reminiscent of a composer of film music screening the movie before standing back to reflect and write his or her score.

15. Cited by Mieczyslaw Tomaszewski in his liner notes for *Penderecki: Orchestral Works, Vol. 1* (Naxos 8.554491, 2000).

16. Lerdahl and Jackendoff, *A Generative Theory of Tonal Music* (Cambridge, Mass. and London: MIT Press, 1983), 296–301; Milton Babbitt, *Words about Music*, ed. Stephen Dembski and Joseph N. Straus (Madison: University of Wisconsin Press, 1987), 167–68. For Lerdahl's more comprehensive commentary on post-tonal music, see his "Cognitive Constraints on Compositional Systems," *Contemporary Music Review* 6, no. 2 (1992): 97–121.

17. In Umberto Eco's view, textual undercoding is even a prerequisite for the aesthetic experience: as he describes it, ambiguity "focuses my attention and urges me to an interpretive effort (while at the same time suggesting how to set about decoding), [and it thereby] incites me toward the discovery of an unexpected flexibility in the language with which I am dealing." Eco, "The Aesthetic Text as Invention," in his *A Theory of Semiotics* (Bloomington, Ind. and London: Indiana University Press, 1976), 263.

18. Panofsky, "Style and Medium in the Motion Pictures" (1934, rev.1947), in *Film Theory and Criticism: Introductory Readings,* 4th edition, ed. Gerald Mast, Marshall Cohen, and Leo Braudy (New York and Oxford: Oxford University Press, 1992), 237. Also see Cook's account, as cited earlier, of the pure music "fiction" outside of film; *Analysing Musical Multimedia,* 92. If what Panofsky said is true, Gorbman's "pure musical codes" are an impossibility: sound and image merge irretrievably, and there can be no purely musical aspect so long as a visual image accompanies the music.

19. Gorbman, *Unheard Melodies,* 6–7.

20. Ibid., 79.

21. Ibid., 6–7.

22. Eisler (with T. W. Adorno), *Composing for the Films,* 32–33.

23. Chion, *Audio-Vision,* 45–47; Tarasti, *A Theory of Musical Semiotics* (Bloomington and Indianapolis: Indiana University Press, 1994), 18. To illustrate, Tarasti refers (p. 25) to Busoni's *Entwurf einer neuen Aesthetik der Tonkunst* where the author refers to symmetrical relationships and architectonic principles as aspects of communicative structure.

24. Cook, *Analysing Musical Multimedia,* 4–7.

25. Lerdahl and Jackendoff, *A Generative Theory of Tonal Music,* 197–98.

26. Ibid., 260.

27. Jonathan W. Bernard, "Inaudible Structures, Audible Music: Ligeti's Problem, and His Solution," *Music Analysis* 6 (1987): 226. My terms for discussing Ligeti here are those advanced by Bernard in this essay, and I am also indebted to Bernard's later

discussion of *Lux aeterna* in "Voice Leading as a Spatial Function in the Music of Ligeti," *Music* Analysis 13 (1994): 227–53. Bernard quotes Ligeti from Péter Várnai, *Ligeti in Conversation*, trans. Gabor J. Schabert (London: Eulenberg, 1983), 44.

28. Ligeti, "Auf dem Weg zu *Lux aeterna*," *Österreichische Musikzeitschrift* 24 (1969): 80–88; cited by Bernard in "Inaudible Structures, Audible Music," 222–224.

29. Chion, *Audio-Vision*, 63.

30. It would be revealing in any event to compare reactions to Ligeti's works to early critical responses to *2001: A Space Odyssey*, a film that at first perplexed, bored, and angered film critic Pauline Kael, among others.

31. Emphasis added. Cited by Piers Bizony in his *2001: Filming the Future* (London: Aurum Press, 1994), 147.

32. Arthur C. Clarke, *2001: A Space Odyssey*, based on a screenplay by Arthur C. Clarke and Stanley Kubrick (New York: New American Library, 1968), 79–80. Note how Kubrick leaves the film scene more ambiguous than the story, just as he artfully edited out a scene later on in the film that would have specifically explained the lethal "malfunctions" of the HAL computer.

33. Sontag, "Theatre and Film," in her *Styles of Radical Will* (New York: Farrar, Straus & Giroux, 1966), 114.

34. *The Berg-Schoenberg Correspondence: Selected Letters*, ed. Juliane Brand, Christopher Hailey, and Donald Harris (New York: W. W. Norton, 1987), 143.

35. Lerdahl and Jackendoff, *A Generative Theory of Tonal Music*, 298.

36. Ibid., 301.

37. Robert Sklar, *Film: An International History of the Medium* (New York: Harry N. Abrams, 1993), 16.

38. T. W. Adorno, "Phantasmagoria," in his *In Search of Wagner*, trans. Rodney Livingstone (London: NLB, 1981), 85–96.

39. Ibid., 95.

40. In his encyclopedic *Anatomy of the Orchestra*, Norman Del Mar cites the restruck glissandos in the "timpani battle" of Nielsen's Fourth Symphony as his only pre-Bartók example. Bartók also used glissandos in the *Cantata profana* (1930), Sonata for Two Pianos and Percussion (1937), and Violin Concerto (1938). See Del Mar, *Anatomy of the Orchestra*, paperback edition with revisions (Berkeley and Los Angeles: University of California Press, 1983), 368–69; and James Blades, "Timpani, §4: Repertory," *New Grove Dictionary of Music and Musicians*, ed. Stanley Sadie (London: Macmillan, 1980), 18:833–37.

41. Naturally, the extent of such associations depends on how much the ondes is brought out in the overall texture; the performances by the composer's sister-in-law Jeanne Loriod, for example on Kent Nagano's recording of the *Petites liturgies de la présence divine* and André Previn's rendition of the *Turangalîla Symphonie*, are discreetly balanced.

42. Cook, *Analysing Musical Multimedia*, 93–94. On Fröhlich, also see Cook, *Beethoven: Symphony No. 9* (Cambridge and New York: Cambridge University Press, 1993), 12–13.

43. Wardell, "Music to Commit Murder By," cited by Steven C. Smith, *A Heart at Fire's Center: The Life and Music of Bernard Herrmann* (Berkeley, Los Angeles, and Oxford: University of California Press, 1991), 229.

44. Ted Gilling, "The Colour of Music: An Interview with Bernard Herrmann," *Sight and Sound*, winter 1971–72; cited by Smith, *A Heart at Fire's Center*, 165.

45. In his liner note for the New World recording of Corigliano's Clarinet Concerto, composer and New York Philharmonic program annotator Philip Ramey remembered Leonard Bernstein saying after a rehearsal of this piece "how taken he was with the way [the composer] had used avant-garde techniques and color effects to musical ends." Ramey, "A Talk with John Corigliano," *John Corigliano: Clarinet Concerto* (New World 309-2, 1981), 10. As if to substantiate such descriptions of his style and means, Corigliano has recently written a piece for cello and piano with the title *Phantasmagoria*!

46. Corigliano, notes to *John Corigliano: Pied Piper Fantasy* (RCA Red Seal 6602, 1987), 4. Regarding my point about the *Pied Piper Fantasy* being more a concert work than a theatrical one, I draw attention to the composer's firm but undoctrinaire separation of "theatrical aspects" from "the original concept": "The evolution of theatrical aspects [in performances] seems to me a healthy and inventive addition to the original concept, and I have no doubt that the physical trappings of future performances will continue to change and grow. Because the *Fantasy* is a truly programmatic and theatrical work, these additions are not artificial but grow naturally from the initial idea. As long as the musical integrity of the work is preserved, such creative extensions are to be encouraged."

47. Hush, "Modes of Continuity in Schoenberg's *Begleitungsmusik* [sic] *zu einer Lichtspielscene*[sic]," *Journal of the Arnold Schoenberg Institute* suppl. to vol. 8, no. 1 (1984): 5.

48. Rognoni, *The Second Vienna School*, trans. Robert W. Mann (London: J. Calder, 1977), 279; cited in Jeremy Tambling, "Mechanical Reproduction in Opera," in *Opera, Ideology, and Film* (New York: St. Martin's Press, 1987), p.70.

49. Meyer, *Style and Music: Theory, History, and Ideology* (Philadelphia: University of Pennsylvania Press, 1989), 208–9.

50. Ibid., 14–16.

51. Ibid., 209.

52. Ibid.

53. Baudrillard, "The Ecstasy of Communication," in *The Anti-Aesthetic: Essays on Postmodern Culture*, ed. Hal Foster, 126–34 (Seattle: Bay Press, 1983).

54. Henry Pleasants writes: ". . . it was not until they had practically destroyed the implications of tonality that composers suddenly discovered that emancipation had brought them, not freedom of musical speech, but the inability to speak musically at all. The tonal framework they had so hopefully destroyed proved to have been the very substance of their creative language." Pleasants, *The Agony of Modern Music* (New York: Simon and Schuster, 1955), 104. As a point of contrast with avant-garde concert composers, Susan McClary writes: "The fact that [Earth Wind and Fire's 'System of Survival'] reaches a wide audience, that it speaks in a comprehensible language of exuberant hope in the face of hardship is regarded not as evidence of selling out, but as a mark of success in an economy of prestige that rewards communication and political effectiveness" (McClary, "Terminal Prestige: The Case of Avant-Garde Music Composition," *Cultural Critique* 12 [Spring 1989]: 81).

55. Eisler (with T. W. Adorno), *Composing for the Films*, 37.

56. From a letter to Will Grohmann dated 21 November, 1925. Grohmann, *Wassily Kandinsky: Life and Work*, trans. Norbert Guterman (New York: Harry N. Abrams, 1958), 180.

Contributors

ARVED ASHBY is Associate Professor of Musicology at the Ohio State University. Much of his work has centered on Alban Berg and the historiography of twelve-tone music, and in 1996 he received the Alfred Einstein Award from the American Musicological Society for an article involving these subjects (*Journal of the American Musicological Society,* Spring 1995). In addition to interests in modernism and popular culture, he is also interested in phenomenological, McLuhanesque correlations between twentieth-century concert art music and the mass media. To this end, he is now writing a book titled *Absolute Music in the Age of Mechanical Reproduction.* He wrote criticism for the *American Record Guide* between 1987 and 2001, and now contributes regularly to *Gramophone* magazine.

AMY BAUER earned her Ph.D. in Music Theory at Yale University. She is Assistant Professor of Music at Washington University and has also taught at the University of Colorado at Boulder, the University of Missouri-Kansas City, and West Chester University. She is currently writing a book on the music of György Ligeti. Her other research interests include jazz history and analysis, cross-cultural influences in contemporary music, the history of music theory, non-Western music and its pedagogical applications, and psychoanalytic and other critical approaches to the theory and analysis of music.

JONATHAN W. BERNARD is Professor of Music (Theory) in the School of Music at the University of Washington, Seattle. He has published extensively in the theory, analysis, criticism, and aesthetics of twentieth-century music (specifically on the work of Varèse, Bartók, Elliott Carter, Messiaen, Ligeti, Feldman, and Frank Zappa; more generally on the repertoires of minimalism, serialism of the 1940s and 1950s, and recent tonal music), and in the history of theory. He is the editor of *Elliott Carter: Collected Essays and Lectures, 1937–1995* and co-editor of *Music Theory in Concept and Practice* (both published by the University of Rochester Press in 1997).

WILLIAM BOLCOM, composer and pianist, studied with Darius Milhaud at Mills College in California, and later in Paris at the Conservatoire de Musique. Compositions from every period of his life have earned him many honors, including the Pulitzer Prize for music in 1988, for 12 New Etudes for Piano. In January 1995 Bolcom was composer-in-residence for a week with the New York Philharmonic under the direction of Leonard Slatkin. The Lyric Opera of Chicago gave the premiere of his *McTeague* in October

1992. The Lyric Opera also premiered *A View from the Bridge,* his second opera, based on the play by Arthur Miller. It was also performed at the Metropolitan Opera in December 2002. The latest of his seven symphonies (7th Symphony: A Symphonic Concerto) was presented in May 2002 by James Levine and the Metropolitan Opera Orchestra. Bolcom has recorded twenty albums with his wife, soprano Joan Morris, including two recent albums of songs by Vincent Youmans. Bolcom has taught at the University of Michigan since 1973, where he has been a full professor since 1983. In the fall of 1994 the university named him Ross Lee Finney Distinguished University Professor of Music.

PIERRE BOULEZ attended the Conservatoire de Musique in Paris under the tutelage of Olivier Messiaen and René Leibowitz. In 1954 he founded the Domaine musical in Paris, and remained their director until 1967. He was principal guest conductor of the Cleveland Orchestra (1967–72), and principal conductor of the BBC Symphony Orchestra (1971–75) and the New York Philharmonic (1971–77). In 1995 Boulez was named principal guest conductor of the Chicago Symphony Orchestra. In 1974, French President George Pompidou invited him to found and direct a music-research agency; the result was the Institut de Recherche et de Coordination Acoustique/ Musique (IRCAM), which Boulez directed from 1977 to 1992. He is also the founder and president of the Ensemble InterContemporain and co-founder of the newly-created music center Cité de la Musique in Paris. Among his recent compositional projects and completions are *Sur incises, Anthèmes* for solo violin, an orchestration of his own complete *Notations* for piano, and a new version of . . . *explosante-fixe* . . . , which conjoins real-time computer technology with acoustic instrumental production. Translated volumes of his writings and lectures include *Notes of an Apprenticeship, Boulez on Music Today, Pierre Boulez: Conversations with Célestin Deliège, Conversations with Boulez: Thoughts on Conducting* (edited by Jean Vermeil), and *Orientations* (edited by Jean-Jacques Nattiez).

JUDY LOCHHEAD, Professor of Music at the State University of New York at Stony Brook, teaches the history and theory of recent musical practices. She has published articles on the music of Berg, Cage, Carter, Kolb, and Tower. Her current research project is a book-length study, *Reconceiving Structure: Recent Music/Music Analysis,* which focuses on the implications of postmodern philosophy on the practice and significance of music analysis. She is the co-editor, with Joseph Auner, of the collection *Postmodern Music/Postmodern Thought* (Garland/Routledge).

FRED EVERETT MAUS teaches at the University of Virginia. He has written on musical narrative, gender, sexuality, performance, and other issues; publications include "Music as Drama" (*Music Theory Spectrum* 1988),

"Hanslick's Animism" (*Journal of Musicology* 1992), "Learning from 'Occasional' Writing" (*repercussions* 2000), "Concepts of Musical Unity" (in *Rethinking Music,* Oxford University Press, 1999), "Glamour and Evasion: The Fabulous Ambivalence of the Pet Shop Boys" (*Popular Music* 2001), and other essays. A founding member of the editorial board of *Women and Music* and an associate editor of *Perspectives of New Music,* he was a director of the conferences Feminist Theory and Music 4 (Charlottesville) and 5 (London), and has helped create a Gay and Lesbian Discussion Group in the Society for Music Theory.

ANDREW MEAD is Professor and Chair of Music Theory at the University of Michigan, and earned his Ph.D. in composition at Princeton University. He has published a book on Babbitt (*An Introduction to the Music of Milton Babbitt,* Princeton University Press) as well as articles on Elliott Carter, Schoenberg, Webern, and abstract twelve-tone theory. Recent essays include "Physiological Metaphors and Musical Understanding" (*Journal of Music Theory* 1999). He is also active as a composer.

GREG SANDOW writes about classical music for *The Wall Street Journal* and has taught graduate courses at Juilliard since 1997. From 1980 to 1986 he wrote a classical music column for the *Village Voice,* concentrating on new and experimental work and on the position of classical music in contemporary culture. In 1988 he became chief pop music critic for the *Los Angeles Herald-Examiner,* and after that was music critic and senior music editor for *Entertainment Weekly.* His writing has appeared in many other publications, including the *New York Times* and *Vanity Fair,* and he has contributed to the *New Grove Dictionary of American Music* and the *Spin Encyclopedia of Alternative Rock.* He has taught at Yale and at the University of Minnesota, where he was Visiting Professor of Musicology, and has served as panelist and consultant for organizations that include the American Symphony Orchestra League, Opera America, the Cleveland Orchestra, the National Endowment for the Arts, and the Rock & Roll Hall of Fame. He received the M.M. in composition from the Yale School of Music, and is the composer of four operas, all successfully produced. He is writing a book on the future of classical music.

MARTIN SCHERZINGER is Assistant Professor of Musicology at the Eastman School of Music. He recently completed his Ph.D. at Columbia University, and holds B.M. and B.A. degrees from the University of the Witwatersrand, South Africa. He is winner of the Emerging Scholar Award from the Society of Music Theory (2002–3), as well as a Mellon Fellowship from the American Council of Learned Societies (ACLS), AMS 50 Fellowship from the American Musicological Society, President's Fellowship from Columbia University, H. Hutner Fellowship, Mellon Summer Research Fellowship,

International Scholarship for Music from the Foundation for the Creative Arts (South Africa), and other awards for scholarship as well as composition. His publications include articles in *Music Analysis, Yearbook of Traditional Music, repercussions, Perspectives of New Music, Journal of the American Musicological Society, Disclosure, South African Journal of Musicology,* and *Conference,* and his compositions have been widely performed in Europe, the United States, Canada, and Africa.

JEREMY TAMBLING is Professor of Comparative Literature at the University of Hong Kong and author of *Opera, Ideology and Film* (Manchester University Press, 1987), and *Opera and the Culture of Fascism* (Oxford University Press, 1996). His most recent book is *Becoming Posthumous: Life and Death in Literary and Cultural Studies* (Edinburgh University Press, 2001). He has written on literary topics connected with modernism, including a monograph on Henry James (Macmillan 2000), and is currently working further on representations of madness within the modern.

RICHARD TOOP is Reader and Chair of Musicology at the Sydney Conservatorium (University of Sydney). English-born, he studied at Hull University, and was Stockhausen's teaching assistant at the Staatliche Hochschule für Musik in Cologne from 1973 to 1974. He emigrated to Australia in 1975. He writes primarily about post-1945 European modernism, and especially Stockhausen and Ferneyhough. His biography of György Ligeti was published recently by Phaidon Press.

LLOYD WHITESELL has taught at the University of Virginia, the University of Southern California, the State University of New York at Stony Brook, and the University of Minnesota. His published articles include work on Benjamin Britten, Charles Ives, Maurice Ravel, Joni Mitchell, minimalism, and the Bloomian theory of the "anxiety of influence." Now on the music faculty at McGill University, he has co-edited a volume of essays on musical modernism and queer identities, *Queer Episodes in Music and Modern Identity* (University of Illinois Press, 2002). His chapter in the present book reflects interests in audience-oriented criticism and multilinear histories of musical style.

Index

absolute music, 7, 15, 24, 131, 139, 145. *See also* autonomy

academia and academicism, 24, 46, 50, 51, 87, 90, 93, 153–54, 155, 159, 165, 168, 169–70, 224, 257–58, 269, 347–49. *See also* educators and education, music; music, schools of; prestige

"acquired situational narcissism" (Millman), 3

Adams, John, 106, 113, 119n38

Adorno, Theodor W., 6, 15, 18n1, 28–29, 68, 69, 74–76, 78, 88, 91, 94, 95n6, 96n20, 100n77, 107, 112, 194n47, 310; on Berg, 185–88, 189; on commodification, 74–76, 91–95, 98n53, 105–6, 111, 367; on the culture industry, 87, 307–8; on modernism, 1, 16, 97n48, 187; on "phantasmagoria," 367, 369–70, 376; on Schoenberg, 69–70, 79–83, 95n6, 97n48; on Strauss, 117n2; on Stravinsky, 105, 186; on tonality, 81, 105–6, 111, 119n39; *Philosophy of New Music*, 29, 65, 67n15, 185, 186–87; *Dialectic of Enlightenment*, 92; *Introduction to the Sociology of Music*, 94, 99n76, 223, 226; *Aesthetic Theory*, 186–87; "On the Fetish-Character of Music and the Regression of Listening," 90

aesthetics. *See* modernist aesthetics, postmodernism

aggregates, twelve-tone, 63, 82, 260, 270–22. *See also* atonality; chromaticism; twelve–tone music

AIDS, 92

Albright, Daniel, 70, 78

aleatoric music. *See* indeterminacy

alienation (*Verfremdung*), 185–88, 286, 289

Althusser, Louis, 91

ambient music, 306

analysis, musical, 41, 43n8, 55–56, 57, 59–62, 63–64, 66, 100n77, 131, 152n74; assumptions in analytic-theoretic discourse, 61, 64–65, 259–62, 268–72; as objectifying musical experience, 62, 63–64, 261–69. *See also* listening; metaphor; modernist jargon or terminology; theory, music

Anderson, Laurie, 286

Andriessen, Louis, 47, 246–47

Antheil, George, 287

Arrowsmith, William, 348

Artaud, Antonin, 99n73

atonality, 33, 36, 63, 106, 108, 111–12, 113, 115–16, 118n20, 118n24, 119n47, 122, 153–55, 161, 163–68, 270, 383–84n13; atonal and non-tonal forms, 358–59, 365; atonal theory and analysis, 163–68, 259–61, 267–69; listener perception in, 147n15, 355; as peculiar or pathological, 124, 125, 132, 156, 159, 173n24, 383–84n13. *See also* aggregates; Forte; hexachord; modernism; twelve-tone; chromaticism; politics; schizophrenia; tonality

attitude formation, 345–47, 382n2

Augenmusik. See compositional ciphers and cryptology

authorship, 27, 29, 30, 32–33, 38, 40, 44n19. *See also* Barthes; hermeneutics; intention; listening; writing

autonomy, 15, 24, 68–95, 130, 346

avant-gardism, 10, 16, 26, 45n32, 130, 145, 152n73, 224, 278, 282–85, 286, 287, 288, 290, 292, 295, 300, 301, 304, 305, 308–9, 315n8, 325, 326, 327; defined, 8, 9, 32, 279. *See also* modernism

ethnomusicology, 90, 93
evolution. *See* progress
exchange value. *See* Marxism
expressionism, 72

facture, 40–41
fascism. *See* totalitarianism
Fats Domino, 281
Fauconnier, Gilles, 14, 134–25
Feldman, Morton, 41, 340n1
feminism, 28, 37, 158–59, 171n5
Fernandez-Duque, Diego, and Mark L.
  Johnson, 133
Ferneyhough, Brian, 3, 18n1, 31, 243–
  44, 246, 381
film, 17, 49, 52, 98n60, 295, 297–99,
  345–82
film music, 10, 16, 347, 353, 355, 356,
  357–72, 377–78, 380, 384n14
Fink, Bruce, 18n8
Fischer, David Hackett, 3
Five Americans, the, 288
Flaubert, Gustave, 88
Fluxus, 286, 287, 292, 301, 304
form, musical, 75, 79–81, 159, 187,
  202–7, 209–10, 224–25, 330; form
  and hearing/listening, 13, 14, 35–36,
  121–24, 138, 144, 145, 197–222,
  225–30, 238, 325–29, 334–40, 357–
  59, 379–81; inaudible, invisible, or
  subconscious aspects of, 121–22,
  124, 138–39, 243, 326; objective
  properties of, 328–29, 331, 332,
  339. *See also* composition;
  formalism; perception; process
  forms; sonata form; structuralism
formalism, 77, 138, 145, 346, 353. *See
  also* structuralism
Forte, Allen, 27, 43n8, 161, 163, 164
Foster, Hal, 328, 344n55
Francesca, Piero della, 47
Foucault, Michel, 30, 44n19, 86, 89,
  91, 151n69; *History of Sexuality*,
  13, 160. *See also* authorship
Freud, Sigmund, 95n6, 182; *Beyond
  the Pleasure Principle*, 179
Fripp, Robert, 206
Fröhlich, Franz, 24, 25, 370

Fuseli, Henry, 49

Gann, Kyle, 97–98n51
Gaudí, Antonio, 49
gender, 158–59, 166–67
Gesualdo, Carlo, 49, 87
Gielen, Michael, 257
Gilmour, Dave. *See* Pink Floyd
Glass, Philip, 89, 119n38, 289,
  342n16; film music, 10, 367. *See
  also* minimalism
Goehr, Lydia, 9, 69, 148n32
Goethe, Johann Wolfgang von, 108
Gorbman, Claudia, 349, 355, 356,
  357, 364–65, 369, 371, 384n18
grammar, musical, 14, 33–34, 70, 368.
  See also cognition; composition;
  compositional grammar; Lerdahl;
  listening; listening grammar; music
Grateful Dead, the, 285, 292, 293, 319
Griffiths, Paul, 54–55, 57, 58–59, 61,
  67n9, 253–54
Grosz, George, 51
Guattari, Félix, 95n6, 176, 180, 182
Guck, Marion A., 131, 139, 148n33
Guilbaut, Serge, 88
guitar, electric, 281, 282, 315n3
Guitar Slim, 281
Gutknecht, Dieter, 41

Haimo, Ethan, 27, 43n8
Halen, Eddie van
Hand People, the, 288
Hanslick, Eduard, 26, 42n5
happenings, 286, 287, 304
Harrison, George, 284, 316n17
Haydn, Franz Joseph; Symphony No.
  94, "Surprise," 36
hearing in 20th-century music, 14, 31,
  122, 130, 145, 261, 270–72, 325–
  40, 368, 379–81; hearing defined, 5;
  development of, 226–27; structural
  hearing, 16, 122–24, 223–48; 325,
  326, 328, 331–33, 340–41n4. *See
  also* listening, perception
Heartfield, John, 91
Hegel, G. F., 26, 41, 79, 81, 95n6
Heidegger, Martin, 70, 82, 95n6

Mayall, John, 281
McCartney, Paul, 284, 285, 323n94.
 See also Beatles, the
McClary, Malcolm, 100n76
McClary, Susan, 1, 3, 37, 45n32,
 45n33, 54, 145, 159, 167, 171n7,
 271n6, 381, 386n54
McLuhan, Marshall: *Understanding
 Media*, 381
Mead, Andrew, 12, 37–38, 259–72
meaning, musical, 2, 14, 17, 18n1,
 19n20, 23–24, 29, 31, 37, 38–40,
 45n32, 50, 51, 145, 221, 222–23,
 254, 256–57, 339, 346, 348–49;
 defined, 24–26, 116; in modernist
 music, 55, 58–67, 69, 350–82. *See
 also* compositional authority over
 interpretation and meaning;
 hermeneutics; language, music as;
 listening
Mendelssohn, Felix, 93–94
Merleau-Ponty, Maurice, 19n22
Messiaen, Olivier, 7, 30, 51, 369, 370
metaphor, 13, 14, 33, 39–41, 106–16,
 122, 130–44, 145, 148n38, 150n59,
 150–51n60, 267; concept-
 metaphors, 72. *See also* conceptual
 metaphor; language, music as;
 semiotics
Meyer, Leonard, 5, 379–81
Michelangelo, 219
micropolyphony. *See* Ligeti
Milhaud, Darius, 15
Millman, Robert B., 3
minimalism, 47, 49, 59, 89, 118–
 19n31, 289, 317n35, 326, 341n10,
 342n33, 343n49
Mitchell, Donald, 112
Mitchell, Joni, 12
modernism, 8–11, 14, 15, 16–17, 24,
 29, 46, 47, 48, 49, 70, 72–74, 88,
 115–16, 124, 130, 153–54, 176,
 191, 223, 257, 279–80, 297, 307,
 309–10, 325–26, 328, 340n1, 376;
 and academia, 10, 16, 168, 169–70;
 as response to crisis, 103; and avant-
 gardism, 8, 9; as disjunction between
 signifier and signified, 124–25, 176,

180; and mass (popular) culture,
 98n60, 278, 296, 345–46, 349–53,
 378–82; and modernization, 278–
 79, 307; and postmodernism, 8, 9,
 16, 18n4, 24, 68–95, 97n51, 114,
 116, 124, 144–45, 156, 325, 326,
 335–40, 341n5, 344n58, 356–57,
 381–82; as private or disrupted
 language, 9, 14, 42, 47, 65, 66, 70–
 72, 78, 99n73, 103, 110, 112,
 119n47, 124–25, 145, 187, 191,
 257, 381, 386n54; as social or
 political critique, 69–72, 74, 75, 78,
 79–80, 81, 82, 186–87, 191. *See
 also* aesthetics; attitude formation;
 avant-gardism; form; Lacan;
 language, music as; mannerism;
 metaphor; monism; perception;
 sadomasochism; schizophrenia;
 structuralism
modernist aesthetics, 3, 4–5, 11, 15,
 31, 38, 55, 97n48, 145, 180, 190,
 326, 334, 336, 340, 341n4, 342n16,
 346–49, 351;
modernist jargon or terminology, 12,
 37, 44n20, 167, 260, 268–69;
Molino, Jean, 346
moment form, 225, 238
monad (Leibniz, Benjamin), 76
monism, 29, 32, 36, 37
Monteverdi, Claudio, 49
Moon, Keith, 286. *See also* Who, the
Moore, Allan F., 145
Moravec, Paul, 113
Morgan, Robert P., 9, 110–11, 116,
 119n36
Morrison, Jim, 298, 299, 321n71
Mosolov, Alexander, 287
Move, the, 317n26
movies. *See* film
Mozart, Wolfgang Amadeus, 9, 51, 62,
 90, 131, 224, 255, 261, 358
MTV, 98n60
Murdoch, Rupert, 92
museum-style concert life, 13. *See*
 concerts
music, difficulties and problems in
 discussing, 45n31, 259–72. *See*

Eastman Studies in Music

(ISSN 1071–9989)

CPSIA information can be obtained
at www.ICGtesting.com
Printed in the USA
FFOW03n1807110817
38713FF